Adventuring

~~~~ *IN THE* ~~~~

Chesapeake Bay
Area

The Sierra Club Adventure Travel Guides

Adventuring Along the Gulf of Mexico,
  by Donald G. Schueler

Adventuring in Alaska, Completely revised and updated,
  by Peggy Wayburn

Adventuring in Arizona, by John Annerino

Adventuring in Belize, by Eric Hoffman

Adventuring in Australia, by Eric Hoffman

Adventuring in British Columbia, by Isabel Nanton
  and Mary Simpson

Adventuring in East Africa, by Allen Bechky

Adventuring in North Africa, by Scott Wayne

Adventuring in the Alps, by William E. Reifsnyder
  and Marylou Reifsnyder

Adventuring in the Andes, by Charles Frazier
  with Donald Secreast

Adventuring in the California Desert, by Lynne Foster

Adventuring in the Caribbean, by Carrol B. Fleming

Adventuring in the Chesapeake Bay Area, by John Bowen

Adventuring in Florida, by Allen de Hart

Adventuring in New Zealand, by Margaret Jefferies

Adventuring in the Pacific, by Susanna Margolis

Adventuring in the Rockies, Completely revised and updated,
  by Jeremy Schmidt

Adventuring in the San Francisco Bay Area,
  by Peggy Wayburn

Trekking in Nepal, West Tibet, and Bhutan, by Hugh Swift

Trekking in Pakistan and India, by Hugh Swift

Walking Europe from Top to Bottom, by Susanna Margolis
  and Ginger Harmon

JOHN BOWEN

Adventuring

~~~~~ IN THE ~~~~~

Chesapeake Bay Area

THE SIERRA CLUB TRAVEL GUIDE
TO THE TIDEWATER COUNTRY
OF MARYLAND, VIRGINIA, AND WASHINGTON, D.C.,
FROM BALTIMORE TO THE VIRGINIA CAPES

SIERRA CLUB BOOKS • SAN FRANCISCO

The Sierra Club, founded in 1892 by John Muir, has devoted itself to the study and protection of the earth's scenic and ecological resources—mountains, wetlands, woodlands, wild shores and rivers, deserts and plains. The publishing program of the Sierra Club offers books to the public as a nonprofit educational service in the hope that they may enlarge the public's understanding of the Club's basic concerns. The point of view expressed in each book, however, does not necessarily represent that of the Club. The Sierra Club has some sixty chapters coast to coast, in Canada, Hawaii, and Alaska. For information about how you may participate in its programs to preserve wilderness and the quality of life, please address inquiries to Sierra Club, 730 Polk Street, San Francisco, CA 94109.

Library of Congress Cataloging-in-Publication Data

Bowen, John, 1929–
   Adventuring in the Chesapeake Bay Area / by John Bowen.
      p. cm.
   Includes bibliographical references.
   ISBN 0-87156-680-X
   1. Chesapeake Bay Region (Md. and Va.)—Description and travel—
Guide-books. 2. Natural areas—Chesapeake Bay Region (Md. and
Va.)—Guide-books. I. Title.
F187.C5B68 1989
917.55′18—dc20   89–10551
                                                                                                    CIP

Production by Felicity Gorden
Cover design by Bonnie Smetts
Book design by Seventeenth Street Studio/Lorrie Fink
Printed in the United States of America on acid-free paper containing a minimum of 50% recovered waste paper, of which at least 10% of the fiber content is post-consumer waste
10 9 8 7 6 5 4 3

Contents

CONTENTS

CONTENTS

CONTENTS

Foreword

DEGRADATION CREEPS ALONG ALMOST UNNOTICED UNTIL IT OVERWHELMS us. That has almost been the fate of Chesapeake Bay, a beautiful and bountiful waterway that now is struggling to cope with our past mistakes while continuing to provide the contemporary pleasures and profits we expect. For much of our human tenure on the Bay, we have accepted its grandeur and largesse without considering the consequences. Even watermen, whose lives depend on the abundance of the Bay, at times disregarded laws and prudent behavior in order to satisfy the demands of the moment. The rest of us were no better, contributing in various ways to the decline in seafood, the damage to wildfowl, the disappearance of open shoreline, and the increase in the number of people trying to experience Bay life.

An extensive tour—I traveled more than 8,000 miles to revisit every section of the region while researching this book—is a rude awakening. Those who use the Bay frequently, and have recognized the changes at their favorite places, will be painfully aware that the total impact is much greater than the sum of the individual parts. Those who have not experienced the Bay for a decade or two will be shocked by the degradation that has taken place.

The Bay will continue to exist in some fashion, no matter how destructive we are. Nature will make changes, too, just as it has every year since it created the Bay. Indeed, the dynamic quality of the Bay region is one of its most striking, and most attractive, features.

Fortunately, at long last, the problems human beings have produced for Chesapeake Bay have caused concern among those who live and recreate along its shores. The states of Virginia, Maryland, and Pennsylvania have joined the District of Columbia and federal agencies, including the Chesapeake Bay Commission, in a massive effort to clean up the waterway and restore its vitality. Objectives include a 40 percent reduction in nutrient pollution and significant reduction of toxics by the year 2000 to improve natural habitats, acquisition of more park and open spaces, management plans for fisheries and population, and a uniform policy for protecting wetlands. Both individuals and private organizations such as The Nature

Conservancy and the Wildlife Trust of North America also have accepted partial responsibility for preserving the Bay.

The Chesapeake Bay described in this book is the natural Bay area, the area where the impact of the waterway is dominant. This includes all of eastern Maryland, or about two-thirds of the state, and the tidewater area of Virginia, roughly the land inland as far as tidal action on tributaries. The book divides the region into locally recognized sections within the two states that border on the Bay. In Maryland, these include Baltimore; Annapolis and Anne Arundel County; Southern Maryland, the lower part of the giant claw of land appended to Baltimore and Washington, D.C.; the upper Chesapeake Bay region; and the Eastern Shore, including the ocean side, which is so close culturally that it is inseparable. In Virginia, the sections are the Eastern Shore, Hampton Roads, Middle Peninsula, and Northern Neck. The distinctive national capital area, which includes Washington, D.C., and suburban areas of Virginia and Maryland, is treated as one unit. This creates a more or less circular tour of the Bay.

Virginia's capital city, Richmond, stands on the border between the tidewater and piedmont regions. Although secondary tidal action reaches as far as the falls (the water is fresh, not brackish, and rises and falls because tidal action downstream impedes the flow), the city is customarily not regarded as part of Chesapeake Bay country. Similarly, Delaware, which shares the Delmarva Peninsula with sections of Maryland and Virginia, is oriented more toward Delaware Bay to the east.

Local descriptive terminology can be confusing. Both Virginia and Maryland have features with identical names — Wicomico River, for example. The name Eastern Shore, which Maryland and Virginia share, describes the landmass opposite the original settlements on the mainland, or western shore. Invariably, a resident of one of the states will be talking about his own river or section of the Eastern Shore. When a Marylander mentions the "south Eastern Shore" or just "south Shore," more than likely he is referring to the southern end of the Maryland Eastern Shore, not the Virginia section south of it. In Hampton Roads, "South Shore" means the landmass south of the water, principally Norfolk.

The Chesapeake Bay area is such a vast, complex arrangement of land, water, and people relating to each other that it is impossible to include every detail in one book. This book seeks to explore the highlights, especially those related to the outdoors, in a historical, social, and cultural context, to "feel" the region as well as catalogue its features. Many people were helpful in this endeavor, including rangers, government officials, attendants, and people who gave generously of their time and knowledge to discuss particular refuges, parks, facilities, or attractions. Among them are Tom Burton, Jr., of New Church, Virginia; the late Arthur "Buck" Briscoe and Mrs. Briscoe of St. Mary's County, Maryland; Dr. Mitchell Byrd and Dr. Gerald H. Johnson of the College of William and Mary; Gloria Frost of St. Michael's; Linda Cunningham Goldstein of Woodlawn Plantation; Buddy Harrison of Tilghman's Island; Mike Harrison of Smith Island; Jay Munday of the Newport News *Daily Press* sports staff; Thomas G. Murphy of Washington, D.C.; Dr. Paul Opler of the U.S. Fish and Wildlife Service; Don Perkutchin at Blackwater National Wildlife Refuge; Jeffrey S. Ruark of Sandy Point State Park; Diane Stutz of Norfolk; Barry Truitt and John M. Hall of The Nature Conservancy; and Sandy Marriner and Susan Bounds of Somerset County.

Chesapeake Bay, even in diminished form, is one of the richest bodies of water in the world. It may be the greatest waterway in the United States; at the least, it ranks among the top few. The Bay area is at the same time a highway for ocean-going ships, the most productive seafood area in the United States, one of the most versatile recreation areas in the country, and the home of millions of people.

The wonder is not that it has been able to survive maltreatment and disinterest in so many ways for so long, but that it has done so so well. The challenge is to use it wisely and preserve its beauty and its bounty indefinitely. It is with the hope of furthering these aims that this book is written.

John Bowen
Newport News, Virginia

PART ONE

~~~~~~~~

The Ways of the Bay

CHESAPEAKE BAY AREA

Rhythms and Riches

CAPT. JOHN SMITH WAS ASTONISHED. NEVER, IN ALL OF HIS TRAVELS, HAD he seen anything like it. The water around his boat churned with the writhing bodies of so many fish that he needed only a skillet to catch them. He continued to experience such bounty as he further explored the Chesapeake Bay coastline and many of its tributaries, feasting in Indian villages littered with piles of oyster and crab shells. "Neither better fish, more plenty, nor more variety of small fish, had any of us ever seen," he later wrote.

The "Chesepiook," the "great shellfish bay" of the Algonkin Indians, has over the intervening centuries retained its early reputation for size, dynamism, and productivity. In July 1746, the *London Magazine* described the Chesapeake as "the noblest bay in the universe. . . . In this Bay, the whole Navies of Great Britain, Holland and France might ride at anchor." Something of that nature did occur during the 1893 International Naval Rendezvous, when ships representing nine of the ten major world naval powers anchored in the lower end of the Bay. More recently, the bounteous Bay has been described as the most useful estuary in the world and the "crown jewel" among 850 estuaries in the United States.

Chesapeake Bay is, indeed, an estuary or drowned valley through which the Susquehanna River flowed in antiquity. Geologists say the region has had four upheavals, but the Bay was created in the Pleistocene era about 10,000 years ago. It differs from the estuaries of the northwestern United States, which were dug by glaciers; San Francisco Bay, which was created by violent earthquake action; and Biscayne Bay in Miami, which developed behind a barrier reef.

The largest bay in North America is 195 miles long on a north–south axis, more than 25 miles wide at its broadest point and nearly 4 miles wide at the narrowest point, near Annapolis, Maryland. The greatest depth is 174 feet, off Bloody Point at the southern end of Kent Island, Maryland, but the average is 21 feet. The water surface covers an area four times that of Rhode Island, our smallest state.

However, the Bay lies wholly within two states—Maryland and Virginia. Its 8,000-mile shoreline, serrated by scores of rivers, subbays, and coves, hides more than five hundred safe harbors.

The Bay drains about 64,000 square miles in Maryland, Pennsylvania, New York, Virginia, Delaware, and West Virginia, an area larger than many countries. About four hundred small streams feed 48 main tributaries, 19 of them navigable. Although many tributaries are short, three are major systems in themselves. The Susquehanna begins in New York and flows through Pennsylvania and Maryland, amassing a waterflow that at times exceeds that of the Mississippi. Branches of the Potomac reach deep into the valleys of West Virginia. The James River, whose 5-mile-wide mouth hosts a deepwater port and shipyard, begins in the mountains of Virginia. These three streams provide 80 percent of the fresh water that enters the Bay.

The mixing and layering of this flow with salt water from the Atlantic Ocean—the salinity of the Bay varies widely, increasing closer to the mouth—creates a relatively rare but productive environment. Tributaries feed minerals and salts into the Bay, where they mix with plants and tiny animals under the surface. More than 500,000 acres of tidal marshes contribute food in the form of leaves, seeds, roots, and detritus. Plants in shallow water convert sunlight into microscopic food for numerous tiny lifeforms, which in turn feed larger resident and transient animals.

It is impossible to visit the Chesapeake Bay area and not be impressed by the richness of nature's bounty. Both the shore and the water pulsate with the rhythms of reproduction, growth, and migration. The 1.2 million acres of wetlands remaining—substantially less than once existed—provide habitat and protection for diverse resident and migratory sea life and birds. Marshes feed about two-thirds of the Bay's commercially valuable marine resources. Flocks of waterfowl, shorebirds, and songbirds rotate according to the seasons; the movement of finfish and shellfish is less noticeable but just as substantial. Many waterfowl depend on underwater plants for food in winter.

More than two thousand marine plants and animals, including microscopic forms, live in and around the Bay. The bright colors of berries and wildflowers glisten among the 1,150 kinds of plants that thrive in the combination upland-lowland terrain. About a hundred species of land animals, such as deer, rabbits, and squirrels, inhabit softwood and hardwood forests lush with ground cover that extends from the edible royal fern to honeysuckle and mountain

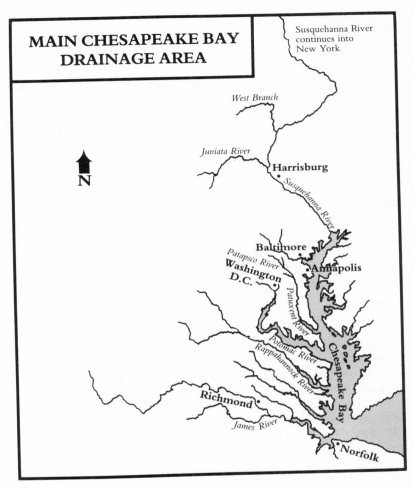

MAIN CHESAPEAKE BAY DRAINAGE AREA

Susquehanna River continues into New York

West Branch

Juniata River

Harrisburg

Susquehanna River

N

Baltimore

Patapsco River

Washington D.C.

Annapolis

Patuxent River

Potomac River

Rappahannock River

Chesapeake Bay

Richmond

James River

Norfolk

laurel. Population growth and destruction of habitats has caused large predators like bear and panther, familiar to early human inhabitants, to decline or relocate. The Bay region is the second most productive area in the United States for commercial hunting of muskrat.

Human beings, standing at the top of the chain, traditionally have used the Bay as an economic resource. Capt. John Smith wrote of the "plentie of good Oysters, Fish, Flesh, Wild-foule and good bread." Author H. L. Mencken described the Bay, which teems with more than 250 varieties of fish and shellfish, as an "immense protein factory." More than forty salable species of aquatic life, including blue crab, oysters, clams, and finfish worth hundreds of millions of dollars annually, make it one of the richest commercial seafood areas in the world.

The 95 million pounds of blue crab taken each year is not matched anywhere in the world. The harvesting of blue crabs has almost produced a Bay subculture. Watermen speak of the crustacean with a respect they show no other aquatic creature. "Crab yarns" often endow the crawler with legendary intelligence, strength, and determination. Watermen time their lives according to seasonal migrations — north in summer, south in winter — and from shallow to deep water. Every aspect of the crab's curious life and its hide-and-seek relationship with watermen has been researched. The crab's habits are an economic barometer. Ask restaurant staff in the Upper Bay in early May for the crabmeat listed on a menu, and you're likely to get the answer, "They're not catching many now. They're too expensive."

Although crabs prefer deep water in cold weather, a few boats pursue them into the winter. Virginia has no closed season, and Maryland bans catches only in the depth of winter, when few crabs are found. Deal, Smith, and Tangier Island crabbers frequently haul pots as long as weather and the number of crabs permit, sometimes moving their operations to places like Hampton, Virginia, in the southern end of the Bay.

Others, while waiting for return of the crab, fill the time by tonging for oysters. Some shift their attention as early as September. Chesapeake Bay watermen produce one-fourth of the oysters and half of the clams consumed in the United States. About 17,000 people earn their livelihood as watermen, seafood processors, packers, and laborers.

The crab-oyster chase has influenced the design of boats and specialized equipment. Pursuing moulting crabs into shoal waters requires shallow boats; hunting for them in the depths they prefer in winter demands special gear and techniques. A unique nomenclature exists; words like "Jimmies" (male crabs), "doublers" (mating crabs), "bar cats," "one-sail bateaus," "dinky skifts," "Jenkins Creekers," and "Hooper Island draketails," which are unfamiliar to the uninitiated, roll glibly off the tongues of watermen. A specialized terminology also includes corruptions like "drudge" for oyster dredge, "kay-ners" or "kay-noos" for Chesapeake Bay log canoes, and "arsters" for oysters. And when Smith Islanders mention "outhouses," they are not talking about dry toilets but crab and/or utility sheds.

The Bay is the spawning, nursery, and feeding ground for a Number of ocean-dwelling fish, including 90 percent of the striped bass (rockfish) on the East Coast. Ocean spawners, such as the game bluefish, sea trout, spot, and croaker, use protected Bay waters as a nursery. As adults, they enter the Bay to feed. Bluefish, sea trout, cobia, and other species abundant in the Bay during the summer seek out ocean depths in winter. The eel population goes largely unnoticed by all except the watermen, but they slither into every nook and cranny and grow to large sizes. In November, they make one of the great migrations by Bay creatures, ending in the Sargasso Sea in the central Atlantic.

The tributaries are extensions of the Bay's wealth. The shad from the Susquehanna River, whose numbers have dwindled drastically, has been called the finest eating fish in the world. Chincoteague salt oysters are especially flavorful. Terrapin, plentiful in the area, has grown in culinary fame since it was the everyday diet of slaves.

Next to fishing, the Bay is best known for its wildfowl. Even the casual observer is instantly aware of the abundant birdlife. The graceful ospreys soar over the marshes and byways, while the cautious blue herons stay a safe distance from intruders into their habitat. Peregrine falcon wheel over nests built on platforms in isolated areas. Red-winged blackbird and numerous other smaller fowl can easily be observed on most trails and farmlands. The bald eagle, once scarce in the region, now nests safely in a number of parks and forests.

The waterfowl are the "glory" of the Chesapeake, in the view of author William W. Warner. The Bay is a key point on the Atlantic flyway for hundreds of thousands of migratory birds. Many of the forty-three species of native waterfowl winter on the Bay. The skies begin to come alive in September, as shorebirds leave for winter quarters in Central and South America and the first waterfowl arrive from their summer places in northern Canada and Greenland. Later, geese, swans, and ducks migrating south fill the skies, ponds, and marshes around the Bay, which provide both food and protection during the cold months. By December, the presence of noisy waterfowl is overwhelming as many of them settle down for the winter along accommodating shorelines. Their standard diet is supplemented in places by great numbers of clams cast on the beach by storms.

Accommodating these flocks requires enormous areas of open and green spaces. Federal, state, and local refuges and parks — more than thirty on the Eastern Shore alone — range in size from a few hundred to thousands of acres. In recent decades, private organizations like The Nature Conservancy and the Wildlife Trust of North America have added a new dimension to the conservation effort by acquiring additional large tracts of land in strategic wildfowl areas.

Chesapeake Bay is one of the most important shipping lanes in the United States. More than ten thousand ocean-going vessels carry at least 100 million tons of cargo to Bay ports, principally Baltimore and Hampton roads. Port-related activities account for at least one-fifth of Maryland's employment and about 15 percent of the gross state product. The staple of the colonial era, tobacco, still moves through Virginia ports, primarily Hampton Roads, but now ranks far behind coal, grain, and petroleum. Virginia figures that inland areas benefit from the ports almost as much as coastal areas. The Newport News shipyard, which constructs nuclear-powered warships, is the largest single employer in the Commonwealth of Virginia.

Chesapeake Bay's strategic location makes it attractive to dozens of military bases. Virginia hosts, among others, the largest naval base in the world at Norfolk, U.S. Marines headquarters at Quantico, a Coast Guard training station at Yorktown, Army doctrine and Air Force continental protection commands at Hampton, and the Army Transportation Center at Newport News. Weapons and equipment of all kinds are tested at Aberdeen Proving Ground in Maryland, while seaborne aircraft are put through rigorous tests at the Patuxent Naval Air Station. A few former bases have been converted into wildlife refuges and historic sites. The relationship between the bases and civilians generally is good, although friction sometimes is created by disclosures of dumped waste or training exercises that disturb nature or those enjoying it.

Thomas Jefferson's inquiring mind has modern-day counterparts. Scientific study in the Bay region ranges from the fossils in the cliffs of Calvert County, Maryland, to the mating habits of the blue crab at prestigious institutions such as the Virginia Institute of Marine Science at Gloucester Point and the Chesapeake Marine Biology Laboratory at Solomons, Maryland. Agricultural experimentation also is intensive, especially on farms near the national capital. The area contributes to nuclear research through the Continuous Electron Beam Accelerator Facility (CEBAF) at Newport News, Virginia.

Everyday life, which includes a sharp urban-rural division, has its own kind of charm. A majority of the more than 10 million residents are concentrated in metroplexes at the ends of the Bay —

Baltimore, the national capital region, and Hampton Roads. Other communities are small fishing or farming centers for lightly populated rural hinterlands, a few with a newfound affinity for light industry. In out-of-the-way fishing villages, watermen unload bushel baskets of blue crab or oysters and tend their boats amid a jumble of masts and power boat superstructures.

To millions of sports enthusiasts and casual users, the Bay is the friendly place depicted years ago in a television commercial by the lovable gull, Chester Peake, but recreation competes with commerce to such a degree that no self-respecting governor can mention one without citing the other. Charter and "head" fishing boats leave ports that also shelter crabbers and tongers. Personal boats launched from public and private ramps turn streams into scenes of graceful motion, but workboats are never far away. Skipjacks that may have raced police patrols in the days of oyster "pirates" hoist billowing sails for racing prizes during the summer, and sometimes dredge for oysters in the winter. Commercial and sport fishers are aided by submerged hulks, numerous marshy islands, and abundant sources of food for the finfish and shellfish. Swimmers, sunbathers, and surfcasters crowd substantial beaches near oyster or fishing grounds. Hunters stalk deer and game birds on the land, lure wildfowl on the water. The carving of duck decoys has emerged as a folk art form. The flat terrain is ideal for hikers and bikers, while large forested areas, standing among fertile farmlands, appeal to bird-watchers, photographers, and campers.

The only sporting dog to originate in the United States, the Chesapeake Bay retriever, developed on the shores of the Bay, apparently by accident. Two Labrador retrievers that survived the wreck of an English brig on the Maryland shore in 1807 bred with local dogs, many of which were water spaniels from England. Since these were working dogs, owners were interested in the fittest and most intelligent, and the breed quickly spread to other parts of the country. It had become a distinct breed by 1885 and was later accepted by the American Kennel Association. The Chessie, known for its individualism, willingness to work hard, loyalty to its owners, sturdiness, and love of the water, was exported to Great Britain and several continental countries following World War II.

Some of the most historic cities in America, including Williamsburg in Virginia and Chestertown in Maryland, balance a natural orientation toward the water. Historic town districts thrive with modernized homes, chic shops, offices, colonial-style inns, and exhibit mansions filled with antiques. Old courthouses, a few of which hold records dating back to the seventeenth century, stand near churches built by founders of the country. Hundreds of serene seventeenth-, eighteenth-, and nineteenth-century plantations dot the countryside, many of them open to the public. A few have been converted into picturesque bed-and-breakfast establishments. Some historic private homes are opened for public visitation on special occasions, such as Maryland House and Garden Pilgrimage during Virginia Historic Garden Week in late April.

Dozens of maritime, military, commercial, historic, and science museums reflect the personality of the region. Among historical relics are sailing warships, trend-setting workboats used by watermen and oyster "pirates," and shallow, outlawed hunting craft. In some places, prehistoric fossils emerge from eroding cliffs.

Contemporary history is manifest at three aviation and space centers, where tiny moon rocks attract as much attention as mammoth experimental and operational craft; military bases that offer concerts as well as tours; waterfront cruises that pass the active wharves of ports, ship bases, and shipyards or explore beautiful rivers, offshore islands, and the Bay itself; and numerous water-related festivals at all seasons of the year.

The combination of population, farming, commercial, and recreational uses places an unbelievable burden on the ecology of the Bay area. A decline of underwater vegetation and living resources has reduced the ability of the water to sustain life. Overharvesting, pollution, and shellfish diseases have decimated seafood populations in whole areas of the Bay and its tributaries. Bay oyster harvests have dropped by one-third in the last twenty years; soft-shelled clam production has fallen even more. Decline in the commercial harvest of striped bass from nearly 15 million pounds to around 2 million in a single decade prompted Maryland to ban catch of this fish, prized by commercial and sport fishermen alike. Declines in other Bay spawners, like the Atlantic sturgeon, also have been noticed.

Dams on the tributaries have altered life cycles of certain species. Nearly a thousand blockages have affected historic migration patterns. The impounding of areas of the Susquehanna has been especially damaging to the reproduction of shad. In the early nineteenth century, the fish went as far inland as the New York state border to spawn, but a dam built at Columbia, Pennsylvania, in 1835 began to restrict their movement. Spawning migration was made nearly impossible by the 100-foot dam at Conowingo, constructed in 1928.

Damming the James River at Richmond has been somewhat less damaging to the shad population. A recent multistate Chesapeake Bay Agreement promises to provide fish passages at dams and to rebuild stocks.

A few hardy species seem to thrive under even the most adverse circumstances. The tiny menhaden—too oily for most human tastes but used extensively for fertilizer and catfood—has become big business in certain Bay communities as use has expanded to steel, cement, perfume, and cosmetics. Research is being done on using this cheap fish as a substitute for more expensive crab, shrimp, and lobster. The bluefish, pound for pound the hardest fighting fish in the Bay, feasts on menhaden.

The comfortable mix of land and water cultures is being tested as housing development absorbs waterfront land at a rate alarming to many conservationists. According to a U.S. Fish and Wildlife pamphlet, "Shoreline development and resulting habitat destruction create obvious problems for Chesapeake Bay wildlife. Secluded nesting grounds and feeding areas required by many animals are disappearing rapidly in the Bay area." Bay area human population is projected to reach 16 million by the year 2020.

The traditional attitude that the Bay can continue to provide, no matter what, is slowly being abandoned. In the last decade, a multi-faceted Save-the-Bay movement has been mounted to restore its vitality and preserve it for the future. Among the organizations working toward that end are the Chesapeake Bay Foundation, Citizens' Program for the Chesapeake Bay, Inc., Save Our Streams, Maryland Department of Natural Resources, Virginia Council on the Environment, the District of Columbia Department of Consumer and Regulatory Affairs, the Chesapeake Bay Commission, and the federal government.

History

THE WINDS ON CHESAPEAKE BAY HAVE FILLED THE SAILS OF SOME OF the great historic caravans of American society, as well as a number of lesser flotillas. Not the least of these expeditions are various movements for individual and corporate rights.

Although a theory exists that Leif Eriksson's Vinland was located along the James River in Virginia, the first recorded European explorer in the Chesapeake Bay region was Giovanni da Verrazano in 1524. While exploring the East Coast in the service of the king of France, Verrazano anchored near Chincoteague Island on the Eastern Shore and marched overland as far as the swamps of the Upper Pocomoke River in Worcester County, Maryland. He stopped short of discovering the Bay but was impressed by the abundance of trees and named the land Arcadia. He left an account of his contacts with the Assateagues, a peaceful people who hunted, fished, picked wild fruit and berries, and cultivated the soil. They lived in semipermanent settlements, but traveled substantial distances in dugout canoes. The points of their arrows were made of bone.

The Spanish, who came next, settled among the more aggressive mainland tribes at what is now Hampton, Virginia. Primarily interested in converting the Indians, the priests soon antagonized them and were wiped out. The British colonized the region, starting at Jamestown on the broad James River. Many of the original colonists perished, so many in fact that the survivors were ready to abandon the settlement until dissuaded by the last-minute arrival of relief ships. New settlers were lured by fanciful stories that the beaches of the region were strewn with semiprecious stones.

Among the first settlers was the great explorer of the Chesapeake Bay region, Capt. John Smith. In June 1608, less than a year after the establishment of Jamestown, he landed at Cape Charles on the Virginia Eastern Shore with a party of fourteen men. Two weeks later, with a number of his men seriously ill, Smith reluctantly turned back. On a second voyage, Smith reached the head of the Bay and explored the rivers there, including the Susquehanna and the beautiful Sassafras. The Susquehannock Indians, who welcomed Smith with gifts, "seemed like giants to the English, yea, and to their neighbors, yet seemed of an honest and simple disposition."

The Algonkin Indian tribes, whose lifestyle was founded on the abundance of wildlife in the water and forests, were well organized into a tight federation when the English arrived. The pattern of settler-Indian contact was much like that among the tribes: alternate periods of war and peace. The depredations of strong, warlike tribes encouraged weak, peaceful ones to side with the new arrivals, foreshadowing both the conflict that dominated the westward movement of whites and the willingness of some Indian tribes to side with whites against other Indians.

The assistance of the Indians was crucial to the survival of the white settlements. Plots of Indian chiefs to kill the white settlers might have succeeded had not friendly natives warned many intended victims. The advice provided by Indians on growing corn and new varieties of beans and squashes, the use of wild fruits and berries, and methods of freshwater fishing, shellfishing, hunting, and boatbuilding may well have enabled the early colony to survive. The Indians also introduced the settlers to tobacco, which soon became the cash crop on which colonial affluence was founded.

Conflicts also arose among the settlers. An early dispute between the Virginia and Maryland colonies over unclear boundaries required intervention by the king in England. Similar territorial disagreements between the two continued well into the twentieth century. No monarch could resolve the differences between Lord Baltimore, head of the Maryland colony, and William Claiborne, who defended his independent settlement of Kent Island. James Michener's novel *Chesapeake* fictionalizes the prototype property battle between land grant and prior settlement that characterized expansion westward. Every Western movie fan is aware of the conflicts between ranchers who opened vast territories and "squatters" who came later.

The colonies were joined to England by ships. From numerous Chesapeake Bay ports, tobacco, furs, and grain sailed to satisfy European tastes; the ships returned with the necessities and luxuries that Virginia and Maryland could not produce — and more settlers. In the eighteenth century, the gentry sent their children to England for their education, and a few hardy souls ventured across the ocean as pure travelers.

As a result of legitimate commerce and extensive, two-way smuggling to evade taxes, shipbuilding quickly developed as a major industry. Long before the American Revolution, Chesapeake Bay shipyards were producing vessels not only for American use, but for shipowners in Great Britain as well. Innovative designs, like those that appeared in the early 1800s and later became famous as the Baltimore clipper, had a universal appeal and laid the groundwork for the clipper era, when larger but still fast clippers dominated commercial sea lanes. In the nineteenth century, regular trans-Atlantic travel by packet boat became frequent. Great lines were built on this combined passenger-cargo trade, despite what Alexis de Tocqueville called the "droll life one lives in this great stagecoach one calls a ship." Ralph Waldo Emerson, who traveled to Europe in 1847, declared "sea-life an acquired taste."

Many of the roots of national independence drew nourishment from the Bay area. The tradition of self-government was founded at Jamestown and nurtured at Williamsburg after it became the colonial capital of Virginia. Much of the intellectual ferment that led to American independence occurred within a few miles of one of the most loyalist sections of the country, the great plantations that lay along the James River. Thomas Jefferson, James Madison, George Wythe, George Washington, and Patrick Henry, philosophical founders of the new country, were familiar sights in the taverns and legislative chambers of Williamsburg. Physical opposition to unjust laws was widespread. "Tea parties" were held at Chestertown (then known as New Towne) and Annapolis only months after Bostonians destroyed a shipload of tea to protest taxes imposed in Britain. Virginia and Maryland united to boycott British goods and to withhold tobacco, a lucrative commodity that Britain resold to other European countries, as part of their prewar efforts to force British moderation.

During the Revolutionary War, Virginia and Maryland created credible navies and engaged both the British and the strong force of Tory marauders on Chesapeake Bay. One of the naval heroes of the Revolutionary War, Joshua Barney, had assumed his first command at age 15, when the master of the Baltimore ship *Sidney* died at sea. As commander of the wartime *Hyder Ally,* his skillful maneuvering and boldness grounded one British attacking vessel and captured a second, which he later commanded as the rechristened *General Washington.* On a return voyage from France, he carried the secret draft of the peace treaty ending the war.

The capital of Virginia was moved from Williamsburg to Richmond for greater protection—insufficient, as it turned out, because the turncoat Benedict Arnold burned Richmond. Annapolis, Maryland's capital then and now, sent capable leaders to the Continental Congress and worked with Virginia to protect the Bay. Independence, proclaimed at Philadelphia, became a reality with the defeat of Lord Cornwallis and the British army at Yorktown, Virginia.

During the War of 1812, British naval and military activity was centered in the Bay area. The British raided and burned numerous communities, including the national capital, from bases on Chesapeake Bay islands. The aging Barney once again arose to the occasion; his command of 600 sailors earned the admiration of British Rear Adm. George Cockburn. However, an American defeat at Bladensburg allowed the British army under Maj. Gen. Robert Ross to burn Washington. The British were less successful at Baltimore, where the determined defense of Fort McHenry salvaged national pride and produced the national anthem, "The Star-Spangled Banner."

In the early nineteenth century, vital transportation links were established. The first steamboat, a paddlewheeler appropriately named *Chesapeake,* sailed from Bowley's Wharf in Baltimore to Annapolis in 1813. Two year later, the *Surprise* connected the Patuxent River and Baltimore and the heyday of the Bay steamer had begun; soon, dozens of steamboats built for the trade linked scores of formerly isolated communities with major cities around the Bay. There was an air of romance about overnight trips from Baltimore to Tolchester and Cambridge, between Hampton Roads and Washington. A miniature cruise was supplemented by stops at numerous landings in communities otherwise outside the mainstream of life. Cargo crowded the wharves while curious spectators, alerted by the steamboat whistle, lined nearby riverbanks to watch the proceedings. Uncertain weather provided another form of adventure, but boats normally could seek shelter in one of the hundreds of rivers and sheltered coves. The names of the boats — the *Piankatank, Emma Giles, Westmoreland,* and *Louise* among them — became household words along their routes.

The Bay was a vital transportation link in Union prosecution of the Civil War. Ships carrying combatants, supplies, and wounded steamed back and forth. The peninsula campaign against Richmond was possible only because the federal navy controlled on the Bay. Two great battles were fought at Manassas, on a tributary named Bull Run. Confederates harassed Union shipping, sent spies sailing across at night, and illegally imported vast quantities of medical and military supplies from Maryland. Hampton Roads witnessed the historic battle between the ironclads *U.S.S. Monitor* and *C.S.S. Virginia (Merrimack),* which changed the nature of naval warfare for all time.

Post-Civil War expansion brought a surge of activity. The restlessness that drove people westward in search of a better life drove those who remained at home to seek recreation and excitement. Steamboat travel reached its peak in the latter part of the nineteenth century, depositing vacationers at resorts far removed from their urban habitats. Train depots and new hotels increased the popularity of the developing Atlantic Coast beach resorts.

In the affluent period after the Civil War, a series of unrelated events led to the Chesapeake Bay oyster "wars." The development of an easy and reliable method of steam canning, combined with a booming economy, created unprecedented demand for oysters in major cities and raised the prospect of quick fortunes. Tongers, hard pressed to meet demand by scooping up oysters with hand tools, soon faced competition from mechanical dredgers, many of whom shifted from Long Island when those beds became depleted. As Bay harvests declined, some dredgers turned to piracy, illegally invading the Potomac River, Pocomoke Sound, Chester River, and other streams. So many pirate boats were involved that a Baltimore reporter, sailing into Breton Bay on a "buy boat," at first thought the night lights of the pirate flotilla were the lights of a city.

What began as antagonism between Maryland hand tongers and dredgers soon became a confusing multicornered conflict between Maryland and Virginia watermen, oyster police, and militia, governments of the two states, and ordinary citizens of the affected areas that lasted from 1871 into modern times. The "war" produced frequent murder, shanghaiing, and mistreatment of crews, organized defiance of authority, running gun battles between police and oyster pirates, attacks and threats on towns, political intrigue, and legal conflict between the states. State and local governments attempted to control the situation by creating oyster police and militias and by legislative and court action, but depletion of the oyster beds from overuse, pollution, and natural diseases did as much as improved police training and equipment and new state compacts to end the fighting in the mid-1950s. The resolution came in 1962 when the Potomac River Fisheries Commission bill, negotiated by Virginia and Maryland, was approved by Congress and signed into law by President John F. Kennedy.

As the nation grew to maturity, the region continued to make its mark. The Bay remained an important transportation link in the first half of the twentieth century. Overnight runs between Baltimore and Hampton Roads, operated by the Old Bay Line until after World War II, were festive, often sleepless, occasions that still evoke nostalgia in those who remember them, but the liners could not compete against fast interstate highways and air travel. Millions of fighting men boarded transports in Newport News and Norfolk for the battlefields of Europe and North Africa during World Wars I and II. The invasion of North Africa during World War II virtually was launched from the ports of Hampton Roads. Merchant vessels sustained the farflung troops with millions of tons of cargo. Aircraft carriers, other warships, and merchant vessels slid in a steady stream down the ways of the Newport News shipyard. After the war, the yard built the fastest passenger liner ever built, the S.S. *United States,* whose exact speed is still a national secret.

The Bay region has a long association with aviation. The first successful plane flight from a flat-deck vessel occurred off Norfolk. Newport News was the site of significant lighter-than-air experimentation. The Langley Research Center of the National Aeronautics and Space Administration at Hampton was a pioneer in modern aviation research. The space age dawned in the region as the original astronauts—the Mercury Seven, who set the standard for the program—trained at Langley for their rendezvous with destiny in space. Rocket launches from Wallops Island, Virginia, provided part of the information needed to develop effective and safe hardware and techniques.

Tourways

HIGHWAYS PARALLELING THE SHORELINES IN BOTH VIRGINIA AND MARYland create a circular route that puts almost every city, fishing village, and wilderness area in the region within a few minutes drive of a main route. Interstate 95 between the metropolitan areas of Washington, D.C., and Baltimore is supplemented by U.S. 40 between Baltimore and Elkton, at the head of the Bay. From Elkton, Maryland Route 213 meanders southward through the historic communities of Chesapeake City and Chestertown before meeting U.S. 301, which passes Annapolis and cuts through the heart of Southern Maryland. U.S. 50 continues down the Eastern Shore through Cambridge, Princess Anne, and Salisbury to coastal Assateague Island and the chic Ocean City resort.

U.S. Route 13 completes the Eastern Shore run from Salisbury down the center of the narrow Virginia portion of the peninsula to enter Norfolk, part of the Hampton Roads metroplex. Interstate 64 continues the circular route to Hampton, Newport News and Yorktown, Williamsburg, and Jamestown. Then, U.S. Route 17 turns northward to provide access to the Virginia Middle Peninsula and Northern Neck, which are in entirety part of the Bay territory. At

Fredericksburg, Interstate 95 runs past Civil War battlegrounds, natural forests, and historic cities such as Alexandria to Washington.

Modern bridges open most of the islands, including Kent, Tilghman, and Hooper, to vehicular traffic, but the most picturesque islands are accessible only by boat. Among these are Smith Island and Tangier Island, which have developed into tourist attractions; Bloodworth Island, a former bombing range; and South Marsh Island, now a wildlife management area.

The same kind of circular journey is even easier by boat and has a longer tradition. Modern pleasure craft follow the trails opened by Capt. John Smith's exploration in the seventeenth century, subsequent voyages of settlement, and the golden age of Bay passenger travel. Water routes provide access to almost all the principal cities and towns, just as they did during the formative years. Rivers sometimes are navigable far into the interior, and most can accommodate boats of considerable size. Individual cruises from Norfolk to Baltimore just for a festive holiday are now ordinary.

A round-the-Bay cruise can start anywhere, but should include some or all of the most beautiful and most interesting landfalls on both sides of the Bay. Starting at Baltimore's attractive Inner Harbor on the Patapsco River, a clockwise trip could include a diversion up the varied Susquehanna and inspection of the historic community of Havre de Grace before skirting the Susquehanna Flats to reach the Eastern Shore.

Continuing the journey, boaters discover a different kind of river on the Maryland Eastern Shore, often short but beautiful streams, where boaters sometimes can still find temporary solitude. Among them are the Elk, better known in the eighteenth century when it was a lifeline of Washington's army during the Revolutionary War; the incomparable Sassafras, handsome Chester, and nature-bound Wye; the Choptank and Little Choptank, with mile after mile of forested shoreline; the calm Miles and Tred Avon; the commerce-dominated Wicomico; the Manokin, considered by some as the most beautiful; the Pocomoke, which reaches across the peninsula almost to the ocean; Fishing Bay, the way to isolated areas of the Fishing Bay Wildlife Management Area; and the coves and fishing harbors on the Virginia Eastern Shore, including tiny Saxis, Onancock, and bustling Cape Charles.

Around Hampton Roads are Virginia Beach, the naval vessels on the Elizabeth River at Norfolk, and the broad James River, home of the Newport News shipyard and a mothballed fleet of merchant vessels. Turning north, the boater can inspect the handsome low shoreline of the York River; the unspoiled Piankatank; the historic shoreline of the Rappahannock; the well-developed bank of the Potomac River, where George Washington's hilltop home, Mount Vernon, is clearly visible; the Patuxent, which reaches deep into Southern Maryland, site of Maryland's first settlement and great plantations; Annapolis; and the handsome high banks of the Severn River where dogwoods bloom in May.

Knowledge of the Bay is important, and boaters should possess current charts and tidal information and keep in mind the unpredictable nature of weather on Bay waters. The advice of locals, whose wisdom is born of experience, on silting, channels, and the like is important. For example, improper anchoring off an island can lead to considerable delay if the tide recedes.

Major airports are located at Washington (National, Dulles), Baltimore (Baltimore-Washington), Norfolk, and Newport News (Patrick Henry). Commuter service also reaches Salisbury, Maryland. Runways for small planes are located at Chesapeake, Fredericksburg, Melfa, Manassas, Portsmouth, Saluda, Suffolk, and Williamsburg in Virginia and at Annapolis, Baltimore County, Bel Air, Cambridge, Cecil County, Chestertown, College Park, Conowingo, Crisfield, Easton, Fallston, Forest Hills, Kent Island, Middle River, Newburg, Ocean City, Raintree, Ridgely, St. Mary's County, Salisbury, Suburban Washington, and Waldorf in Maryland.

Amtrak service connects Baltimore, Washington, and the Hampton Roads area.

Recreational Uses

THE RECREATIONAL ATTRIBUTES OF THE BAY ARE LEGENDARY: SPORT-fishing, boating, hunting, swimming, biking, hiking, canoeing, waterskiing, bird and animal watching, picnicking, camping. In a few places, local residents even go cross-country skiing on those rare occasions when sufficient snow survives long enough on the ground.

The seasons are not as important as one might imagine. Some fish are biting, some birds are singing, some wildflowers are blooming at least two-thirds of the time. The weather is milder at the southern end of the Bay, but usually fair enough even at the northern extreme to make the Bay accessible year round.

Summers are hot and humid, but there is usually a breeze on the water. Autumn often is the most pleasant season of the year. The Bay has a surprising flair in winter; the weather is just erratic enough to be interesting. The stark limbs of leafless trees are framed by the dark green of evergreens, while the holly berries and the cranefly orchid, which in deep winter puts up a single leaf, purple on the bottom and green on top, brighten the ground level. Wintering waterfowl are everywhere along the water. Inland, sparrows and blackbirds maraud the decayed fruit of wild trees and even the flies remain active at times. Normally, snowfalls are light and do not remain long on the ground. Festivals related to the water or Bay produce last into the winter. However, few sports enthusiasts other than hunters venture out during the coldest winter months. Temperature dips into the teens, or below, are tempered by warmer days. Occasionally, a severe winter will freeze ponds, and even streams, for the benefit of ice skaters. Old-timers remember when ice on the broad James River was so thick people could walk across, but it has not happened in half a century. Even in the most severe periods, the filtered sun may break through to promise relief. Spring can also be erratic, but compensates with a gradual emergence of color.

Federal, state, local, and private parks, nature areas, and historic sites provide a variety of outdoor experiences, from trails through woods and marshes to gardens. Maryland has thirteen state parks in the region; Virginia has nine, and local parks sometimes have all the variety of state parks.

Boating

During the warm months, danger increases on any highway overlooking a waterway because varicolored spinnakers, colonies of ballooning white sails, and forests of masts distract drivers. No one minds. Boating is a subculture, if not a cult, in the Chesapeake Bay area. Preparation for the season is an annual ritual for those who do own boats. Those who do not, perform a different kind of ritual by turning to commercial operators who provide harbor or Bay tours, charter boats for fishing and excursion groups, and "head" boats that put unrelated people together for trips.

This affection is not only natural, it is historically sanctified. The Indians drew sustenance from the water of the Bay and its tributaries before Europeans began to colonize the coasts. The Europeans, who came as farmers and artisans, were drawn to the Bay by necessity. Once there, they began to evolve a lifestyle that was, directly and indirectly, dependent on the Bay as a source of food and social organization and as an outlet to the world.

For more than three hundred years, until fiberglass created a new kind of hull, Bay watermen depended on boats that evolved from the Indian dugout canoe. Almost immediately, they began to make the canoe larger and more efficient. Soon, they were putting two or more logs together to increase the size of the vessels, which in time evolved into boats that were distinctive to the Bay region or even to subregions. Boats in the lower Bay often are slightly different from those of the same class in the northern Bay. Even today, these are called "log canoes" in the vernacular.

Adaptations frequently met the needs of the watermen. The oyster industry, which became a cash crop in the nineteenth century when depletion of northern beds increased demand for Chesapeake Bay oysters, has been responsible for major modifications. The two-masted pungy, which appeared in the 1840s, was a scaled-down version of the Baltimore clipper. The later bugeye, whose name remains something of a mystery but may have evolved from "buckie," the Scottish word for oyster shell, were less expensive and more versatile. The small, flat-bottomed centerboard schooner with an aft cabin dominated the oyster fleet by the 1880s.

None has ever rivaled the fast, sleek skipjack in the affection of the watermen. The single-masted vessel, which appeared in the 1890s and was named after bluefish that at times "skip" across the water, could be handled by one person. Although many watermen have turned to more efficient powerboats, they speak of the skipjack with much the same reverence they reserve for the blue crab. The tilted masts of perhaps twenty skipjacks still rise above the harbors of a few ports, including those on Maryland's Deal Island, but their most popular use now is cruising and racing. Skipjack races are held annually at Deal Island. Log canoe races are run in July, August, and September in the Miles, Chester, and Tred Avon rivers in Maryland.

Adaptation and innovation have not been limited to commercial boats. The *Hampton One* sloop, designed in the 1930s by boatworks owners Harry A. Bullifant and Vincent J. Serio, Jr., represents an attempt to meet the specific needs of the region. The small, inexpensive racing sailboat is both fast and able.

Boat building is a fading but not a lost art. Although factories have replaced the hand-hewn methods, it is still possible to find a persistent builder on Tilghman Island and a few other places, but it is simply easier and cheaper to purchase a factory boat.

About 240,000 boats are registered on Chesapeake Bay, the second largest concentration on the East Coast. Only Long Island Sound has more. The number of craft using the Bay is even larger. The Chesapeake is part of the Intracoastal Waterway, a protected route for pleasure craft that extends from New Jersey to Florida. The waterway passes through the Chesapeake and Delaware Canal, traverses the Bay, and departs for Albermarle Sound in North Carolina by way of the historic Albermarle and Chesapeake Canal at the Dismal Swamp. The spring and autumn migration of "snowbirds" along this route emulates the flights of waterfowl.

Most visitors are impressed by the physical qualities of the Bay, in particular the expanses of water for maneuvering and the extensive system of tributaries. More than two hundred harbors where boats drawing 6 feet can safely stop stand along the shoreline, bays, and streams. Hundreds more can handle boats with 5-foot drafts. Marinas, boat ramps, piers, docks, landings, marine railways, and ship's stores inhabit every navigable stream and cove, many of them near historic cities or homes. Virginia and Maryland maintain scores of boat-launching ramps and docking facilities, and most private wharves permit landings and make slips available to transients.

Sailboaters regard the Bay as one of the best in the continental United States. A fairly good breeze blows winter and summer, especially in the lower end of the Bay, including an afternoon sea breeze in summer. Summers are hot, but even in July and August there usually is enough breeze to move sailboats. At least one regatta is held each week throughout the sailing season, and a "Frostbite Series" of races pushes off in November.

Although it is for the most part user-friendly, the Bay is not a place for unwary sailors. The long coastline and large number of tributaries affect the tides, which move 2 or 3 feet and in certain areas may vary as much as twelve hours from normal. Currents sometimes are strong, especially in narrow channels. Weather is unpredictable. Squalls are a problem, although clouds usually provide ample warning for those who can read them. Winds out of the northeast can make the water choppy. Winds on the Potomac River vary considerably from section to section. Mud flats and shoals line large sections of shoreline. Silting is a continuing problem and channels may move suddenly, especially during a storm. Boaters should be wary of restricted areas. Hazards contributed by humans include crab pots and the hulks of abandoned boats.

Boating season runs from April through November, but the prime period is May–June and September–October.

Regulations are pretty standard. Boats remaining in Virginia more than ninety days must be registered. A lifejacket is required for each person on board all sailing craft and motorboats operating in Virginia waters, as well as canoes, kayaks, and inflatable boats. Fire extinguishers are required on all inboards, all outboards measuring 26 feet and over, and certain craft under 26 feet. Inboard gasoline engines must have flame arrestors on carburetors, and those in enclosed compartments must be ventilated. Operators of boats 16 feet and longer must carry a horn or whistle on board.

Navigation lights are required on international and inland waters for both motorboats and sailing vessels, but sailboats under 22 feet 10 inches (7 meters) and rowboats may substitute a flashlight or lantern. Smaller vessels must give way to deep-draft ships in channels.

Maryland regulations are a bit complicated, but generally follow Coast Guard procedures. Nonresident boaters visiting the state for ninety days or less are not required to obtain a certificate of boating safety education, as are residents born after July 1, 1972. Engines must have backfire flame arrestors and vessels must carry flame extinguishers, a sound signaling device, and visual distress signals. Wearable floating devices are required for each person on board; boats 16 feet or over also must carry one throwable preserver. Kayakers, canoers, and others also must have life jackets.

Buoys are red on the right and green or black on the left going upstream (RRR or red right returning); midchannel markers have red and white vertical stripes. Meeting boaters pass to the right; when crossing, the boat on the right has the right of way; sailboats have the right of way over motorboats, unless they are the overtaking vessel, and canoes and rowboats have the right of way over sailboats.

NOAA Weather radio broadcasts on 162.400, 162.475, and 162.55 MHz. National weather service numbers include Washington, D.C. (202/471–1741), Norfolk, Virginia (804/853–3013), and Baltimore, Point Lookout, and Salisbury, Maryland.

Brightly colored sailboards increasingly mix with the larger sailboats, in protected waters from the mud flats off Havre de Grace to the busy waters of the James River. The growing popularity of windsurfing, waterskiing, or aquaplaning in rivers and small bays has prompted the organization of schools that offer instruction in handling and safety. Waterskiing and aquaplaning are permitted from one hour before sunrise to one hour after sunset, provided the towing boat has an observer in addition to the driver; skiers should wear floatation jackets.

The placid waters of many Chesapeake Bay tributaries are as amenable to modern canoeing as they were to the crude boats of the Algonkin Indians. Canoeists paddle courses of varying degrees of difficulty on more than a score of streams lined with trees and bushes.

Some are surprisingly close to population centers. The Gunpowder River system, north and east of Baltimore, offers several predictable trails. A Patapsco River run, also near Baltimore, passes through a gorge in Patapsco State Park, the remnants of industries along the shoreline, and requires portage at two dams. A whitewater area is located between U.S. 40 and Ellicott City, with easier rapids below. Stretches of the Potomac northwest of Washington, including the Great Falls, are too wild for ordinary trips, but the section between Great Falls and Little Falls (levels 4 feet and above are regarded as hazardous) has both navigable rapids and wilderness appearance. Canoeing also is permitted in the Tidal Basin and on the Anacostia River.

Three trails begin near the Conowingo Dam at U.S. Route 1. Below the dam, canoeists on the Susquehanna River pass over rocky shallows and around small islands that are major hazards, share the Susquehanna State Park with fishers in boats and along the shoreline, and take up at the park's boat ramp. Conowingo and Octoraro Creeks have diverse trails just before they empty into the Susquehanna River. The Conowingo below U.S. Route 222 has jagged rocks at low water, better condition at high water. The Octoraro below U.S. Route 1 lives up to its Indian name, which means "rushing waters."

In the Upper Bay area, the Big Elk Creek is tame near Elkton, rougher closer to the Pennsylvania border. Along Great Bohemia Creek, canoeists experience an easy, peaceful trip past marshes, forests broken by rolling farmlands, narrow sandy beaches, tidal action, and handsome cottages and piers. The upper reaches of the Choptank River, between the Delaware border and Denton, are also scenic, and Tuckahoe Creek, which empties into the Choptank west of Denton, explores the wooded splendor of Tuckahoe State Park. Kings Creek and Miles Creek, which enter the Choptank near

Easton, are flat but beautiful. Other scenic Eastern Shore canoeing streams include Worlds End Creek, Farm Creek, Blackwater River (which traverses a swampy wildlife refuge), Transquaking River, Nanticoke River and its tributaries, Pocomoke River, and the Assateague Island National Seashore.

The upper reaches of the Patuxent River serenely dissect the twin urban explosions at Washington and Annapolis, creating a 10-mile wilderness stretch that starts near the Washington-Baltimore Parkway, crosses the Patuxent Wildlife Refuge and follows the boundary of Fort George G. Meade. Nanjenoy Creek in Charles County features marshes and wooded bluffs until it broadens into Hill Top Fork. Zekiah Swamp Run, which extends 11 miles from Cedarville State Forest in Southern Maryland, is one of the roughest and wildest places for canoers in the Chesapeake Bay area.

Canoe rentals are available in some state parks and along some lakes and rivers and the Chesapeake and Ohio Canal north of Washington, D.C., for leisurely paddling.

The Virginia mainland is broken into peninsulas by major river systems, but even the wide, active James River attracts canoers on occasion. More popular are the smaller rivers like the Severn and Chickahmony. The ideal Virginia stream for canoers is Dragon Run, one of the last pristine stretches of water in the region, which flows gently through a wilderness area and empties into the Severn River (see the section on the Middle Peninsula). Another is Dismal Swamp, where a feeder canal leads to isolated Lake Drummond.

The shoreline of Virginia's Eastern Shore is corrugated with shallow bays and inlets that present few challenges.

Sportfishing

Fishing attracts more people than any other competitive Bay water sport. An estimated 900,000 people land at least 10 million pounds of fish each year. Surfcasting is done on many beaches, and anglers sometimes stand shoulder to shoulder on fishing piers, but most take to their boats in the numerous coves, bays, and rivers of the region.

Fishing continues year round in some fashion in some place, but rough seas and icy weather during January and February deter all but the most hardy. Virginia bans rockfish catches from December 1 through May 31, and Maryland has since 1985 imposed a year-round moratorium because of a population decline.

Anglers begin to appear in large numbers in late March or early

April as the weather improves and the fish return from the Atlantic Ocean or rise from the depths of the Bay. Returning or rising fish tend to be large. Early catches include tautog and bluefish, which become active from mid- to late-April. Bluefish of 12 to 15 pounds are common in May and run through December. A few gray trout and shad may show earlier, but these species don't appear in large numbers until the water temperature approaches the sixties, normally in late April or early May. At the same time, black drum and red drum (channel bass) arrive in the lower Bay area and speckled trout appear farther up in Mobjack Bay and its tributaries.

Warming weather increases finfish activity. Warm, sunny days with light winds are best for flounder. Croaker and spot are plentiful from late April through early September, with the biggest catches often coming later. October and November are excellent for sea trout, sea bass, tautog, croaker, spot, and sea bass. Bluefish usually begin migrating to open seas in late October, while striped bass normally are back by late November.

Tides are a factor. Fish follow the movement of their food on incoming and outgoing tides. Some species actually feed better when tide is moving in and out. In addition, tidal action affects water levels on sandbars, shoals, and streams and bays.

Just like fishers, Chesapeake Bay finfish haunt favorite spots. Stripers, as rockfish are often called, favor the mid- and upper-Bay sections, including Tangier Sound. Black and red drum frequent the James River off Newport News and Tangier Sound during summer. Wrecks or artificial reefs and the shoals off Onancock Creek attract cobia, while largemouth bass, crappie, and bluegill ranging in size from 1 to 6 pounds select brackish rivers like the Choptank, Pocomoke, and Wicomico in Maryland. Blue catfish like the Susquehanna River flats and Potomac and other rivers. Smallmouth bass are plentiful in the Potomac and Susquehanna rivers; carp gravitate toward brackish and fresh water; and the chain pickerel (pike) frequents the Tuckahoe, Pocomoke, South, Severn, and Magothy rivers in Maryland.

The greatest fishing place in the Bay may be the Chesapeake Bay Bridge-Tunnel. Located near the entrance to the Bay, it spans the route used by migratory fish. In addition, its underwater structures are covered with marine life that attracts fish, including flounder, speckled trout, striped bass, and gray trout. The barrier islands off the Eastern Shore are one of the best places on the East Coast for flounder. Mobjack Bay in Virginia is known for speckled trout. Bluefish Rock, an underwater wall about 2 miles off Grandview in Hampton formed by ballast discarded by sailing vessels entering Hampton Roads, is a favorite feeding place. Other artificial reefs are located at Goodwin's Island, Parramore Island, and Ocean View.

All types of bait—bloodworms, peelers, clams, whelk, minnows, crayfish, plastic worms and minnows, and small artificial lures—are used.

The proximity of the Gulf Stream to the mouth of Chesapeake Bay makes the Hampton Roads area a headquarters for Atlantic deep-sea fishing. Although many residents prefer to try their luck off North Carolina's Outer Banks, Hampton Roads marinas also operate charter and "head" boats in search of white and blue marlin, sailfish, dolphin, tuna, wahoo, and other varieties. Artificial reefs at Thimble Shoals Light, about 12 miles offshore, and Triangle Wrecks about 30 miles offshore, are popular sites. The season extends from April through October, with June and July the peak period for bluefin and yellowfin tuna.

Virginia and Maryland present concurrent Governor's Cup prizes in late July, with cooperation from Pennsylvania, the District of Columbia, the Chesapeake Bay Commission, and the U.S. Environmental Protection Agency. The tournament sends fishers at all skill levels onto the Bay, beaches, and piers in search of prize-winning blues, flounder, gray trout, speckled trout, croaker, and spot. Prizes are awarded at tournament ports—Chesapeake Beach, Tilghman Island, Solomons Island, and Crisfield in Maryland; and Norfolk, Cape Charles, Onancock, Reedville, Deltaville, and Virginia Beach in Virginia—and Maryland and Virginia winners each receive a Governor's Cup. Special awards are reserved for young people under 16 years of age. Proceeds from the tournament are being used to restore the Bay.

The Virginia Salt Water Fishing Tournament is held annually from May 1 through the end of November. More than 3,500 awards are made.

Freshwater fishing is available in lakes, reservoir ponds, and small streams in the Chesapeake Bay region, although only a fraction of Virginia's 421,000 licensed freshwater fishers are in the Bay area.

Virginia does not require a license for saltwater fishing. Maryland does, except at designated free fishing points in North East, Chestertown, Cambridge, Denton, Sharptown, Salisbury, Snow Hill, Pocomoke City, Havre de Grace, Baltimore County, Baltimore City, Annapolis, Worton, Tysakin Park, and Friendship Landing. Both states require freshwater fishing licenses.

Lists of freshwater and saltwater fishing guides are available from the Fisheries Division, Department of Natural Resources, 69 Prince George Street, Annapolis, MD 21401 (301/974-3765), and the Virginia Division of Tourism, 202 North 9th Street Suite 500, Richmond, VA 23219 (804/786-2051).

Hunting

The unsavory reputation that hunters in the Bay area acquired prior to World War II still haunts the more considerate practitioner of today. Museums at St. Michaels, Maryland, and elsewhere display the devices formerly used to bag commercial quantities of wildfowl, including huge guns that could kill scores of birds at a time, crippling traps, and illegal boats that gave hunters more advantage than they needed.

Hunting is not as prevalent as it was a generation or two ago, but it is still a major sport. Since both land and air game is abundant, shooting of some kind goes on year round. Hunting occurs on public grounds as conservation measures, at private clubs, and on farms whose owners want to hold down the deer population. Licenses are required, and seasons and limits are strictly enforced. Guide service is available at the most popular locations.

Since Chesapeake Bay is a major component of the Atlantic flyway, waterfowl is a popular target. The hundreds of thousands of ducks and geese that winter there or rest before continuing longer flights provide the finest hunting on the East Coast. Taking wild turkeys is allowed in most of the Virginia counties adjacent to the Bay and in a few Maryland counties, including Calvert and Worcester. Other game birds include quail, grouse, rails, pheasants, doves, woodcock, and jacksnipe.

White-tailed deer is the most popular land game—more are killed in the Bay area of Virginia each year than in the rest of the state—but rabbit, squirrel, raccoon, and opossum also are hunted. Exotic animals such as bear and bobcat may be taken in certain areas of Virginia, but are rarely seen these days. The Delmarva fox squirrel is regarded as an endangered species and cannot be hunted.

Maryland has separate firearms, bow, and muzzle-loading hunting seasons. The Maryland Department of Natural Resources, Maryland Forest, Park and Wildlife Service, Tawes State Office Building, Annapolis, MD 21401 (301/974-3195), administers the hunting laws.

Licenses also are available through hunting goods stores. Licenses run from August 1 through July 31.

Maryland seasons and limits vary somewhat by county, but seasons generally are as follows: quail, mid-November to February; rabbits, mid-November to end of January; squirrels, October to end of January; pheasant, mid-November to late December; white-tailed and sika deer, late November to early December for firearms, mid-September to late November and early December to early January for bows; mourning dove, September to mid-October and a few days in November and December; rails, September to early November; snipe, October to mid-January; Canada, snow, and blue geese, mid-October to mid-November and mid-December to February; sea ducks, October to January; muskrat and mink, mid-November to mid-February; raccoon and opossum, mid-October to mid-February (no-kill chasing early August to mid-October), and wild turkey, mid-April to mid-May.

Under state law, fox hunting with dogs is banned during firearms deer season, except in Charles and Dorchester counties. Riding to hounds is legal all year. Queen Anne's and Caroline counties impose additional restrictions.

In Virginia, seasons and limits may vary from county to county. Deer may be hunted throughout the Bay region when in season, which starts as early as October 1 in Virginia Beach and Chesapeake but runs from mid-November to early January throughout most of the region. One-per-day bags are standard, but per-year totals may be either two or three, depending on the county. In most areas, either sex may be taken the last six days of the season. Turkeys may be hunted statewide in the spring and in certain counties, including Middlesex, York, and those in the Northern Neck, in the autumn as well. Fox hunting with dogs is legal year round in most areas; Newport News and Fairfax County shorten the season. Virginia has an early season for archers, from mid-October through early November.

The administering agency is the Department of Game and Island Fisheries, P.O. Box 11104, Richmond, VA 23230 (804/257-1000). Licenses, good from July 1 through June 30, are sold by clerks of court and authorized agencies such as hunting supply stores.

Rabies is periodically a problem throughout the Chesapeake Bay region, primarily in raccoon. Hunters should consult local health departments and their physicians.

Bird-Watching

The Chesapeake Bay area is living proof of Charles Dickens's pronouncement that "nature gives every time and season some beauties of its own." The varied habitats of the Bay area — upland and lowland forests, cultivated fields, saltwater and freshwater marshes, sand dunes, ocean beaches, shrublands, and islands — attract a diverse bird population. Maryland has a larger nesting variety than any state of similar size, while the forests, pristine reserves, and barrier islands of the Virginia coastal plain attract as many species.

Bird-watching is a year-round event on the Bay and its tributaries, but is especially good in spring and summer when songbirds and shorebirds are migrating. Compiling a single list for Bay viewing is difficult because of seasonal changes and habitat variations from section to section. Sometimes uplands and lowlands are in close proximity, thus bringing normally distant birds together, and sometimes not. Altogether, as many as three hundred species of birds are seen throughout the area, including about forty vireos and warblers and more than thirty kinds of geese, ducks, and swans. The tidal marshes and creeks, which provide abundant grasses, wild rice, and cattails, attract many species; as many as one hundred kinds of birds, including migrating shorebirds, king rail, and woodpeckers, have been counted on a single day by the National Audubon Society.

The northern and southern breeding limits of a number of species overlap in the Chesapeake Bay area, including such southern birds as the Louisiana heron, Wilson's plover, and boat-tailed grackle. Rarely seen birds that nest in the area include the red-cockaded woodpecker and Swainson's warbler. Soras and bobolink interrupt their southward journeys in the area. Herons, egrets, pelicans, rails, kestrels, and osprey are common.

The eagle is demonstrating its toughness, as well as its devotion to the region. Some refuges have substantial numbers. The flock at Aberdeen Proving Ground in Maryland, a major weapons-testing center, is growing despite the explosions that take place there on a regular basis. The Caledon Natural Area and Mason Neck National Wildlife Refuge in Virginia have seen major gains in short periods. Sightings are reported less frequently in other parts of the Bay.

Dr. Mitchell Byrd, who teaches ornithology at the College of William and Mary in Williamsburg and is a former president of the Virginia Society of Ornithology, rates Kiptopeke, Chincoteague, and Blackwater National Wildlife Refuges, and the George Washington

Birthplace National Monument among the best places for bird-watching. Kiptopeke is a good area for raptors and more than 150 species of songbirds. Chincoteague hosts a varied list, including a large number of shorebirds; piping plover, a protected species, nests there. Blackwater is crowded with waterfowl during the fall and winter and has a sizable population of bald eagle. Washington's Birthplace in Virginia's Westmoreland County is noted for swans and geese, as well as a few bald eagle.

Conditions are conducive to bird-watching even in some metropolitan areas, like Washington, D.C., and Hampton Roads (see individual chapters).

Seasonal migrations are mind-boggling. In the spring and summer, songbirds on northward movements pause to rest or nest, their tones providing background music for the resurgence of life in the forests and lowlands. Shorebirds appear from the south, followed by wading and marsh birds. Blue-winged teal nest in the saltwater marshes before wintering in the West Indies or South America. Autumn fills the skies with wildfowl. Whistling swan, canvasback, American wigeon, and other wildfowl follow the Susquehanna River and Chesapeake Bay southward, while snow goose, scoter, brant, cormorant, red-breasted merganser, and others favor the ocean coastline. Flying both routes are Canada goose, American black duck, and scaup. About a million waterfowl, 25 percent of those using the Atlantic flyway, winter on Chesapeake Bay, using virtually every waterway. The greatest concentrations occur on the eastern shore of the Bay, particularly the Chester River, Eastern Bay, and Choptank River areas. As many as 100,000 waterfowl may visit the Blackwater area south of Cambridge, Maryland, including the national wildlife refuge. Significant numbers of Canada and snow goose, brant, and whistling swan settle at the Chincoteague and/or Back Bay National Wildlife Refuges in Virginia. Winter land residents include the Carolina chickadee, northern mockingbird, brown-headed nuthatch, sedge wren, pine warbler, gray catbird, and common yellowthroat.

Specific migratory movements vary somewhat but have the following general pattern: waterfowl, mid-October to early December and late February to early April; shorebirds, late April to early June and mid-August to October; and land birds, mid-April to mid-May and early September to early November.

Bird-watchers of the Bay area are heirs to a great tradition. Settlers at Jamestown, including Capt. John Smith and George Percy, made brief comments on birds in their early reports. The first systematic study began in 1712, when Mark Catesby began to document and draw birds and plants along the shores of the James River.

Pollution problems that discourage wildfowl from returning to the area or force them to raid farmlands and pastures for food are being addressed. The states of Virginia, Maryland, and Pennsylvania, as well as Washington, D.C., and federal agencies, are working to reduce the use of pesticides and the flow of effluents that seriously affect the food chain, thus protecting the aquatic vegetation and other lifeforms on which birds feed.

Biking

The Chesapeake Bay area can easily pass a breath test. Stop a biker on any roadway; few will be panting or fatigued. Even hot summer days do not discourage those who pedal the byways past forests and horse and cattle farms, to fishing villages, wildlife refuges, crab feasts, to fishing, swimming, and boating sites, and over bridges spanning Bay tributaries. The flat, varied terrain and an extensive network of side roads create favorable conditions. So favorable, in fact, that three-day and six-day guided tours, using historic inns located 20 to 40 miles apart, pedal across the upper, middle, and lower sections of the Eastern Shore. Bikers can duplicate these tours on their own, of course.

Maryland has mapped out scenic routes, described later in the Eastern Shore and Southern Maryland sections of this book. For the most part, these routes use the shoulders, some of them 10 feet wide, of highways with light automobile traffic. A statewide trail starts in the western mountains, crosses the Bay at Annapolis and splits; one arm extends northward to Elkton, where it links up with another branch that parallels the Maryland-Pennsylvania border, and the other arm moves southward through the Eastern Shore to Ocean City or Crisfield or connects with trails on the Virginia Eastern Shore.

In Maryland, bikers may not use highway travel lanes when speeds of 50 mph or more are posted, expressways, and controlled-access roads and toll facilities. Bikers must use shoulder areas or bike lanes if they are paved. Most rural and small communities can be easily traversed with a little patience, but biking in metropolitan areas is not recommended unless trails have been marked.

State and national parks have biking trails. The C&O Canal Tow Path from Washington to Cumberland, Maryland, the Baltimore and

Annapolis Railroad Trail between those two cities, and the North Central Railroad Trail north of Baltimore, from Ashland to Monkton, follow abandoned public transportation beds. The 3-mile-long boardwalk at Ocean City is an early-morning possibility during the warm months and an all-day route the rest of the year.

Bikes must be equipped with working brakes, bell or horn, rear red reflector, and, if ridden at night, a white beam headlight. Helmet, rear-view mirror, and red taillight also are recommended.

Virginia's long-run routes lie mostly outside the Chesapeake Bay region. However, Yorktown is at one end of the Trans-America Trail that follows Route 76, while the Virginia-to-Florida Trail, which starts at Richmond, passes through Surry and Isle of Wight counties and the city of Suffolk.

One of the most scenic regional bike routes in America is the Colonial National Parkway, which links the Jamestown-Williamsburg-Yorktown Historic Triangle. Other well-used paths are marked in and around Williamsburg, Newport News, and Virginia Beach. Northern Virginia, adjacent to the nation's capital, has an extensive network of bikeways, some of which tie in with Washington and Maryland trails. National and state parks have shorter trails. These are described in appropriate sections.

Virginia highways generally do not have paved shoulders comparable to those in Maryland. However, many rural routes on the Eastern Shore and elsewhere carry light traffic and are popular with biking clubs.

Under Virginia law, bicyclists basically have the same responsibilities as automobile drivers, but must operate as close to the right-hand edge or curb as possible. Bicycle paths adjacent to highways must be used where available. Necessary equipment includes brakes that skid wheels on clean, dry pavement and lights (a reflector may be substituted for a rear red light) at night. Off-limits roads are marked.

Both Maryland and Virginia prohibit riding bikes across major river crossings, but provide courtesy transportation on request.

Camping

When defined as living outdoors in a portable shelter including recreation vehicles, camping is the third most popular sporting activity in the United States. The reasons are obvious: it is an adventure that reinforces family values, provides relief from daily pressures, and is a natural learning experience.

Despite idyllic conditions for both primitive and comfortable participation, the activity does not rate as highly around resource-rich Chesapeake Bay as it does in some other areas, probably because so many other options exist. Nevertheless, it is a rapidly growing activity.

The Bay country is dotted with wilderness camping areas, which have varied characteristics, ranging from seashore sites to forests. Possible on-site activities extend far beyond the gather-round-the-campfire routine and include fishing, hunting, hiking, and nature walks for observation of flora and fauna.

Infrastructure for camping is well developed. Numerous campgrounds and RV (recreational vehicle) parks exist on both shores. Privately operated facilities predominate in Virginia, but many are strategically located on waterways or in forests to facilitate activities. Maryland has a mix of public and private camping possibilities, especially on the Eastern Shore where a large number of wildlife preserves exist.

Beaches and Resorts

The excellent natural beaches, where major and minor resorts and the summer cottages of the well-to-do mingle comfortably with seafood operations, have gone through a number of changes of life.

The resort tradition expanded in the nineteenth century as steamboats, and then railroads, carried city dwellers to isolated riverside and bayfront communities where they could wade in sun-warmed water and relax in cool breezes. Steamboat resorts along the Potomac, at Lookout Point in Maryland, and other places struggled against the vicissitudes of changing interests, economic recessions, and wars. In the late nineteenth century, railroads made waterfront resorts such as Chesapeake Beach popular with residents of large cities such as Washington, D.C.

The latter half of the twentieth century is witnessing another transformation, as single-use centers replace traditional public-private combinations. Some like Buckroe Beach in Hampton, Virginia, which once appealed to middle-class visitors from Richmond and other inland cities, are being absorbed largely by private development. Nevertheless, large resorts such as Virginia Beach and Ocean City, Maryland, both with long oceanfront public beaches, continue the tradition. The Tides Inn is a small but highly regarded resort on the Rappahannock River at Irvington. Bayside beaches, some as isolated as the seldom-visited Mathews County Beach, tend to be smaller but are no less significant.

In hot weather, jellyfish, Portuguese man-o-wars, and nettles (all frequently referred to locally as "stinger nettles") sometimes bother bathers. They can be dangerous to people allergic to their stings; local beachgoers apply topical treatments.

Swimmers should exercise caution. Swimming alone or at a posted beach is dangerous. In some places at low tides, especially in Hampton Roads, people can walk out almost to the channels for deep-water vessels. Almost every year, a few people disappear into those channel currents. Swimmers may want to take heed: locals prefer pools to the Bay and its tributaries.

Insects are a nuisance in most coastal areas during the summer months.

~~~~~~~~~

PART TWO

Maryland

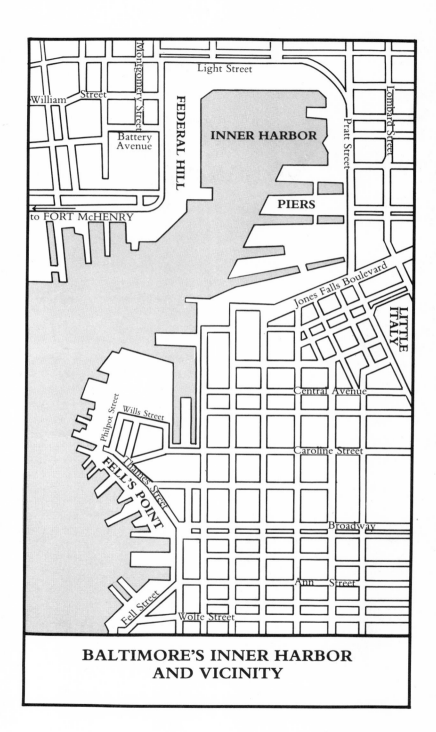

**BALTIMORE'S INNER HARBOR
AND VICINITY**

Baltimore

Office of Promotion & Tourism, 110 West Baltimore Street, Baltimore, MD 21201. Tel.: 301/752-8632.

BALTIMORE IS UNQUESTIONABLY THE "CAPITAL" OF THE BAY COUNTRY, but that status results more from accident than preference. The principal actor in Baltimore history has been, and continues to be, its port. Founded in 1729 as an outlet for grain and tobacco grown in the region, Baltimore soon developed into a crossroads with dual exposure. Since it was situated farther west than any other East Coast port, it drew much of the trade associated with the westward expansion of the nation. Its location on the cusp between North and South was another source of vitality.

Although largely bypassed by the Revolutionary War, meetings of the Continental Congress in Baltimore in 1775 made it for a short time the temporary capital of the new nation. It had a much bigger role in the War of 1812, which was basically a dispute over maritime rights. At least 125 privateers sailed from Baltimore to harass British shipping — more than from any other American port — and they captured or sank more than 500 British vessels. The *Rossie*, Capt. James Barney commanding, on a single voyage took eighteen vessels, of various sizes, whose cargoes were worth $1.5 million, a fortune in those days. Britain sent its fastest vessels, without success, after Capt. Thomas Boyle, the most famous of the Baltimore privateers, who took a total of sixty prizes.

So prominent was the city's role that London newspapers demanded the British navy attack the city in order to stop the "legalized piracy." Vice Adm. Sir Alexander Cochrane, overall British commander in America, was attracted by the potential booty of the rich city and a belief the city "ought to be laid in ashes." Baltimore thus became a major target when the British fleet in the Chesapeake became strong enough to act. The campaign against the city ended when the failure to capture Fort McHenry, the city's coastal guardian, inspired the writing of the national anthem, "The Star-Spangled Banner."

Baltimore once again lapsed into profitable commercialism, only to be aroused by the Civil War. To avoid possible trouble, President Abraham Lincoln surreptitiously passed through the city on his journey to Washington to be inaugurated. Later, pro-Confederate citizens stoned Union troops in transit to Washington and Baltimore, and Maryland spent the war under virtual military occupation. A postwar decline was halted by activity on the Baltimore and Ohio Railway, principally the shipment of grain, and Bay passenger liner traffic.

The city once again declined as modern residential flight to the suburbs brought on urban blight. Twenty-five years ago, Baltimore was, in the words of one native, "the town that nobody wanted to come and see because we were a dirty, boring, industrial, blue-collar city, with a run-down downtown." Coordinated action by government, business, and citizen groups gradually has transformed the downtown area into a place that about 7 million Baltimoreans and visitors a year enjoy, built around a multifaceted Inner Harbor. The outer harbor, where the maritime industry is concentrated, continues to dominate the commercial life of Baltimore despite the decline of shipbuilding.

The relationship between corporate Baltimore and the individual is familial, natural, and casual, not forced or strained. When citizens speak of "Bawlmer," their revelations are unadorned, even understated at times, and arise not from expected loyalty but from genuine affection for their city.

Through triumph and tragedy, a consistent intellectual tolerance has accompanied crass commercialism. Baltimore cared, but with a seafarer's lust for alternating the sensual and the intellectual. The once infamous strip joints along East Baltimore Street coexisted with one of the nation's most famous performing and teaching institutions, the Peabody Conservatory of Music, founded in 1866. The Lyric Opera House, a replica of the Leipzig Music Hall in Germany, has been joined by 2,458-seat Meyerhoff Symphony Hall, dedicated in 1982 as the home of the Baltimore Symphony Orchestra. Lighter musical interests are satisfied at popular concerts in the Pier Six Concert Pavilion at the Inner Harbor, which includes summer performances by nationally known performers and the annual Jazz Festival in September, and the Eubie Blake Cultural Center, which honors Baltimore native James Hubert "Eubie" Blake, the great ragtime pianist and composer. The state theater of Maryland performs at Center Stage in a nineteenth-century theater in the Mount Vernon district. Discotheques, pubs, and dinner theaters, including the Vagabond Players, which claims to be the oldest continuously operated "little theater" in the United States, also help provide a healthy cultural agenda.

The city that provided material for the works of Edgar Allen Poe listened to a home-grown philosopher in the twentieth century, H. L. Mencken, who championed journalistic freedom and challenged conventional wisdom, became a respected intellectual voice in America in the 1920s and 1930s.

Baltimore may no longer be "the gastronomic capital of the world," as essayist Ralph Waldo Emerson suggested it was, but close association with Chesapeake Bay and ethnic diversity — small enclaves of Poles, Czechs, European Jews, and Germans still exist — combine to create a large number of interesting restaurants all over the city, especially along South High Street in Little Italy. Baltimoreans also return to their commercial roots in their gustatory pleasures. The 204-year-old indoor Lexington Market is as well known for its raw oyster bars as for its grocery and ethnic shops. Mencken frequented Hollins Market in search of soft crabs, oysters, and beaten biscuits, which, together with Maryland fried chicken, constitute the state's contribution to the nation's culinary catalogue. The 200-year-old Broadway Market near the waterfront is noted for its Chesapeake Bay seafood. The outdoor Farmer's Market at Holiday and Saratoga Streets is the most prosaic, but fills with the bright colors of flowers and the sweet smells of farm produce.

Official literature claims more than 260 neighborhoods in all, including twenty-three historic districts. Federal Hill, which overlooks the Inner Harbor, and Fell's Point are the best known. Federal Hill, the site of a huge celebration recognizing the ratification of the U.S. Constitution, is one of the oldest neighborhoods. It features revitalized row houses, new shops, and the small Cross Street Market, famous for both raw oyster bars and imported delicacies. Fell's Point, a national historic district with cobblestone streets and 350 original residences, chronicles the city's periods of transition. A fleet of tugboats, reminders that the reputation of the area was built on merchant shipping and shipbuilding, ties up near the yachts of new "yuppie" residents. The Maritime Center, which monitors Chesapeake Bay shipping, stands near structures from periods as far back as 1750, some of which have been converted into townhouses, specialty shops, pubs, and urban inns. Old tobacco warehouses, later used as packing houses, are being restored as condominiums. Ethnic enclaves cluster around churches and a savings and loan institution that enabled new immigrants to buy houses.

The white frame and natural stone homes of Dickeyville, created in 1772 for employees of nearby cotton and flour mills, form a preservation district near Forst Park and Windsorville Road.

The twelfth largest city in the United States, populationwise, is quite approachable. Although more than 750,000 people live within its 79 square miles, Baltimore does not seem too big to handle. Major highways, including Jones Falls Expressway, cross the heart of the city. However, parking lots fill early on warm summer days, and it is best to walk or use public transportation in the downtown area, then drive to outlying points.

City-owned trolleys operate approximately every 15 minutes year round along two circular, intersecting downtown routes. The Inner Harbor trolley (11 A.M.–7 P.M. daily) extends from Greene Street to Fell's Point, following Pratt Street along the Inner Harbor and Lombard Street past Museum Row and Market Place. The Charles Street route (same hours except on Sunday) covers the city's business heart, which includes the stores, restaurants, and specialty shops along variously styled Charles Street and the Mount Vernon district and returns via Howard and Cathedral streets and Maryland Avenue.

Guided tours supplement self-propelled adventures (see Appendix for contact information). The Women's Civic League conducts daily walks to downtown historic structures and the Center for Urban Archeology. An escorted walking tour of Federal Hill and Fell's Point is led by the Society for the Preservation of Federal Hill and Fell's Point personnel, on request. Zeporah (Zippy) Larson leads two-hour Saturday Shoe Leather Safaris to different districts: Fell's Point, Little Italy, Federal Hill, and the "homestead" Otterbein area. A candlelight walking tour by About Town Tours, Inc., covers the Inner Harbor and nearby neighborhoods. Bus tours by About Town Tours, Baltimore Good Time Tours, Alexander Tours, and others cover highlights and include stops during the April–November period. A late-night Insomniacs Tour is among the offerings of Baltimore Rent-a-Tour. Zippy Larson narrates specialty bus tours — markets, chocolate (old German recipes), mansions ("'drop dead' Victorian houses that take the breath away"), Hampden (remnants of a mill town a few miles north of Inner Harbor), and a tour of important sites in Jewish history.

Baltimore's seaward orientation makes it an ideal harbor for boaters. Transient slips are available at the Inner Harbor. Nine other marinas also provide docking and supplies for transients (see Appendix). Several provide travel lift and repair services. Boat ramps are located at Fort Armistead Park and at Broening Park on separate branches of the Patapsco River.

Most maritime supply stores stock navigational aids, including government charts and light lists. The U.S. Power Squadron, U.S. Coast Guard Auxiliary, and Maryland Department of Natural Resources offer free courses in boating and regulations.

Downtown

Baltimore's ability to mix antiquity and modernity shows best at the Inner Harbor, nearby Jonesville, and the Mount Vernon district, where the nation's first monument to honor George Washington was erected in 1842. These areas are within easy walking distance of each other.

On any warm day, the Inner Harbor, the epicenter of modern Baltimore life, is motion personified. People in shorts and sneakers stroll the esplanade to gorge on gustatory specialties and natural visual delights, watch boats from many mid-Atlantic communities ease up to docks, take harbor cruises, visit museums, ride an elevator to the twenty-seventh-floor observation level of the World Trade Center (designed by architect I. M. Pei), climb Federal Hill for a bird's-eye view of the area, attend performances at the open-air theater, and patronize various commercial enterprises.

The wooden frigate *Constellation,* launched in 1797 at Fell's Point and one of the world's oldest ships continually afloat, provides a historical focus for the complex. During its long, active career, the historic vessel fought pirates off Tripoli, saw action during the Civil War, and even served as an auxiliary flagship during World War II. A tour of the vessel is a step back into the romantic era when sailing ships dominated the seas, from the masts and rigging of the recently restored top deck to the swinging hammocks on the berth deck where enlisted men slept. Quarters of the captain, still spartan but outfitted with bunks, chest, and desk, and of the subordinate officers and the Orlop Deck, used for storage, also can be visited. During the summer months, historical interpreters demonstrate handling the ship's 18-pounder guns.

The ship opens daily at 10 A.M. Closing times vary: 4 P.M. between mid-October and mid-May, 8 p.m. end of June to Labor Day, and 6 p.m. the rest of the time.

The 157-foot *Pride of Baltimore II*, whose home port is the Inner Harbor, made its first voyage as city-state ambassador in 1988, visiting Bermuda, Colombia, and Puerto Rico, as well as several destinations in the United States. The topsail schooner, built to the lines and rigging of an early nineteenth-century Baltimore clipper, is on display whenever docked. An earlier ambassadorial vessel, *Pride of Baltimore*, was lost at sea in 1986.

The Baltimore clipper was born of necessity. The wars of the late nineteenth and early nineteenth century, combined with the lack of a large American navy, created a demand for fast ships that could keep open the lanes of ocean commerce. Responding to that demand, Chesapeake Bay builders produced the first class of ships built specifically for speed and the first vessel to be wholly designed in the United States. The early small Baltimore clippers influenced the design of the more famous clipper ships that dominated the peaceful sea lanes of the 1840s and 1850s.

On special occasions, Bay seafood boats from the maritime museum at St. Michaels visit the Inner Harbor.

Those who want to do more than ogle the boats may cruise on sailing vessels, a motor yacht, and harbor cruise ships or charter sail and power boats ranging in length from 25 to 125 feet.

Among sailing vessels carrying passengers is the 45-foot skipjack *Minnie V.*, which in winter works as an oyster boat. Its 1½-hour cruises down the Patapsco River pass the city's waterfront industrial zones, harbor piers, and historic Fort McHenry. Built in 1906 at Deal Island, the city-owned vessel unfurls six times a day on weekends and twice on weekdays, except Monday, from mid-June through Labor Day and on weekends the remainder of the cruise season, always weather permitting. The 158-foot topsail schooner *Clipper City*, a larger-than-life, modernized replica of an 1854 ship with the same name, sails downriver past Fort McHenry and the anchorage of the bombarding British ships to the Francis Scott Key Bridge each afternoon from mid-May to November, plus theme trips on Sunday morning and Friday and Saturday night. The two-masted steel vessel (the original was wooden), the largest tall ship licensed for passengers in the United States, also takes all-day charters to Annapolis, St. Michaels, or other points. The three-masted *Eagle* circles the port area daily from mid-May to November, and the schooner *Nighthawk* makes a similar trip from Fell's Point.

Motor vessels and their itineraries are just as varied. The *Baltimore Patriot II* and *III* operate frequent 1½-hour narrated harbor cruises, while the *Bay Lady* and *Lady Baltimore* offer daily lunch and dinner cruises May–September. The 50-foot motor yacht *Gatsby*, built in 1930, provides daily seasonal service to Annapolis and St. Michaels. American Cruise Lines operates seven-day trips from Baltimore to Savannah and back along the Intracoastal Waterway.

Three shuttle boats leave the Inner Harbor about every 30 minutes from Memorial Day to Labor Day for Fort McHenry and Fell's Point, where visitors may debark for sightseeing.

Three major museums — the Science Center, a broad-spectrum view of Maryland's role in modern science, the National Aquarium, and two vessels of the Maritime Museum — front on the Inner Harbor.

A distorted room, where (for example) a child standing on one side appears larger than an adult standing on the other, illustrates the kind of innovative, hands-on presentation typical of the Science Center. An IMAX Theater, planetarium, demonstrations, games, movies, and static displays deal with energy, space, motion, sound, computers, Chesapeake Bay, and other subjects. The museum opens at 10 A.M. Monday–Saturday and closes at 5 P.M. Monday–Thursday and 10 P.M. Friday–Saturday. Sunday hours are noon to 6 P.M.

Guided tours of the World War II submarine *U.S.S. Torsk,* which made an 11,884-dive world record during its twenty-three-year career, follow the narrow passageways to the cramped quarters and operational compartments of the sub. The cramped quarters on the *Chesapeake Light Ship,* built in 1930 in Charleston, South Carolina, show how the crew lived when the ship served as a navigational aid off the Maryland and Delaware coasts. Both vessels are docked at Pier 3 and are open from 10 A.M. to 8 P.M. daily May–October, 10 A.M. to 5 P.M. Thursday–Monday the rest of the year.

The eyes of Inner Harbor visitors invariably are drawn to the bright colored panels on the National Aquarium, also a model of innovative design. Moving belts carry people through a rain forest with more than four hundred tropical plants and Great Egg Island in the rooftop glass pyramid, while circular ramps descend deep into a tank filled with coral reef and other specimens of marine life. In all, the museum houses more than 8,000 fish, reptiles, amphibians, plants, and other wildlife. It opens at 10 A.M. daily and closes at 5 P.M. most of the time, but stays open until 8 P.M. Friday–Sunday from mid-May to mid-September and Friday the rest of the year.

In the 1793 Flag House on East Pratt Street, a modest brick structure decorated with Federal-style furniture, Mary Pickersgill sewed the 30- by 42-foot flag that Francis Scott Key saw flying "by the dawn's early light" over Fort McHenry. An adjacent museum features an audiovisual program on the War of 1812. The garden contains a map of the United States, made of native stones.

The nearby 243-foot Shot Tower came later, in 1828, and shows by exhibits, audiovisuals, and a sound-and-light presentation how 12.5 million round balls for muskets could be made each year by dropping molten lead into cold water. The Holocaust Memorial at Lombard and Gay streets pays tribute to Jews murdered by Nazis during World War II.

The Peale Museum, not far from the architecturally eclectic City Hall, is the oldest original museum building in the country. Built in 1814 by Rembrandt Peale, it houses Baltimore memorabilia, paintings by the Peale family, and photographs by noted marine photographer A. Aubrey Bodine.

A skywalk provides a scenic route between the Inner Harbor and Charles Center, in the heart of the downtown business area. The elevated route, which can be strolled in 15 to 20 minutes, overlooks street-level activities, fountains, and modern art and passes through plazas decorated with lilies and other flowers, vines, English ivy, euonymus Manhattan, trees, and a dancing fountain at Hopkins Plaza. Poppies decorate the square at Charles Center.

Four attractions in the historic Jonestown area, just west of the Inner Harbor, are collectively known as the Courtyard Sites. The Carroll Mansion on East Lombard Street was the winter home of Charles Carroll, the last surviving signer of the Declaration of Independence, during the final decade of his life. The three-story brick structure, with a marble entrance hall floor and winding staircase, is the city's finest surviving early nineteenth-century town house. An iron door protects the wall safe in the counting room on the first floor. The courtyard also includes the Center for Urban Archeology, the Courtyard Exhibition Center, and the 1840 House. Single and combination tickets are available from 10 A.M. to 5 P.M. (4 P.M. October–March) Tuesday–Saturday and from noon to 5 P.M. Sunday.

Old Otterbein United Methodist Church at the corner of Conway and Sharp streets, built in 1785–86, is the oldest church in continuous use in the city. The handsome brick building is open at noon every Sunday and from 10 A.M. to 4 P.M. Saturday, April–October.

Charles Street rises gently from the Inner Harbor past basilica-style St. Paul's Episcopal Church, erected in 1856 by a congregation dating back to 1692 and noted for its Tiffany windows and peaceful garden, to the Mount Vernon area. The section is not impressive at first, but grows on the visitor. The Walters Art Gallery at North Charles and Centre streets currently divides its collection of 28,000 ancient artifacts, tapestries, illuminated manuscripts, old masters, and art nouveau among two buildings, the oldest built in 1904. The museum owns a valuable and extensive collection of Asian art, but only a small portion is on display. The museum is open from 11 A.M. to 5 P.M. Tuesday through Sunday, except major holidays. Guided tours by arrangement cover subjects that vary from images in ivory to jewelry through the ages.

Around Mount Vernon Place, whose gleaming, 178-foot column honoring George Washington is complemented by nineteenth-century sculptures, fountains, and trees, are scores of old buildings restored as homes, museums, and shops, including the antique shops on North Howard and West Read streets. An 1850 Greek revival mansion, the Hackman House on West Mount Vernon Place, will house the Walters Gallery Asian collection after 1991.

The Maryland Historical Society Museum on West Monument Street is noted for its extensive collection of ship models, nineteenth-century rooms of the Enoch Pratt mansion, 700 pieces of antique furniture, Young People's Gallery featuring dioramas of the history of Maryland, and silver pieces. The museum is open from 11 A.M. to 4:30 P.M. Tuesday–Friday, 9 A.M. to 4:30 P.M. Saturday, and 1 to 5 P.M. Sunday from October to May. Ornate cast iron balconies identify the nineteenth-century library of Peabody Institute of Johns Hopkins University. A monument at Calvert and Fayette streets memorializes those who lost their lives in the War of 1812, and also houses a memorial to black heroes.

History Elsewhere

Away from the downtown area, Baltimore is best covered by vehicle. Although traffic is slow and some routes are complicated, major streets extend to within a short distance of most outlying attractions.

Fort McHenry: Star-shaped Fort McHenry, Baltimore's leading historical attraction, looks much as it did when Francis Scott Key, peering through a smoky dawn, drew inspiration for a poem, which later became the national anthem, from the U.S. flag flying over the defiant fort.

A river approach reveals the five-point brick fort, completed in 1802, much as Key knew it, minus the sound and fury of gunfire. The walk from the dock climbs a grassy knoll. Visits to the four barracks, guardhouse, and powder magazine, which now house historical exhibits and audio stations, are basically self-guided. The ramparts provide an exceptional view of the busy river and sections of Baltimore. The fort that stood in 1814 when the battle raged now has no cannon. Civil War Rodman cannons fortify an outer battery constructed later.

Every hour during the summer months, rangers narrate tours on a variety of subjects, such as the Battle of Baltimore, how the fort has changed over the years, French influence on the fort, and the fort during the Civil War. As part of the living history program, the volunteer Fort McHenry Guards recreate a day in an 1814 soldier's life, including drilling and demonstrations of musket firing.

By presidential proclamation, the U.S. flag flies over the fort twenty-four hours a day. Rangers raise an 1814-style flag at 9:30 A.M. and replace it at 4:30 P.M. with a 50-star flag. On Defender's Day, the Sunday closest to the September 13 anniversary of the battle, a mock bombardment and fireworks light up the sky over the river. Music, military drills, and a tattoo ceremony complete the program.

Fort McHenry is open from 8 A.M. to 5 P.M. daily, except Christmas and New Year's Days, and closes later during the summer months.
Mount Clare Mansion: This handsome 1760 Georgian house on a rise in 110-acre Carroll Park is the only pre-Revolutionary War home remaining in the city. The home of Charles Carroll, attorney and Revolutionary War patriot, has handsome arches in the entrance hall and many of the original furnishings, including silver, crystal, and Chinese export porcelain used by the family. An orchard of 220 apple, cherry, pear, and plum trees has been recreated. The five terraces where formal gardens stood in the eighteenth century are being excavated in the hope the gardens can be restored. The mansion is open from 10 A.M. to 4:30 P.M. Tuesday–Friday, noon to 4:30 P.M. weekends.
Robert Long House: Located on South Ann Street, the oldest surviving urban residence, built in 1765, is open from 10 A.M. to 4 P.M. Thursday or by appointment.

Evergreen House: The classic revival home at 4545 North Charles Street, built about 1855 and enlarged in 1870, houses a rare book and Tiffany glass collection. It is now part of Johns Hopkins University. The library is open daily and guided tours of the mansion are held the second Tuesday of each month.

Homewood House: Located at Charles and 34th streets on the wooded campus of Johns Hopkins, this 1801 Federal-period building is open by appointment Monday, Wednesday, and Thursday.

Baltimore Museum of Art: French impressionists are impressive among the 120,000 pieces of art. Located at Charles and 32nd streets, the museum is open from 10 A.M. to 4 P.M. Tuesday through Friday, Thursday evening from 6 to 10 P.M., and from 11 A.M. to 6 P.M. weekends.

Poe House: The garret room where the tragic author and poet Edgar Allen Poe lived from 1832 to 1835 while completing many of his early works is preserved at the 2½-story house at 203 North Amity Street. The house is open from noon to 4 P.M. Wednesday–Saturday from April through mid-December. Poe is buried at Westminster Church, built on arches over an old graveyard. These catacombs, opened on guided tours the first and third weekends of each month, may well have provided material for his macabre works.

Basilica of the Assumption: The first Roman Catholic cathedral in the United States, begun in 1805 and completed in 1821, is a handsome neoclassical structure with twin spires and a porch with fluted columns. Guided tours are offered at 1:30 P.M. the second and fourth Sunday of each month.

Mother Seton House: The small Federal period brick structure at 600 North Paca Street was the site of the first school founded in 1808 by America's first native-born Roman Catholic saint. The house and adjacent Chapel of Old St. Mary's Seminary are open from 1 to 5 P.M. Saturday and Sunday, except Easter, Christmas, and New Year's.

Zion Lutheran Church: The beautiful stained-glass windows in this church, founded in 1755, include one memorializing Ottmar Mergenthaler, inventor of the linotype machine, which revolutionized typesetting.

Jewish Heritage Center: The 1845 Lloyd Street Synagogue, Maryland's oldest, is part of this complex, which also includes the new museum of the Jewish Historical Society of Maryland and 1876 B'nai Israel Synagogue. The museum is open from 10 A.M. to 4 P.M. Wednesday–Friday and the synagogue from 1:30 to 4 P.M. the first and third Sunday of each month.

Babe Ruth Birthplace Museum/Maryland Baseball Hall of Fame: A row house at 216 Emory Street combines graphic displays, film clips, and memorabilia in the home where the baseball immortal was born and information on the Baltimore Orioles and other Maryland players in adjacent row houses. The conglomerate opens at 10 A.M. daily and closes at 5 P.M. April–October, 4 P.M. the rest of the year, except major holidays.

H. L. Mencken House: Another nineteenth-century row house on Union Square was the home of the author and social satirist, often called the "Sage of Baltimore," for sixty-eight years. It is furnished much as he left it when he died in 1956. A filmstrip relates his life. The house and orderly garden are open from 10 A.M. to 5 P.M. Wednesday–Sunday.

B&O Railroad Museum: Steam engines of various types hover over exhibits of smaller equipment, the first station erected in 1830, and other railroad memorabilia in an old repair house at Pratt and Poppleton streets. The museum is open from 10 A.M. to 4 P.M. Wednesday through Sunday.

Streetcar Museum: An opportunity to ride more than a mile on a vintage streetcar in the city where the first electric streetcar was put into service in 1855. Other streetcars are on display in the carhouse at 1901 Falls Road, open from noon to 5 P.M. Sunday and, in summer, from 7 A.M. to 9 P.M. Thursday and noon to 5 P.M. Saturday.

The Green Side

Like most sailors, Baltimoreans have always loved the land at their backs. This side of their nature has created a landscape that literally breaks out in green spaces, both large and small. Federal Hill and Mount Vernon Place are only introductions to thirty areas of outdoors color within the Beltway (I-695).

Sherwood Gardens, 7 acres in the Guilford section near Johns Hopkins University, present their best face in late April and early May when the tulips, azaleas, and flowering shrubs are in bloom. These once were the grounds of a private estate.

The Cylburn Arboretum on Greenspring Avenue, 179 acres of gardens and forest around a mansion built in 1888, has beds of herbs, annuals, and perennials that are at their best during spring, including tulips, delphiniums, chrysanthemums, geraniums, Chinese carnations, and peonies. A small plot raised about 3 feet above the ground is designed to accommodate handicapped people; it has signs in braille and includes flowers and plants with distinctive scents, such as wild garlic. Trails strewn with woodchips pass through a forest of conifers, hardwoods, crabapples, maples, ferns, and wildflowers that hosts numerous species of birds and small animals. Signboards along the route identify various kinds of trees and plants. Six large greenhouses grow plants for the city of Baltimore. A naturalist conducts tours by arrangement. The grounds are open from dawn to dusk daily, while the mansion, which houses a nature museum and bird room, is open from 8 A.M. to 3:30 P.M. every day, except holidays.

Druid Hill Park, about 10 minutes northwest of the Inner Harbor via the Jones Falls Expressway, traces its origins to 1688 but was developed primarily in the nineteenth century. It concentrates a variety of activities in 648 acres of forest and meadows, but is best known for the Baltimore Zoo with more than 1,200 birds, mammals, and reptiles. The Children's Zoo has a petting area, a place to view baby farm animals, a mechanical cow for children to milk, and an area where they can watch chickens lay and hatch eggs. Other activities and facilities include jogging around a freshwater lake, pavilions, athletic fields, picnic areas, tennis courts, and the William Donald Schaefer Conservatory, built in 1888 to house a permanent collection of native and tropical plants and flowers. The conservatory has special displays at Easter and Christmas.

Fifteen miles of forested hiking trails run through Gwynns Falls and Leakin Park, located a little farther west on Windsor Mill Road. Naturalists lead daily summer walks through the woods, where small animals and eagles are sometimes seen. A few bikers use the roads in the park. A miniature steam engine hauls passengers. A small stream in the southern end of the park is stocked with freshwater trout. In addition, outdoor workshops, classes, and summer camps are sponsored by the Carrie Murray Outdoor Education Center, which has a small animal zoo.

Middle Branch Park has more water than land—446 acres to 205 acres—and thus is oriented toward boating. The Baltimore Rowing and Water Resource Center, which offers a program of instruction in safety and handling of shells and different kinds of boats, is the headquarters of the park. Canoers and windsurfers use the Middle Branch of the Patapsco River during the summer months. The park has a public boat ramp and a marina with slips for transients. An extensive environmental program, featuring both slide-illustrated lectures and field activity, deals especially with the interaction of the city and Chesapeake Bay and includes the historical and biological sides of the park, bird banding, how to catch crabs, and wildlife research. People can be involved on a one-time or ongoing basis. Six miles of biking trails cover the grassy park and follow the bank of the river, where cherry trees were planted in 1988, and through other areas of the park. The route ultimately will connect with trails in elongated Patapsco State Park, which follows the river far inland. A new Vietnam Memorial was opened in 1989.

Robert E. Lee Park, just north of the city line near Falls Road (SR 25) and the Jones Falls Expressway, is a bird sanctuary, as well as a park. Unmarked bird-watching and hiking trails explore a forested area, and boating and fishing are allowed on Lake Roland. The falls, created by a dam, are attractive.

A Chinese-style pagoda, built in 1891 as an ornamental observation tower and now guarded by two stone lions donated in 1984 by the people of Taiwan, makes Patterson Park off Eastern Avenue the most distinctive in the city. It was also one of the first, but has been enlarged several times since 1827, when William Patterson set aside almost 6 acres as a "public walk." Neglect in the 1950s was overcome by private initiative, especially the Butcher's Hill and Linwood improvement associations, and Parks and Recreation official Virginia Baker. The goldfish pond was restocked, the boat lake was revived, and rose bushes, plants, trees, and shrubs were replanted in the grassland park, which also has bike paths along paved roads and an outdoor ice-skating rink that normally operates from 7 to 9 P.M. daily and on Saturday afternoons from November to March.

Herring Run Park follows a stream valley across a heavily populated part of the city. The stream fills with runoff during rainy periods, but relapses to trickles over a rocky bed at other times. An 8-mile bikeway follows the course of the river.

Around Baltimore

BALTIMORE COUNTY, WHICH ABUTS THE CITY, HAS A SPLIT PERSONALITY. The area closest to the shore is part of the Bay country. Inland, the county begins the transition to mountainous western Maryland. The Bay side shines brightest. No other place in the Chesapeake area is quite like it. Freshwater tributaries, small by Bay standards, wind through uneven ground, wearing at the land and watering upland forests until they encounter brackish penetrations.

These useful streams have been harnessed one way or another. Loch Raven Reservoir, since 1875 the principal source of water for the city and county, stretches for 7 miles along Gunpowder Falls above a dam near Loch Raven Road. A fishing center, which has rental boats, is located east of the reservoir on Dulaney Valley Road. The lake in the 4,500-acre watershed area, with an average depth of 45 to 50 feet, is stocked with bass, pickerel, perch, crappie, bluegill, northern pike, and walleye, caught by thousands of anglers each year. The bottom is littered with tree stumps, boulders, and foundations of artificial structures, and the surface of the lake is interrupted by a number of small islands. A Maryland Department of Natural Resources map shows nearly fifteen sites noted for seasonal catches, as well as year-round spots such as the Peach Orchard, Glenn Ellen Foundation, Feather Island, Oak Tree Foundation, Merriman's Hump, and Old Faithful Log Jam.

On Saturdays and Sundays, a section of roadway in the reservoir area is closed to vehicular traffic so kids can ride their bicycles in safety and pedestrians can walk to the shore of the lake.

Oregon Ridge Park, 838 acres at Cockeysville, has a nature center and trails near its lake. At Soldiers Delight Natural Environment Area at Owings Mills, hiking and bridle trails cover exposed mineral deposits, an unusual geographical feature in the Bay area.

In Towson, on the outskirts of Baltimore, Hampton National Historic Site is an early monument to the mix of agriculture, waterfront, and industry that has characterized the western shore of the region throughout its history. Originally known as Northhampton, the 1,500-acre tract was similar to the "iron plantations" that existed in Virginia and Pennsylvania. It operated from 1762 to 1829 and was an important source of cannon and shot for the patriot cause during the Revolutionary War. Loch Raven Reservoir now covers the site of the ironworks, but the chimney of the furnace protrudes above the water in the lake.

The Hampton mansion, the principal building among twenty-eight structures on the 60-acre national monument, is an example of elegant country living in the last decades of the eighteenth century. It was constructed by an early entrepreneur, Charles Ridgely. One of the largest and most ornate of the remaining post-Revolutionary War structures in the country, the late Georgian house was home to six generations of the Ridgely family.

Some aspects of the mansion, including progress from candles to gas lights to electricity and boys' initials carved on furniture, reflect this continuous use, but for the most part the house is frozen in its formative years. Corner cabinets were used instead of closets, which were taxed; casters on chairs enabled readers to easily move them to better light; guest bedrooms often had several beds because visitors usually had to stay overnight; suitcases sometimes doubled as traveling bathtubs; Federal-style mirrors were convex to better reflect dim light; and brides scratched their initials on window panes to test their diamond rings.

The grounds of the estate, including the formal gardens first laid out in the 1790s, are struggling against the pollution emanating from the nearby Beltway. The natural foliage has decreased perceptibly in the last decade, either because of age or pollution. Nevertheless, a walking tour of the grounds, guided by a printed brochure showing the principal features, remains one of the best aspects of the national monument. The terraced gardens are laid out, European-style, in geometric parterres, approximately according to their original design. Boxwoods frame the upper parterres, where one pair is planted with ground coverings and seasonal flowers and the second features roses. Peonies predominate in the lowest terrace. An herb garden stands near the mansion, just as it did in the eighteenth century. At that time, a kitchen garden was planted below the formal gardens and an orchard stood to the east.

The trees on the estate are just as interesting. One giant cedar of Lebanon, whose branches grow close to the ground to create a natural nook, is a state champion and one of the largest of its kind in the country. The gnarled catalpas nearby are more than two hundred years old. Also growing close to the mansion are red cedar, purple European beech, saucer magnolia, tulip, and pecan trees. During Hampton Farm Day in mid-September, the estate demonstrates crafts and activities common in the eighteenth and nineteenth centuries.

Annual events in Baltimore County, like those in other areas of Chesapeake Bay country, emphasize the outdoors. The Oregon Woods Nature Center at Cockeysville sponsors seasonal woodland walks in April, May, June, September, October, and November. Irvine Natural Science Center at St. Timothy's School, Stevenson, conducts environmental and natural history programs and trips on a nature trail. Outdoor concerts are held at Heritage Park in Dundalk in July and August.

Wildlife artists and carvers and craftspeople gather at the Chesapeake Wildlife Exposition in Essex in September. A community fishing rodeo is held each June in Landsdowne, while powerboats compete for the Maryland Governor's Cup in September at Essex on the Back River. Boordy Vineyards at Hydes, Maryland's oldest and largest winery, hosts a barrel-tasting and vintage preview in March. Towson has a flower mart in April, and farmers' markets in July, August, and October. Dundalk has farmers' markets in August, September, and October. Weber's Cider Mill Farm at Parkville opens in October for cider- and scarecrow-making demonstrations and pumpkin exhibitions.

Each May, some of the best horses in the nation run for the black-eyed Susans at Pimlico's Preakness. The State Fair Grounds at Timonium, just off I-83, host a number of annual events, in addition to the State Fair at the end of August and early September. Among them are the Bass Expo in January and a Rites of Spring exhibition of garden products.

Christmas programs include a tree lighting and caroling in Towson, Ballestone Holly Tours, a Christmas crafts festival in Dundalk, Yuletide at Hampton, and a community tree lighting in Essex.

History is not forgotten. In early September, the War of 1812 Battle of North Point is re-enacted at 62-acre Fort Howard Park in Dundalk. Essex has two intriguing historical events — the annual Civil War encampment at Ballestone Manor in early October and a retelling of the Legend of Cox's Point, a witch's tale, at Cox Point Park in late October. Lutherville Festival emphasizes that community's historic district.

Gunpowder Falls State Park: The bits and pieces of this dismembered park cover more than 15,000 acres in the Big and Little

Gunpowder Falls River valleys. Five separate sections of park extend from Chesapeake Bay almost to the Pennsylvania border, three of them near the Bay along the course of the Big and Little Gunpowder Falls, which empty into the Gunpowder River.

The Hammerman area on Gunpowder River, the closest to the Bay, is used primarily for picnicking and swimming, but also has one beach for windsurfing. Saltwater fishers cast from the shore and boats in the Dundee Creek fishing area. Wildfowl frequent the area during fall and winter.

The Big Gunpowder Falls section, an inverted boot-shaped wilderness about 3 miles from the Beltway, extends from near U.S. Route 40 northwestward to Harford Road. Hiking trails follow the undulating shores of the meandering river from one end of the park to the other; offshoots explore the heavily forested areas north of the river. A 10-mile stretch of the capricious stream at the southern end of the park is open to canoeing, depending on water conditions. The rocky river changes character completely when rainfall is heavy. It is much milder west of Route 1, with a short drop at Route 147 and riffles at two places farther downstream in water up to 2 feet. Currents increase considerably and the riffles become rapids with easily recognizable passages above two feet, however. The 4 miles below the gauge on U.S. Route 1 are best left to experienced boaters. The river is Class III (difficult) up to 2 feet of water, with one sharp drop and a long rapids, and more difficult above that level, with unpredictable, violent rapids and rock hazards. Ledge Falls has to be portaged. Neither section should be attempted when the water level is above 3½ feet. River access points are located at Cromwell Bridge and U.S. Routes 1 and 40 and Maryland Routes 147 and 7.

Farther east, a stringbean section of parkland along more than 20 miles of the Little Gunpowder Falls is crossed by hiking trails that follow the banks of the river and divert in places for considerable distances into the hardwood forest, which in spring is alive with the bright colors of wildflowers. A covered bridge, still in use, spans the river on the Jericho Road east of Route 1. Certain sections of both streams are stocked with trout in the spring. Smallmouth bass also are caught occasionally.

Three interconnecting primary trails in the Sweet Air area off Dalton-Bevard Road cross wooded areas, river bottomland, and open plateaus. The 2.6-mile Big Rock Trail crosses the Little Gunpowder Falls and ends at the Big Rock Landmark — which, as its name states, is a large rock. From there, the 2.4-mile Sweet Air Trail takes another route back past Green Glade Pond to the starting point. The 2-mile Park Loop Trail explores the headwater of a tributary and Barley Pond.

North of Lock Raven Reservoir, about 9 miles of North Central Railroad bed has been improved with a stone base for hiking, biking, and horseback riding along the Little Falls. The trail is almost flat, although the surrounding terrain is hilly. The route is most popular in spring and fall because of scenery along the Big Gunpowder River and Little Falls tributary, which traverse forests of oak, hickory, gum, sycamore, and a few pines and hemlocks where small animals, deer, and even an occasional bobcat wandering down from Pennsylvania may be seen. In winter, when there is sufficient snow, the trail also is used for cross-country skiing.

The state, which owns 66 feet width of the former roadbed as far as the Pennsylvania line, is slowly developing the entire length. Parking currently is available on Ashland, Phoenix, and Monkton roads.

Canoeing, rafting, and tubing are possible on a 2-mile stretch of the Gunpowder Falls River just off Interstate 83 north of Hereford when the water is between 1 and 3 feet high. A gauge under the York Road Bridge indicates current levels. The course includes a bend, which is rated Class II (medium difficulty) when water approaches the upper limit. Access points exist at Masemore Road, Bunker Hill Road, and Big Falls Road, which is the boundary of the upper portion of the park.

Hikers may use the same parking areas and those at Falls Road and York Road to reach color-coded trails that follow the river and explore hilly woods reminiscent of western Maryland, mostly along the southern bank of the river. The Gunpowder South Trail follows the meandering river about 6.5 miles from Big Falls Road to Prettyboy Reservoir and passes the falls. Some sections between York Road and reservoir are quite steep. Offshoots include the Highland Trail, which climbs the high ground covered with pine and hemlock, and the Bunker Hill–Mingo Branch loop. The north shore path, which also passes the falls, stops at Falls Road.

Horseback riding is permitted along portions of the trails. An archery range is located on Bunker Hill Road.

Year-round fishing for rainbow and brown trout is possible in this area. Nearby fishing places include 62-acre Fort Howard Park, overlooking the Bay in Dundalk; 25-acre Cox's Park in Essex, which has a boat ramp; and Rocky Point Beach and Park in Essex, also with boat-launching facilities. Fifty-nine-acre Miami Beach Park in Middle River has a nature area with marshland and trails.

Annapolis and Vicinity

Tourism Council of Annapolis and Anne Arundel County,
152 Main Street, Annapolis, MD 21401. Tel.: 301/268-8687.

ANNAPOLIS, THE CAPITAL OF MARYLAND, LIVES IN A TIME WARP, CON-ducting modern state business in an eighteenth-century setting. More than that, the city has never really exhausted the mental image of its origins.

It is difficult to imagine a city with more advantages than Annapolis. It occupies a beautiful site on the Severn River, with sailboats and power boats docking within sight of the dome of the old Capitol building. The roots of its history reach deep into both the nearby land and the Bay. One of the oldest cities in Maryland, Annapolis was settled in 1640 by Puritans from Virginia. First named Provincetown, it was also Arundel Town for a few years before choosing the name that has stuck for more than three hundred years. Annapolis was only the second state capital, succeeding St. Mary's City in 1694.

The first impression of Annapolis is one of too much bustle and movement. Government, handsome residences, and commercial establishments share the hillside sloping toward the harbor. Walkers, many of them eating snacks, crowd the narrow streets of the old section. A steady stream of motorboats and sailboats enter and leave the City Dock, including tour boats that offer cruises of various lengths in the Severn River and Chesapeake Bay. On the grounds of the U.S. Naval Academy, visitors and midshipmen mingle beside massive light-colored buildings or in shaded open spaces while bikers negotiate the streets.

This is the exterior Annapolis. The interior city is quite different. The historic buildings, private and public, exude much of the pleasant ambience that endeared the city to members of the Continental Congress, who met in the State House during some of the most fateful days of the Revolutionary War and its aftermath. On State House Circle and in the streets radiating from it, eighteenth-century homes offer bed and breakfast to modern tourists in much the same manner that boardinghouses and owners of mansions provided accommodations for those early congressmen, who horrified one of their pious members from Rhode Island by preferring card games to prayer.

At least three activities should be on everyone's list — visits to the waterfront, the historic area, and the Naval Academy.

The ideal way to arrive in Annapolis is by boat. The approach from the Chesapeake Bay exposes the shoreline of the Severn River, which remains beautiful despite the intrusion of industrial uses and radio towers, and the water side of the U.S. Naval Academy. In the warm months, the river and Spa and Back creeks are a panorama of white sails, colorful spinnakers, and the wakes of power boats. Boaters can tie up for short periods at the City Dock on Spa Creek within minutes of the historic homes and government buildings and find space at nearby marinas, including the City Marina across Spa Creek.

For those who don't arrive by boat, cruises on the river and Bay lasting from 40 minutes to 7½ hours are conducted daily from Memorial Day through Labor Day and on weekends in the spring and September. The *Lady Sarah,* built in 1919 as an oyster buy boat, is used on 90-minute cruises of the river and Spa Creek; Chesapeake Marine Tour's all-day cruises on the Bay to St. Michaels or Baltimore give day-trippers the same experiences that boat owners have as they move about the Bay and its tributaries. The same can be said of chartering sail or power yachts at Annapolis or Edgewater, south of the city. Several companies provide this service (see Appendix).

Annapolis' devotion to sailing is evident elsewhere, as well. Rental sailboat fleets — Rainbows, Sunfish, Windsurfers, Hobie cats, Annapolis 26s, Newport 30s and 41-Ss, O'Day 37s, and Gulfstar 50s — come with or without sailing instruction. Sailing schools train beginners, as well as experienced sailors wishing to operate their own charter boats. The Maritime Museum on Main Street concentrates on seafaring in the last half of the eighteenth century and includes a number of colonial sailing artifacts. It is open daily from 11 A.M. to 4:30 P.M., except on Thanksgiving and Christmas Day.

The historic district of Annapolis, just as compelling as the waterfront, is an ideal place for walking. The historic sights are situated in a compact area that, while hilly, has gentle slopes.

The hilltop State House on State Circle dominates the historic section and harbor. Constructed between 1772 and 1779, it is the oldest state capitol in continuous use and the only one also to have served as the national capitol. A uniformed mannequin occupies the spot in the Old Senate Chamber where George Washington stood before the Continental Congress on December 23, 1783, to resign as commander-in-chief of the Continental Army. Several pieces of furniture still in the room were in use during the period from November 26, 1783, to August 13, 1784, when Congress met there. Hanging on one wall is a valuable portrait, entitled "Washington at the Battle of Yorktown," by Charles Wilson Peale.

A painting of Mistress Margaret Brent, a colonist who was so active in public affairs that she was officially classed as a "gentleman," hangs in the Old House Chamber alongside portraits of the early Governors Calvert. Other historical exhibits cover the Treaty of Paris ending the Revolutionary War, ratified while Congress was sitting in the State House, and the lifestyle of the members of Congress. Photographs of many of the buildings in which they lived, including the Paca and Hammond-Harwood houses, which are currently open to public inspection, and details of their active social lives are on display. Virginia's Arthur Lee got into trouble with the ladies by planning a ball at the same time another was scheduled, but all the members of Congress ate "good fat turkie, the fine fish and delightful oysters" that Annapolis is still famous for.

Also on display is the silver service donated by the state to the cruiser *Maryland* in 1906 and later transferred to the battleship *U.S.S. Maryland*. On the silver service are depicted 167 scenes from all the counties in the state. Chambers in which the bicameral legislature meets today also are open for sightseeing. Guided tours start from a visitors center in the lobby.

The Old Treasury Building also is located on State Circle. State office buildings are scattered in nearby blocks.

Historic structures such as the 1727 Calvert House, 1765 Robert Johnson House, and the 1820 State House Inn, now commercial hostelries, also front on State Circle. The 1776 Maryland Inn and 1647 Annapolis front on St. Anne's Circle.

A number of historic homes, decorated with period furniture and open to the public on various days of the week, stand on streets radiating from State Circle and smaller St. Anne's Circle. The well-proportioned, wall-enclosed, red brick Governor William Paca House on Prince George Street, built in 1765 by a signer of the Declaration of Independence, is noted for its 2-acre colonial pleasure garden, whose decorations include a Chinese Chippendale bridge and domed pavilion. The Chase-Lloyd House, begun in 1769 by another signer of the Declaration of Independence, Samuel Chase, and finished by Edward Lloyd, and the Hammond-Harwood House, a 1774 structure whose handsome doorway with tall Ionic columns has been described as the most beautiful in America, stand on opposite sides of Maryland Avenue, near the Visitors Gate to the U.S. Naval Academy.

St. Anne's Episcopal Church was founded in 1692 and has silver communion service donated by King William III, but the present structure with two Tiffany windows was completed in the mid-nineteenth century. Reynolds Tavern, which dates from 1747, faces St. Anne's Circle, while the Banneker-Douglass Museum, housed in the Victorian-Gothic former Old Mount Moriah African Methodist Episcopal Church on Franklin Street, depicts the historical and cultural experience of black people in Maryland.

The quiet 300-acre grounds of the Naval Academy are an oasis from the bustle of nearby streets. Conducted tours begin at the Visitors Center in Ricketts Hall, but visitors may use a free map to visit the same sights on their own from 9 A.M. to 5 P.M. A sample midshipman's room is displayed in one wing of giant Bancroft Hall, where musters are held each day at noon during warm months. Visitors stand near the famous statue of Shawnee Indian Chief Tecumseh, who frequently is colorfully decorated with warpaint (and painted slogans) during football season. Full-dress parades are held three times each semester and during Commissioning Week in the spring. A museum in Preble Hall exhibits flags, ship models, portraits, and weapons, while weapons ranging from a jet fighter plane and small experimental submarine to cannons and torpedoes are spotted around the grounds. Naval hero John Paul Jones lies in a crypt in the large Naval Academy Chapel.

Annapolis maintains a convenient Visitors Center at the City Dock. An inexpensive trolley shuttle runs year round to the historic area and City Dock from Navy-Marine Corps Memorial Stadium, where visitors may park free.

Anne Arundel County, which stretches for more than 80 miles along Chesapeake Bay, is essentially a land bridge—beteen Baltimore and Annapolis, between Annapolis and Southern Maryland, between Annapolis and the rapidly filling Maryland suburbs of the national capital. The soaring, and extensively used, Bay Bridge connects the county to the Maryland Eastern Shore. The county is indented by numerous minor bays and streams, creating a series of small, odd-shaped peninsulas and small communities conducive to waterfront activities. The words *beach* and *harbor* figure in the names of at least a dozen communities.

Sandy Point State Park, at the western entrance to the Bay Bridge, has the main public beaches in the Annapolis area, staffed by life-guards during the summer months. The 2 miles of beachfront have two swimming areas, a launching area for Hobie cats, windsurfers, and small sailboats, and a surfcasting section mainly for spot, perch, and bluefish. A marina on Mezick Pond has eleven double boat ramps and day slips, as well as rental boats in the summer. A crabbing and fishing pier is located on the pond. Fishing and crabbing are excellent near the Bay Bridge. Short nature trails run through the marsh and pine woodland, whose thickets provide cover for numerous cottontail rabbits. The park also has a growing population of deer, red fox, opossum, and raccoon, as well as all types of reptiles, including snapping and painted turtles. Sizable flocks of waterfowl, shorebirds, and land birds, such as Canada goose, canvasback, mallard, scaup, and bufflehead, use the park.

Hour-long interpretive programs, offered throughout the year, relate nature to crafts, such as using pinecone birdhouses to attract birds. An early 1800s brick and frame building is being restored as a nature center. The park is open year round, except Thanksgiving, Christmas, and New Year's.

The natural beauty of the Severn River west of Annapolis has resulted in substantial upscale private residential development, with each community having its own beaches and piers. However, the headwaters of the Severn River, located in the 1,600-acre Severn Run Natural Environment Area, are stocked with trout, and fishing is permitted for about two weeks in April. A well-defined but un-marked foot trail originates at Dicus Mill Road, crosses forest and marsh habitats, and provides access to the river for trout fishers. A trail off Indian Landing Road follows the scenic headwaters of the Severn River, while a third starts at a parking site on Burns Crossing Road. A 3-mile-long bridle trail, maintained by an organization named Preserve Anne Arundel's Trails for Horses (PATH), extends through a forest visited mostly by perching birds and across the stream. Primitive campsites are available to youth groups.

Although there is no fishing on the Annapolis Reservoir, fishermen sometimes use the headwaters of the South River south of U.S. Route 50.

The Annapolis hinterland along U.S. 301 and 50 is an expanding suburban zone, where someday soon the overflows from Annapolis and the national capital will meet. At racetrack-minded Bowie, U.S. 301 turns south through a mix of forests, farmlands, and small communities to the section known as Southern Maryland. South of Annapolis, Route 2 moves out of suburban clutter and parallels the Chesapeake Bay coastline through sparsely settled countryside hiding resorts and captivating natural reserves.

About 18 miles south of Annapolis, red brick All Saints Episcopal Church sits on a knoll overlooking the intersection of state Routes 2 and 4. It was built in 1744.

The Smithsonian Institution of Washington, D.C., owns a 2,600-acre tract south of the Rhode River where its scientists study estuarine life, including trees, crabs, ants, migratory birds, vines, and grass shrimp, and the effects of human activities on natural ecological systems. The estuary is productive—twenty-seven fish species have been identified in the creek alone—but activity in the vicinity is largely seasonal. Fish spawn in spring; shellfish, sea nettles, and small numbers of black duck, mallard, and wood duck are present in summer, and waterfowl by the thousands settle down in late autumn and winter. Itinerants include tundra swan, Canada goose, canvasback, redhead, ruddy duck, lesser scaup, oldsquaw, green-winged teal, and pintail.

A 2-mile self-guided nature trail, open to the public from 8 A.M. to 4:30 P.M. Monday through Friday except holidays, explores natural and modified habitats, as well as some of the work of the center. Thirteen numbered points explain the relationship between vines and trees, the natural process of regenerating forests, tree diversity (sixteen varieties in one 25-yard area), ecology along Muddy Creek where the salinity changes continuously, animal signs from white-tailed deer and small species, tidal and high marshes, insects such as gypsy moth and Japanese beetle, and a fish weir.

Plants along the route include poison ivy, Japanese honeysuckle, Virginia creeper, wild grapevine, greenbrier, reed canary grass, salt marsh hay, cinnamon fern, highbush blueberry, common reed, narrowleaf cattail, multiflora rose, tulip poplar, persimmon, sycamore, red juniper, Virginia and loblolly pine, red cedar, black cherry, red maple, sassafras, sweet gum, American beech, pignut and mockernut hickory, white and willow oak, and princess tree.

Southern Maryland

*Tri-County Council for Southern Maryland, P.O. Box 1634,
Charlotte Hall, MD 20622. Tel.: 301/884-2144.*

THE SERVICE STATION ATTENDANT IN LEONARDTOWN WAS A MAN OF FEW
words. Asked about the location of a good motel, he responded,
"Motels are better in Lexington Park, same price." No embellishment,
no explanation, no concern about his rating with the Chamber of
Commerce.

Outsiders do not always receive such frank advice in clannish
Southern Maryland, but that man's laconic comment is a reminder
that simple virtues are still one of the most evident qualities of this in-
triguing, and sometimes mystifying, section. As the oldest section of
Maryland, history is ingrained and tradition is hidebound in Southern
Marylanders. It was here that the first English settlers came ashore and
built a society that survived many hardships to reach maturity. The
relationship with Virginians on the opposite shore of the Potomac
River is in some ways just as strong as the relationship with other
Marylanders, despite a history of periodic conflict over water rights.

The substantial and often isolated wilderness areas are among the
most unique in the state, from the northernmost stand of bald cypress
to the prehistoric fossils in the Calvert Cliffs. Solomons is one of
the state's premier aquatic centers.

When natives speak of Southern Maryland, they refer to a three-
county area. Calvert (pronounced "Culvert" locally) County is bisected
by Maryland Route 2 south of Annapolis. St. Mary's County can be
reached across the Patuxent River Bridge on Route 2 or via state
Route 5 east of U.S. Route 301. Charles County straddles U.S. 301.

Prince Georges County west of the highway is split between the
rural south, which is closely related to Southern Maryland (but not
considered part of it), and the urban north oriented toward the District of Columbia.

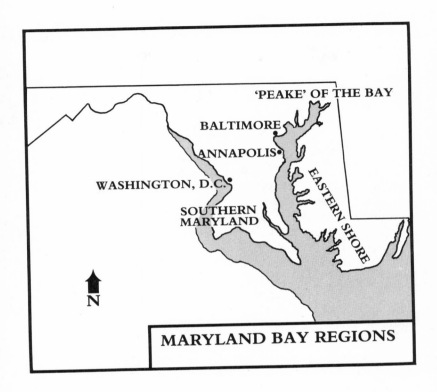

MARYLAND BAY REGIONS

Calvert County

*Tourism Council of Calvert County, Inc., P.O. Box 190,
Owings, MD 20736. Tel.: 301/535-1013.*

SPARSELY SETTLED CALVERT COUNTY, WHICH OCCUPIES A PENINSULA
created by the Patuxent River and the Bay, is quintessential Bay
country, better known to boaters than to motorists. Indeed, the
number of sailboats and motorboats in the water at times matches
the number of vehicles traversing the rare combination of seashore,
spectacular fossil cliffs, and inland wilderness settings, which remained

semi-isolated until the Governor Thomas Johnson Memorial Bridge opened near the tip of the peninsula.

Calvert County is still predominately rural in nature, with agriculture and seafood as primary industries. The character of the county is rapidly changing, however, as tourism, services, and retail business gain. Calvert has a number of unusual features along its dual coastline that create superlative recreational sites.

Chesapeake Beach

In 1900, the completion of the Chesapeake Beach Railway gave fun-starved residents of Washington, D.C., ready access to this resort city. In large numbers, they forsook the humidity of the nation's capital for the breezes and beaches of Chesapeake Bay. In 1927, the Potomac Anglers Association sponsored its eighth annual excursion, offering $10 prizes funded by the competing *Washington Post* and *Times-Herald* to the man and woman catching the largest fish. At the same time, steamers from Baltimore deposited boatloads of eager sunseekers and patrons of the casino.

The elite of both cities went elsewhere after the Depression of the 1930s closed the railroad and steamers were replaced by private automobiles and other forms of transportation. Chesapeake Beach waned, only to revive as the passion for waterfront land, condos, charter boat fishing, and seafood restaurants developed in recent years.

The aura of its glory days is preserved at the Chesapeake Beach Railway Museum, housed in the original eastern terminal of the railroad and half of the parlor car *Delores,* one of four used by the railway. The station looks much as it did when it welcomed droves of summer passengers, with barrels and hand carts stored on its platforms. Inside are the familiar roll-top desk, a pot-bellied stove with a coffee pot on top, and a variety of exhibits that illustrate activities at the station and resort. The resort lifestyle of the era is vividly captured in photographs. Sunbathers lounge on the beach and pose for photographers, while more circumspect vacationers stroll along the boardwalk. In the evenings, dancers enjoy the conviviality of the grand ballroom. A 1922 photo shows dozens of automobiles parked near the station, a harbinger of things to come, while another taken in 1916 shows the Great Derby rollercoaster that titillated thousands of thrill-seekers year after year.

In its heyday, the terminal had tracks ending on both sides. Those are gone, but the truncated *Delores,* the only piece of rolling stock to survive, stands silently where it once paused amid the happy talk of passengers. The car was recovered in Washington, where it was being used as an office. When it rolled on the railroad, it held thirty-six plush seats and thirty-six wicker chairs.

Among current operations continuing the resort tradition is Rod 'n' Reel Marina, which claims its twenty-eight boats constitute the largest charter boat fleet on Chesapeake Bay. The marina also operates "head" boats from June 1 through Labor Day in search of bluefish that may range from 5 to 14 pounds, striped bass from 3 to 42 pounds (which must be released), sea trout from 7 to 11 pounds, and black drum that exceed 40 pounds. Both half-day and full-day trips are offered.

Battle Creek Cypress Swamp Sanctuary

Nature reveals many secrets in the "primordial world" that survives at Battle Creek Cypress Swamp Sanctuary, on state Route 506 (Sixes Road) and Grey's Road off Route 2-4.

The seasons change dramatically along the self-guided circular, quarter-mile Cypress Knee Nature Trail, which follows an elevated boardwalk through a swampy area supporting the northernmost stand of naturally occurring bald cypress trees in the United States. A 100-foot-high leafy canopy shades the swamp, which largely dries up in summer and refills in autumn and winter. Mysterious "knees" or rootlike protuberances surround the flared base of bald cypress trees, perhaps to furnish oxygen or help stabilize tall trees in mud. The trees shed their leathery needle leaves in autumn. In the bushy undercover are the slender, pointed leaves and the strawberry-red seed pods, which hold orange seeds.

White-tailed deer, muskrat, raccoon, opossum, squirrels, frogs, and other small animals rustle leaves as they forage for food. Tracks or the paw prints of raccoon digging for crayfish may be seen at times. In spring, the silence of the forest is broken by the songs of warblers, who either nest or pause on the refuge, and other songbirds. In winter, woodpeckers hammer at trunks and wood ducks nest in tree cavities, sometimes near the boardwalk. More than a hundred species of birds have been identified in the refuge.

Wildflowers, such as lady's slipper, mayapple, bloodroot, wild violet, and cardinal flower, rotate from late spring into autumn. Pink turtlehead in small patches brightens the trail from August to October. In late autumn, the ripening banana-shaped fruit of paw-paw trees perfumes the air.

Audiovisual presentations, demonstrations, and exhibits in the nature center tell the history and topography of the swamp, which may be similar to the appearance of the entire coastal plain 70,000 to 120,000 years ago. In addition, a glass hive reveals bees hard at work producing honey, while live turtles and a black snake and static exhibits represent denizens of the wild—now less imposing than the extinct saber-toothed tigers and mammoths that roamed the land 100,000 years ago.

The interpretive program is aimed primarily at schoolchildren, and includes walks that identify edible wild plants, samplings of natural foods, and natural dyes and crafts programs. Others may join guided tours of the swamp and participate in the annual Open House and Nature Celebration in late September. The park is owned by The Nature Conservancy (nonprofit), which leases it to Calvert County. It is open Tuesdays through Sundays at varying hours year round. Programs sometimes are conducted jointly with Flag Ponds Nature Park.

Flag Ponds Nature Park

Often overlooked by visitors but intensively used by Calvert Countians, Flag Ponds Nature Park crowds an unusual diversity of features within its 327 acres—wooded uplands, fossilized cliffs, ponds, freshwater marshes, swamps, and a sandy Chesapeake Bay beach.

The Calvert Cliffs, in this section covered with vegetation and thus protected from erosion, dominate the park. A substantial section of the waterfront is a restricted natural heritage area, open primarily to hiking and fossil collection. Fossilized shark teeth, scallop shells, and whale and porpoise bones have been found, but are not common. A mile-long strip of beach is available for swimming, sunbathing, fishing, crabbing, and searching for fossils. A fishing pier extends from the south end of the beach.

Reaching the beach requires a half-mile walk through lowlands woods. In addition, the park has four established and interconnecting trails that cross upland and wetlands vegetation sustaining a balance of birds, mammals, fish, amphibians, reptiles, and insects. Furthermore, the park has a local reputation as having an "absolutely unbelievable" collection of wildflowers. The mile-long North Ridge Trail and 0.8-mile South Ridge Trail, as their names imply, pass through the forests along the face of the cliff. A 0.6-mile loop extends the former, and the 0.4-mile Duncan Pond Trail skirts the pond and stops at an observation deck and passes through a swampy area.

Flag Ponds was used as a fishing area until about 1955. One of three shanties used by fishermen during the pound net season has been renovated to interpret the use of nets to catch croaker, trout, herring, and other fish offshore. Displays at "Buoy Hotel No. 2" include nets, net-tarring equipment, and boats.

Flag Ponds is open daily from Memorial Day to Labor Day and on weekends the rest of the year.

Jefferson Patterson Park and Museum

The surprising Jefferson Patterson Park and Museum at the end of Route 265 is a kaleidoscope of human life on the Chesapeake Bay. A contemporary working 512-acre farm with a 2½-mile riverfront, it preserves relics of many periods of civilization along the Patuxent River.

From mid-April to mid-October, costumed interpreters explore the daily tasks of seventeenth-century Indians and settlers, the influence of technology on culture at various periods, and the techniques and ethics of contemporary archeology. Although geared primarily to groups, and especially schoolchildren, the park has much to offer people and families who visit it. Patterson Farm is primarily an outdoor experience. Visitors may lean on rail fences to watch activities at barns or walk, as well as drive, the roadways past fields and clumps of trees with signboards explaining conservation methods and natural erosion of topsoil and riverbanks.

The park especially provides an insight into the Indian presence on Chesapeake Bay. The site of an Indian village that may have been the "Quomocac" visited by Capt. John Smith in 1608 is part of a short archeology trail through farm fields on a bluff overlooking the river. Indians lived and hunted in the area for more than 9,000 years before European settlers arrived in 1651 to create great tobacco farms. Displays in the museum include stone implements from the Indian culture, as well as information on the five Pawtuxent Indian villages that existed in what is now Calvert County. Archeological exploration has confirmed the existence of only two palisaded villages in the tidewater area of Maryland, one of which is the "Cumberland" site a few miles downstream from the park. It may have been the village of "Opament" visited by Smith in 1608.

The excavated site of Kings Reach farmhouse and ancillaries, the center of a tobacco plantation from 1680 to 1710, represents the early colonial period. The buried remains of seventeenth-century St. Leonard Town also are located in the park. During the War of 1812, cannon placed on shore in the present park helped an American flotilla drive off British naval units in the Battle of St. Leonard Creek. Altogether, at least sixty archeology sites have been identified. A few relics of Lord Baltimore, Maryland's founder, are displayed in the museum alongside relics of later periods, including a 1929 Ford Model A farm truck.

The circular Cove Nature Trail, which starts near the Visitors Center and passes Mackall Cove, highlights the continuous changes in forests, water, and landscape that result from natural causes and human activities, including the seasonal patterns of renewal and decay—the spring leaves and blossoms, the sprouting of seeds, the changing colors of the jack-in-the-pulpit, the ripening and dropping of fruit, the autumnal coloring and subsequent fall of leaves.

The self-guided walking trail begins at an overlook of the hand-some Patuxent River Valley, created by glacial ice and erosion over a long period of time. Grazing or cutting keep the pasture, where deer sometimes are seen in the early morning or evening, from revert-ing to shrubs, vines, and trees. Animals, including raccoons, ground-hogs, frogs, turtles, and snakes, frequent the stream bottom, while a mixture of tall pines, oaks, sycamores, beech, and tulip poplars soar above the beautiful blossoms of dogwood and wild cherry trees and the ferns, mountain laurel, and jack-in-the-pulpit on the forest floor. In one tree, the remains of a deer stand recall hunting techniques that may date back to the Indians and early settlers, who hunted deer, rabbits, squirrels, ducks, and geese for food and clothing. In another, holes made by the yellow-bellied sapsucker's search for sap and in-sects demonstrate the interdependence of nature's various elements.

The Patuxent riverfront near the farm provides a glimpse of the still-thriving Maryland seafood industry. From harbors like Broomes Island, filled with squat, white boats, watermen venture forth on almost a daily basis most of the year to tend crab pots or dredge or tong for oysters on offshore flats.

Calvert Cliffs State Park

Although Route 2–4 is a heavily traveled four-lane, divided high-way, it traverses forested countryside that attracts occasional shoulder lane bikers and joggers and invites frequent diversions to both natural and artificial sights.

The fossil-studded cliffs facing Chesapeake Bay, readily accessible at Calvert Cliffs State Park, are easily Calvert County's most famous feature and have inspired conservationists to action against the incursion of industry, principally a nuclear-powered electric plant and an offshore natural gas unloading terminal. Calvert Cliffs State Park has facilities for day use and fishing, but is primarily a place for walkers. All vehicles must be left in the parking lot just off Route 2-4. However, the 13 miles of trails are not difficult and attract family groups as well as confirmed hikers. The woods, swamps, and beach have enough diversions to capture the imagination of even the most active child.

Six color-coded, interconnecting trails, ranging in length from 1.2 miles to 3.7 miles, cover all the principal features of the 1,600-acre park, but the 1.8-mile (each way) Cliff Trail (red code) meanders over a fairly level course to the beach below the cliffs. The trip through woods, over wooden bridges spanning small brooks, and past a marshy area takes about 40 minutes to an hour each way, depending on the ability to resist temptation to watch small animals and frogs, listen to songbirds, ogle migratory waterfowl, linger on benches along the trail, or spend time at the beach on Chesapeake Bay.

The trail ends at a narrow beach, where a signboard describes the origins of the surroundings. The strata of the cliffs belong to the Choptank and St. Mary's formations, created 10–13 million years ago in the middle to late Miocene period, and contain more than 600 species of fossils. The Choptank formation, the lowest 6 feet, is light gray in color, marked by iron stains, and contains fossil shells; the St. Mary's formation above it is mostly dark gray, weakly laminated, and topped by a weathered zone. Most visitors spend some time searching for fossils at the water's edge; fossils that wash ashore may be kept, but digging in or climbing on the cliffs is forbidden.

The beach looks in one direction toward weathered cliffs and in the other toward the 1820 Cove Point Lighthouse, the oldest brick tower lighthouse on Chesapeake Bay still in active use. A closer look at the lighthouse may be gained along state Route 497, but the tower is not open to the public.

The green trail, which traverses rolling upland terrain covered mostly by hardwood forests and skirts a number of open fields, is the longest and most rugged. It meets the Cliff Trail not far from the beach.

A nineteenth-century tobacco barn houses the visitors' center of the Calvert Cliffs Nuclear Power Plant north of the park. Fossils uncovered in construction of the plant are displayed in historical and natural context, alongside a working model of a nuclear reactor and other energy devices and information. The nearby ruins of the eighteenth-century plantation home of Charles Giff also may be visited.

West of Route 2-4, along state Routes 264 and 265, is Port Republic School No. 7, a one-room schoolhouse built about 1870, still outfitted with the double desks and slates that served about 30 children a year in grades 1 through 7 until it closed in 1922. Children walked as far as 3 miles to attend this school and 59 similar ones in Calvert County.

Near the school is one of Maryland's original Episcopal parishes and Calvert County's oldest continuously worshipping congregation, established in 1672 in a log church. The present church dates from 1772.

Solomons Island Area

Solomons Island may have had trouble with its identity over the years, but its mission as a safe and active harbor has never been in doubt. Its deep, protected harbor gained its reputation as early as 1680, when it was named Bourne's Island. During the War of 1812, Joshua Barney's small flotilla sailed from the island to attack British vessels on Chesapeake Bay. After more than a century as Somervell's Island, the name was changed again in 1867 when Isaac Solomon's oyster house initiated a renaissance in commercial fishing and shipbuilding. The workhorse bugeye was created at Solomons Island in the late nineteenth century.

Now a handsome resort and fishing center, whose few streets are jammed with cars and people most of the time, Solomons has outgrown the island onto the mainland near the Johnson Bridge, which crosses the Patuxent to St. Mary's County.

The Calvert Marine Museum, sited near the end of the bridge, becomes a beehive of recreated eighteenth-century activity on a mid-September Saturday known as Faire Day. Men dress in ancient sailors' outfits, women don period dresses and caps, performers recreate colonial entertainment, children play eighteenth-century games, cooks and bakers serve colonial-style food, and crafts- and tradespeople offer their wares.

The pace at the museum is more leisurely at other times of the year. The museum is divided into two parts: (1) the main complex of a museum and floating exhibits and (2) the J. C. Lore & Sons Oyster House in the legendary seafaring community on the island.

The museum's emphasis on boatbuilding and related crafts is a good orientation to Bay maritime activities, as well as a good introduction to the remainder of the museum's presentations. A superior collection of vessel nameplates, such as *Bay Belle* and *Kathryn N.*, hang on the walls above a 28-foot, three-log canoe built in 1905 at Poquoson, Virginia, and models of other typical Bay vessels. Among them are the log canoe *Tigress,* built in 1936 at Olivet, Maryland, which won three first-place racing trophies; Potomac River dory *Doris C.,* representing a type of vessel that was developed in 1880 near the mouth of the Potomac River; a Chesapeake pungy; the 67-foot bugeye *Lizzie J. Cox,* constructed in 1905 at Fishing Island, Maryland; the 72.9-foot schooner *Rattler,* built in 1881 in Worcester County, Maryland; a Bay sharpie circa 1885; the skipjack *Gertrude Wands,* built in 1899 at Deal Island, Maryland; a 1900 Bay skiff; and steamboats *Dorchester* and *Calvert.*

Decoys, compasses and other tools, and visual displays depict Bay life, including methods of harvesting and processing finfish and shellfish. The significance of the Bay in the War of 1812 also is explored.

An estuarium demonstrates the importance and diversity of estuarine life on the Bay and Patuxent River through hands-on exhibits, including touching various lifeforms and looking through a microscope at lifeforms invisible to the naked eye. Other exhibits provide a short course in sportfishing with shrimp, alewives, perch, crabs, and artificial lures as bait at Sandy Point, Block Buoy, Deep Point, Lighthouse Lump, Chinese Mud, Cedar Point, and Point Patience and cover the habits and growth of the blue crab, the protection of eagles, and the work of the Audubon Society.

Among the vessels tied up at the museum dock is the 60-foot *William B. Tennyson,* one of the oldest surviving chunk bugeyes on the Bay and the oldest Coast Guard–approved vessel carrying passengers on excursions (Wednesday through Sunday, May through October "weather permitting," around Solomons Harbor and the Patuxent River). The *Tennyson,* built in 1899 at Crabb Island, Maryland, with a 9-inch-thick log hull, originally carried sail when she served as an oyster dredge boat but was converted to diesel power in 1911 and operated as an oyster "buy boat" until acquired by the museum in 1979.

Among other floating exhibits are the "oyster pirate" *Marie Theresa,* a small, fast version of the skipjack used to poach on oyster beds, and the 51-foot skipjack Maggie Lee, built in 1903 at Pocomoke City, Maryland, and still used by her owner to dredge oysters under sail in wintertime. A shed holds examples of smaller craft.

Drum Point Lighthouse, constructed in 1883 as one of 45 that marked strategic Bay points, overlooks the museum's waterfront area. Visitors may ascend stairs to the three levels of the restored lighthouse, including the cupola holding the light. Boardwalks extend into freshwater and saltwater marshes.

The J. C. Lore and Sons Oyster House, situated a half-mile south of the main museum on Solomons Island, features restored oyster-shucking and -processing rooms, clam house, net shanty, and a display illustrating the historical uncertainties of a waterman's life. It is open May through September.

Landlubbers at first may wonder about the fuss over Solomons Island, connected to the mainland by a causeway built about 1870. It is a water-oriented resort, which since 1925 has been the home of one of the Bay's most prestigious maritime research institutions — the Chesapeake Biological Laboratory, which now functions as a unit of the University of Maryland's Center for Environmental and Estuarine Studies. One of its missions is to study the effects of pollutants and human activities on the Bay.

Solomons Island grows on landlubbers. It occupies a spectacular setting where the Patuxent River flows into Chesapeake Bay and thus is a good place for ship watching. Even a confirmed landlubber will appreciate the sight of sailboats crossing the tip of the island to find sheltered harbor in Back Creek and the numerous seafood restaurants. The island has ideal pleasure boating conditions and makes the most of them, with excellent facilities extending from the Solomons Island Pier on the Patuxent River to the sheltered marinas on Back Creek. Rental sailboats and motorboats are available, as are bikes and mopeds for leisurely riding on the streets of the island.

The twenty-passenger *Mystique* leaves Solomons twice daily Wednesdays, Saturdays, and Sundays from mid-April to mid-November and crosses the Bay (1½ hours) to Hoopers Island, where visitors may wander around the village of Fishing Creek, visit Rippons Crab House, or make more distant excursions, including Blackwater National Wildlife Refuge and Cambridge, by bike or van. Departures alternate between Ship Point Research Park on state Route 670 and the Oyster House Museum dock. Tours also may be taken in the opposite direction, leaving the Dorchester County Dock in Fishing Creek.

Drum Point Lighthouse at the Calvert Marine Museum, Solomons Islands,
Maryland. PHOTO BY JOHN BOWEN.

Patuxent River

THE PATUXENT RIVER IS SECOND ONLY TO THE POTOMAC IN INFLUENCE on Maryland, past and present. Indeed, some believe it should be first. It is now, after a long period of neglect, regarded as one of the most important natural resources in the state.

The river drains the bulk of the Southern Maryland peninsula, extending inland almost to Frederick and changing from a woodland stream to tidal wetlands on its way to Chesapeake Bay. It is navigable for about half its 100-mile length — the British fleet sailed up the river in support of army troops marching to attack Washington during the War of 1812 — and has valuable oyster beds. Sports enthusiasts sit down to feasts of venison, raccoon, muskrat, opossum, ducks, geese, oysters, and crabs taken from the basin. Along the shoreline are small parks, a marina at Sandgates, the Patuxent Naval Air Test Center, and waterfront communities like Golden Beach on the western bank. On the eastern bank, fishing communities dominate from Solomons Island to beyond Broomes Island.

For more than two decades, the Maryland Department of Parks and Recreation, the Maryland–National Capital Park and Planning Commission, and Prince Georges County have been acquiring land along the river as a conservation measure. In recent years, most of the acquisition has been accomplished by Maryland's Program Open Space.

Conservation does not mean the land is idle. Eleven natural areas totaling 6,000 acres are open to limited use. Large segments are leased for restricted farming, while smaller tracts are leased to the Girl Scouts of Washington, the 4-H Foundation, and the Isaak Walton League. A few areas of the Patuxent River Park and the Merkle Wildlife Management area are available for public day use. Programs also include managed hunting, waterway improvements, wildlife conservation, and surface mining reclamation.

Patuxent River Park

On a map, the green color identifying Patuxent River Park seems to cover most of the river. The expansiveness of the park will mean little to the visitor, who can visit only certain sections of it.

The 2,000-acre Jug Bay Natural Area, reached via Croom Road (state Route 382) and Croom Airport Road from U.S. 301 south of Upper Marlboro, provides a variety of ways to explore the natural attributes of the upland forests, fields, swamps, and marshes.

Three widely separated boat ramps provide access to the river for boats up to 18 feet in length. A mixture of freshwater and tidal fish, especially catfish, bass, perch, and rockfish, frequent the river. Black Walnut Creek, while it has some tidal fish, mostly has freshwater fish. A half-dozen duck blinds are located along the waterfront. In addition, upland small game hunting is allowed off the park in a state-county cooperative program.

Canoeists can observe the change from upland stream to tidal wetlands on the 8-mile stretch of river between Jug Bay and Queen Anne Bridge, which takes about five hours. The park rents canoes from March to the end of October (out before noon, back by 3:30). Canoeists may use their own hulls year round, but park rangers discourage going out on the river during hunting season. They also advise checking the tidal charts and floating with the tide.

Jug Bay has trails for hikers and horseriders. For hikers, Swan Point Trail starts near the park office and leads to the boardwalk across marshy Black Walnut Creek, then connects with Chapman trail, which extends through a forested area. An 8-mile bridle trail winds through the forest and crosses the entrance road. Primitive camping areas are available for youth groups as large as 200 people.

The interpretive program includes boat tours aboard the electrically powered *Otter* (any day April–October when eight or more people are available) to explore the marshland ecology. Other events, some in cooperation with other organizations, include sky watches for meteor showers, Audubon wildlife field trips and lectures, nature walks, and crafts.

"Patuxent Village," a living history exhibit in a forest setting, includes a 150-year-old log cabin brought to the site from Aquasco; a tobacco "prize," which was used to stuff tobacco leaves into barrels; and a smokehouse. The Chesapeake Bay influence is represented by a 28-foot log canoe built about 1900, which is typical of the type used for oystering and crabbing in the nineteenth and twentieth centuries, and another boat with a gill net. More than a thousand nineteenth-century tools, farm implements, and domestic items also are on display. During Patuxent Discovery Day the first weekend in May, the buildings are used to demonstrate old-style activities, such as trapping and preparation of food.

A 4½-mile driving trail, open from noon to 3 P.M. Sundays, connects the Jug Bay Natural Area and nearby Merkle Wildlife Sanctuary. The route highlights important areas through narrative signboards, crosses a 1,000-foot bridge over Mattaponi Creek, and stops at a lookout tower past which waterfowl fly.

An alternate route when the driving trail is closed uses Croom Road and St. Thomas Church Road.

Merkle Wildlife Sanctuary

In autumn, the meadow below the Visitors Center of the Merkle Wildlife Sanctuary is carpeted with strutting and honking Canada goose. Occasionally, a new gaggle wheels over observation decks at the center and slips to a landing near Lookout Creek or in scattered open spaces in the meadow.

Between 5,000 and 10,000 of them, the largest concentration on the western shore of Chesapeake Bay in Maryland, come each year. October is the peak month, but the geese stay around until the end of February or the middle of March, depending on the weather.

Despite this concentration, the Merkle Sanctuary is not a one-bird park. Bluebirds nest there in large numbers, partly along a trail of fifty-eight boxes that have been erected in fields behind the Visitors Center. Bald eagles, great blue heron, winter wrens, tree swallows, and sparrows also are regular tenants. A few osprey nest in dead trees along the shoreline.

Nature programs, naturally emphasizing the bird population, include walks that frequently spot as many as forty species, lectures on waterfowl, backyard bird feeding, and deer hunting, and an annual Goose Greet in late October. The Green Wings program sponsored by Ducks Unlimited features naturalists, wildlife artists, decoy carvers, bird-banding demonstrations, and puppets.

A large selection of bird photographs hangs in the Visitors Center, alongside handsome carvings of ducks and flowers, displays on how to make bluebird nests, and information on bees, butterflies, and hummingbirds. Live turtles, small fish, and snakes inhabit the Nature

Discovery Room, which also has an exhibit on tree leaves. A bee and butterfly garden is located in front of the center.

The Paw-Paw hiking trail, one of three on the sanctuary, is divided almost evenly between fields and woods. The mile-long trail is open all year, but hikers are cautioned to avoid areas where geese may be feeding. Another short walk leads to Lookout Creek, while the longer Poplar Springs Trail, a continuation of a trail that begins in the Jug Bay Area of Patuxent River Park, winds through upland forest, across Mattaponi Creek, and past wildflower meadows.

Merkle Sanctuary's varied terrain is bright with wildflowers in the spring–October period, including pink lady's slipper orchid, cardinal flower, ivy-leafed morning glory, arrowhead, buckwheat, partridge pea, flowering spruce, jimsonweed, climbing hempweed, black-eyed Susan, roe marigold, daisy fleabane, swamp mallow, wild columbine, yellow water lily, and ironweed.

Merkle's bridle trail also is a continuation of one that begins in Patuxent River Park.

The sanctuary is open daily from 8 A.M. to 5 P.M. The Visitors Center opens Tuesday through Sunday from 10 A.M. to 4 P.M.

Cedarville Natural Resources Management Area

A wilderness eagerly sought by deer hunters less than three miles from heavily traveled Route 301? It seems illogical, but it's true. White-tailed deer are so abundant in the area they can be seen at night even along Cedarville Road, the side road just north of Waldorf that leads to Cedarville Natural Resources Management Area. Although bucks are rare, does in the 100- to 150-pound range are common.

Hunters sign up at the Charcoal Kiln, on the edge of the section of the forest where hunting is allowed in season. (The kiln, a 1930s relic, also is used by the rangers to demonstrate the method of making charcoal, as part of the forest's interpretive program.) Small animals such as rabbits and squirrel also are abundant in the state forest.

The abundance of game may have been one reason the Piscataway Indians chose the area for their winter quarters before European settlers arrived. Camping is still part of the Cedarville program, with Scouts using a primitive campground and families signing up for more comfortable but still wooded sites. Signs along a short forest resources walk identify conservation practices.

Five hiking trails, most of which have some wet areas, cover the diverse features of the forest. The 3-mile-long Birdwatchers Trail traverses an area where food patches attract songbirds, hawks, owls, and other birds and wildlife. Holly and magnolia dominate the forest along the 3-mile Holly Trail, which also passes examples of marsh plants and wildflowers. The 2-mile Swamp Trail passes through the headwaters of Zekiah Swamp, the largest freshwater swamp in Maryland, and areas of ferns and dense underbrush. The hilly, 3.5-mile Heritage Trail, with a 60-foot change in elevation, passes streams and springs once used for the manufacture of "moonshine" whiskey, crosses abandoned farmland, and goes past the kiln. The 2.5-mile Plantation Trail is the driest and most level as it winds through a pine forest planted in the 1930s and circles Cedarville Pond.

The 4-acre pond is the only fishing area in the forest. It is stocked with bass, bluegill, and catfish. Bikers use the six paved roads in the forest. Other facilities include an archery practice range, fish hatchery, playground, and picnic tables and pavilions.

St. Mary's County

Economic Development Commission, P.O. Box 351, Leonardtown, MD 20650. Tel.: 301/475-5621.

Chamber of Commerce, Route 5, Box 41A, Mechanicsville, MD 20659. Tel.: 301/884-2148.

IN AUTUMN, WHEN BLACK-EYED SUSAN PROLIFERATES, THE BYWAYS OF St. Mary's County are among the most beautiful in Maryland — and the least traveled. Patches of brilliant yellow blossoms color mile after mile of roadway designated as scenic by the state and fill whole fields at farms and isolated residences. There is an air of expectancy, as well, for soon the air will turn crisp and waterfowl nestling down for the winter will begin to crowd the shorelines of the Potomac and the Patuxent rivers.

This side of St. Mary's is not altogether indicative of the composite character of a county that believes, to a large extent, that beauty is as beauty does. Behind the façade of flowers lie well-worked farmlands and quaint harbors, where crab boats chug slowly out in the dim predawn, often followed by charter boats heading Bayward on fishing expeditions. History overlays everything else. As the site of the first English settlement, St. Mary's is also the most historic county in Maryland. No one forgets that, least of all the visitor.

The most concentrated residential-business complex in St. Mary's County lies a few miles south of the Patuxent River Bridge (officially the Governor Thomas Johnson Memorial Bridge) from Solomons. Lexington Park is built in large measure around the Patuxent Naval Air Test Center, whose mission is to test and evaluate all aircraft and systems for operational efficiency and safety. The station's activities are on view Tuesday through Saturday at the Naval Air Test and Evaluation Museum, conveniently located on Route 235.

The museum, the only one of its kind in the nation, provides a cockpit view of naval test evaluation activities. A map indicates the airspace over the Maryland, Virginia, and Delaware coasts, including Chesapeake Bay, periodically used for aircraft testing. Ground aids, such as an F-4 cockpit procedures trainer and computers, stand beside exhibits on successful and unsuccessful ideas, including an inflatable airplane built in 1957 as a potential rescue device and the Skyhook method of rescue. Other exhibits include a model of the aircraft carrier *U.S.S. Commencement Bay*, built at Tacoma, Washington, in 1944; helicopter engines; a portable helicopter; and information on the moon landing program and the Navy test pilot school.

Volunteers guide tours of outdoors static exhibits by appointment. Five once-active aircraft, including a Douglas F-6A jet fighter, the F-4 "Salty Dog 100," and examples of the Sidewinder missile and MK-82 Snakeye bomb, whose anchor was designed to make low-level bombing safer, share the grounds with the wooden cupola of the Cedar Point Lighthouse, which marked the confluence of the Patuxent River and Chesapeake Bay from 1896 to 1954.

North of Lexington Park, what may be the nation's oldest plantation in continuous operation occupies a rolling hillside beside the Patuxent River. Sotterly, at the end of Sotterly Gate Road and also accessible by boat, retains much of its colonial ambience. The rambling manor house with shingle roof, massive chimneys, and a 100-foot-long, columned porch with stone floor, whose oldest part dates from about 1717, overlooks grazing pastures that slope to the tree-lined Patuxent River. The fine wood paneling and Chinese Chippendale staircase, from about 1750, were the works of an indentured servant, Richard Boulton, who according to legend left some work unfinished when his term expired. The Great Hall, notable for its woodwork and shell-capped alcoves and still lighted by candles, has been described as "one of the 100 most beautiful rooms in America." A secret ladder passage connects the ornate sitting room with one of the upstairs bedrooms, now decorated with nineteeth-century furniture.

The formal garden beside the house is planted in annuals and perennials, which bloom in succession, starting with daffodils in April and lilacs, tulips, hyacinths, peonies, and irises in May. Other flowers include Harrison roses, oriental poppies, Shasta daisies, fall asters, evening primrose, black-eyed Susan, sweet shrub, veronica, and phlox. A section of the garden is planted in typical colonial crops of tobacco, corn, and herbs.

The 1757 brick customs house, active when Sotterly was a port of entry, houses a small museum of Indian artifacts and colonial farm implements. One pre-Civil War slave cabin survives.

Although Sotterly is still used as a residence, the house and garden are open daily June–September, and by appointment April–May and October–November. It also hosts a series of candlelight dinners, an art festival and musical in June, a Thanksgiving dinner, and a Christmas open house.

George B. Cecil Memorial Park, at the end of Forrest Landing Road off Sotterly Gate Road, is small but has a boat ramp on a handsome cove whose shoreline also has a number of private landings.

Beyond Sotterly is Charlotte Hall, a crossroads community with a farmers' market on Wednesday and Saturday year round, a few horsedrawn Amish carts on the roads at most times, and faint memories of its historic importance. Preserved at the veterans home are the White House, built around 1803, and the 1883 red stone Dent Memorial Chapel. From Charlotte Hall, state Route 6 makes a straight run to U.S. 301 at LaPlata, key to the western part of Southern Maryland. State Route 5, decorated in some places by crepe myrtle trees, turns north to Hughesville where visitors may listen to the almost indecipherable drone of auctioneers at tobacco auctions. The circa 1830 home of Dr. Samuel A. Mudd, who treated President Lincoln's assassin, John Wilkes Booth, stands on state Route 232, not far from high-roller Waldorf on U.S. Route 301.

South of Lexington Park, state Route 235 (also known as Three Notch Road) passes country homes and farms with fields of black-eyed Susan; marinas on St. Jerome Creek; the point on Chesapeake Bay with perhaps the most unusual name, Point No Point; and little-known attractions like the county-operated Elms Beach, which has the unusual combination of public beach and an environmental education center. At Ridge, the self-styled "bluefish capital of the Chesapeake," it unites with state Route 5 to complete the run to Point Lookout, the southernmost tip of the peninsula.

Point Lookout

Point Lookout, the sandy tip of a narrow peninsula at the confluence of Chesapeake Bay and Potomac River, has had a succession of highs and lows. It was part of St. Michael's Manor, one of three estates owned by pioneer Leonard Calvert. Remote and mysterious in its formative years, it was largely ignored by the rest of Maryland, except during times of conflict. Lookouts were stationed there during both the Revolutionary War and the War of 1812 to report on the movements of British warships in Chesapeake Bay. The British, in turn, chased away the lookouts and used the point as a supply base during the capture of Washington, D.C., and the unsuccessful attack on Baltimore.

Point Lookout achieved its first high point as a resort area prior to the outbreak of the Civil War. Its popular hotel, about a hundred beach cottages, and a lighthouse produced an unprecedented interest in the peninsula and relative prosperity. The war changed that, drying up the resort trade and creating financial difficulties for resort proprietors. In 1862, the federal government leased the hotel and converted it into Hammond General Hospital. The first prisoners, largely Southern Maryland civilians sympathetic to the Confederacy, were confined on the hospital grounds early in 1863 and a full-size prisoner-of-war camp was set up after the Battle of Gettysburg.

Camp Hoffman ultimately became the largest of the war, housing more than 52,000 Confederate prisoners and Maryland civilians. The tents in which the prisoners lived, each with only a single blanket, were inadequate for the winters, and thousands of prisoners literally froze to death. Even when prisoners built shacks, camp officers ordered them demolished. Other POWs suffered from exposure, disease, contaminated wells, and lack of adequate rations. By the end of the war, Point Lookout's reputation was comparable to the infamous Confederate camp at Andersonville, Georgia.

In the early 1900s, a contrite nation erected a monument to the 3,384 Southerners who died there; the tall, handsome obelisk stands in a small park beside state Route 5 that goes to the tip of the peninsula. A smaller monument erected earlier by Maryland stands on the same site. The marks of the tent camp have long since disappeared, but the partially restored remains of one of the three earthen forts erected to guard the prisoners are located in a picnic area overlooking the river about half a mile off the main roadway. Little remains of the hospital building.

Point Lookout State Park, although devoted primarily to outdoors activities, recalls the Civil War history at its Visitors Center. For example, a 12-minute audiovisual recalls that, on New Year's Day 1864, hungry Confederate prisoners caught and cooked a rat. In the summer, they supplemented their inadequate rations by catching crabs and fish. Thieves, called "tent cutters" because of their modus operandi, were made to wear barrel shirts and carry balls on chains when caught. Watercolors painted by prisoners and other illustrations depict the gentler, as well as the harsher, moments in camp life, such as prisoners trading valuables and handmade crafts to guards for food and clothing. The poet Sidney Lanier was one of those who survived to return home after the war. Contemporary photographs and relics, such as swords, are used to create static displays.

The Visitors Center museum also has photographic displays on commercial oystering and historical uses of the Bay for recreation.

Point Lookout State Park, which doubles as headquarters for state parks in the region, crowds rugged natural beauty and extensive facilities into a 495-acre site. The flat terrain hosts sandy beaches, marshland, and forests of pine, oak, and gum indented by numerous creeks and inlets. Facilities permit sunbathing, swimming, camping, hiking, boating, fishing, crabbing, oystering, and nature observation.

The park has three focal points: Lake Conoy, the bayfront, and the beach area.

Centered on Lake Conoy are the year-round campsite where RVs park among trees, with its own pier; a separate launching ramp and boat and canoe rental facility; and the Visitors Center, which is the jumping-off place for two short trails. The short Sand Fiddler Alley Nature Trail takes visitors through tall reeds and marsh grass to the muddy shore of Lake Conoy. The longer Periwinkle Point Nature

Trail divides into ¼-mile branches, one ending at marshy Point Lookout Creek and the other terminating in the woods. The Junior Ranger program includes canoeing on the lake, as well as instruction on poison ivy and other nature-oriented subjects.

Surf fishers, using the riprap barrier, dominate the Chesapeake Bay shoreline along Route 5. The highway ends at a naval station on which the 1839 lighthouse is located.

Sunbathers and migratory osprey nesting on offshore poles coexist at the beach area overlooking the Potomac River. Walkers can follow the beach to the restricted nature area beside Cornfield Harbor or hike a half-mile to the Civil War earthworks. The 25-foot *Miss Lookout,* commanded by Capt. Brady Bounds, operates day charter fishing trips to Tangier and Pocomoke sounds and other Bay fishing grounds. Fishers troll, chum, and bottom fish for sea trout, speckled trout, croaker, bluefish, flounder, spot, sea bass, and perch. Trips may include stops at Smith Island or Crisfield.

The First Maryland

Maryland got off to a quick start. In March 1634, two small ships anchored off St. Clement's Island in Chesapeake Bay and sent the first Marylanders ashore. The 140 foresighted colonists had brought along the implements that would help them tame the wilderness, but they must have marveled at the abundance of migratory wildfowl that soon invaded the area and the wealth of the forests on the near-by mainland.

The island hesitation was typical of early English settlements — it provided natural protection against an unpredictable indigenous population and the uncertainties of the forest — but it did not facilitate the establishment of farms. The settlement remained at St. Clement's only a short time before a permanent colony was established at St. Mary's City, a hospitable area on the mainland. Within a year, the new colony loaded one of the vessels, the *Dove,* with grain — Maryland's first export. That same vessel would later carry a cargo of beaver pelts and lumber to the mother country, only to be lost in a storm off the English coast.

Maryland's early history was written largely at two sites — St. Clement's Island, opposite Colton's Point at the end of state Route 242, and St. Mary's City on Route 5 southeast of Leonardtown, the county seat.

Reconstructed 17th century sailing vessel Dove, *which carried Maryland's first settlers, rides the dock at St. Mary's City.* PHOTO BY JOHN BOWEN.

St. Clement's Island and Vicinity

St. Clement's Island, in the Potomac River at the end of state Route 242, is accessible only to boaters, just as it was when the 72-foot *Ark* and 42-foot *Dove* discharged the first colonists in 1634. Private boats may tie up at its two docks. An excursion boat shuttles from the Potomac River Museum at Colton's Point to St. Clement's on weekends from Memorial Day to July 4, and Thursday through Sunday thereafter through the last Sunday in September. The 20-minute boat trip includes a turn around the small island before debarkation.

Maryland's first conservation law concerned St. Clement's. Today, after an up and down career, the island is preserved in a near-natural state as a sanctuary for wildlife, especially migratory wildfowl and small animals. Trails explore the island, which has picnic facilities and piers for crabbing. A 40-foot cross was erected in 1934 to commemorate the first Roman Catholic Mass in England's American colonies. Like earlier Anglican pioneers in Virginia, one of the first acts of the settlers was to offer thanks to God for their safe voyage. In winter, watermen tong for oysters around the island.

Maryland Day in late March features laying a wreath at the landing site on St. Clement's Island. A Sail-by Mass is read in late May and the Blessing of the Fleet is held in late June.

A 10-minute audiovisual program in the Potomac River Museum, which is open daily during the warm months and Wednesday–Sunday in winter, relates the off-and-on use of the island after it served as a stepping-stone for the settlers. The British landed troops there during the War of 1812; steamboats brought hundreds of tourists to the island and resorts at Colton's Point in the nineteenth century; the "oyster wars" on the Potomac from the mid-nineteenth-century until after World War II turned the entire region into a "hell on the half-shell"; and for a time after 1919, the U.S. government used the island as a practice target range before returning it to the state in 1962.

The museum's diverse collection of relics includes human skulls dating from A.D. 1200 excavated at nearby Brushwood; Indian arrowheads, pottery, and jewelry; a pre-Revolutionary home front from St. Patrick's Creek; colonial costumes; and photographs of Potomac River lighthouses. On the lawn is the Potomac River dory *Doris C.,* built in 1919, which is typical of a type of workboat that was constructed after the Civil War on nearby St. Patrick's and White Neck creeks. Ocean Hall on the Wicomico River, one of the oldest brick houses in North America, can be visited by arrangement with the museum. The Georgian house, built in 1703, has a colonial upper cruck roof, classical box cornice, and other unusual features.

A public dock stands in front of the museum. Marinas are located on St. Patrick's Creek, an arm of St. Clement's Bay, whose eastern shoreline hosts St. Clement's Shores Park. Also across the Bay, on Route 243, is the oldest Roman Catholic Church in continuous use in English America. St. Francis Xavier at Newtown was founded in 1640, but the current church was built in 1731 and restored in 1984. The bell in the vestibule is dated 1691 and may have been used in the church at St. Mary's for a time, while the stained-glass windows were installed in the early twentieth century. The adjacent 1789 Manor of Little Brittaine (Bretton), also known as Newtown Manor, is the successor to a house acquired in 1668 by the Jesuits as a center of missionary work among the colonists and Indians.

St. Mary's City

It is possible to visit St. Mary's City, the first capital of Maryland, with a minimal exposure to the modern side of the community.

Indeed, no place conveys the atmosphere of seventeeth-century Maryland better than the separate phases of historical St. Mary's City that triangulate around the Brentland Visitors Center on Rosecroft Road. Trails lead in two directions from the center, which is open daily year round. A half-mile path crosses a field and follows the high riverbank to the historic restoration at Governor's Field. Visitors also may descend the embankment and walk a way along the shoreline. The second path extends in the opposite direction about three-quarters of a mile through a built-up area and woods to the Godiah Spray Plantation; from the plantation, the trail meanders more than 1½ miles through a wooded area to Chancellor's Point Natural History Area. The historical sites are open daily from Memorial Day to Labor Day and on weekends from Maryland Day (last weekend in March) through November.

The settlers obtained the site, situated on a "naturally fortified" bluff above the St. Mary's River, by trading axes, hoes, cloth, and hatchets to the Yaocomico Indians, who were ready to abandon it because of attacks by the stronger Susquehannock tribe. The first permanent English settlement in Maryland was a substantial city of sturdy homes and government buildings, housing a commercial center for tobacco farms along nearby waterways.

Reconstructed elements at Governor's Field recall the social organization and day-to-day activities of citizens of the first capital. Government is represented by the Jacobean State House of 1676, reconstructed as part of Maryland's Tricentennial celebration in 1934. In the original, Maryland's first brick public building, delegates met for eighteen years in a large downstairs chamber to enact the laws governing the colony, while the governor and his privy council occupied the second floor. Daily living history market and court days demonstrations from Memorial Day to Labor Day and annual Christmas concerts and madrigal singing now share the building with historical exhibits.

The original State House stood among the oaks, walnuts, and poplars of nearby Church Point, but reconstruction on that site might have disturbed old graves. Old Trinity Parish, founded on Smith's Creek but moved to St. Mary's when it became the capital, acquired the State House after the capital was relocated to Annapolis in 1694. The present Old Trinity Church dates from 1851 but incorporates bricks from an older structure.

The scattered sites of other buildings, including 1638 St. John's mansion on Fisher's Road, where Mistress Margaret Brent made her plea to the Maryland Assembly for the right to vote, and the 1765 Tolle-Tabbs House, off Route 5 north of the city, have been excavated. Mistress Brent, who was actually given the title of "gentleman" in court records, acted as treasurer of the colony and agent for Lord Baltimore, the proprietor, after the death of Governor Leonard Calvert and used ingenuity, courage, and diplomacy to head off hunger and disorder.

At William Farthing's Ordinary, waitresses in period costumes serve "pottage," planter's lunch, seafood stew, "sallatt," crab pie, and more modern favorites, either in a tavern setting or under the grape arbors that grow outside. Food is prepared in a separate kitchen typical of the period. The frolicsome side of seventeenth-century living is demonstrated during autumn Tavern Nights, when entertainment ranges from bluegrass to sixteenth-century sea chanties.

The path from the State House past the ordinary to the Village Center overlays a seventeenth-century village road named Aldermanbury Street. Seventeenth-century buildings, split-rail fences, lots, and roads form the Village Center site. Another period inn, van Swearingen's, has been partially reconstructed. The Brome-Howard House, whose garden honors Margaret Brent, dates from the early nineteenth century. The 1840 Greek revival manor house was built by Dr. John Brome on a 3,000-acre plantation.

Although St. Mary's had some commerce with the colony of Virginia, it remained dependent on the home country of England for manufactured products such as axes, hoes, muskets, and printed material, including Bibles. A path leads to the banks of the St. Mary's River, much as it did when the colonists created their capital. The reconstructed three-masted *Maryland Dove,* typical of the slow, small vessels that linked the colony to England in 1634, rides easily at dock when it is not demonstrating to twentieth-century passengers how difficult passage across the stormy North Atlantic must have been in the early seventeenth century.

Godiah Spray Tobacco Plantation is worked as a seventeenth-century farm, with attendants performing seasonal chores under the watchful eyes of guided tours. The dwelling house, tenant house, and tobacco barn, where leaves are stored and cured, are supported by vegetable and herb gardens, an orchard where apples are raised for cider, and an old field and a new field where trees have been cut to allow planting. March through May, planting is one of the farm's demonstration programs.

Indian life is one of the facets at multipurpose Chancellor's Point

Natural History Area. An Indian longhouse is the centerpiece of an annual Indian Culture Day in early October.

The 66 largely unspoiled acres at Chancellor's Point include bluffs, beaches, fields, woodlands, marshes, and a garden growing medicinal plants and vegetables. A natural history center combines a beautiful view of the river with exhibits on beekeeping, archeology, local plants and animals, and snail, clamlike, and other fossils deposited in the sediment 12 million years ago when the sea covered the Chesapeake as far inland as Washington, D.C. The *Life of St. Mary's River* mural by artist Earl Hoffman capsules the history of the river from settlement to the present day.

A mile-long trail loops along the shore and through the woodlands. The hour-long walk overlooks the brackish water habitats of osprey, heron, and bald eagle and meanders through a second-growth forest with mixed pine, tupelo, hickory, and sweet gum predominating.

St. Mary's City hosts a number of other festivals associated with history and the water, including a Grand Militia Muster/Charter Days in late June, Maritime Heritage Festival in mid-September, the Oyster Festival and Harvest Home Celebration in mid-October, and a Christmas Shopping Fair in late October.

The impressive Religious Freedom Monument at the northern entrance to St. Mary's City, adjacent to the busy walkways of St. Mary's College of Maryland, recognizes one of the important legislative initiatives approved by the government of a colony founded as a haven for Roman Catholics. The 1649 Toleration Act, officially titled "An Act Concerning Religion," was the first law in America to grant freedom of conscience to all Christians.

St. Ignatius Roman Catholic Church at St. Inigoes, off Route 5 south of St. Mary's City, dates from 1786 and is the second church on the site. It is noted for its stained-glass windows and altar.

The Potomac Shore

St. Mary's County is oriented primarily toward the mighty Potomac River, whose many coves and tributaries provide some of the finest small-boat harbors accessible to Chesapeake Bay. Like other areas around the Bay, the St. Mary's waterfront mixes commercial and sport fishing. A combination of state Routes 5 and 234 parallels the Potomac all the way from Point Lookout to U.S. 301, the main north–south highway through the region. Supplementing the maritime presence are historic homes, churches, and wilderness areas.

The small peninsula that ends at St. George's Island is historic as well as handsome. Cornfields and stands of trees alternate along state Route 249, but the most beautiful area is Valley Lee, through which state Route 244 passes to provide access to McKay Beach and Potomac Shores. Valley Lee was part of St. George's Hundred, established in 1638 as settlement moved outward from its base at St. Mary's City. The present white brick St. George's Episcopal Church was built in 1799 and altered in 1884, but the first church was erected between 1638 and 1642. Known locally as "Poplar Hill" Church, the present building has a separate bell tower (steeples have twice been placed on the church and each time removed) and box pews.

Piney Point and St. George's Island combine to provide a nostalgic glimpse of the way many seafood-procuring and -preparing communities used to look. Seafood firms line St. George's Creek, just off the highway, and a primitive public park extends across the highway to front on both the Potomac and St. George's rivers. In season, local crabbers use the boat ramp daily to retrieve a few bushels, while some patiently drop hand nets from the nearby pier. St. George's was not always as placid as it is today. During the Revolutionary War, the British occupied the island; an effort in 1776 to land on the mainland was repulsed.

At inland St. Mary's River State Park, down Camp Cosoma Road from Route 5, a double boat-launching ramp near a stand of drowned tree trunks provides access to an impounded lake widely known for trophy-size largemouth bass. Boy Scout volunteers helped lay out short trails in the nearby woods, one of which takes the hiker below the dam while another leads to a point overlooking the lake. Sections of the park accessed by Indian Ridge and Chancellor's Run roads are open to upland game hunting, mostly white-tailed deer, squirrels, rabbits, doves, and pheasants, between mid-October and mid-February.

Leonardtown, the seat of St. Mary's County since 1708, touches Breton Bay, which long has been a favorite fishing hole. However, the city is best known for its historical relics. The two-story, brick and granite mid-nineteenth-century Old Jail, located on the courthouse lawn, was managed in a casual fashion when local mores did not agree with law. For example, during the Prohibition era, "bootleggers" assigned to the jail sometimes spent the days playing cards at the St. Mary's Hotel or fishing in Breton Bay and went home at night. The building now houses a museum of local artifacts, including the office of Dr. Philip Bean, who practiced medicine in

Leonardtown for more than sixty-five years, and serves as a tourist information center and headquarters of the historical society. The cannon in front of the Old Jail was brought to Maryland on the *Ark*. Tudor Hall, which dates from around the end of the eighteenth century, features a hanging staircase, recessed portico, and captain's walk. Among annual Leonardtown events are the Crab Festival at mid-June and the Oyster Festival on the third weekend in October. The latter, starting in 1967, includes the men's and women's U.S. National Oyster Shucking Championships (the overall winner goes to the international contest in Ireland), and an oyster cook-off, which attracts entries from as many as thirty states in quest of a $1,000 grand prize. Visitors receive oyster-shucking lessons.

A number of historic structures are located near Chaptico, including Christ Episcopal Church of King and Queen Parish, whose sanctuary dates from 1736 and steeple from 1913. A local tradition exists that the church, which is open by appointment, was designed by Sir Christopher Wren. Privately owned historic homes near Chaptico include (1) Bachelor's Hope, off Route 238, built in the latter half of the eighteenth century with an unusual exterior staircase to the second floor, and (2) Deep Falls, off Route 234, a 1745 frame house that was the home of the 1835–1836 governor of Maryland, Maj. William Thomas.

State Route 234 west of Chaptico fully deserves its designation as a state scenic highway as it enters Charles County, the last of the Southern Maryland triumvirate. It passes a farm specializing in Arabian horses, Allens Fresh Run and other waterways bordered with marsh grass, and rolling farmlands planted in grain, vegetables, and tobacco. The 6,492-yard, 18-hole, par 71 St. Mary's County Municipal Golf Course is located at Wicomico Shores.

Entering Charles County

Maryland Route 257, en route to Cobb Island, is in a way a condensation of Charles County. The roadway passes modern white hilltop houses, farms with tractors pulling wagons laden with tobacco leaves, fields yellow with blooming black-eyed Susan, and privately owned plantation houses with signs on the highway dating their lineage to the 1700s. Among the historic buildings are circa 1792 Mount Republican, 1760 Maiden Point Farm, and Christ Church of William and Mary Parish, at Wayside, constructed in 1690 and enlarged in 1750 and, thus, the oldest public building in Charles

County. At the end of the highway lies Rock Point, with a beautiful overlook of the Wicomico River.

Intersecting state Route 254 leads to the maritime community of Cobb Island, which has marinas with about two hundred slips, restaurants and signs offering steamed and peeler crabs on both sides of Neale Sound, and a boat parked in almost every yard. A small park at the end of Bridge Boulevard, which overlooks the scenic river and Virginia shoreline in the distance, marks the island's moment in modern history. The historical marker reads, "Here, on Cobb Island, in December 1900, Reginald Aubrey Fessenden, assisted by Frank W. Very, while experimenting in wireless telephony, for the first time sent and received intelligible speech by electromagnetic waves between two masts 50 feet high and one mile apart."

On U.S. 301, Southern Maryland makes its affinity for the outdoors known immediately. Just north of the Potomac River Bridge (officially the Governor Nice Bridge) is a private Good Sam campground, which has a riverfront beach, boat ramp, and boat lift. On the opposite side of the road is Crain Memorial Park, a hilltop picnic area where tall trees hide the river from view. A marker at the entrance to the park identifies the highway as an historic route between Maryland and Fredericksburg and Williamsburg in Virginia. Laidler's Ferry, which crossed the river at this point, was mentioned in George Washington's diary.

West of Route 301

NO AREA OF MARYLAND SHOWS AS MUCH STARK CONTRAST AS THE sections of Charles and Prince Georges counties lying between U.S. Route 301 and the stretch of the Potomac River south of Washington, D.C. The national capital dominates the urbanized area of Prince Georges County well beyond the Beltway (Interstate 95) and along the shoreline beyond Indian Head in Charles County. In contrast, the southern section of Charles County remains surprisingly pastoral, with farms and forests and occasional signs for pick-your-own strawberries and other produce. La Plata, the largest town in Charles County, has a population of about 2,500.

The area has a long history of association with the water, but the influence is waning. Boats sally forth from marinas along the creeks and inlets of the area, but the area does not have the heavy concentration of commercial fishing evident farther downstream.

La Plata on Route 301, founded in 1872 along the route of a new railroad, is the county seat and from mid-March to early May a tobacco auction center. At Mount Carmel Convent off Mitchell Road, two buildings survive from the first community of religious women established in the original thirteen colonies in 1790. The old monastery and Pilgrim's Chapel are open daily. The present boundaries of Charles County, named in honor of Charles Calvert, third Lord Baltimore, date back to 1658.

La Plata also is the turnoff point for exploring the byways of the section of Charles County west of U.S. 301. A combination of state highways 6, 344, 224, and 210 bypasses the bulge caused by a bend in the Potomac River and leads in a rough arc along the riverfront to the Washington suburbs.

Port Tobacco, just off Route 6, is typical of the anomalies of the area. Capt. John Smith visited the Indian village of Potopac during one of his exploration voyages from Jamestown, Virginia. One of the earliest settlements in Maryland, the name probably derives not from tobacco but from the Potopac Indians who lived there. Tobacco put in a later appearance and, from 1770 to 1775, the port was one of the busiest in the New World. It was officially known as Chandler's Town until 1822, when the name already in common use among local residents was adopted. The town also was on a ferry route to the South, but silting of the river and movement of the county seat to La Plata caused its decline.

The early era is recalled by the reconstructed 1815 brick courthouse, which now houses a museum with displays on tobacco growing and processing and regional archeology, and the circa 1732 Stagg Hall and 1765 Chimney House. The courthouse is open Wednesday–Sunday during the warm months, on weekends September–December and March–May.

Chapel Point State Park, untended and administered from Smallwood State Park, has a dirt boat landing on the Port Tobacco River, but is best known for hunting. White-tailed deer, rabbit, squirrel, quail, and dove can be taken on a 500-acre section of the park. Seven duck blinds, available on a first-come, first-serve basis in season, stand along the river shoreline. The park is located on Chapel Point Road

(Maryland Route 427), which also curves past Port Tobacco's historic structures, about 5 miles from La Plata.

Chapel Point gets its name from St. Ignatius Roman Catholic Church, founded in 1641 by the Rev. Andrew White, who is regarded as Maryland's first historian. The present church building, which commands a majestic view of the Port Tobacco and Potomac rivers, was constructed in 1798 and reconstructed using the original Flemish bond brick walls after it was gutted by a fire in 1866. The interior features colonial iron railings and chandelier. St. Thomas Manor House, built in 1741 and also restored after the fire, has ceilings more than 12 feet high.

Another historic structure is 1732 Old Durham Chapel (Christ Church) on state Route 425 at Ironsides, a simple brick church with wide aisles.

Pope's Creek, once a gathering place for Indians and site of the first county courthouse, gathers fishing boats laden with catches for its processing houses. The area also is known for its restaurants.

Doncaster State Forest

During July, hikers and picnickers seldom bring dessert to Doncaster State Forest, about 13 miles west of La Plata along Route 6. Instead, they pick from the abundance of wild blueberry and huckleberry bushes and blackberry vines that blanket the ground in places.

Visitor use is not incidental, but has never been the primary purpose for the 1,445-acre forest, which began in the mid-1930s as a Civilian Conservation Corps (CCC) camp. With the departure of the CCC, the forest was left pretty much in a natural state until a management plan that included visitor facilities was devised in the early 1970s. Doncaster, divided by Route 6, is now a demonstration area for modern forest management.

Hiking trails dissect both the 840-acre tract north of the highway and the 605 acres south of the highway. Two interconnecting, circular blazed hiking trails, laid out in the late 1950s north of the highway, are maintained by the National Capital Hiking Club. Both the 1.75-mile circular Burnt Pine Trail and a 2.8-mile unnamed circular trail cross wooded areas, with features such as a spring and berry vines. Primitive trails include the short Maiden Fair and Shortcut trails near the eastern boundary of the park and Y Trail in the northeastern corner. All are accessed from the paved entrance road.

An east–west trail extends the length of the northern section of the forest and crosses Routes 6 and 344 to enter the southern section, where three interconnecting primitive trails parallel and cross Beaver Dam Creek. The hiking link between the two sections of the park is sometimes closed off. The boundaries of the park, like those in all Maryland parks, are marked and can be hiked.

Equestrians also use more than 13 miles of trail in the forest. These paths temporarily are marked with ribbons when local groups sponsor rides. Hunters come in season primarily to stalk white-tailed deer, but also find squirrel, dove, and other small game.

Doncaster's terrain varies from 70 to 150 feet above sea level and includes productive bottomland, as well as areas where clay beds are too thick for tree roots to penetrate. Although one-third of the forest is Virginia pine, a large percentage of the trees are aged and are being cut and replaced by faster-growing loblolly pine. Hardwoods include tulip poplar, red maple, several kinds of oak, hickory, and American beech.

A few miles west of Doncaster, Route 6 curves southward down a peninsula to Riverside, where state Route 224 begins its run northward parallel to the Potomac River and passes undeveloped Purse State Park, which is available for hiking, fishing, and hunting. Route 334 provides a shortcut to avoid the peninsula.

Although it is a main highway, Route 224 has characteristics of a country road, including an occasional bike rider on its paved shoulders. Short diversions lead to small communities where down-home events can be seen from time to time. For example, in autumn members of Pisgah Methodist Church on state Route 425 light outdoor fires, set up large kettles, and stir apple butter, which they sell to passers-by.

Smallwood State Park

The plantation of Maryland's superpatriot, Maj. Gen. William Smallwood, is now a 630-acre state park and memorial to the dependable commander of Old Line troops during the Revolutionary War.

Smallwood State Park, located off state Route 224 on Sweden Point Road, is first of all a historical experience. The plantation home, popularly known as Smallwood's Retreat, sits on a knoll in the forest of Mattawoman Plantation. Meticulously reconstructed, using three surviving corners of the original circa 1760 home, the mansion reflects the lifestyle of the family of a wealthy gentleman farmer of the Revolutionary War period and afterward, when Smallwood served as governor and leader in civic and church affairs. The eighteenth-century antique furnishings, including three dining room chairs owned by Smallwood, are the kind that made Washington feel at home when he visited there after the war.

General Smallwood, whose troops played crucial roles in battles at Long Island and White Plains, New York, and Camden, South Carolina, is buried on the slope near his mansion.

Some of the outbuildings, including the colonial kitchen and nearby herb garden and tobacco barn, have been restored, too. An eighteenth-century vegetable garden is part of the living history presentation, which from time to time includes firing of muskets at military encampments and crafts and cooking demonstrations. Costumed guides take visitors through the mansion and grounds on weekends and holidays from Memorial Day to Labor Day and at other times by appointment. Christmas candlelight tours are conducted on two successive Sundays in mid-December.

A nature trail extends about 0.7-mile from the lawn of the mansion along the forested shoreline of Mattawoman Creek and across a bridged marsh to the marina, fishing pier, and boat-launching ramps. The park has many snakes; only the copperhead is poisonous. The paved circular road from the parking lot at the picnic area also provides a scenic walk that passes some of the bird nesting boxes placed in the woods.

Sweden Point boat ramps, open from 8 A.M. to sunset year round, provide access to excellent fishing for bass, crappie, perch, bluegill, and other species in the Potomac River and Mattawoman Creek. The headwaters of the creek are also used for canoeing and sailboating. However, boaters are warned that hazardous explosions may occur at any time in areas adjacent to a nearby naval ordnance station.

Fragmented Mattawoman Natural Environment Area, which straddles Maryland 224 north of Smallwood Park and touches Mattawoman Creek, is undeveloped but open for fishing (including freshwater at the Mason Springs area) and hiking on a use-as-is basis. It is administered from Smallwood Park.

Nature is gradually recovering the slender, 834-acre Myrtle Grove Wildlife Management Area, which requires a short detour along state Route 225. Except for a graveled road down the center of the forested park, a target-shooting area, and a water treatment plant, there are no prepared facilities. However, the park never closes and is used for a variety of activities by small numbers of people.

The conditions near a 23-acre freshwater lake are ideal for bird-watching and photography; bald eagle, pileated woodpecker, osprey, marsh hawk, and other species have been seen, as well as waterfowl and songbirds. Beaver, muskrat, and other small animals live nearby. Fishers use the shoreline and electric motor-powered boats. Hikers and equestrians follow primitive trails through the oak-hickory forest and along the park boundaries, across the fields and past the water areas. Joggers, and cross-country skiers when snow covers the ground, use the road. Hunters shoot white-tailed deer, rabbit, squirrel, quail, and other small prey in season near the fields and hedgerows around an old barn.

At Indian Head, site of a naval installation and Tuesday and Thursday farmers' markets, Southern Maryland begins to turn urban. Some outdoor surprises remain off state Route 201 before the trend is confirmed, however.

Piscataway Park–National Colonial Farm

More than 4,000 acres of prime Potomac Riverfront land at Accokeek preserve the view from Mount Vernon on the Virginia Shore much as it was in George Washington's time. The separate elements of the complex, strung out along the Accokeek Road about 3½ miles from Route 210, are Piscataway Park, the National Colonial Farm, and Marshall Hall, a restored colonial mansion.

The graveled road in Piscataway Park passes an old barn filled with bundles of hay, and crosses a field. A path from the parking lot leads through the woods to the shore of Piscataway Creek. The park is open from 8 A.M. to dusk year round.

The adjacent National Colonial Farm, founded in 1958, recreates a middle-class mid-eighteenth-century tobacco farm, complete with log buildings, costumed attendants, feeding animals, and growing crops. A half-dozen structures of various size stand along lanes bordered by split rail fences and trees. A barn about 280 years old and held together by wooden pegs, brought to the site from Anne Arundel County, displays tobacco grown on the farm and an old "prize" used to press tobacco into large barrels. A circa 1770 house was recently moved from Laurel Branch, Maryland, to give added authenticity to the presentation, which also includes a rebuilt out-kitchen, smokehouse, barn, stable, and "necessary."

Visitors may stroll the lanes or paths leading to the pond and waterfront, but must take potluck on farming demonstrations, which occur mainly for school or bus groups or on Sundays in the warm months. Red Devon cows, pigs, Hog Island and Dorset horn sheep, turkeys, ducks, geese, chickens, guinea hens, and peafowl share the barnyard, while demonstration crops of tobacco, corn, grain, and vegetables grow in the fields. The orchard has apple and cherry trees.

A grove of rare American chestnut trees is one of the experiments carried on by Accokeek Foundation, Inc., which administers the farm for the National Park Service. The foundation also directs studies in agricultural history and experiments with land preservation techniques and plant preservation from offices on the farm. The farm is open Tuesday–Sunday, year round, except on Thanksgiving, Christmas, and New Year's Day.

Nearby "Hard Bargain" Farm can be toured by appointment. The farm is owned and operated by the Alice Ferguson Foundation to promote environmental study.

Fort Washington

In front of Fort Washington, the Potomac River bends outward. Northward, the river runs straight to the nation's capital, its marble spires and low waterfront discernible on a clear day. In the other direction, the river turns southwestward and is visible for miles. This commanding position on the approach to Washington recommended the bluff as the site of a fort to protect the nation's capital.

The first fort, a 13-gun bastion on the river's edge, was erected after the Revolutionary War. It was there when the British burned Washington in 1814; the British merely landed troops and bypassed the fort, which protected the water approaches. With Washington gone, the American commander destroyed the fort to keep it out of British hands and retreated. Only 12 days later, planning for construction of a new fort began. Maj. Pierre L'Enfant, who designed the national capital, began the task, only to be dismissed after a disagreement with the War Department. The present enclosed masonry fort designed for thirty 24-pounders was completed in 1824 under the direction of Lt. Col. Walter K. Armistead.

Although rifling of cannon soon diminished its value, the stone fort has been manned in several wars, but has never fired a shot in anger. It stands today virtually as it was in 1824. Walking the ramparts shows both the strength of the fort and the way the site dominates the bend in the river. The eye travels down the wooded opposite bank of the Potomac in the direction of Mount Vernon. Motorboats, sailboats, and river cruise vessels from Washington and Alexandria, Virginia, follow the course that invading warships might have taken.

Living history demonstrations recreate the lifestyles of soldiers manning the fort during its active periods. Every Sunday, rangers dressed in the blue and red uniforms of the first half of the nineteenth century guide visitors through the officers' quarters and barracks and other features inside the fort, discuss the life of soldiers at the time, and demonstrate the loading and firing of muskets, the standard shoulder weapon of the period. At other times on regular schedules, programs cover the Civil War period when the fort was part of the ring of fortifications defending Washington and include demonstrations of cannon firing.

The Visitors Center is the 1824 commandant's home, near the site of Warburton Manor when the land was a plantation. Its exhibits, which include historical relics, detail the history of the fort through its easy wartime periods and the lean peacetime years. For a time before 1941, it housed the headquarters of the Old Guard, the unit that guards the Tomb of the Unknown Soldier in Arlington. One road and a path descend to the riverfront, where a short trail passes around the base of the hill on which the imposing fort sits and goes to a point on the riverbank. Another path leads to Piscataway Creek.

A number of later structures share the riverbluff with the old fort, including huge concrete and steel bastions constructed during the short Spanish-American War. Battery Decatur, inspected on guided tours, also can be visited on an individual basis. Old buildings from later periods, around a parade ground now used as a park, are boarded up.

The fort is open from 7:30 A.M. to 8 P.M. May 1 through August 31 and from 7:30 A.M. to 5 P.M. the rest of the year, except on Christmas Day. The Visitors Center is open daily from 7:30 A.M. to 4:30 P.M. from June 1 to Labor Day and on weekends and holidays the rest of the year. The park is open daily from 7:30 until dark.

"Peake" of the Bay

Discover Harford County, P.O. Box 635, Bel Air, MD 21014.
Tel.: 301/836–8986;

Cecil County Office of Planning & Economic Development,
County Office Building Room 300, Elkton, MD 21621.
Tel.: 301/398–0200.

THE UPPER BAY REGION OF MARYLAND, THE SELF-STYLED "PEAKE OF THE Chesapeake," is clearly a transitional zone with characteristics of both the Bay area and its industrial and urban hinterland. It is also the link between the urbanized northwestern shoreline and the waterman's way of life on the Eastern Shore.

Traditionally, traffic has flowed through the region rather than to it. Washington's soldiers and supplies passed by; so did the ocean-going commerce using the canal on the Susquehanna River to reach the hinterlands of Pennsylvania and New York. Interstate 95 is typical of the way thoroughfares have whisked people past the head of the Bay since the invention of mass transportation.

The Susquehanna River flows into the Chesapeake at Havre de Grace, 35 miles northeast of Baltimore. The father of Chesapeake waters, which extends more than 600 miles inland through some of the most rugged terrain in the eastern United States, continues to exert a powerful influence on both the land and the water. It discharges more fresh water than any other stream, at least a billion gallons a day. Periods of heavy runoff change the nature of the Upper Bay by reducing the salinity of the water. With more than 440 miles suitable only for small boats, the Susquehanna is the longest nonnavigable river in the United States.

The upper bay region consists of two counties. Harford County, entirely on the western side of the Bay, balances intense shoreline activity with a more relaxed inland atmosphere. Cecil County, which folds around the northern tip of the Bay, is sometimes included as part of the Eastern Shore, but is transparently transitional in nature. The principal city of the "peake" of the Bay is Havre de Grace, which is historically and culturally an integral part of the Bay country.

Havre de Grace

Havre de Grace has all the hallmarks of a Bay city — waterfront seafood restaurants, marinas and marine railways, and public waterfront areas where people fish, launch boats, and idle away hours mesmerized by the soft breezes and movement of the water — but is becoming more and more industrialized. It is a bit commercialized for the tastes of true outdoorspeople, but that commercialization creates many opportunities to experience the adventures of the Bay.

Capt. A. L. Price, a native of the region who returned from Florida in 1984, takes passengers aboard his boat, *Friendship I,* every Sunday during the warm months for a four-hour cruise into the most pristine areas of the upper bay. The first Sunday he sails to the opposite shore of the Bay and up the beautiful Sassafras River, which he describes as the last unspoiled tributary of the Bay; the second, he visits the Chesapeake and Delaware Canal; and the third, he explores the Still Pond area. Bay exploration by air began in 1988, when a sail-making firm acquired an amphibian airplane.

Although Havre de Grace predates the Revolutionary War, it was by its own assessment a sleepy fishing village when British fire during the War of 1812 severely damaged more than 60 percent of the buildings. As a result, the 1787 Rodgers House, a Georgian brick townhouse now occupied by a barber shop, is the most significant eighteenth-century structure listed in the city's self-guided tour brochure. The remaining buildings are largely from the early nineteenth-century canal era, which gave the city its greatest impetus, and the Victorian period.

The historic district includes about 800 structures, but twenty identified as particularly significant by local historians are concentrated in an eight-block stretch along Union Street, with additional key buildings on Washington and St. John streets. Many are private homes, which can be viewed from outside, while others house boutiques and antique shops. Carriage rides tour the historic area "the old-fashioned way."

A walk through the historic district shows the city's affinity for the Bay. The considerably altered O'Neill House, parts of which may date back to 1814, remained in the family of the "defender of Havre de Grace" for more than 156 years. The original owner, John O'Neill, earned the title for single-handedly resisting the British invasion in 1814. The 1835 Hall House is among a number of brick structures dating from the early nineteenth-century canal era. The 1885 Seneca Mansion and 1895 Spencer-Silver Mansion represent the ornate tastes of the Victorian era.

The city's oldest church is St. John's Episcopal Church, an 1809 Flemish bond brick structure whose construction was financed by a lottery authorized in 1802. Although damaged by the British in 1814 and gutted by fire in 1832, it retains its simple early eighteenth-century appearance.

The waterfront adjacent to the historic area remains largely a workaday place dominated by marinas and seafood restaurants.

The commercial value of Chesapeake Bay waterways is emphasized by remnants from the 45-mile-long Susquehanna and Tidewater Canal, which are displayed at the Susquehanna Museum at the end of Conesteo Street. The red brick lock tender's house, built in 1840, and small segments of the lock, towpath along which mules muscled the barges, gates, and pivot bridge over the lock provide an insight into the immensity of the project—which, like other canals of the era, opened vast areas of hinterland to oceangoing commerce. The canal remained in operation until 1900. The museum is open 1–5 P.M. Sunday, April to end of December.

At the opposite end of the city are the Decoy Museum (open 1–5 P.M. Tuesday through Sunday), which displays and demonstrates a handicraft that has been elevated to the status of folk art, and the Concord Point Lighthouse, an excellent example of another Bay trademark. A new pathway beside tidal marshes connects the two. The nearby Bayou Villa Hotel was a luxury hotel during the 1920s when the city had a modest reputation as a resort; it is now an apartment building.

Decoys are a focus of annual celebrations in Havre de Grace. The annual Decoy Festival in early May features a carving contest and demonstrates the way self-taught skills and imagination can turn a workaday activity into an art form. Master carvers show their talents at the Decoy Museum at the foot of Giles Street and talk informally about their work. Carvers also work at the July Duck Fair at the museum.

Tydings Park is the setting of the annual mid-August Harford County Seafood Festival, whose primary activity is dispensing Bay delicacies such as steamed and soft-shelled crabs, fried oysters, clams on the half shell or fried, and fish fillets. Other water-oriented events include bass-fishing tournaments in early June and early October, a boat exhibit and display in late July, power boat races in late August, and Susquehanna Appreciation Day in late September. Another major festival occurs on Indpendence Day; Christmas events range from a candlelight tour to a tree-decorating contest and crafts program.

Havre de Grace has two areas where sport fishing is allowed without permits: the city marina at Tydings Park and the fishing pier at Frank Hutchins Memorial Park. Other fishing piers are located at Jean S. Roberts Memorial Park, while boat-launching ramps are located at Roberts and Tydings parks.

Susquehanna State Park

The trails and open areas of Susquehanna State Park, 3 miles up-river off state Route 155, provide access to an unusual collection of flora, fauna, activities, and history. The hilly park has one of the largest collections of trillium on the East Coast, as well as significant stands of white, red, and swamp oak, honey locust, sycamore, spice-bush, honeysuckle, and wild raspberry. It is especially beautiful in spring, when the tulip poplar, dogwood, and paulownia bloom.

Bird-watchers are likely to spot bluebird, pileated woodpecker, chickadee, bald and golden eagles, osprey, blue heron, kingfishers, and ducks, all of which nest in or visit the park. The forest also has large numbers of snakes, especially blacksnakes, but few are poisonous. Small turtles thrive in the remnant of the Susquehanna Canal.

The nature trail leaves from the picnic area beside Deer Creek and is divided into two loops. A 2-mile loop between the parking lot and campground is bisected by an old farm road that can be used to cut the walk in half. This trail is marked by red blazes or red arrows, while blue markings direct cross-country skiers in winter. A 4-mile hiking trail covers all the main sectors of the park, including the Rock Run historical area and the Steppingstone Museum.

The dynamics of a riverside community are reflected in buildings from different periods. A four-story grist mill with a 12-ton water wheel, where John Stump began grinding grain in 1794, now demonstrates on weekends, from 2 to 4 in the afternoon, the procedure followed for nearly two centuries. Related structures include the late eighteenth-century Miller's House and carriage barn, a detached stone privy, and a springhouse erected between 1794 and 1804. The largest building is a thirteen-room manor house, completed in 1804.

Rock Run's role as a transportation hub is represented principally by a white frame Toll House, where resident managers collected four cents from each horserider and six to 12 cents from farmers herding various kinds of animals across the mile-long toll bridge, built to facilitate travel to New Jersey in the nineteenth century. Fire, the vibrations caused by crossing animals, and ice floes each destroyed part of the bridge before it was finally closed in 1856. You can also see some of the stonework of three Susquehanna and Tidewater Canal locks that were located within the boundaries of the park.

The park also has a boat ramp, with people fishing from shore and from boats; an archery range; pullouts along Deer Creek; and campsites.

At Steppingstone Museum, reached by a scenic uphill drive through the woods along Rock Run, whose name obviously derives from the huge boulders in the small stream, volunteers demonstrate the rural arts and crafts of the 1880–1920 period. The farmhouse is furnished as a turn-of-the-century country home, while shops house blacksmithing, woodworking, coopering, tinsmithing, and leatherworking activities.

The hilltop site overlooks the river and the orchards and stone-fenced fields of nearby farms. Steppingstone is open weekends from May to the first Sunday in October.

The Rest of Harford County

Harford County has a variety of outdoor attractions and activities, as well as the usual picnicking and playground facilities. Thirty-five parks have undeveloped natural areas, while walking trails are found at the Parks and Recreation Administration Office and Liriodendron Mansion in Bel Air; Mariner Point Park and Robert Copenhaver Park in Joppatowne; and the Norrisville Recreation Complex. Seven parks have ice-skating rinks, and five have ponds.

A total of sixteen parks allow fishing, with piers located at Broad Creek north of Darlington, Bynum Run Park near Bel Air, Flying Point Park in Edgewood, Friends Park near Forest Hill, Mariner Point Park in Joppatowne, and Otter Point Creek Landing off U.S.

Route 40 near Edgewood Meadows. Boat-launching ramps are located at Broad Creek, Flying Point Park, Mariner Point Park, Otter Point, and Willoughby Beach.

The 100-foot-high hydroelectric Conowingo Dam on U.S. Route 1 blocks nearly 300 miles of the Susquehanna River formerly used by shad and other herring. The annual shad catch in the river has fallen from 7 million pounds in 1890 to about 35,000 pounds. At Fishermen's Park below the dam, line fishing for smallmouth bass, white perch, catfish, and other varieties remains good enough to attract dozens of fishers to the shoreline and dam catwalk even on cold, overcast early spring days. The first warm, sunny weekend brings hundreds into the small park, which has boat ramps, rest rooms, and a sandwich and souvenir shop. The park is open from March through September. Camping, fires, and trailers are not permitted.

Fishing also is allowed in the 14-mile-long lake behind the dam. Ramps at Glen Cove and Broad Creek provide access from the western shore. On the opposite shore, in Cecil County, fishers can walk upriver about a quarter-mile to a small cove by which local fishers swear.

The peaceful Ladew Topiary Gardens, designed and developed by Harvey S. Ladew over three-quarters of a century, provide sharp contrast. The 22 acres provide a short course in the art of shaping shrubs into animal and geometric shapes by training and trimming. Colorful flowers, trees, and bushes complement the shrubbery. The white, frame Ladew house is furnished with antiques, fox-hunting memorabilia, and paintings. The Oval Library, which contains more than 3,000 books, has been cited as one of the "hundred most beautiful rooms in America." Both the gardens and house are listed on the National Register of Historic Places.

Rocks State Park, 8 miles north of Bel Air on Route 24, is primarily known for the massive boulders strewn along Deer Creek and a thronelike formation known as King and Queen Seats, where (according to legend) Susquehannock Indian tribal councils were held. The park encompasses 600 acres of stream valley.

The Equestrian Center at Bel Air, the county seat, hosts the annual tournament of Maryland's official sport, jousting. On the first Saturday in October, knights in shining armor, encouraged by pageantry and costumed ladies, try to spear a small ring while riding at a gallop. The winner has the honor of selecting the Queen of Honor and Beauty. The State Championship Jousting and Horse Fair also includes a mock medieval battle and horse-pulling and similar contests.

The logic for holding a medieval event in Maryland runs something like this: Jousting, originally a form of combat, had been pacified by the time Maryland was founded and was a favorite sport of the early settlers; the fascination with the equestrian sport has persisted through both wartime and peacetime and has raised funds for Civil War monuments and civic and church organizations. In 1950, the Maryland Jousting Tournament Association was formed to formalize rules and promote the sport and, in 1962, the Maryland legislature made jousting the official state sport.

Bel Air has a number of historic buildings. The Hays House at 324 Kenmore Avenue, maintained by the Harford County Historical Society, dates back to the late 1700s. Liriodendron, a palladial mansion built in 1898 by one of the founders of Baltimore's Johns Hopkins University Hospital and now operated by Bel Air as a cultural center, reflects the comfortable lifestyle of the Victorian era. Just outside the city is Tudor Hall, the ancestral home of the famous Booth acting family, one of whom, John Wilkes Booth, assassinated President Lincoln. Armor used in modern combat is displayed at the U.S. Army Ordnance Museum at the Aberdeen Proving Ground, just a few miles off Interstate 95. The comprehensive collection of weapons includes some that made history, including a World War II V-2 German rocket and "Anzio Annie," the huge German railroad gun used so effectively against the Allied invasion of Italy; a tank park with hundreds of armored vehicles ranging from a fragile World War I tank to an atomic cannon; and Gen. John J. (Blackjack) Pershing's Locomobile. The museum is open noon to 4:45 P.M. Tuesday through Sunday, except for some holidays.

Cecil County

The personality of Cecil County is split several ways. The Susquehanna River strongly influences the adjacent countryside, while Interstate 95 and U.S. Route 40 dominate the central and northern parts. The remainder relates to the Eastern Shore, where people are more attuned to natural seasonal rhythms than to the hum of engines along highways, spaces are more open, industrialization is less prominent, and communities are smaller and more closely tied to the water.

The transition is gradual between Port Deposit and Perryville on the banks of the Susquehanna and Elkton, the county seat, near the Delaware border. The distinction increases as the visitor turns south to follow less-traveled state roads along the Bay shoreline.

Perryville, the first community encountered along U.S. 40, is a workaday town that nevertheless treasures restored Rodgers Tavern, a favorite stopping place on the Old Post Road in the eighteenth century. It was originally operated by a Revolutionary War hero, Col. John Rodgers. The tavern is open to afternoon tours on the second Sunday of each month, May through October, or by appointment.

Port Deposit, first settled about 1729 as a river ferry station named Creswell's Landing, had become a major cargo discharge port on the Susquehanna River by 1813 and was a major rival to Havre de Grace. By the middle of the century, the community, jammed between the riverbank and steep cliffs, also had become a major source of coarse-grained, granitic gneiss for construction. A dozen churches in Philadelphia and five in Baltimore obtained building blocks from the Port Deposit quarry. It also was used at the U.S. Naval Academy and Fort McHenry.

Both adventures have withered. The port's cranes have stood idle for years. Among nearby historic structures are ruins of the Jacob Tome Institute and School, founded in 1889 by an entrepreneur who made a fortune in lumber and banking. They include a stone arch that once framed the entrance to Washington Hall, one of the main buildings, and the copper tower on the nearby hilltop. (The institute and school, now located in North East, continue their mission of educating children of Port Deposit and Cecil County.)

Others are 1834 Jefferson Hall, now an apartment building, and the Paw Paw Building, which served as both a Methodist Church and school and is being restored by the Maryland Historical Trust to house an historical library and small museum. The Revolutionary War hero the Marquis de Lafayette was entertained in 1834 at the Gerry Building, built in 1813 and now privately owned, during his return visit to the United States. Port Deposit also remembers Snow's Battery, organized by men of the region in 1861, which served with distinction on the Union side in a number of Civil War battles, including Malvern Hill and Antietam.

Fishing, especially for shad and rock, also was a major industry, and the community had a sizable reputation as a sport fishing center. One marina remains along the community's excellent waterfront.

Other upriver digressions include the West Nottingham Presbyterian Church at Colora, whose present building was constructed in 1804 but that celebrated its 250th anniversary in 1974; 1761 Rock Presbyterian Church at Fair Hill; and the brick East Nottingham Friends Meeting House at Calvert, which was built in 1724 and enlarged in 1752. The Meeting House was used as a Revolutionary War hospital, and a number of soldiers who died there are buried near the south door.

Cecil County lists forty-nine historic sites in all, including Carpenter's Point, where the first permanent settlement in the county was located, and 500-year-old Richards Oak, where Lafayette's army camped in 1781. Among other historic structures are the 1764 Mitchell House in Fair Hill, the 1710 Red Ball Tavern between Calvert and Fair Hill, and Perry Point Mansion, a recently restored eighteenth-century structure whose grist mill stands at the mouth of the Susquehanna River.

Charlestown, which requires a diversion off U.S. 40 onto state Route 267, was well known in the early years of the nation, when it was visited frequently by George Washington. Lt. Col. Nathaniel Ramsey, a Revolutionary War soldier, and his brother-in-law, the famous painter Charles Wilson Peale, experimented there with the manufacture of gunpowder for the Continental army. After the war, Ramsey served two terms in Congress.

Charlestown retains its substantial memories and a few historic structures, principally the gray, frame Tory House managed by the Maryland Historical Trust (the restored colonial kitchen and tavern is open the third Sunday afternoon each month from May through September) and the stone wharf, which served as a Revolutionary War supply depot.

North East, a few miles east on Route 267, typifies the transitional nature of the area. The Upper Bay Museum, which is operated by the Cecil County Hunters Association, contrasts with a factory that has produced handmade oak baskets since 1876 and the Cecil County Auto Dragway, which operates March through November. The museum, located at the end of Walnut Street at the head of the North East River and open on Sunday, provides a candid insight into waterfowl hunting and fishing, good and bad, through the centuries. The museum has a sizable collection of hunting, boating, and fishing artifacts native to the Upper Chesapeake, including punt (oversized) shotguns, outlawed sink box floats that helped hunters decimate canvasback populations before 1934, a rare carved swan among a collection of decoys used on the Susquehanna Flats, and antique marine engines.

The Elk Neck peninsula south of North East combines private and park lands, including a number of private marinas at Hance Point. Fragmented Elk Neck State Park and Forest (follow state Route 272) is one of the best outdoors facilities in the Upper Bay area, with cabins and camping areas, boating, fishing, swimming, a shooting range, and four hiking trails.

The trails reveal all the principal features of the park. The 0.7-mile Thackery Swamp Nature Trail near the camp store covers a frequent and ecologically important feature of the Chesapeake Bay coast. Along the Blue Trail at Turkey Point are overgrown fields that provide food and shelter for deer and other wildlife and a manmade relic, the old Turkey Point lighthouse on a point that overlooks the Bay and Elk River. The Black Trail, at 2 miles the longest in the park, winds through a forest of oak, hickory, and tulip poplar and beside a marsh and the shoreline of the Elk River. The mile-long Green Trail loop, which can be entered either at the Visitors Center or one of the camping areas, passes a lake that in autumn and winter is a resting place for flocks of teal, black duck, mallard, and Canadian goose; at other times, the main attraction is the abundance of mountain laurel.

Elkton, the county seat of Cecil County, is the dividing line between the Bay country and the Northeast. Once named Head of Elk, in recognition of its location on the Elk River, it was a vital Revolutionary War transshipment point that circumvented the British naval blockade along the East Coast. Supplies landed at Elkton were carried 12 miles by wagon to the Delaware River, and then shipped to Philadelphia to help sustain the American army under Washington.

No longer a major commercial center, Elkton's main Bay orientation is historical. Downtown Elkton has a number of historic structures, most of which are used for commercial or organizational purposes and can be viewed only from the exterior. American Legion Cecil Post 15 occupies architecturally interesting Patridge Hall, built in 1768 by Col. Henry Hollingsworth, who raised the Elk Militia Battalion in the Revolutionary War. Holly Hall, built in 1832, is now a business office, while the old façade of Howard House Tavern, established in 1844, covers a modern restaurant. The museum of the city's historical society, located on Main Street, exhibits relics of the region's past—a country store, early American kitchen, and a log country schoolhouse. It is open Thursdays from 1 to 5 P.M. or by appointment.

Sinking Springs Herb Farm on Blair Shore Road conducts guided tours of the gardens and colonial house by appointment.

State Route 213 leads southward away from the transitional area and through one of the most traditional sections of the Upper Bay region, one that shows the elements that shaped the character and history of the region—remnants of the great grain and tobacco plantations and the urge to join natural waterways in more useful patterns by digging canals.

Chesapeake City

As the eastern terminus of the Chesapeake and Delaware Canal, Chesapeake City reflects its early nineteenth-century heritage. Every street reveals to some degree the extensive restoration that preserves buildings erected to service the canal, which opened October 17, 1829. Seafood restaurants, shops, arts council, and other commercial and cultural adventures have breathed new life into the community.

Typical structures include the 1790 Polk House; the adjacent 1833 Cropper, 1831 Riley, and circa 1830 Layton houses; the Bayard House, a restored Federal-style tavern; the small circa 1830 Olde Wharf building; and the circa 1861 Back Creek General Store, all on Bohemia Avenue.

The canal, which reduces the distance between the ocean and the Upper Chesapeake by hundreds of miles, was a long time in coming, as the Chesapeake and Delaware Canal Museum at the Army Corps of Engineers station shows. The canal idea was conceived in 1661 by August Herrman, an immigrant from Bohemia, but not until 1799 did the states of Maryland, Pennsylvania, and Delaware and the federal government create a canal company. The first lock was only 14 miles long, but extensions connected Delaware and Chesapeake bays.

Exhibits in the museum, located in the former lift wheel pumping plant equidistant between the two bays, cover four areas of interest: old photographs of the people involved in constructing the canal and operating the facility; models of boats and a canal lock; fossils of the region; and the huge, mid-nineteenth-century lift wheel and engines, which have been preserved virtually intact.

Scale models of vessels include a number of sailboats typical of the Chesapeake Bay area, as well as a showboat and dredges that operated in the Bay. Among the sailboat models are a bateau or skipjack, outfitted as a "night scraper" or oyster poacher; a bugeye principally used for oyster fishing and now virtually extinct, a descendant of the log canoes used by Indians in 1607 when the first English colony was founded; a Bay pungie, a scaled-down descendant of the Baltimore clipper; the Virginia pilot boat *Swift* from about 1803; a

Chesapeake Bay crab "drudger" named *Quick Step,* home port Delta-ville, Virginia; and the auxiliary cutter *Southern Cross,* a pilot boat that operated out of Georgetown, Maryland.

The steam-powered lift wheel was installed in 1851 and had only one recorded breakdown in seventy-five years of operation. A second steam engine was installed in 1854, and both were used until the sea-level canal was completed in 1927.

Fossils found in the canal area include ostrea, turtle shells, fish vertebrae, a porpoise tooth, dinosaur bone, crab claws, and remnants of other shellfish.

A walkway outside the museum overlooks the parade of ocean-going cargo ships and pleasure boats that use the canal. The road from the city to the museum passes a typical Bay country marshland. A small area on the northern bank of the canal west of Chesapeake City is open to hunting by permit during the season. Hunting also is permitted along stretches of the canal in Delaware.

Route 213 south of Chesapeake City traverses beautiful green farmlands, where side roads pass points overlooking the Elk River and the small Elk Forest, Courthouse, Earleville, and Stemmers Run wildlife management areas. State Route 310 west from Cayots Cor-ner forks near the confluence of the Elk and Bohemia rivers. The right fork ends at a residential area, with the kind of small, private pier that once was standard throughout the Chesapeake Bay region. The other goes to three marinas.

Mount Harmon

Mount Harmon, built in the eighteenth century on a rise at the confluence of the beautiful Sassafras River and two of its tributaries, is typical of the tobacco and grain plantations that dotted the Chesa-peake Bay shoreline in the colonial and early American periods. Now owned and operated by the National Lands Trust, about 200 of the 386 acres of the farm still are being worked; four parcels, ranging in size from 23 to 36 acres, will be developed in a limited and con-trolled way — four mansions and a central boating facility within a 40-acre park of fields, woodland, and a pond.

This development will not intrude on the plantation manor house, which is open to the public on Tuesdays and Thursdays from April through the end of October and Sundays from May 15 through October.

Mount Harmon may be visited either by water or land. Boaters can anchor at Knights Island in the Sassafras River, much as vessels did in the eighteenth century. Ships sailed up the Bay and stopped to unload finished goods and take on farm products destined for England. Visitors arriving by automobile have an equally attractive approach along a tree-lined graveled road where osage-orange trees have overgrown the roadway to create a natural quarter-mile-long arch. In addition, the drive to Mount Harmon east from Cecilton passes other historic but privately owned structures, including Mount Pleasant and Woodlawn.

The site of Mount Harmon is known locally as "World's End" because it overlooks water on three sides — the wooded banks of the Sassafras River and Back and Foreman creeks, all green with foliage in summer. The site of the mansion has been enhanced by planting, with English yew trees more than two hundred years old; holly, sugar maple, and white ash in the yard; and a formal garden of boxwood and flowering plants in the rear at the bottom of a curved, double stairway. When the trees are barren, one can see all the way to Rose Hill, an 850-acre, eighteenth-century landmark on the opposite shore of Foreman Creek that is protected by the Maryland Environmental Trust.

Mount Harmon was restored to its 1760 appearance by Mrs. Henry Clark Boden IV, whose ancestors had owned the plantation in the late eighteenth century. Furnishings in the wide central hallway, dining room, and drawing rooms on the first floor and bedrooms on the second floor are not original, but conform to an inventory of the house recorded in an ancient diary, including silk wallpaper in the wide entrance hall and a staircase with twenty-one distinct Chippendale panels. After completing the restoration and refurnishing in 1973, Mrs. Boden donated the property to the National Trust for Historic Preservation, which turned it over to the National Lands Trust in 1982.

Wildlife, abundant on the plantation, appears along the ¾-mile Shinai Woods Nature Trail, which starts about 0.8 mile from the mansion. You may see deer, rabbits, squirrels, barred and horned owl, hawks, orioles, Acadian flycatcher, eastern pee-wee, wood thrush, wood warbler, blue grosbeak, and a nest of bald eagles.

The trail (ask for a guidesheet at the mansion) is easy, but sometimes muddy in spots. It passes through woodland stands at various stages of development, starting with a young woodland, where nature is recovering once-worked land with tulip poplars (*Liriodendron tulipifera*) and ash, some hung with wild grapes. In spring, dogwood and wildflowers such as *Claytonia virginica* and cut-leaf toothwort enliven the forest.with bright colors. Paw-paws, whose purple May flowers later become a fruit, are plentiful farther along. In the more mature forest sections are dogwood, hickory, oaks, locusts, beech, bellflower, rare cranefly orchid; New York, cinnamon, and rattlesnake fern; jack-in-the-pulpit, mayapple, honeysuckle, starry campion, trillium, and marsh marigold.

The trail also passes the site where, according to tradition, a Roman Catholic chapel once stood. A more prestigious and better-identified early Catholic structure is St. Frances Xavier Church, originally known as the Old Bohemia Mission, 2 miles north of Warwick not far from the Delaware border. The first Roman Catholic bishop in the United States, John Carroll, attended the academy established there in 1745. A museum is housed in the former rectory. Not far away is St. Augustine Episcopal Church, a handsomely restored 1838 church built on the site of a chapel erected more than 145 years earlier.

The Bay's influence reaches inland for a considerable distance.

The Eastern Shore

THE EASTERN SHORE IS FIRST OF ALL A GEOGRAPHICAL DEFINITION. WHEN the first settlers of Virginia explored the vast countryside around them, they soon discovered the long, thin peninsula to the east. As settlement moved up the shore of the mainland, these lands were appropriately identified as the Eastern Shore. Marylanders, who started a bit later, also looked eastward from their original placement in St. Mary's County.

Geographical definition does not adequately explain this area, however. The Eastern Shore is also a kind of lifestyle, a down-to-earth existence closely connected to the Bay. It is, perhaps to a lesser degree, a state of mind. Until the advent of mass transportation, the Eastern Shores of Maryland and Virginia were isolated from their mainlands. Even the steamboats that discharged passengers and cargo were occasional visitors, making relatively little impact on the lifestyle.

The construction of new bridges, particularly the Chesapeake Bay Bridge in Maryland and the Chesapeake Bay Bridge-Tunnel in Virginia, did more than anything else to join the regions mentally, as well as physically, to their respective mainlands. With the bridges came an improvement in the roads that parallel the shoreline the length of the peninsula—Maryland Route 213 from Elkton to Wye Mills, then U.S. 50 to Salisbury, and next U.S. 13 through the Virginia Eastern Shore to Hampton Roads. The psychological change they wrought has been profound. Nevertheless, to a certain extent, the people of the region still feel isolated.

What does this mean for the visitor? Some of the uniqueness of the area has dissipated in the last few decades, but enough remains to make the region distinctive. And visiting the beaches and resorts, the numerous wilderness areas teeming with wildlife, the picturesque fishing villages, and historical structures is much easier than it formerly was.

The Maryland Eastern Shore divides easily into upper and middle Bay segments (Virginia owns the lower end). Kent, Queen Anne's, Caroline, and Talbot counties form the upper segment, while the remainder of Maryland's Eastern Shore—Dorchester, Wicomico, Somerset, and Worcester counties—constitute the lower.

Upper Eastern Shore

Tourism Council of the Upper Chesapeake, P.O. Box 66, Centreville, MD 21617. Tel.: 301/758-2300.

ACCORDING TO ONE BROCHURE, KENT COUNTY "SITS SERENELY OFF THE beaten track." That is only partially true. U.S. Route 301, heavily traveled by trucks and private automobiles, crosses the Chesapeake Bay Bridge at Annapolis and cuts across portions of both Queen Anne's and Kent counties en route to the populous Northeast.

The influence of the highway is limited to its immediate environs, however, and the remainder of the predominantly agricultural county is relatively isolated and available for discovery. The county is the smallest in Maryland, but it makes up in charm what it lacks in size. It is especially attractive to outdoorspeople because it is a favorite wintering or resting place for ducks and geese on the flyway between Canada and their winter havens. It is especially noted for boating, fishing, hunting, and bird-watching. Millington Wildlife Management Area, east of U.S. 301 near the Delaware border, is one of the few places that the Maryland Forest, Park and Wildlife Service opens to dove hunting in late November and December.

Natural and historical discoveries are equally appealing. Although the county graciously has outlined a 110-mile circular driving tour, state Route 223 is the main artery for the adventurous. It passes through historic Chestertown, which bustles for no apparent reason. Side roads lead to the waterfront wilderness areas and outdoors facilities, including small but active Rock Hall, a drive-through nature experience created and managed by an ammunition manufacturer, and the exceptional Eastern Neck Island National Wildlife Refuge.

Actually, the major features of the county are concentrated in the handle of the pistol-shaped county, but the beautiful Sassafras River along the northern boundary should not be ignored. Neither should the numerous historic homes that offer bed and breakfast in settings frozen in an earlier time frame.

The Baltimore Bicycling Club has mapped out a number of routes, ranging from 10 to 81 miles, which provide a more intimate relationship with the handsome Chester River, the flat to gently rolling countryside, and many historical sights. The shortest, from Chestertown to Pomona, rolls on a number of side roads through forests and farmlands and follows the course of the river on the final leg. A 20-mile run follows the river downstream through Pomona and ends at Cliff City, a major source of river crabs; the route can be extended by a side trip to Quaker Neck Landing. The watermen's community of Rock Hall and nearby Eastern Neck Refuge are objectives of a 50-mile bike ride along the river and through flat countryside.

Georgetown, south on Route 213, is the port of entry. Although the name may suggest history, it actually is a workaday community dominated by marinas on the Sassafras River. Courageous women, as well as men, helped form the individualistic lifestyle that pervades the Bay region. One of the most courageous was Kitty Knight; the house where she stood at the door to deny entry to the British soldiers during the War of 1812 stands 3 miles north out of the town.

Despite its name, which probably results from the discovery of silver nearby in 1813, Galena has a soft side. Rosehill Farm, the fourth largest miniature rose nursery in the United States, is a bed-and-breakfast place where visitors may explore the working nursery and idle on the banks of the Sassafras River.

Downstream, past 1832 Shrewsbury Church and Turner Creek public boat landing, where the Kent Museum is located, lies the early nineteenth-century resort of Betterton. It occupies an advantageous location overlooking the mouth of the river. Discoveries of buried skulls under the floor of buildings torn down to make way for the resort revealed the persistence of medieval superstition in some areas of Bay country; the skulls were supposed to ward off spooks.

Still Pond on state Route 292 shows the way the Elizabethan language, which was strong in a few isolated places in Chesapeake Bay right into the twentieth century, has been corrupted with time. It was originally named Steele's Pone, meaning the favorite place of its first settler. Still Pond made history in May 1908 when it became the first place in Maryland where women exercised the right to vote.

Rockfish is the dominant game fish in the Upper Bay, so the state moratorium on catching it has hurt Rock Hall, long a commercial and sport fishing center. Nine marinas have slips, six provide some sort of repairs, and five have bareboats or charter boats, but most boat owners have turned to the profitable clamming industry. Capt. Naudain Francis, one of the few to continue charter boat operations, often heads for the Chesapeake Bay Bridge or Love Point on Kent Island to seek bluefish and white perch, or sails into the Chester River. Five marinas offer some form of sailing instruction; the sailing school at Pelorus, for example, provides five days of textbook and hands-on instruction.

Hunting has not declined. Deer are so plentiful that drivers on side roads must stay alert at night. Canada goose, ducks, quail, and small animals such as rabbits and squirrels also are hunted. Some public lands are open at times for deer hunting, but most hunting occurs on private farmlands, which can be rented. Guides are available in Chestertown. Decoys are carved for use in the water or for decoration.

The Bay orientation of Rock Hall also is apparent at the museum located in the municipal building on Main Street (state Route 445S), where models of typical Chesapeake Bay boats such as the bugeye, log canoe, pungy, dory, and a 1917 sailing yacht are displayed alongside oyster tongs and buckets, paintings and prints, toys, and quilts. It is open Wednesday, Friday, and Sunday from 2 to 4:30 P.M. Rock Hall's major festival is its annual Waterman's Day in September.

Main Street also leads to the Eastern Neck Island National Wildlife Reserve 6 miles away, which provides an insight into the nature and importance of marshlands and woodlands in the cycles of life that produce the richness of the Bay.

The orientation of Eastern Neck National Wildlife Refuge on the mouth of the Chester River is apparent when the visitor crosses the one-lane bridge over Eastern Neck Narrows onto the island. Although open to a variety of day uses, ranging from trails to crabbing and boating, these are strictly controlled so they do not infringe on the preservation objective of the refuge. Camping, fires, off-road vehicles, and use of firearms (except during hunting season) are not permitted.

Four trails, all short, flat, and easy to walk, are well marked and provide more variety than might be expected. The 1.2-mile Boxes Point Trail, only a short distance from the entrance to the refuge, traverses low land with diverse habitats and, for a distance, skirts Fryingpan Cove to Boxes Point on the Chester River side of the island.

The shortest and easiest, the Boardwalk Trail at Tubby Cove, is exactly what the name implies. The boardwalk extends across a shallow coastal area where the marsh grass is visible underwater even when the water level is abnormally high. An interesting phenomenon occurs when the water is high enough, as the weight of people on the boardwalk liberates air trapped in the grass and causes the surface to bubble. Explanatory panels on the boardwalk cite the importance of marshes in the life of mallard, Virginia rail, muskrat, and other wildlife, as well as the danger to humans of poison ivy, whose leaves are eaten by cottontail rabbit and whose fruit is swallowed by a number of birds, including ring-tailed pheasant, grouse, and wild turkey. The observation platform on a hammock at the end of the boardwalk provides an excellent view of the teeming life of the marshland and Bay. The uprooted tree on the hammock is an example of the power of nature. In the autumn, the skies and ponds are filled with ducks and geese seeking food or rest.

A 0.6-mile wildlife trail winds through a bottomland hardwood forest where Delmarva fox squirrels, deer, and other mammals and a variety of birds live. Panels on the trail provide general information about the surroundings, rather than information on specific forms of wildlife in the area.

Eastern Neck Wildlife Refuge is noted for bird watching. Among species that have nested there are the American and least bittern, great blue and green-backed heron, mute swan, wood duck, mallard, blue-winged teal, osprey, bald eagle, red-tailed and red-shouldered hawks, northern bobwhite, king and Virginia rail, killdeer; several kinds of owls, doves, and cuckoos; belted kingfisher, ruby-throated hummingbird; red-bellied, downy, and hairy woodpecker; Acadian and great crested flycatcher, northern rough-winged swallow, white-breasted nuthatch, wood thrush, ovenbird, prothronotary warbler, Louisiana waterthrush, Kentucky warbler, summer and scarlet tanagers, and blue grosbeak.

Among birds that are abundant or common during at least three seasons are the green-backed heron, mute swan, wood duck, American black duck, canvasback, Canada goose, northern pintail, black and turkey vultures, northern harrier, northern bobwhite, king and Virginia rail, killdeer, semipalmated and least sandpiper, ring-billed and herring gull, mourning dove, great horned owl, chimney swift, red-bellied and downy woodpecker, northern flicker, eastern wood-pewee, eastern kingbird, American crow, Carolina chickadee, tufted titmouse, Carolina and marsh wren, wood thrush, and northern mockingbird.

Those making less frequent appearances include the loon, several types of grebes and bitterns, cattle egret, fulvous whistling duck, tundra swan, snow goose, Eurasian wigeon, ring-necked duck, black and surf scoters, sora, black-bellied and semipalmated plovers, Western and pectoral sandpipers, common and least terns, rock dove, black-billed cuckoo, barred and short-eared owl, common nighthawk, yellow-bellied sapsucker, red-headed woodpecker, purple martin, cliff swallow, black-capped ckickadee, red-breasted nuthatch, brown creeper, winter wren, warbling vireo, hermit thrush, Tennessee and other warblers, vesper sparrow, bobolink, red crossbill, and pine siskin.

The half-mile-long Duck Inn Trail leads to a shell midden, evidence of ancient Indian occupation of the island. Indians entered the area 2,700 years ago and were present in 1608 when Capt. John Smith first recorded the abundance of seafood and wildlife.

Eastern Neck Island was one of the first places on the Eastern Shore to be settled by Europeans. The Wickes Memorial at the end of the main road marks the site of Wickliffe House, built in the 1650s, and honors Capt. Lambert Wickes, a Revolutionary War hero and descendant of the original settler of the island.

The refuge headquarters, where considerable information about the sanctuary is available, overlooks the confluence of the Chester River and the Bay. Osprey, bald eagle, and other birds also frequent the area. A boat ramp is available at Bogie's Wharf, a stopping place for packet boats until 1929, while crabbing and picnicking are favorite activities at Ingleside recreation area.

Hunting of white-tailed deer is permitted at times in order to clear off surplus animals. Hunters must obtain a federal permit and are restricted to bows and arrows and shotguns, to daylight hours, and to only one kill.

Three miles north of Rock Hall, state Route 20 divides the two phases of Remington Farms Wildlife Management Demonstration Area, a conference center owned by an arms manufacturer, which incorporates eighteenth-century Broadnax Mansion and newer structures. Guidebooks for a driving exposure to waterfowl and other wildlife and their habitats are available at the office on Richauds Branch–Langford Road, a major route during the Revolutionary War along which the courier rode to notify Congress of Lord Cornwallis's surrender at Yorktown, Virginia.

From October through early March, visitors may sit in their cars beside a pond near the office and watch the flight, movement, and antics of thousands of Canada goose and mallard, pintail, and other types of ducks. Management practices reduce the possibility of disease by draining the pond and aerating it with disc harrows during the warm months.

Across Route 20 is a more comprehensive, 4-mile drive-through exposure to wildlife and the conservation methods practiced on the farm. Open February 1 to October 10, the fourteen stops include a cornfield, tilled in summer and left covered with stubble and other harvesting residue to protect the soil and provide food for the ducks and geese; multiflora rosebushes, hedges, and fencerows, which provide cover and food for deer and smaller animals; a 40-acre flooded woodland; crabapple trees, shrubs, pines, oaks, and other species of nut-bearing trees; and a variety of ponds where blue heron, osprey, ducks, geese, and numerous smaller birds, raccoons, rabbits, turtles, and other animals can easily be seen.

The farm has placed artificial nesting houses at strategic places, primarily to attract wood ducks, generally regarded as the most beautifully plumaged North American duck.

Farther east on Richauds Branch–Langford Road is handsome, brick St. Paul's Episcopal Church, built in 1713 and used as a barrack by the British during the War of 1812. Actress Tallulah Bankhead is buried in the church cemetery. In the parking lot stands an American Bicentennial tree older than the country.

The nearby pond, part of the Remington Farms property, is open to fishing.

A roadside marker at the intersection of Route 21 and Caulk's Field Road recognizes a little-known battle of the War of 1812, the only significant engagement fought on the Eastern Shore. At Caulk's Field, not far from the original farmhouse, a modest monument commemorates the standoff victory that Maryland militia achieved over British regulars in August 1814.

Chestertown

Chestertown, the Kent County seat on the banks of the Chester River, retains a pleasant, eighteenth-century appearance that it eagerly shares with visitors. It wasn't always so peaceful: on May 23, 1774, near the brick Customs House that had been built about 28 years earlier, irate citizens protested the tax on tea imposed by the Parliament in Great Britain by boarding Port Collector William Geddes's brigantine and tossing its cargo overboard. This "tea party," which occurred only a few months after the more famous one in Boston, is re-enacted annually in late May, accompanied by a parade, visits to *Bernice J.* (a 75-year-old skipjack) and other typical Bay boats, and typical Bayside feasting on seafood and Maryland fried chicken from farms in the region.

The Chamber of Commerce thoughtfully provides a walking tour guide to the historic structures, most of which are private homes and open only one night each September for a candlelight tour. The Geddes-Piper House, which is the headquarters of the Historical Society, is open for visits during the Chestertown Tea Party Festival. A few of the historic structures—including circa 1725 Radcliffe Cross, which is framed by ancient boxwoods—are open as bed-and-breakfast inns.

A walk around the historic district shows what the founders of the nation saw in their everyday lives at home, inn, and church. Although the twenty-eight historic structures on the tour extend as far inland as Washington College, founded in 1782 and named for the Father of the Country, most are concentrated in a few blocks of Water, Queen, and High streets and on Lawyer's Row. Narrow Queen Street has numerous examples of late eighteenth-century and

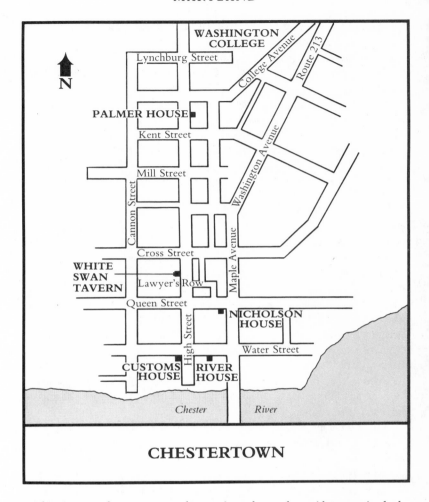

CHESTERTOWN

early nineteenth-century tradesmen's and merchants' houses, including the Nicholson House, built in 1788 by Capt. John Nicholson, who served in the Continental Navy in command of the first of many vessels to carry the name *Hornet.* Among important buildings on Water and High streets are Wide Hall, built circa 1770 by merchant Thomas Smylie, who also headed Maryland's revolutionary provisional government; the circa 1735 William Barroll House; the Flemish bond River House, built 1784–1787; and the architecturally interesting 1770 Frisby House, which has wide chimneys and curvilinear windows.

Emmanuel Protestant Episcopal Church, erected in 1768 but significantly altered in the 1860s, originally was a chapel in Chester Parish. The minister, the Rev. Dr. William Smith, presided over the convention that changed the name of the Anglican Church in the United States to Protestant Episcopal Church. He also was founder of Washington College. White Swan Tavern, across High Street, has been restored to its 1795 residential appearance and continues its role as a tavern that began in 1803. Another Episcopal clergyman, the Rev. William H. Wilmer, rector of St. Paul's in Alexandria, Virginia, and of Bruton Parish in Williamsburg, Virginia, was one of the nineteenth-century owners.

Queen Anne's and Caroline Counties

The comfortable mix of agriculture and waterfront continues south of the Chester River. Route 213 passes many of the 900 farms in the county, which are among the most productive in the state of raising corn, wheat, hay, oats, barley, and soybeans. Historic churches, like 1732 St. Luke's Episcopal Church at Church Hill, stand near the road. Side roads lead to the county's 450 miles of shoreline, over which about 90 million pounds of seafood are hauled in annually.

Queen Anne County, named in 1706 after her "gracious majesty," typifies the divided loyalties that troubled many Marylanders during the break from the Mother Country of Great Britain. The county retained the name, even during the Revolutionary War when such things were not popular, but sent five citizens to the Continental Congress and raised troops to help control the strong Tory sympathy in counties to the south. Native son William Paca not only signed the Declaration of Independence, but served as a wartime governor of the state (1782–1785).

Picturesque Centreville, so compact that all historical attractions can easily be visited on a single walk, has the oldest courthouse in continuous use in Maryland and a Lawyer's Row almost as old. Town Hall, located in the same block as Lawyer's Row, dates from a much later period. The county seat since 1782 continues to honor its namesake with a statue on the courthouse green.

The 1794 Tucker House on Commerce Street, whose brick sidewalks and herb garden testify to its heritage, houses a collection of photographs, genealogical files, old documents, and Federal-period furniture. Wright's Chance, cited in official records as early as 1744, retains original wood paneling and antique glass windows;

its eighteenth-century furnishings include some furniture and china owned by William Paca. Now the headquarters of the Queen Anne's County Historical Society, Wright's Chance was relocated to Commerce Street from its original site 4 miles from town.

The antiquity of St. Paul's Episcopal Church is apparent in the communion silver, which dates to 1717. The oldest part of the church was built in the late seventeenth century.

Boat-launching ramps provide access to Reed's Creek. Archery ranges are located at 20-acre Roundtop Park, north of Centreville, and Route 18 Park, a 52-acre facility noted for model airplane flying.

South of Centreville a marked change takes place. It is not as much a physical change—the comfortable mixture of farmlands and waterfront continues—as a mental transition required by the infusion of traffic and commerce along U.S. Route 301. There, the traveler has a choice to make—between the westward rush on Route 301 to Annapolis and beyond and continuing on Route 213 and later U.S. 50 in the more casual atmosphere of the Eastern Shore.

Route 301 leads past Queenstown, the first county seat and such an important port during the War of 1812 that it became a British target. The original one-room wooden section of the old courthouse, used as a jail, was built in 1708; the middle frame and brick courthouse sections were added in the 1800s.

The Wye Island Natural Resource Management Area, set aside by the state, is located on Carmichael Road 6 miles south of U.S. 50 and past a number of privately owned historic homes. Not designed primarily as a public facility, its tree-shaded dirt roads, across which blacksnakes slither from time to time, traverse a primitive woodlands area. Among the limited facilities are four trails for hiking, nature viewing, and visiting the waterfront.

At Grasonville, Horsehead Sanctuary preserves six wetlands habitats visited by almost all types of migratory waterfowl and shorebirds on the Bay. White-tailed deer, muskrat, otter, and red fox also roam the preserve.

Two short, self-guided trails in the 310-acre natural wetlands area, whose oyster shell parking lot recalls a side of Bay living once much more prevalent than it is today, enter habitats varying from ponds to woods to marsh. The Marshy Creek Trail, the newest, passes a meadowland that is periodically flooded, then moves through a loblolly pine woodland to reach an enclosed blind on reed-lined Lake Knapp. Farther on, the trail passes uprooted and dead trees and reed grass and goes to a lookout tower on the edge of Marshy Creek.

Along the other trail are examples of nesting boxes; a meadow aviary where a collection of resident ducks, geese, and swan can be seen year round; a pond demonstrating the cohabitation of aquatic and land species; and a blind overlooking the other side of the lake.

The multipurpose preserve, operated by the Wildlife Trust of North America, is open from 9 A.M. to 5 P.M. Friday, Saturday, and Sunday. The trust also raises native breeding waterfowl for release and conducts an educational program, including birding bus trips.

Heavily traveled Route 301 continues to Kent Island, where the first settlement in Maryland was founded in 1629 by William Claiborne, whose subsequent trials have been chronicled by James Michener in his novel *Chesapeake*. The island remained somewhat isolated, with the narrows populated mainly by ducks and a few men hunting them, until after World War II.

The opening of the Chesapeake Bay Bridge, which connects the Annapolis-Washington-Baltimore triangle directly to the Eastern Shore, drastically changed life on Kent Island. The subsequent rush to the suburbs is hastening the metamorphosis from an isolated farming district and crabbing center to a waterfront residential and marina center. Although the interior of the claw-shaped island still has extensive farmlands and the island remains famous for steamed crabs, residents admit the island is "not like it used to be." Kent Narrows bustles with waterfront activity, including marinas and a boat ramp. (Seven boat ramps are located at various places on the island.)

Roads leading off U.S. 301 pass through the neat, green farmlands of the interior of Kent Island and end at isolated points, some of which are being developed for housing. State Route 8, which crosses Route 301, is the principal north–south road on the island. A section of Stevensville has been designated a historic district, including the 185-year-old Cray House and the Schoolhouse Commons, an old school converted to offices and retail shops. The community gradually is being restored to a basic Victorian appearance. Mowbray Park includes a fitness trail among its facilities. Love Point, at the northern tip of the island, divides its attention between an industrial area, a 30-acre park, and offshore fishing.

Matapeake State Park, south of Route 301 and beyond a small-plane airport, has an excellent location facing the Bay but a minimum of facilities—a fishing pier and boat ramp. Camping is not allowed.

Kent Island remains true to its heritage in at least one regard. The blue crab is still the core of the diet. A self-styled "old-style Maryland crabhouse" at Kentmorr Harbour, south of the Matapeake Park, sells crabs the traditional way—either steamed for immediate eating or by the bushel for individual cooking. The harbor also is the site of two marinas and windsurfing schooling managed by an Annapolis firm, Windsurfing Unlimited.

Nine-hole Blue Heron Golf Course, 5 miles south of U.S. 301, is open to the public seven days a week. Romancoke Pier, open for fishing and crabbing from 6 A.M. to 9 P.M. during warm months, dominates a small park at the end of Route 8 that also has picnicking facilities.

Travelers turning east from Route 213 onto state Route 404 will enter Caroline County, the only landlocked county on the Eastern Shore. Side roads lead to the historic crownstone of the Mason-Dixon Line at Marydel and to two state parks.

Martinak State Park, three-quarters of a mile off state Route 404 at Denton on land known to have been frequented by Algonkin Indians at the time of European settlement, has a boat ramp and dock on Watts Creek, an arm of the Choptank River. The tidal waters in the 100-acre park surrender bigmouth bass, pickerel, yellow and white perch, and catfish. Other facilities include campsites for tents or RVs, a single cabin, picnic shelters, river swimming, and standard playground equipment.

Tuckahoe State Park, on the Queen Anne's-Caroline border about 2 miles north of Route 404, possesses the kind of natural, little-used habitat that attracts wildfowl and animals. Nestboxes for wood duck are not necessary because of the large number of trees with cavities made by nature. This same setting also attracts prothonotary warblers, which are relatively rare where these conditions do not exist, and woodpeckers. Bald eagle, osprey, mallard, pintail, woodcock, oriole, doves, cuckoos, owls, kingfishers, ovenbird, and eastern bluebird also frequent the park. The near-natural state of Tuckahoe Creek, both above and below a dam, attracts large numbers of beaver, whose lodges and dams are easier to spot than the animals themselves, turtles, muskrat, and even an occasional otter.

The park is an example of both the growing conservation trend in the region and the way human beings and nature can work together to create attractive and unusual sights. Trish Gruber, naturalist, and Wilbur Rittenhouse, curator of the Adkins Arboretum, are engaged in a long-range project to cultivate and propagate along loop trails all the major trees indigenous to Maryland. The trails have been laid out, and several thousand of the 13,000 seedlings required have been planted. In addition, a 1.1-mile-long Piney Branch Trail leaves

This footbridged trail meanders through the forest at Tuckahoe State Park, Maryland. PHOTO BY JOHN BOWEN.

the Central Maryland arboretum loop and meanders through the forest to the lake; a Lake Trail then follows the shoreline to the campgrounds. Some sections of the trails have been laid out to accommodate wheelchair users. The park also has a fitness trail.

Another trail, about 30 minutes of easy walking, leads past black walnut, black cherry, pignut hickory, black and white oak, American beech, American holly, mountain laurel, flowering dogwood, river birch, and sweet gum to a giant overcup oak, the Maryland champion. Park forests also are havens for an endangered holly, *ilex decidua,* as well as red maple, green ash, and tulip trees.

The active naturalist program includes bird walks, native tree identification workshops, moonlight walks and campfires, bird-banding demonstrations, antipollution lectures, and amateur archeology. An annual triathlon in August includes a 2-mile run, 10-mile bicycle course, and 1-mile canoe trip.

Canoeists can use either the 60-acre lake, where 40 swampy acres have obstacles that can be avoided without portage, or the creek below the dam, which is not recommended for beginners. The 3-foot tidal range extends inland as far as Hillsboro, requiring awareness of the tidal chart, but the creek between Hillsboro and about 2 miles from the park is usable, especially at high tide. Conducted canoe trips for amateurs are offered periodically.

The campground and fishing areas are separated from the arboretum. Likewise, types of fishing are divided by the dam—above, a freshwater license is required on the lake, stocked especially with striped bass, while a saltwater license is required to catch perch, catfish, and other species below the dam. Fishing tournaments are held on special occasions, such as Father's Day or Mother's Day, and children are allowed to fish in the arboretum pond on occasion.

Hunting for deer and small animals is permitted in designated woodland areas of the park after October 15. The five pits available are assigned by lottery.

Travelers going south who stay on state Route 213 after it intersects with 301 will soon shift to U.S. Route 50 but will remain in the low-key atmosphere of the Eastern Shore. Dove hunting is allowed at Idylwild Wildlife Management Area near Federalsburg in Caroline County.

The old Wye Grist Mill, located near the boundary of Talbot County, has been in operation since 1671 and still produces commercial water-ground cornmeal—just as it did for Washington's army during the Revolutionary War. Governor William Paca owned Wye Plantation on the border between Queen Anne's and Talbot counties. A commemorative program is held there every July Fourth. Wye Oak, which is 400 years old and believed to be the largest white oak in the United States, stands in tiny Wye Oak State Park, just over the line in Talbot County.

Middle Ground

THERE IS NO SPECIFIC DELINEATION OF THE BOUNDARY BETWEEN THE Upper and Mid-Bay regions. Neither the character of the land and shore nor the use of them changes much. The same mix of agriculture, forests, and seafaring exists. There is not even a common terminology; pilots who guide ocean-going commercial vessels through Chesapeake Bay sometimes refer to the mid-Bay region as the "Middle Ground," while landlubbers talk about the Middle Bay. But the separation has existed since the earliest days of European settlement.

There is general acceptance to the idea that Kent Island forms the line between the two regions. This sets the Eastern Bay River, the northern boundary of Talbot County, as the practical dividing line between Upper and Middle Bay. Talbot County, which has 602 miles of shoreline and about 25,000 population, sometimes advertises itself as the "heart" of Chesapeake Bay County. The claim may be just as true psychologically as it is geographically.

The Middle Bay region of Maryland adds a special élan to its earthy, provincial atmosphere. Water lore is deeply ingrained in the culture, and people think more about their association with Cambridge and Salisbury to the south than their ties with Washington, Baltimore, or Annapolis. Regional names that do not appear on maps—such as Bay Hundred, the name of the odd-shaped peninsula that leads to Tilghman Island—are common currency, and certain families have remained prominent for a century or more—and not always because of money. Where the Bay or river stops the highway, drivers of farm pickup trucks wave a friendly greeting to almost any oncoming vehicle.

Indeed, the region takes advantage of its earthiness and provincialism as it struggles to harmonize past and present. Horses begin to replace cattle in grazing fields and corn and soybeans dominate the farm fields. Hogs Neck Golf Course (open to the public) stands near an ice- and roller-skating arena, the ice aspect certainly a new-found interest. And one of the few remaining small ferries that once were essential to highway communication continues to ply between Oxford and Bellevue, offering a 15-minute water ride to incorrigible automobile travelers who don't want to stop longer for the numerous day trips on the Bay from St. Michaels or elsewhere.

Waterfowl are so important to the people of the Middle Bay that they sponsor an annual Waterfowl Festival, which attracts scores of artists and carvers and, on occasion, television coverage. ABC's *Good Morning, America* featured the fifteenth festival on its "Backroads of America" segment. More than $1 million in profits has been contributed to waterfowl conservation since the festival began in 1971.

Talbot County has mapped two scenic bike trails between its principal historic attractions. One covers the 10 miles between Easton and St. Michaels on Maryland Route 33, a flat route with paved shoulders through sparsely settled, wooded, and historic countryside. The other is a more interesting 10.5-mile run along state Route 333 between Easton and Oxford, where a small ferry crosses the Tred Avon River.

Traveling south on U.S. 50, drivers have a choice to make at the outskirts of Easton: will they survey land history or waterfront lore first? Those enamored with the Bay will go first to St. Michaels and Tilghman Island and then return to Easton, perhaps after a ferry ride among sailboats and oyster boats on the Tred Avon River to Oxford, once a bustling port and pirate haven but now just a quiet repository of historic memories with a riverfront beach named The Strand.

At Tilghman Island, the visitor gets a sense of both the deep roots of residents of the area and the rhythm of the Middle Bay region. Islanders have reached a modus vivendi with visitors; a few operate marinas at Knapp Narrows, conduct fishing and waterfowl hunting trips, and operate hotels and restaurants, while the majority continue the aquatic ways of their ancestors. Watermen take their workboats out winter and summer to bring in mountains of crabs, oysters, and finfish. Despite its small population, the island continues to produce more shellfish than any other single place in Maryland.

Buddy Harrison, who captains the charter boat *Pleasure Merchant* when not managing his Harrison's Chesapeake House, observes the seasonal variations and the changes in habits of the fish in the Bay. "It's a funny situation," he says. "We lose some species, but we gain others." In recent years, fishers have hauled in more pounds of fish than ever before, but bluefish, drumfish, and sea trout have replaced the "loads" of Norfolk spot, herring, and shad that were caught when "Cap'n" Harrison first got his license. The Tilghman Volunteer Fire Department sponsors an annual seafood festival in June.

Several major sport fishing sites are located off Tilghman, including the Stone Rock near Sharp's Island Lighthouse; Poplar Islands area (once inhabited but now visible only at low tide); Cook's Point, the Sands, and the Diamonds in the Choptank River; and the Gooses (pronounced "goosies") in the middle of the Bay. A typical sport fishing cruise leaves Tilghman about 7:15 A.M. in order to reach the fishing grounds by 8 A.M.; the boat remains out until 3 P.M. or may return earlier if the fish are biting. Lures are used in May to troll for bluefish. In early June, soft crabs are used to catch channel bass; from the Fourth of July until late October, the principal quarry is trout and bluefish.

At least ten other captains operate charter boats — a few of which are skipjacks — from Tilghman Island, Oxford, St. Michaels, and Trappe. In addition, marinas decorate almost every cove, including five in Tilghman, five in Oxford, three in St. Michaels, two in Trappe, and one in Easton, and public landings exist at a number of places.

Waterfowl hunting also is a favorite pastime on the island, with late November and December being a good period for ducks and January a good time for geese. As many as twenty-five "rigs" (boats and decoys) may be seen in the water around Tilghman on a single day during the season. In addition to regular goose and duck shoots, a new type of "sea duck" hunting has developed in recent years. "Sea duck" hunters trail plastic bottles painted black behind their boats to attract the curiosity of the ducks; the ducks descend to take a look and are shot as they shy away and start climbing again. Out of season, many goose hunters feed their favorite prey when extremes of cold weather threaten to deprive geese of their normal diet.

On occasion, "chicken neckers" (as they are known locally) crowd 2 miles of beach below the old steamboat pier and the cove at Fairbanks to catch crabs. The island also has RV camping at the southern end of the island.

Deer hunting occurs in the area known as Bay Hundred, the claw-shaped mainland that lies between Tilghman and St. Michaels. More than seventeen hunting guides were included in a recent Chamber of Commerce directory. Claiborne, at the northern tip of Bay Hundred, has a boat ramp and county rental slips, as well as a pier that can be used for fishing.

A sense of history also runs deep elsewhere in Talbot County, even if it often has a commercial base. St. Michaels is the star among a cast that includes restored Victorian homes in Oxford and Trappe and the earlier buildings in Easton.

St. Michaels

The harbor at St. Michaels is one of the most beautiful in the Bay area — and one of the most active. In the warm months, it is filled with boats from Annapolis, Washington, and points farther away, as well as local craft. The 40-foot schooner *Farewell,* docked at the Higgins Yacht Yard, offers visitors a sample of sailing on the Miles River, while the *Mildred Belle,* a 55-foot Bay workboat built in 1955 at Odd, Virginia, conducts daily private charters. Between May and October, the 65-foot *Patriot* departs twice daily on 90-minute narrated cruises down the Miles River that explore the characteristics and history of Talbot County. Condos, hotels, and restaurants stand on the shoreline.

St. Michaels reflects its colorful history in a variety of ways. The Cannonball House — the only home damaged by British bombardment during the War of 1812 — stands as a reminder of the cleverness of the town's early citizens, who saved their homes by blacking out the town and hanging lanterns in a nearby forest to draw the British fire. The Tarr House, built about 1661, and St. Mary's Square, a small, green oasis where the town museum is located in a mid-eighteenth-century house, also reflect the town's formative years. Historic structures, dating from the earliest days of the country through the Victorian period, house chic shops.

St. Michaels almost inevitably lies at the midpoint of a Bay trip. That is unfortunate, because the Chesapeake Bay Maritime Museum on Navy Point provides a short course on the rich resources of the Bay and the ways they have been used for work and play. Historic or reconstructed buildings house an extensive collection of artifacts and memorabilia. In addition, the museum is a working place, where methods and sheds typical of the region are used to make repairs on operating vessels owned by the museum under the watchful eyes of visitors.

Exhibits and models in the Chesapeake Bay Building, built in 1979 but patterned after the historic home Otwell, provide an overview of the Bay from its geological history to boat design inventions and adaptations produced on the Bay.

Many residents of the Bay area were dependent on their boats, not only for their livelihood but also for social intercourse, right into the automobile age. The original settlers used shallops imported from England, but these were ill suited to penetrate the marshlands and numerous shoals. The shipbuilding industry thus became an integral part of their lives. Colonists soon adapted the simple Indian log canoes to their special environmental and economic needs and progressed to two-, five-, and even seven-log canoes. The installation of sails and redesign of the bows to improve efficiency and maneuverability made them the workboats of crabbers and oystermen. The larger brogan, which had fixed masts and a forward cabin, was a mid-nineteenth-century improvement. The even larger bugeye appeared after the Civil War as the railroad, steam canning, and the legalization of the oyster dredge combined with depletion of New England beds to create a seafood boom on the Chesapeake.

Models of the 28-foot, one-log canoe *Methodist,* the smaller *Magic,* and the bugeye *Lizzie J. Cox* demonstrate how adaptation produced larger and more efficient vessels. The last bugeye in the Bay oyster-dredging fleet, the *Edna J. Lockwood,* was taken out of service in the 1960s and is now one of the floating exhibits at the museum. The motorized, seven-log, 47½-foot *Old Point,* built by J. G. Wornom of Poquoson, Virginia, in 1909, is another working vessel owned by the museum.

The improvement in the reputation of oysters, eaten locally but not regarded as a commercial shellfish until the 1840s, influenced the design of Bay vessels. The famous skipjack, designed specifically for oystering, appeared around 1890 and was an improvement over smaller, V-hulled skiffs used for crabbing. Like earlier Bay craft, the shipjack had staying power; according to the museum, it is "the only type of commercial craft working under sails in the United States."

A model of the oyster sloop *Agnes,* built by John B. Harrison of Tilghman Island, Maryland, in 1898, illustrates the early period of the skipjack, while a model of the *Geneva May,* a bateau constructed in 1908 at Wenona, Maryland, shows the downsizing of the skipjack that sometimes occurred on Maryland's Eastern Shore. A typical Bay crabbing skiff, the V-bottom *Lark,* built in 1918 on the West River, also is on display.

The sleek Baltimore clipper, considered by many as the most beautiful ship ever built, was an ocean-going sailing vessel that worked out of Bay ports such as Baltimore and Norfolk during the first half of the nineteenth century. As the model of the 1807 *Nonpareil* shows, the design sacrificed cargo space for speed. This allowed the clippers to show their heels to most vessels of the era, including those of the British navy blockading Chesapeake Bay during the War of 1812. Their elusiveness was one of the reasons the British attacked Baltimore.

The clipper had virtually disappeared by mid-nineteenth century, but was followed by shallower draft, ocean-going schooners that remained in operation well into the twentieth century. A smaller version of the clipper, the pungy schooner, survived until the 1940s.

The museum also has an excellent collection of small craft used to give hunters an advantage over waterfowl. Among them are sneak boats and the now-outlawed sink box, which sat flush with the water level and was surrounded by decoys. The icebox, used in winter, was inserted into a hole cut in a frozen stream.

The Waterfowl Building supplements this collection with dozens of decoys (one nineteenth-century swan by Sam Barnes may be worth as much as $25,000) and various types of guns used by hunters, including big guns that could kill as many as 100 ducks at a time and a homemade version fashioned from steel pipe after use of the big fowling piece was outlawed in 1918. Another unusual duck killer was the multibarreled gun.

The military presence on the Bay historically has been as strong as it is today. The first naval battle took place in 1635, only twenty-eight years after the establishment of the first settlement, as other European countries sought to challenge Britain's monopoly of the new tobacco trade. A model of the ship *Reprisal,* built in 1776, recalls an ineffective defense against depredations by the British navy and Loyalist privateers during the Revolutionary War. The wheel from the *River Queen,* used by Union Gen. Ulysses S. Grant, and models of the *U.S.S. Monitor* and *C.S.S. Virginia* (former *U.S.S. Merrimack*) illustrate the importance of the Bay during the Civil War.

Other displays include a binnacle from the *U.S.S. Maryland* and information on the U.S. Naval Academy, which has been located at Annapolis since its founding in 1845.

The museum sponsors a variety of events, from lectures and chanty singing to festivals. Among annual events are Crab Day in mid-

August, traditional sailboat races and the Bartlett Cup Race in mid-September, the Mid-Atlantic Small Craft Festival in early October, and Oyster Day in early November. It also demonstrates special hunting methods in conjunction with Easton's mid-November Waterfowl Festival.

Easton

In Easton, the more things change, the more they are the same. A form of controlled dynamism permits the city to function and grow, without ever losing sight of its origins. Founded on the banks of the Tred Avon River in the eighteenth century, it quickly expanded inland to develop the section now preserved as a historical district.

The historical heart, located near the courthouse whose south wing was constructed in 1712, is neither static nor sterile. It reflects changes in subsequent periods. A number of showplace buildings, such as the 1814 James Neall building and the 1780 Seven Stars Tavern, retain their original forms; numerous others have been converted into shops, including a row of buildings across from the courthouse.

The historic structures are spread over a fourteen-block area, but can be easily viewed on a self-guided walking tour mapped by the Talbot County Historical Society. The society also maintains a museum, housed in two buildings on Washington Street, that has a superior collection of maps from the colonial and Revolutionary periods. Handsome, tree-shaded Christ Episcopal Church, built in 1842, stands on South Street near the pre-1794 Benjamin Stevens House and the 1790 Bullitt Mansion. One of the oldest frame houses of worship in the United States is the 1682 Third Haven Meetinghouse; William Penn was among the divines who preached there.

Easton is a center of major activity. It is the county seat and Talbot County's most important commercial center. Three-fourths of the events on the county's annual calendar, or more than thirty-five in number, take place in and around the city of 8,500 people. The Academy of Arts operates an active year-round program from the 1820 primary school, while the 8-acre Warner Wildflower Sanctuary, operated by the Talbot County Garden Club, brings vegetation from the surrounding countryside right into the city.

Easton also is the headquarters for visits to the 400-acre Talbot County Shooting Preserve near Denton, where quail is stocked and pheasant and ducks are common. The Talbot County Bird Club sponsors periodic wilderness walks in places such as the Third Haven Woods Wildlife Preserve, Easton, and the Brookside Nature Center in Wheaton, as well as hikes, butterfly surveys, and nature sketching.

Oxford's quiet demeanor belies its lusty beginnings in 1694 as an official Port of Entry and shipbuilding center, where according to legend pirates posed as Quakers to disarm their prey. A gentler side was apparent in its willingness to become a haven for Acadians, who emigrated from Canada when French territory was ceded to Britain. Part of the mansion of Robert Morris, a rich merchant whose son is often known as the "financier of the Revolution," is now a hotel. Lt. Col. Tench Tilghman, a Talbot County native who carried to the Continental Congress news of the British surrender at Yorktown, is buried there. A reconstruction of the original customs house and the town museum recall the town's beginnings as a port and shipbuilding center. A huge grapevine in the front yard of a home on Morris Street, planted in 1810, still bears.

The Tred Avon Yacht Club at Oxford and the Chesapeake Bay Yacht Club of Easton combine to sponsor a three-day regatta at Oxford in August.

The Southern Middle

Like as not, when Marylanders refer to the "southern Eastern Shore," they are describing the southernmost four counties—Dorchester, Wicomico, Somerset, and Worcester. The descriptive ignores the Virginia Eastern Shore, which is the anchor end. However, in reality, the complete southern Eastern Shore, which includes the tip of the peninsula in Virginia, is integrated mentally and commercially. Residents of both states cite nearby communities in the neighboring state as though they were their own. Brochures from one place often include attractions or events from neighboring communities, even across the state line. Thus, an information sheet from Wicomico County may list events at Deal Island in Maryland's Somerset County and Chincoteague in Virginia's Accomack County.

History has washed like an incoming tide over the region. The land was occupied by peaceful Indian communities when Verazzano and Capt. John Smith made their separate explorations. By the mid-1660s, European settlers had institutionalized government. Along these coasts sailed wartime profiteers and pirates, the distinction not always being obvious; during the War of 1812, the British set up an operating base on the Bay island of Tangier and raided liberally in search of provisions and success at arms. One result is evident at Taylor's Island, where a cannon captured during the war is displayed as a memorial. The southern mid-Bay has a liberal sprinkling of historic structures, including designated historic areas in Cambridge, Vienna, East New Market, Princess Anne, and Snow Hill. Old Trinity Church, a small, one-room red brick structure built about 1675 on Route 16 six miles west of Cambridge, claims to be the oldest church in the nation still in active use.

But Maryland's Eastern Shore South is unabashedly outdoors country. No other section of the Bay has more dedicated green space. The elongated Blackwater National Wildlife Refuge and a number of Wildlife Management Areas stretch across southern Dorchester County from Taylor's Island to the Nanticoke River. This preservation zone continues south along the Bay coast of Somerset County and includes several offshore islands. Inland, up the Pocomoke River, saltwater fishing licenses are required in the fragmented Pocomoke River State Park because of tidal action. On the ocean side is Assateague Island National Seashore, part of which is open to the public as a state park.

The region also has a strong commercial identification. The influence of the watermen is strong, as it has been since the first settlers arrived. Hoopers Island, famed for boats prized for style and seaworthiness, is still predominately a crabbing and fishing community. Crisfield is the self-styled crabbing capital of the world. Neat farmlands, green with corn, wheat, soybeans, and vegetables, dominate the interior and sometimes even separate marshlands in soggy coastal areas. Ocean City, on the Atlantic side, is one of the East Coast's most famous resort areas.

Although the Bay coastline is geared more to commercial than recreational boating, marinas for pleasure boats exist in most coastal cities, including Cambridge, Salisbury, and Crisfield, and in a few isolated places. For example, Henry and Tommy Gootee take charter groups from Golden Hill, located at the intersection of state Routes 335 and 336, down the handsome, tree-lined Honga River, and into the Bay in search of bluefish, sea trout, and other finfish. The Atlantic side has a much heavier concentration of recreational boating, including deep-sea fishing, especially at Ocean City.

U.S. Route 50, which crosses the region on an east–west axis from Cambridge, is a heavily traveled weekend corridor to the resort at Ocean City. At Salisbury, U.S. Route 13 takes over for those continuing to Bayfront areas and into the Virginia segment of the Eastern Shore.

Cambridge

Cambridge, on the southern bank of the Choptank River, is a quiet city of more than 11,000 people. Although not representative of the region, where villages and towns predominate, it demonstrates the combination of history and waterfront activities well.

Along the riverfront are a mix of homes, commercial areas, and marinas. A scenic drive looks out on the broad, handsome Choptank River, where the skipjacks and other vessels constitute the last sail fishing fleet in the United States. One of the Shore's most celebrated late immigrants, Annie Oakley, used this waterfront a different way; she practiced sharpshooting from the upstairs windows of her retirement bungalow on Bellevue Avenue.

A walking tour of the historic area, located only a few blocks off U.S. 50, covers scores of eighteenth- and nineteenth-century buildings in a rectangular area stretching from the municipal boat basin to Gay Street. The concentration of more than twenty buildings along High Street includes a nineteenth-century brick townhouse with sawtooth moldings; a tiny law office constructed in 1796, the oldest surviving office building in the city; an 1803 Federal-style building, which was home to four generations of the LeCompte family; a home moved from Annapolis to Cambridge in 1750 by wealthy merchant-court clerk John Calle; and the handsome, white Goldborough house, constructed in the late 1700s and considered the finest example of Federal-style architecture in Cambridge. Christ Episcopal Church has stood on the same site since 1693, but the present greenish stone, steepled church dates from 1883. The graveyard hosts early settlers, Revolutionary War heroes, and several Maryland governors. A guide brochure is available from the Chamber of Commerce office on Route 50 at the northern entrance to the city.

One of Cambridge's most historic buildings, the late eighteenth-century, Georgian-style Meredith House, is not located in this district. The current home of the Dorchester County Historical Society is decorated with furniture of the Chippendale, Hepplewhite, Sheraton, and Victorian styles, portraits of early county residents and of the six Maryland governors from the county, oriental china, and a rare quilt with a star pattern. The Children's Room displays dolls and other early toys, miniature china and furniture, and baby carriages and cradles.

The adjacent Nield Museum, beyond an herb garden and smokehouse that is one of the oldest remaining structures in the county, houses a collection of maritime, Indian, and agricultural artifacts, including an original circa 1834 McCormick reaper.

The small Brannock Maritime Museum on Talbot Avenue emphasizes the city's maritime connection with photographs of the first steamboat on Chesapeake Bay, the *S.S. Chesapeake,* and whaling ships built at Cambridge, as well as relics from the cruiser *U.S.S. Chester.* The "pathfinder of the seas," Matthew Fontaine Maury, is honored in a display on navigation.

The Dorchester Heritage Museum, a few miles west of the city on state Route 343 in what is known as the "Neck District," hosts an antique airplane fly-in in May and an arts and crafts festival each autumn. Permanent displays emphasize the watermen, aviation, and archeology. The museum is open Saturday and Sunday afternoons from 1 to 5 P.M. from April 15 through October 30.

Nearby are the University of Maryland Center for Environmental and Estuarine Studies and the reconstructed Spocott Windmill, an example of the kind used in mid-nineteenth-century milling.

Blackwater

Blackwater National Wildlife Refuge, operated by the U.S. Fish and Wildlife Service, is off the beaten track, but is easily reached by following signs on state Routes 16 and 335. Conservation study programs, including audiovisuals and conducted tours, are directed by rangers at the Visitors Center. The center also houses a series of displays that include sample birdhouses and stuffed owls, eagles, and muskrats.

The refuge has three trails. Two short paths—the ⅓-mile Woods Trail, which traverses a nature hardwood forest, and the half-mile Marsh Edge Trail, which starts in a wooded area and extends along a boardwalk into a marsh—cover the two types of habitat in the park. The 5-mile driving and bike Wildlife Trail, which skirts an impoundment area and the marshy banks of the Blackwater River, is best for wildlife viewing. An observation tower has water on three sides. Waters and fields adjacent to the trail are alive with birds; white-tailed and sika deer and red fox sometimes enter the fields early at morning or at dusk. The number of bald eagles increases. Nesting boxes strategically spotted along the trail are used by wood ducks in spring and smaller birds at other times.

The choice of seasons is important. Summer is the off-season. ("Visit anytime but summer, because of the flies and mosquitos," said a ranger.) However, even at that time of year, a few ducks, Canada goose, herons, and blackbirds can be seen. Spring through autumn is the best time to see the reptiles and amphibians, including snapping and eastern painted turtles, water and land snakes, toads and bullfrogs, and salamanders and lizards. The peak season is late October through December, when more than 110,000 geese, ducks, and whistling swan pass through or winter on the 14,279-acre preserve. Northward-migrating killdeer, robins, and bluebirds begin arriving in February. In March, ducks and geese start winging northward for the summer, while hordes of red-winged blackbird pass through or take up residence. Resident ducks and geese begin incubating in April. Migratory songbird populations peak in late April and early May. The marsh hibiscus begins to bloom in late July, when the swallows, flycatchers, and kingbirds are feasting on swarms of insects. Blue-winged teal fly through in the other direction in August. Osprey or "fish hawk" in September leave nesting platforms constructed at the river's edge and begin the flight to Central and South America.

The refuge shelters three endangered species of birds — the rarely seen red-cockaded woodpecker, the migrant peregrine falcon, and the bald eagle, which rests in a clump of dead trees. More common sightings include the great blue and green-backed herons, Canada goose, American black duck, mallard, northern pintail, tundra swan, turkey vulture, northern bobwhite, king rail, greater and lesser yellowlegs, laughing gull, mourning dove, great horned and eastern screech owls, red-bellied woodpecker, northern flicker, great crested flycatcher, eastern kingbird, purple martin, Carolina chickadee, tufted titmouse, golden-crowned kinglet, northern mockingbird, European starling, white-eyed vireo, northern cardinal, red-winged blackbird, brown-headed cowbird, and common grackle. On rare occasion, a wild turkey invades the forest.

The endangered Delmarva fox squirrel is among the thirty animals identified as living on the refuge. In addition to deer and foxes, the following also have been sighted in the marshes and forests: muskrat, rabbits, squirrels, nutria, shrews, voles, bats, moles, raccoon, opossum, weasel, rats, mice, skunks, and otter.

Southern Dorchester County is an area where aimless wandering can be interesting. Southward along Maple Dam Road, the driver or biker breaks out of the commercial zone into an area of fields green with corn, soybeans, wheat, and vegetables and stands of trees. In a short time, this gives way to marshland with a thick covering of grass and isolated duck blinds. Mysterious lights sometimes appear in the marshes around Robbins. This road (officially, the name changes without being marked) intersects with state Route 336, which leads in one direction through the fishing villages of Bishop Head peninsula and, in the other direction on Route 335, past historic Tubman Roman Catholic Chapel, established in the 1660s by settlers from St. Mary's City on the mainland, to Hoopers Island.

Hoopers Island, settled in the latter part of the seventeenth century, provides an insight into the waterman's lifestyle, past and present. Despite its singular name, Hoopers is really a chain of three islands. Upper Hoopers is a tranquil area of neat houses and streets where children riding bicycles need be concerned only about an occasional vehicle; crab-processing firms where workboats tie up to unload their cargoes; and divers slips and docks, some heavily protected by discarded tires. The 1980 Narrows Ferry Bridge to Middle Hoopers is high enough to provide a panoramic view of the lowland and adjacent waters, as well as Middle Hoopers, which appears less prosperous and even more sparsely settled than its bigger neighbor but supports a country store of the type that has long since disappeared from most Bay areas. Lower Hoopers can be reached only by boat.

Offshore, and reachable only by boat, is Barren Island or "Barn" Island, in the vernacular. The hardy inhabitants abandoned the island early in this century and floated their homes, churches, and stores across Tar Bay to Hoopers Island.

Taylor's Island, another waterman's refuge where most of the homes have a pleasure boat on a trailer parked in the yard or driveway, stands at the end of state Route 16. Its symbol is the 12-pounder Becky Phipps cannon, which was captured by Taylor's Island militia from British raiders during the War of 1812. Other historic sights include the circa 1707 Episcopal Chapel of Ease, a handsome white frame mission established by Old Trinity Church; the oldest county schoolhouse, a one-room frame structure erected about 1785; Bethlehem Methodist Episcopal Church, known locally as the "Old Brick Church," which was established in 1787; and 1857 Ridgeton mansion, with two large chimneys and an unusual widow's walk.

The Taylor's Island Wildlife Management Area anchors a chain of preserves that stretch across the county and protect an abundance of wildlife. The largest is the divided Fishing Bay WMA, whose major segment straddles Chickamacomico River at the head of Fishing Bay and occupies a small segment of Elliott Island on the Nanticoke

River. The Lecomte Wildlife Refuge near Vienna and the Linkwood WMA north of U.S. Route 50 at Linkwood are small.

The limited access to Taylor's Island WMA keeps its 1,020 acres of pine and cedar trees and marshland relatively isolated. For the time being, it is reachable only by water via Slaughter's Creek, which can handle depths only to 4 feet at mean low water because of a bar near the mouth — and thus good territory in which to hunt sika and white-tailed deer and waterfowl and to observe wildlife. Overnight camping is not allowed, but nearby privately owned Tideland Park Campground, with a boat ramp, 50-foot pier, and 500-foot bulkhead, provides access to this preserve and the Blackwater Refuge, as well as other Bay pleasures such as crabbing and fishing, birdwatching, and nature study. A public boat ramp is located on Taylor's Island.

The abundant wildlife in the area also supports a growing number of hunting lodges.

The Little Choptank River is short as Eastern Shore rivers go, but extends into a sparsely settled area and has relatively light boating traffic, despite the five navigable creeks leading off it. Fishing Creek is a substantial waterway in itself, with tree-lined ancillary streams providing numerous pleasant anchorages for those familiar with the shoals. From Church Creek, one of its arms, boaters can see the historic Old Trinity Church. Hudson Creek is another favorite with boaters, because the channel is well marked and shoals are easily avoided. Phillips Creek, in the vicinity of Cedar Point and Cherry Island, provides an alternative.

East New Market, northeast of Cambridge, retains ten impressive structures from its settlement period during the last half of the eighteenth century. Among them are circa 1740 Friendship Hall, a 2½-story Georgian-style brick home noted for its raised paneling, mantels, and floors and for its boxwoods; the 1½-story white frame Smith Cottage, built about 1760; the circa 1750 House of the Hinges, whose name derives from the large hinges on an ancillary building; and the circa 1780 New Market House, after which the town was named, which has an original brick section and a frame addition.

The Secretary area has numerous legends, including the unsavory reputation of the Patty Cannon House at Reliance, where travelers reputedly were robbed and murdered by the proprietors and stolen slaves were resold. Most notable are My Lady Seawell's Manor, built about 1662 and now the parish house of Our Lady of Good Counsel

Catholic Church, and the 1825 Springdale Manor or Sherman Institute, a nineteenth-century private school.

Vienna, on the banks of the Nanticoke River, has been a crossroads since it was settled soon after Capt. John Smith stopped there during his 1608 Bay expedition. The British raided the community during both the Revolutionary War and War of 1812, during the latter firing several volleys at defenders behind riverfront breastworks. In more peaceful periods, sailing ships and steamboats navigated the river in large numbers, creating commercial prosperity. Vienna retains twenty-two early structures in reasonably original form, including the 1768 Old Customs House, whose ground level has brick floors laid in herringbone patterns; Pearcy's Purchase, built about 1796 with exposed ceiling beams and fireplaces with decorative mantels; the 1800 Tavern House, the historic meeting place for the community and lodging for travelers crossing on the nearby ferry; and Governor's Ordinary, built in the 1780–1800 period, which was the home of Maryland's Civil War governor, Thomas Holiday Hicks.

Salisbury

Busy Salisbury, which has a population of more than 17,000, is the largest city on the Eastern Shore and the county seat of Wicomico County. The Eastern Shore's most important commercial center is basically an agricultural market, where the largest employers are food processors and more than sixty truck lines, but it is far from one-dimensional. Salisbury is Maryland's second largest port—not for ocean-going vessels, but for pleasure craft and commercial vessels carrying coal, aggregate, and other bulk commodities. The Salisbury/Wicomico County Airport, second in the state in number of flights, is served by three commuter airlines.

From the compact 47-slip Port of Salisbury Marina, part of a harbor revitalization program, the sidewheel steamboat *Maryland Lady* cruises down the Wicomico River past natural forests, cultivated fields, historic sites, picturesque villages, and modern commercial and residential additions. With specified minimums, 90-minute narrated trips operate six days a week at 3 or 4 P.M. from June through September and on Saturdays and Sundays in April, May, and October; two-hour luncheon and three-hour dinner sailings are made two or three times a week during those periods. *Maryland Lady* also makes fall foliage cruises from Pocomoke City and Snow Hill in

October, and sails from those cities a few times during June, July, and August.

The Ward Foundation's North American Wildfowl Art Museum on the grounds of Salisbury State University is devoted to wildfowl carving, an art form that evolved from carving crude decoys to attract ducks to hunters. Lemuel and Steven Ward of Crisfield, pioneers in the art form, were barbers who worked on decoys between customers. Lem carved and Steven provided the beautiful coloration of the decoys, dating back to the 1928s, which are included in the collection.

In 1970, Lem Ward was asked what he would carve as his "masterpiece" if he had an opportunity to do so. Ward chose a swan, but said he could not afford the kind of wood needed. Leonard Palmisano of New Jersey provided cedar from that state and Lem produced the delicate white preening swan now displayed near earlier examples of his and Steven's work, including a canvasback, the Canada goose used as a logo by the Ward Foundation, mallard, and other fowl.

The two-level museum, open Tuesdays through Sundays, has an extensive collection of championship carvings from recent decades, including reigning champions. Among them are an oldsquaw pair, the 1971 world champion decorative pair, carved by Jules Iski of Bordentown, New Jersey; a black duck, the 1987 Shootin' Stool champion, by John Garton of Jasper, Ontario, Canada; buffleheads, the 1979 champion decorative pair, by Randy Tull of Hayward, Wisconsin; pintail drakes, 1977 world champion decorative pair, by Tan Brunet of Galliano, Louisiana; and wood ducks, the 1988 best in the world decorative pair, by Kent Duff of Rochester, Minnesota. The museum also houses a replica of the workshop of the Ward brothers; an audiovisual presentation and display on carving methods; antique decoys from various states stretching from North Carolina to Michigan; a historical summary of duck hunting, with equipment such as an Indian dugout canoe and hunter's sink box and replicas of decoys dating back to the colonial period, and a display on decoys used to hunt shorebirds such as the plover and curlew.

The Ward Foundation sponsors two major decoy shows each year — the World Championship Wildfowl Carving Competition in April at Ocean City, and the Wildfowl Art Exhibition in October at Salisbury — as well as summer carving and painting seminars at the university.

A walking tour of Salisbury's Newtown Historical District covers twenty-seven structures in a dozen blocks of North Division, East

Isabella, East William, Broad, and Gay streets and Poplar Hill and Park avenues. The oldest structure is Georgian-style, white frame Poplar Hill Mansion, built about 1805, which is open for tours on Sundays from 1 to 4 P.M. The mid-19th century is well represented by brick Wicomico Presbyterian Church, completed in 1859; the circa 1854 Greek revival Alex Toadvine House, with pilasters; Mrs. Herold's School, a Greek revival structure with fluted Doric columns, which dates from about 1860; the colonial revival-style George Humphreys House, circa 1850, and others. As a result of a devastating fire in 1886, the Victorian influence is strong and includes the 1901 Holloway House of Cape Cod design, 1896 Fred A. Grier House noted for its decorative windows and fish-scale central tower, and the L-shaped cottage, "Little Eden." A number of interesting buildings, including the Day-Brewington House at the corner of Elizabeth Street and Poplar Hill Avenue, are not listed in the walking tour brochure.

Salisbury has a 12-acre zoo, open daily year round, with more than 400 animals, birds, and reptiles in natural habitats along walkways lined with exotic plants and shade trees. The adjacent city park, an oasis from the city's bustle, has tennis courts, picnic and games facilities, summertime concerts, and fishing. A riverfront walk meanders along the east prong of the Wicomico River.

The Salisbury Festival is held the first weekend in May to coincide with the blooming of the dogwood trees. Some of Salisbury's historic private homes open to the public during the Newtown Festival in October.

Salisbury also is a way station for visitors to nearby outdoors and historic sights, including the still-quaint villages of Whitehaven (its river ferry has operated for more than 285 years) and Quantico. Green Hill and Spring Hill churches date from 1773. Modest Pemberton Hall, completed in 1741, was one of the earliest brick gambrel-roofed houses in Maryland.

Ellis Bay Wildlife Management Area, a 1,924-acre preserve of marsh and wet woods near the mouth of the Wicomico River that is open year round, is rated excellent for deer and duck hunting, fair for quail, Canada goose, and small animals such as rabbit and squirrel. Trapping, crabbing, fishing, hiking, and bird-watching also are allowed. The preserve can be reached by land along state Routes 349 and 352 and Muddy Hole Road, but is best approached by boat from ramps at Webster Cove or the Mount Vernon Wharf, both on the Wicomico River off state Route 362. The small Johnson WMA, an area of inland woods and fields off state Route 12 on Johnson Road in the southeast corner of the county, is among the dove-hunting areas authorized by the Maryland Forest, Park and Wildlife Service in November and December. Quail, rabbit, and deer hunting also is excellent, and the preserve is open to bird-watchers, photographers, and hikers.

Information on all wildlife management areas is available from Eastern Regional Service Center, Wildlife Management Area, 122 Arlington Road, Salisbury, MD 21801 (301/749-2461).

The Beach-to-Bay Indian Trail that meanders across the peninsula from Crisfield to Ocean City illustrates the strong ties between the two coasts. Both an automobile and a bike trail, it follows state Routes 413, 388, and 12 and U.S. Routes 113 and 50 through the stately trees of the Pocomoke State Forest, a sanctuary for numerous birds and the endangered Delmarva fox squirrel, and over streams. It passes through the historic communities of Princess Anne, Snow Hill, and Berlin, the birthplace of national naval hero Stephen Decatur, who ended the Barbary pirate threat, and provides opportunities to visit museums.

A flat, 100-mile-long circular bike trail — marked by Viewtrail 100 signs — extends on secondary state and county roads from Pocomoke City to Berlin and back. It skirts Chincoteague Bay at Public Landing, crosses a number of streams, swamps, and forests, passes Milburn Landing State Park, and transits farmlands and rural communities.

From Salisbury, U.S. Route 50 makes a straight run to the Atlantic Ocean, with a possible diversion to the Wicomico State Forest for hunting, horseback riding, hiking, and walking on nature trails and Berlin, where a park honors naval hero Stephen Decatur, a native son, and the historic district features early nineteenth-century Taylor House Museum (open Monday, Wednesday, Friday, and Sunday from 1 to 4 P.M.). Also near Berlin are old St. Martin's Church and the Revolutionary War-era Genesar mansion.

This is the only section of Maryland that fronts on both Chesapeake Bay and the Atlantic Ocean.

The Ocean Side

Assateague Island once extended from Chincoteague in Virginia to the Delaware border but was cut in two by a storm in 1933. The 22-mile-long Maryland remnant, which varies from one-third to a mile wide, is now a model of outdoors activity of all kinds, hosting the major resort community of Ocean City, a state park, and a national seashore. Although ocean oriented, it is still tied to Chesapeake Bay by historical and social links.

Ocean City's rise as a resort has been rapid. At the turn of the century, Chincoteague ponies roamed the dirt roads and beaches of a quiet seaside village. Today, the city realizes the full potential of its natural resources — the Atlantic with its border of sand and the more placid waters of the four bays that separate the barrier island from the mainland. Each day during the summer season, between 150,000 and 200,000 fun-seekers fill the city's modern hotels, luxuriate on the beach during the daytime and in the clubs and restaurants at night, listen to top entertainers at the Convention Center, which also sponsors big band dances, or attend flea markets and trade shows. Boardwalk trams run about every 20 minutes along the pencil-thin island, which bulges in places — the largest being at Montego Bay in the northern end of the city. One street runs the entire length of the resort, although its name changes from Philadelphia Avenue to Coastal Highway.

The main season extends from June through Labor Day, and includes surfing, boating, and surfcasting, as well as sun worshipping. The Chamber of Commerce sponsors an annual surf fishing tournament.

For all its glitter, Ocean City has a down-to-earth side. Deep-sea and Bay fishers sail from Talbot Street Pier, Bahia Marina, Dorchester Pier, and White Marlin Marina on charter and "head" boat expeditions for marlin, tuna, black drum, and swordfish in the ocean and mackerel, sea bass, flounder, trout, and croakers in the sound. Public launching facilities are maintained in Commercial Harbor in West Ocean City, at Gum Point Road off state Route 589 and on the bayfront at 87th Street in Ocean City. Evening scenic cruises depart the Talbot Street Pier aboard the *Bay Queen* and Capt. Jack Bunting's *Miss Ocean City*. Sunsets often turn the Bay waters into subdued layers of pink, orange, yellow, and blue colors.

The destructive aspect of the ocean is revealed at the Ocean City Life Saving Station Museum, opened in 1976 in an authentic 1891 lifesaving station. Displays reflect the city's original role as a coastal village and its early history as a resort, including the importance of the railroad, and include marine life indigenous to the area. A four-day bash in mid-September creates a "second season," whose principal attraction is free entertainment every day under big top tents at the inlet between the ocean and Bay.

Cycling supports twelve bike rental shops on the island. Frontiertown, on state Route 611 on the mainland, provides staged diversion—can-can girls, street shootouts, an Indian show—and live rodeo and steam train, riverboat, and stagecoach rides from mid-June through Labor Day. Gold Rush Territory, Jungle Golf, and Jolly Roger Amusement Park, which has a 1902 carousel, also are active places.

A tourist information center is maintained by the Chamber of Commerce on U.S. 50 in West Ocean City landward of the causeway to the island resort. A golf course and small airport, served by Cumberland and Resort commuter airlines, also are located in the area.

Assateague State Park, with protected dunes up to about 22 feet high, is not a seasonal phenomenon. In the summer, it sets aside separate zones on its gently shelving, white sand beach for swimming, surfing, and surfcasting for channel bass, bluefish, stripers, and sea trout. In the late autumn and winter, 660-acre Assateague is a vantage point for viewing flying wildfowl formations and wintering ducks and geese. Sea duck, scoter, and eider congregate along the ocean shoreline, while the salt marshes on the Sinepuxent Bay side of the island attract flocks of mallard, canvasback, black duck, and pintail.

Waterfowl hunting from pit and above-ground blinds is permitted in season, with hunters being selected by lottery each morning when overregistration occurs. Deer hunting presently is restricted to sikas because of a decline in the number of white-tailed deer. Other park activities include biking, flatwater canoeing, and hiking.

Assateague State Park has 311 paved campsites among the dunes supported by shower houses, toilets, laundry units, and a water, air, and sanitary dumping station. A separate site is set aside for group youth camping. Other facilities include a bathhouse for day visitors, concessions, and picnic areas. Park naturalists conduct beach walks and interpretive programs from Memorial Day through Labor Day.

Assateague National Seashore has facilities for fishing, hunting, swimming, and boating, guided and self-guided trails, a Visitors Center with exhibits, and an off-road vehicle (ORV) trail.

Between Shores

The Pocomoke River, one of the longest and most important in Maryland's southern Eastern Shore, begins its meandering journey to Chesapeake Bay not far from the Atlantic Ocean. As a result, it exerts a significant and continuing influence on the southernmost counties in Maryland, Worcester, and Somerset.

The river played a key role in the development of historic Snow Hill, which celebrated its tricentenary in 1986. Snow Hill was an active port serving the prosperous farms of the hinterland from its royal designation in the colonial era until railroads and automobiles began to dominate transportation. Now more oriented toward U.S. Route 113, the community retains numerous structures from its heyday, despite a fire in 1893 that destroyed the original downtown and many records in the courthouse.

More than a hundred historically valuable structures remain. Among the fifty-seven authenticated buildings listed in a tour brochure available from the Chamber of Commerce are 1756 Flemish bond brick All Hallows Episcopal Church, serving a parish that dates from 1692; the 1889 gothic revival Makemie United Presbyterian Church, established in 1693 by Francis Makemie, the founder of the denomination in the United States; the pale yellow frame Mumford House, built about 1710; Greek revival-style Chanceford, built between 1759 and 1795; the Teagle-Thompson House, with a large chimney, built about 1814; a fourteen-room, nine-fireplace home raised in the early nineteenth century; and an L-shaped townhouse in Federal style, built about 1844. A one-room school building, whose furniture and books are authentic, illustrates an early form of education. The Worcester County Historical Society's Julia A. Purnell Museum, which occupies a former frame Catholic Church, displays household artifacts and farm equipment from the colonial period through the Victorian era.

The influence of the river on Snow Hill has declined, but the landing is periodically active. Pocomoke River Canoe Company (open weekends spring and autumn, daily Memorial Day through Labor Day) rents canoes for fishing or a few hours or days of paddling the gentle water through varied scenery in search of eagles, osprey, egrets, herons, and small animals such as otter. The firm also portages serious canoeists to points on the Pocomoke, Nassawango Creek, and Assateague Island backwaters for paddles ranging from a half-day to three days.

Four miles north of Snow Hill off state Route 12 stands the industrial village of Furnace Town, which throve in the nineteenth century in what is now the Pocomoke State Forest. The Nassawango Iron Furnace (perhaps the first hot-blast facility in the United States), broom house, blacksmith shop, smokehouse, print shop, church, company store, and museum are open daily except Mondays from 10 A.M. to 5 P.M., April through October.

Also located in the forest is Pocomoke State Park. The two developed areas, Shad Landing and Milburn Landing, may be farther upstream than Capt. John Smith explored, but the remoteness and inaccessibility of the cypress swamps have made them attractive in the past to a succession of ne'er-do-wells, from Civil War deserters to smugglers and bootleggers. Current motivation is somewhat different—the relative isolation of one of the Eastern Shore's most beautiful rivers, enhanced by recreational possibilities.

Boat ramps in both areas provide access to the river. The Shad Landing area also has a marina on Croakers Creek that has twenty-three slips with hookups and a well-lighted dock, as well as dock and shoreline fishing. The tidal river, an excellent bass stream with a few feisty gar, requires a saltwater license. Minnows, worms, crickets, and lures are used to catch pickerel, shad, yellow and white perch, catfish, crappie, and bluegill. Youngsters may fish for fun in a ¾-acre pond at Shad Landing. Both sections have picnic facilities, some with fireplaces, pavilions, and playground equipment.

The Shad Landing area off U.S. Route 113 between Snow Hill and Pocomoke City offers the most facilities, including a 25-meter swimming pool with bathhouse, six areas with tent or vehicular campsites, two youth group camping areas, boat rentals, and a nature center, which has displays on wetlands, birds, and other life in the cypress swamp and skeletal remains of small animal life in the region.

The theme of Shad Landing's principal trail is the inevitability of change in nature. The ¾-mile Trail of Change, whose marked stops can be thoroughly explored in 45 minutes, begins at the old Shad Landing road and the ruins of the landing once used by commercial fishers. Successive numbered stops identify bayberries, used in the early period of the country to make candles; a former farm being reclaimed by nature, including black walnut and Norway maple trees; ferns, moss, and fungi and the tall, multirooted bald cypress (whose resistance to decay made it valuable for shipbuilding and home construction); Hardship Branch, a tributary of the Pocomoke, which is reduced to mudholes at low tide; the hollow trunks of black gum or tupelo trees where raccoons, squirrels, birds, and other animals live; mountain laurel, an evergreen with light pink flowers; and examples of upland forest.

About 2 miles of fire roads lead to largely untouched parts of the cypress swamp, where the changing abundance of wild blossoms, from dogwood and pink laurel in the spring to the bright colors of holly and red teaberries in the autumn, can be observed. A wide variety of birds, especially the prothonotary warbler and pileated woodpecker, reside in the forest. Also among the more than seventy birds recently identified in the park are seventeen kinds of warblers, seven varieties of sparrows, four vireos, eastern bluebird, northern shrike, starling, ovenbird, eastern meadowlark, red-winged blackbird, Baltimore oriole, scarlet and summer tanagers, indigo bunting, blue and evening grosbeaks, and slate-colored junco.

Interpretive programs (June through August) include 1½-hour guided pontoon and canoe trips (through waters broken by the gnarled stumps of trees), canoe safety lessons, demonstrations on how to make birdhouses and attract birds to home yards, nature walks, fishing competitions, and stargazing and campfire programs.

The smaller Milburn Landing area, accessible by state Route 364, is the oldest section of the park, dating back to the 1930s. It occupies one of the few Pocomoke River banks that tidal waters do not overflow, which made it an important hinterland stop for steamboats in the nineteenth century. The park thus has good stands of both upland pine and cypress and swamp hardwoods. Fifty family campsites and three youth camps are dotted along the heavily wooded shoreline. The 2-mile-long, self-guided Bald Cypress Nature Trail through an inland section of woodlands is also the setting of nature walks during the summer season. The interpretive program also includes campfire programs.

Nine miles south of Snow Hill, on Johnson Bay, the E. A. Vaughn Wildlife Management Area's mixture of marsh, fields, and woodland is easily reached by automobile via state Route 12 and Taylor's Landing Road or by boat from Taylor's Landing or George Island Landing. The 1,750-acre preserve is used for hunting ducks, geese, deer, quail, dove, woodcock, squirrel, and rabbit, as well as for crabbing, trapping, bird-watching, and photography.

Route 13 south of Salisbury runs down the interior of the peninsula and thus bypasses many attractions of the region. However, the extensive network of side roads in the direction of Chesapeake Bay reaches some of the most typical Bay communities and most useful natural areas, as well as historic sites.

A ferry crosses the Wicomico River at Whitehaven, not far from Mount Vernon, which sponsors a mid-August Waterman's Festival.

The Bay Side

The fascinating peninsula between the Wicomico and Manokin Rivers provides an opportunity to experience the lifestyle of the region and indulge in a variety of outdoors activities. State Route 363 skirts Deal Island National Wildlife Refuge, which is actually located on the mainland and is open year round to the public. Activities include duck, goose, and quail hunting in season; trapping of rabbits and other small game; crabbing, fishing, and bird-watching; and photography and collection of wild foods. The road also passes Monie Bay National Estuarine Research Refuge at St. Stephen on the way to road's end at Deal Island.

Deal Island, now connected to the mainland by a high bridge, holds an important place in the history of the Bay islands. It was the home of Joshua Thomas, the "Parson of the Islands," who established the strong Methodist strain that remains to this day on Deal, Tangier, Saxis, and Spring islands. The chapel near his gravesite in the yard of St. John Methodist Church honors him.

In some ways, Deal Island retains the homespun atmosphere that formerly characterized all the fishing villages on the Eastern Shore. The lifestyle revolves around the seasonal movements of the blue crab and the harvesting of oysters. Handsome, tall-masted skipjacks, which once filled the Bay but now are rare, sail from Wenona Harbor to tong for oysters and to compete in the annual Labor Day skipjack races on Tangier Sound, which begin at Deal Island Harbor on the northern end of the island. Six of the sleek vessels, including the *Caleb W. Jones* and *H. M. Krantz* owned by Capt. Dicky Webster, tie up at Wenona. Modern boats also discharge baskets of blue crab and buckets of oysters at the wharfs, while men and women wash and grade shellfish in sheds on the shore.

A number of captains also take out fishing parties, with Arby's General Store facing the harbor sometimes acting as coordinator. Piney Island Swash at the mouth of the Manokin River is a premier area for fishing; trolling areas stand near the shoreline of both Deal Island and Little Deal Island. A number of areas in Tangier Sound also are popular, with red drum reacting to peeler crab bait in shallow water from late April to mid-June and springtime blues averaging about 11 pounds. The popular gray trout or weakfish, which like the depths but sometimes appear in schools 15 to 20 feet below the surface, run 5 to 15 pounds. Other frequent catches include spot, croaker (known locally as *flathead*), and the bottom-dwelling flounder.

Exploring South Marsh WMA, an island 3 miles off Deal Island, requires a seaworthy boat and a small, shallow-draft boat to penetrate the marshes. It is open to hunting (ducks, geese, snipe primarily), fishing, crabbing, bird-watching, and photography. Public launching ramps are located at Wenona, Deal Island Harbor, and Rumbley on Goose Creek (off Route 361).

Route 13 bypasses the historic inland community of Princess Anne, whose brick mansions, tree-lined thoroughfares, and boxwood gardens sparkle brightest during Olde Princess Anne Days in October. Located at the headwaters of the handsome but short Manokin River, Princess Anne was an early seaport and market town, which was incorporated in 1733 and named the county seat in 1744.

Several noteworthy buildings are included on a prepared walking tour. Both Manokin Presbyterian Church, built in 1765 by a congregation started in 1683 (the tower was added in 1888), and 1770 St. Andrews Episcopal Church conduct services every Sunday, the latter with a silver communion service dating from 1717. St. Andrews also has an eighteenth-century library. White, frame Washington Hotel on Somerset Street, which opened in 1745 and is still going, retains the sheepskin-lined ledger on which it registered business transactions during the Revolutionary War period — and separate staircases then used by ladies and gentlemen. The Teackle Mansion, built in 1801 by Littleton Dennis Teackle, an associate of Thomas Jefferson, resembles a Scottish manor house. Symmetrically balanced throughout, it also is noted for its elaborate plaster ceilings, mirrored windows to reflect light from the garden, and a covered 7-foot fireplace and beehive oven. The mansion is open Sundays from 2 to 4 P.M. and by appointment. Nearby Josh House features a collection of early American kitchen utensils and furniture.

During Olde Princess Anne Days, residents dress in period costumes and conduct tours of a number of private homes from the colonial and Federal periods. Among them is 1705 Turnstall Cottage, perhaps the oldest inhabited house in the town. Wicomico Hunt Club performs during Olde Princess Anne Days.

The boxwood gardens at the corner of Washington Street and Somerset Avenue were planted in 1842 by Gen. George Handy.

Two Wildlife Management Areas are located near Princess Anne. Fairmount WMA, 14 miles southwest of the town on state Route 361, is rated excellent for hunting deer, ducks, and Canada geese. Other inhabitants of the 3,846-acre preserve are rabbits, squirrels, snipe, quail, and woodcock. Trapping, crabbing, fishing, photography, and hiking are permitted. The small, 389-acre Wellington WMA, consisting primarily of open fields and woodlands, is rated high for deer, quail, and dove hunting; raccoon, squirrel, rabbit, and woodcock are also present. Hiking, bird-watching, and photography are among other activities.

Crisfield, relatively new as Eastern Shore communities go, has changed drastically since its founding in 1866 as the terminus of a spur off the New York, Philadelphia, and Norfolk Railroad. Completing the railroad through the marshy area to transport fashionable oysters and crabs to the hungry Northeast was not easy and resulted in several blocks of the downtown area being built on oyster shells 6 feet deep in places. The city had a lusty beginning, with places like "Bloody Block" and brothels for sailors existing alongside legitimate theater for the more refined residents. The fishing boats were soon joined by luxurious steamers offering nightly service to Baltimore and Norfolk and, by the turn of the century, Crisfield ranked in the top five in the nation in the number of registered boats.

The self-styled "Crab Capital of the World" is unquestionably a watermen's community, whose life is centered around its docks and fish houses. At the City Dock at the end of state Route 413 (West Main Street), visitors may sit with local people to see low-slung crab and oyster boats and pleasure craft of all sizes come and go or watch the watermen unload crab baskets into waiting refrigerator trucks. Although it is becoming increasingly difficult to locate the former trademark of the industry, the unpainted shacks built on piers over the water, a few stand at Jenkins Creek and Apes Hole Creek, fishing villages before Crisfield was created. Several places continue the practice of putting crabs in floating pens for shedding, including the J. C. Tawes Crab House near Side Street Market.

A boat ramp is located at state-owned, 370-slip Somers Cove Marina. In addition, charter boats head for favorite fishing sites in Tangier and Pocomoke sounds, including the Puppy Hole, Island Rock, and Terrapin Shoal areas.

The J. Millard Tawes Museum and Visitors Center, named for a popular governor from Crisfield, is located in a modern building one block off Main Street. The museum houses a number of permanent exhibits, including Governor Tawes's memorabilia; replicas of decoys carved by the Ward brothers; artifacts from the area; and development of the seafood industry. The workshop on Sackertown Road where barbers Lem and Steve Ward worked also is now a museum. Makepeace, an early eighteenth-century brick home with unusual double front doors, stands on Johnson's Creek Road, while the 1889–1890 Crockett House on Main Street represents the Victorian era.

The J. Millard Tawes Crab and Clambake is held at Crisfield in mid-July; the National Hard Crab Derby and Fair occurs on Labor Day.

Only a few years ago, the only transportation to Smith and Tangier islands in the Bay was a mail boat. Now tour boats leave for both on regular schedules from the City Dock and Somers Cove Marina. Boats leave Crisfield at 12:30 P.M. and depart Smith Island about 4 P.M. daily during warm months, with the *Captain Tyler II* going to Rhodes Point, the *Theresa Anne* and *Island Belle II* (the mailboat) going to Ewell, and the *Captain Jason* going to Tylerton. The boats return to Smith Island at 5:15 P.M. to overnight. The *Steven Thomas* and *Miss Tangier* leave at 12:30 P.M. during the summer for Tangier Island, with only the former returning to the mainland the same day, at 5 P.M.

The larger *City of Crisfield* leaves at 11 A.M. Saturday on a four-hour run down the Bay to Portsmouth, Virginia, which includes an overnight stay in that city. It leaves Portsmouth at 2 P.M. Sunday on the return voyage.

A 7.5-mile circular bicycle trail, which takes about 90 minutes, starts at Somers Cove Marina, sidetracks to the Coast Guard station, passes the home of the Ward Brothers, crosses Jenkins Creek and Apes Hole Creek (which harbor crab shanties where the shedding process can be seen), and moves past stately Victorian houses along Route 413 (Main Street) to the point of origin.

Just outside Crisfield, along Jacksonville Road (state Route 358), Janes Island State Park preserves a section of typical Chesapeake Bay coast where visitors may enjoy the kind of natural isolation that once existed extensively in the region. The park is divided between a small mainland site and the island, accessible only by boat.

The mainland Hodson area, located in a small stand of loblolly pine, hosts the park headquarters; a 25-slip marina for boats up to 24 feet long, available only to campers; 94 campsites for all types of vehicles and tents; four modern waterfront rental log cabins; and picnic facilities. Rental boats are available from May through September. The area has no trails designed for hiking or biking, but devotees can use roads on the site and uncongested highways near the park, including Jacksonville Road, which leads to 1782 St. Peter's Episcopal Church.

A boat ramp provides year-round access to the meandering creeks and ponds on 3,000-acre Janes Island, subject to tides of about 2½ feet and composed mostly of grassy hammocks but including some forested areas. Although deer sometimes are seen on the island, they do not live there but swim out from the mainland. Wildfowl hunting is permitted, in season, away from frequented public areas. The 50-foot-tall chimney of a fish processing factory, which operated from 1880 to the 1930s, serves as a landmark. Occasional discovery of Indian arrowheads along the shoreline proves that Indians boated to the island, too.

During the summer, a park pontoon boat opens part of the large island to those without their own boats. The 10-minute trip leaves the mainland hourly from 1 to 5 P.M. weekdays and 10 A.M. to 5 P.M. weekends by way of the Annemessex Canal between the mainland and the island. It wends along Ward Creek, whose shoreline is frequented by blue heron and interrupted by strings of exposed crab pots, and stops at a "T" pier capable of handling forty boats. Narrow, sandy flat Cap Beach, which extends about 1½ miles along Tangier Sound before being interrupted by a creek, is modestly developed to accommodate boaters, bathers, and fishers. This beach is surprisingly free of mosquitoes but sometimes is infested by flies. Old Island, on the southern coast of Janes Island, also has a protected cove where small boats may be moored and is suitable for bathing.

Cedar Island Wildlife Management Area between Tangier and Pocomoke sounds about 2 miles south of Crisfield is accessible only by boat. Ducks are the primary game, but Canada goose and snipe also inhabit the 2,880 soggy acres. Other uses include fishing, crabbing, bird-watching, and photography. The 1,122-acre Pocomoke Sound WMA, 3 miles southeast of Crisfield and reachable only by boat, has much the same characteristics and activities.

Deer can be hunted at the former Maryland Marine Properties Inc. site at Marumsco, 10 miles east of Crisfield via state Route 667 and Back Shelltown Road. Also present in the wet woodlands area are rabbit, quail, and woodcock. In addition to hunting, bird-watching and photography are permitted.

A prepared driving tour of Somerset County adds to the Princess Anne and Crisfield sites such historic structures as the 1839 Fairmount Academy (open during its May 1800s Festival and by appointment), the hundred-year-old homes in St. Stephens, and 1706 Rehobeth Presbyterian Church, one of the most historic structures in the county. Red brick Rehobeth Church, located on Old Rehobeth

Road a short distance off state Route 667 between Crisfield and Pocomoke City, housed the first congregation started in 1693 by the founder of Presbyterianism in the United States, Francis Makemie. Nearby are the ruins of Coventry Parish Church.

Carvel Hall cutlery factory outlet on state Route 413 one mile north of Crisfield is a monument to a native genius, Charles Bridell, who began his career making crab-picking and oyster-shucking knives and developed a line of cutlery, especially steak knives, which gained a national reputation.

Pocomoke City, the city closest to the Virginia border, located at the intersection of U.S. Routes 13 and 113, is a workaday Pocomoke River community, with harness racing and historic Costen House. Riverfront Cypress Park combines bike trails, water plants, and a wharf for small boats, which is also an interesting river walk.

Somerset County maintains a Visitors Center on Route 13 north of Pocomoke City.

PART THREE

Islands in the Bay

KEDGES STRAITS

MARTIN

WILDLIFE

REFUGE

Ewell

Smith

Island

Tylerton

TANGIER

SOUND

CEDAR
ISLAND
MARSH

MARYLAND
VIRGINIA

Goose Island

Tangier Island

N

ISLANDS IN THE BAY

The Near and the Far

THERE ARE FIFTY-TWO ISLANDS IN CHESAPEAKE BAY, ACCORDING TO A count made by one mapmaker. Many of the islands are uninhabited and have been converted into wildlife sanctuaries or are simply ignored. Some were inhabited for many generations, but were abandoned in the nineteenth and twentieth centuries as the Bay began to reclaim the land. Poplar Island off Bay Hundred, for example, is still visible and solid at low tide; others have become part of the extensive shoal system in the Bay. A few islands are privately owned. The Chesapeake Bay Foundation uses Port Isobel Island as an educational platform for conservationists.

Islands that lie close to the shoreline or are linked to the shore by new high-rise bridges, like North and Middle Hooper islands, interface with those areas and are covered in the appropriate places. Still-isolated South Hooper Island, and others in similar situation, are grouped with their cousins.

But two—Tangier in Virginia and Smith Island in Maryland—are special. Both were settled early in the seventeenth century. Originally viewed as farmland, they have since evolved into a more feasible relationship with the Bay around them. For many generations, the inhabitants have made their living from the water, primarily by harvesting crabs and oysters. Their contacts with outsiders were commercial, as they sailed their boats to Crisfield, to sell their seafood. A mailboat visited the islands once a week.

Isolated from the mainland, they preserved their customs and traditions to a much greater degree than the more exposed mainlanders. Even in the early part of this century, the Elizabethan accent could be detected on Tangier. Crimes such as rape and the use of drugs were unknown. The most noticeable families of both islands are descendants of those who settled there in the seventeenth century. No formal governments existed; community business was conducted as needed at mass meetings called in the local Methodist

Church, the strongest influence on both islands since the "Parson of the Islands" brought religion to the fiercely independent people.

Modern communications and transportation have brought the islands closer to the mainstream of life around the Bay. Television and formal secondary schooling on the mainland have diluted ancient dialects and customs. Tourist boats from both Maryland and Virginia mainlands almost daily disgorge droves of curious tourists, attracted to the islands by the influence of the isolation that is now being lost. Tangier now has a formal government, and Smith Islanders have recently given the idea some thought.

Those who knew, and loved, these islands before the transformation will lament the changes, but will recognize their inevitability. Even in their modern versions, these islands retain a charm and outlook that are refreshing to beleaguered outsiders.

Tangier

The wind-swept appearance and weathered picket fences are for the most part history. So is the delightful absence of vehicles. Neatly painted houses with green grass yards, a few trucks, and construction machines and motorbikes attest to the changed lifestyle of Tangier Islanders. The movie house, once the pride of the island, is gone; it could not compete with television. Islanders now have more than three hundred bicycles. An airport for small planes, opened in 1969, is especially useful when the harbor freezes in winter.

Reception of visitors is much more organized than it was thirty years ago, when Mrs. Hilda Crockett provided food and overnight accommodations in her home to the few visitors who ventured to the island. Between April 15 and October 15, a guide meets cruise boats and leads passengers along the narrow lanes of the town to Hilda Crockett's Chesapeake House, a larger building across the street from the original guest home. Mrs. Crockett's daughters, Bette and Ruth, continue the tradition of hosting overnight guests and providing family-style meals, including soft-shell crabs, which many tourists consider the primary reason for the trip. Signs near the harbor provide directions to other restaurants that serve the traditional crabcake sandwiches and crab platters, as well as less traditional fast foods. Pleasant girl guides conduct golf cart tours of the narrow lanes of the 1- by 3-mile island. Virginia Marine Resources Commission police are on hand, but crime is rare.

Crab pots and work sheds line the harbor at Tangier Island. PHOTO BY
JOHN BOWEN.

Despite its emergence from isolation, Tangier is interesting because
of its ambience. The island pace is different from that on the mainland.
A real community spirit exists. If help is needed, everyone pitches
in, whether it involves fuel for winter or recovering a boat that sank.
The birth of a baby involves the entire community, not just the family.
And that is not entirely because so many of the citizens on Tangier
are related. Crocketts, by one count, account for about a third of
the residents, for example.

Years ago, when the island was isolated, the Tangier dialect was
distinct — and quaint to outsiders. Islander speech still has a musical
quality and is rapid, which a few years ago a British Broadcasting
Corporation documentary described as Elizabethan, but the quaint-
ness of speech is diluted more and more each year.

The waterfront is a jumble of piers, tied-up boats, crab-shedding
racks, ramps, piled crab pots, floats and lines, service facilities, and
moving boats. While visitors wander the community to shop for T-
shirts or handicrafts, refuel in the restaurants, or talk with attendants
at the country store, watermen go silently about the business of tending the crab-shedding racks, which once floated in the water but now
balance on piers, or preparing their boats or crab pots for the next

morning's run, or talking among themselves about prices, weather, and the relative abundance or scarcity of seafood. Youngsters — even young daughters — sometimes accompany the men on these chores. Tangier, like other Bay islands, is subject to severe erosion at times. Thus, the island is slowly shrinking. A $4.2 million plan to stabilize 5,700 feet of coastline with a riprap seawall is designed to preserve the island at about its present size. Water comes from sixteen artesian wells, sunk 1,000 feet under the island.

Narrow lanes lead away from the harbor. Most of the homes front on what is usually described as Main Street, but which is not marked. This paved lane also passes Swain Memorial United Methodist Church and its large cemetery. The church was founded as Lee's Bethel Church in 1835, and the present church was built in 1897. The name was changed in 1900. The island has a second Methodist church and residences at a distance from the harbor, which many visitors do not visit. These churches are the centers of social and corporate life, as well as the spiritual advisers to the islanders.

Tangier's 700 residents do not dote on ancient history, perhaps because a waterman's unpredictable life changes from year to year. However, Tangier is one of the oldest place names in Virginia. Capt. John Smith visited the island during his 1608 exploratory voyage around Chesapeake Bay and named it for a place from his military past. In 1688, John Crockett and sons and their families became the first settlers.

The historical marker on the island recalls the most famous intrusion between the seventeenth-century settlement and the twentieth-century tourist invasion as follows: "In 1814, it was headquarters of a British fleet ravaging Chesapeake Bay. From here, the fleet sailed to attack Fort McHenry near Baltimore. The Rev. Joshua Thomas, in a prayer, predicted the failure of the expedition. It was in that attack that the 'Star-Spangled Banner' was written."

Visitors may walk past the Tangier Historical Museum, attached to a gift shop, and neat homes that front on the narrow lanes and discuss, with the sometimes-shy residents, changes that have taken place. Conversations often are punctuated by the roar of passing motorbikes. Mrs. Eva Pruitt, whose surname is also one of the oldest on the island, believes that tourism now may bring more money into the community than the seafood industry.

The 12-mile cruises to Tangier clear Crisfield Harbor at the same time that other cruise boats, including the mail boat, start for Smith Island. The sudden appearance of so many brightly colored boats is misleading; tourism is only a sideline for Crisfield, whose stock in trade remains the seafood-processing houses lining the shoreline. The 45-minute to 1¼-hour cruise to Tangier is a pleasant mixture of sun, breeze, aquatic birds, and views of passing boats — watermen scooping up crabs with nets or crab pots or stunting pleasure craft. The captain of the 90-foot-long *Steven Thomas,* which has three passenger decks and can carry up to 300 passengers, offers occasional commentary about points along the route. The cruiser sails close to the southern shoreline of Janes Island State Park, whose white sand beach contrasts with the red brick smokestack ruin of a former menhaden-processing plant. Bell Buoy 6 marks the crossing of the boundary between Maryland and Virginia. A privately owned hunting island is seen from a distance; in the autumn, when the ducks and geese migrate, the populated sky shows why hunters also migrate to the island. The cruise ship passes close to 200-acre Port Isobel Island, now a Chesapeake Bay Foundation bird sanctuary and educational center, on the entrance to Tangier Harbor.

The mail boat *Tangier Princess* still runs daily year round (except Sunday, October–May) from Crisfield, Maryland, to Tangier Island, but the best way to visit the island for a short period are the cruise ships that operate daily from Memorial Day through October. The *Steven Thomas* leaves from the City Dock. *Capt. Eulice* departs Onancock, Virginia, while the *Chesapeake Breeze* leaves Reedville, Virginia, on the western shore of the Bay 16 miles from Tangier.

Smith Island

Capt. John Smith, the seventeenth-century explorer who dropped a lot of names around Chesapeake Bay, gave his own to the largest island in the Bay, which he explored in 1608. John Evans and John Tyler were among the first settlers to bring their families to the island. Like Tangier, it was used first for farming — principally cattle — but then developed its own water-based economy. Islanders have been making their living from the sea for more than 300 years, using first sailboats and then power boats to seek the elusive blue crabs and delicate oysters. At one point in the late nineteenth century, more than fifty skipjacks operated from the island's three harbors.

Smith would hardly recognize his namesake today. In the first place, Smith Island is not a single island. The large northern half, or 4,400 acres, is separated from higher ground by a gut known as the Big Thorofare and maintained by the U.S. Fish and Wildlife Service in a pristine state.

An expanding population of aquatic and land animals lives among the waving marsh grasses and tree-covered hammocks of the Glenn L. Martin Nature Refuge. Gulls and grackles by the hundreds peck at shorelines, while six species of herons, three kinds of egrets, and the glossy ibis nest in large areas set aside as rookeries. About 250 great blue heron nests were identified on one forested hammock alone. In all, more than forty species of birds have been seen on the refuge. The herring gull is the most abundant, followed by terns, snowy egret, and the tricolor (Louisiana) heron. Among other birds are the double-crested cormorant, willet, woodcock, sanderling, oyster catcher, black-bellied plover, marsh hawk, and bald eagle. Wintering waterfowl total more than 16,500, principally black duck, pintail, bufflehead, Canada goose, and tundra swan. Black duck, mallard, gadwall, and green-winged teal nest on the refuge. The banks of the waterways at low tide teem with fiddler crab, which attract predators.

The area known as Swan Island is used frequently by organizations for bird walks and watching. Thousands of egrets nest in that area. The Martin refuge has seventy man-made platforms for osprey nests, some clearly visible from waterways; fifty-six were occupied in 1988. In addition, the endangered peregrine falcon has made a comeback and some young birds were "hacked" (cared for until flight stage and then released) in West Virginia. Boaters may use the area known as Swan Island, which has a sandy beach year round.

Small numbers of red fox, mink, otter, and muskrat and greater numbers of northern diamondback terrapin also live on the refuge. Rockfishing is good, but Maryland enforces a ban on rockfish fishing as a conservation measure.

Mike Harrison, ranger in charge, says the refuge is indented by shallow inlets with names like Fishing Creek, Joe's Ridge Creek, Otter Creek, and Well's Ridge Creek. Actually, except for the hammocks on which trees grow, the refuge consists almost entirely of tidal marshland. Watermen make their way through it daily to tend their crab pots or tong for oysters outside the refuge, but the waterways are shallow (as little as 8 inches in some places outside the channels) and deceptive and should not be attempted by outsiders without guidance.

Duck blinds stand in a number of places offshore, but hunting is not allowed within 300 yards of the refuge. Solomons Lump

Lighthouse, also known locally as Kedges Lighthouse, marks the northern boundary of the refuge. Boaters in the area frequently witness lone watermen, who stand in their boats and dip crabs off the shallow bottom. The water around the boats is calmed by pouring oil on it.

A century ago, much of the land inside the refuge was high and dry. Mike's septuagenarian father can remember when people lived in this area and took their boats across the water to farm at what is now the community of Ewell on the main part of the island. Most Smith Island residents now earn a living from the water.

The headquarters of the Martin Refuge at Ewell, sited in a house built in a single week in 1900 from parts shipped from the mainland, doubles as a museum and Visitors Center. Displays include maps of the refuge and the places where waterfowl banded in its boundaries have been checked and photographs of different kinds of birds.

The traffic between Smith Island and the mainland is substantial. The mail boat and private boats haul cargo—bananas, plywood for building, paper bags containing medication brought to the dock by a druggist in Crisfield, frozen chicken breasts, and so on—as well as passengers. The island has an elementary school, but pupils must travel to the mainland and back by boat every day for the higher grades. When Mike Harrison attended school, students remained in Crisfield for the entire school week and the state boarded them in homes.

Cruise ships dock at either Ewell or Rhodes (originally Rogues) Point. Boats leaving Crisfield's City Dock or Somers Cove Marina during the warm months pass near the sandy beach and chimney ruin on Janes Island, whose low-lying terrain is a good preview of Smith Island, and meet a changing assortment of workboats and pleasure craft on the choppy 12-mile crossing. To reach Ewell, the *Capt. Jason* enters water protected by extensions of the two parts of the island and slowly navigates the narrow Big Thorofare to a harbor with numerous piers, including the county dock, where the mail boat ties up. The *Capt. Tyler II* approaches Rhodes Point through more open water, but the shoreline is similarly lined with piers. Each cruise ship allows visitors about 2½ hours ashore to visit the restaurants, wander the streets, or reach other island communities on rented bicycles or in automobiles.

The 150-passenger cruise ship *Capt. Evans* also makes daily trips to Ewell from Reedville, Virginia, from May through September.

On Smith Island, the steeple of the Methodist Church dominates the skyline of both Rhodes Point and Ewell, which are clusters of homes near the church. The tradition of accepting overnight guests in homes continues in both communities, but Ewell is relatively well situated in this regard because it has a small motel. Tylerton, the third community, also built around the Methodist Church, a few years ago rejected the idea of a bridge connecting Ewell and Tylerton because it would mean too much contact. Small boats remain the main means of transportation between the communities.

The Smith Island ambience represents a delicate balance between staunch individualism and corporate assistance to others in need. The island has a small-town atmosphere where "everybody knows too much about everyone else" but nobody takes advantage of it. Community decisions on everything from street lights to helping the elderly are made at mass meetings, usually held in the Methodist Church, and life still is controlled by tides, seasons, and the weather.

The presence of thousands of summer day visitors, accepted by Smith Islanders because of the resulting economic benefits, is making more cultural inroads than islanders recognize. Although today's lifestyle is less picturesque than a generation or more ago, it is still refreshing to outsiders, who climb on the piers to watch watermen work on their boats, walk narrow streets to admire the handsome white frame churches, and inspect model skipjacks and ducks carved by Edward Jones and others.

The welcome that Smith Islanders extend to visitors does not include those who want to build condominiums. A proposal in 1987 to build a hundred vacation and retirement homes aroused both the 500 inhabitants and the Chesapeake Bay Foundation, which had the resources to fight it in court. The never-ceasing search for waterfront sites may exert an influence on the islanders yet; the near-approval by Somerset County authorities of the condominium proposal has made the islanders think in terms of creating a formal government — something they had never before felt they needed.

PART FOUR
~~~~~~~~~
Virginia

Eastern Shore

Chamber of Commerce, Accomac, VA 23301. Tel.: 804/787–2460.

"THE BEST OF WHAT'S LEFT IS RIGHT HERE, SEASIDE AND BAYSIDE," BARRY Truitt of the Virginia Coastal Reserve said as he contemplated the quality of the water on the Eastern Shore of Virginia. The short streams and inlets of the region are the most pristine and have the best remaining submerged aquatic vegetation in the Bay.

This is largely a result of chance. Virginia shore dwellers have not treated natural surroundings any better than other users; there were just fewer of them. Furthermore, isolation retarded migration from metropolitan centers and limited outside access to the creeks and harbors on Chesapeake Bay and the wilds of the Barrier Islands off the Atlantic Coast. Only a few towns have 1,500 or more residents.

The Virginia Eastern Shore is geographically a modified 72-mile extension of the Maryland Eastern Shore. The terrain is flat (the highest point is about 60 feet) and the peninsula is 10 miles wide at its widest point. There are no major rivers, only short creeks and shallow coves, many of them bordered by marshes. More than 135,000 acres are covered by forests. Agriculture and fishing are the dominant industries. Rich soil produces tons of potatoes, soybeans, tomatoes, green beans, cucumbers, and peppers, which are processed at Eastern Shore canneries or shipped fresh through markets in neighboring Maryland. Poultry is another major farm product. The seafood industry is based primarily on the harvesting of oysters, crabs, and clams.

Residents sometimes think of themselves as "baysiders" or "sea-siders" and, indeed, there is marked difference between the two shores. The Chesapeake Bay side is comfortable, with short, pristine rivers and small inlets where droves of sailboats head for the generally placid Bay. The ocean side, although protected by largely undisturbed barrier islands 10 or so miles offshore, has a wild quality that stems

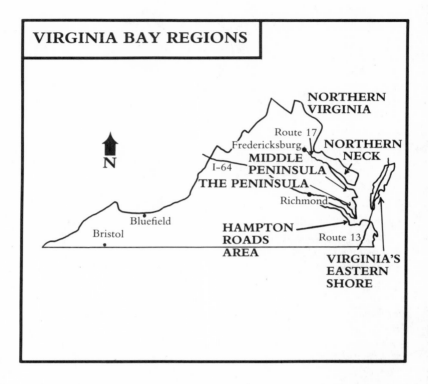

VIRGINIA BAY REGIONS

NORTHERN VIRGINIA

Route 17
Fredericksburg
NORTHERN NECK

N

MIDDLE PENINSULA

I-64

THE PENINSULA

Richmond

Bluefield

HAMPTON ROADS AREA

Bristol

Route 13

VIRGINIA'S EASTERN SHORE

from the unpredictable nature of its winds and weather and tricky marshes and mud flats, where brown pelicans, willets, terns, and oystercatchers compete with working watermen for sustenance.

The Virginia Eastern Shore is divided into two counties — Accomack and Northampton — but the division is not significant for the visitor. Accomac is the county seat of Accomack County (even informed Virginians sometimes miss the spelling distinction). The court seat of Northampton County is Eastville, whose courthouse records, dating back to 1632, are the oldest continuous set of documents in the United States.

The history of the Eastern Shore of Virginia has not occurred in a straight line, but in waves, mostly the result of transportation changes. The region was one of the first places explored by the peripatetic Capt. John Smith, who established good relations with Accomacks and Nussawattocks Indian Chief Debedeavon and his brother, Kiptopeke. Kiptopeke's name survives among other Indian place names, including Nassawadox, Wachapreague, and Onancock, which visitors often have trouble pronouncing but which natives roll off their tongues with drawling authority. It was among the first areas settled by Europeans; Thomas Savage arrived in 1620 to put down roots that are maintained by his descendants. Although many names derive from the family names of landowners, the English heritage is evident in names like Cape Charles and Belle Haven.

The early character of The Shore was shaped by isolation, from the insularity of its residents to their ordeals with pirates. Among the first settlers were the Custises, whose progeny moved to the mainland and became entwined with the families of George Washington and Robert E. Lee. These later generations were more contented than John Custis IV and his wife, whose romantic marriage turned so sour that his tombstone off Route 13 south of Cheriton reads, "Liv'd but Seven Years, which was the space of time He Kept a Bachelors house at Arlington." His wife is buried in Williamsburg.

Steamboats first opened up the region to the outside, bringing visitors and carrying away produce and seafood. The coming of the railroad in the nineteenth century created an unprecedented wave of growth, as whole new towns sprouted along the tracks and once-dominant communities, now bypassed, withered. The railroad has been an integral part of life since it was completed down the center of the peninsula to Cape Charles. The train still hauls away farm products and returns with heavy equipment, but on a limited schedule. In 1988, Parksley, a community created by the railroad, illustrated the declining influence of the silver tracks by converting its train station into a railroad museum.

Many of the communities along the rail line now are more oriented toward four-lane, divided U.S. Route 13 — the Ocean Hiway — which created the latest developmental wave. The steady stream of traffic across the Chesapeake Bay Bridge-Tunnel, which in 1964 made the area readily accessible to tourists and businesspeople, has spawned new motels, aluminum and steel structures for light manufacturing, and burger and broasted chicken stands, and begun to transform the lifestyle. Nowadays, the number of "waterfront property for sale" signs may exceed the number of vegetable patches. Larger and larger audiences collect at natural wonders that until recently were selectively used. More than forty boat captains take fishing parties on charter and/or head boats from Cape Charles, Sanford, Quinby, Wachapreague, Oyster, and Chincoteague. The proliferation of businesses along Route 13 includes a duck decoy "factory" and bronze foundry and wildlife art gallery. Roadside stands offer fruits and vegetables to passers-by.

On the plus side, these trends have heightened awareness among watermen that future use of the Bay depends on current practices, have strengthened the ecology movement in general, and are resulting in the preservation or salvage of historically or architecturally important structures that had deteriorated through neglect. Numerous antique shops, many in restored structures, are ranged along Route 13.

Even today, the Virginia Eastern Shore retains a rustic charm. It is not backward, but demonstrates some of the picturesque straightforwardness that characterized the entire region a few generations back. Residents are supportive of each other in quiet ways and band together when confronted by outsiders.

Points of tourist interest are widely scattered, but the narrowness of the peninsula puts the Route 13 driver only minutes away from both Bay and ocean and most historical sites. In general, the historic attractions are located west of the highway and the natural attractions east. There are exceptions, of course; the Bayside has picturesque fishing villages and Accomac, on the eastern edge of U.S. 13, has a wealth of restored colonial homes. In addition, there are certain concentrations — principally at Accomac, Onancock, Eastville, and Cape Charles.

The nature of the sights on Virginia's Eastern Shore has been shaped as much by environment as history. There are no eighteenth-century brick towns, like Chestertown in Maryland, because there are no long navigable rivers to create ocean-going harbors. Almost all the surviving early structures are wooden. Still, The Shore, as it is known locally, has an incredible diversity of architectural types. More than four hundred structures predate the Civil War, relatively few retaining their original forms.

A few eighteenth-century structures show the modest, but improving, lifestyle of the colonial period. A 1660 law required a house of at least 12 feet square to claim a piece of land; many houses started out about that size and were enlarged as time passed and farm income permitted. Pear Cottage, a one-story clapboard house near Bridgetown, illustrates the humble beginnings of many later plantations. The "big house, little house, colonnade, kitchen," a series of connected additions of varying size and roof height, is considered a distinctive style of architecture for the Virginia Eastern Shore. The Seymour House in Accomac is a good example.

The great waves of building that occurred with the coming of the railroad after the Civil War left a passel of late nineteenth- and early twentieth-century stores, barns, garages, warehouses, and homes of the kind already beginning to make an appearance in Americana museums. Examples are located at Nassawaddox, Keller, Painter, and elsewhere. A few have been turned into specialty shops, especially for antiques, but many are somewhat dilapidated.

Although most of the historic homes are privately owned, a few are opened each year during Historic Garden Week in Virginia.

Aimless exploration of the side roads that shadow Route 13 through rich farmland or head for the coast can have major rewards in the form of early twentieth-century stores, unheralded early nineteenth-century and Victorian homes, and faded relics of the past. Side roads lead to communities where homespun virtues continue to dominate the way of life; marinas that mix commercial and pleasure craft; wildlife areas that are characterized by diversity; peaceful coves where deep hues of red and yellow obscure the horizon at sunrise and sunset; and easily the most impressive natural phenomenon, the Barrier Islands, which guard the peninsula from an unpredictable ocean.

A map showing all the paved roads can be obtained at the Eastern Shore of Virginia Chamber of Commerce in Accomac, but there is little chance of getting lost even without one. All roads lead, as the old-timers say, to the Bay, the ocean, or the "stone road" (the local name for Route 13 when it was graveled and all other roads were dirt). In some instances, lateral roads reduce the time a detour requires.

The barrier islands in the Atlantic Ocean off the Eastern Shore of Virginia, the area's most important natural feature, literally are both a womb and a tomb. Ninety percent of the fish and shellfish caught in the area depend at some point in their lives on the marshes and tidal flats that lie between the mainland and the islands. The barrier islands also provide physical protection for the mainland from the stormy Atlantic, which has periodically destroyed farms and communities on the islands.

The Virginia and Maryland coastal islands are part of the chain that extends along the East and Gulf Coasts, some of which have been developed into major resort cities like Miami Beach, Atlantic City, and Ocean City. Most of the Virginia-Maryland islands remain largely undeveloped, however, and governments and nonprofit conservation organizations are cooperating in an effort to use them wisely and preserve the natural heritage. All or major portions of thirteen islands are owned by The Nature Conservancy, a national nonprofit conservation organization, which permits limited access to the islands. Wreck Island is a Virginia state park, while Assateague, Assawoman, Mockhorn, and Fisherman's islands are owned by federal agencies. Wallops Island is part of a National and Aeronautics Space Administration station.

Boaters can explore almost the entire chain, if they wish. Ramps and charter boats are available at a number of places on the mainland, but the waters are tricky and guides are advisable (see Appendix). Drivers will find their access more limited; they can drive to Assateague, take a limited-access boat tour from Brownsville near Nassawaddox, and go with rangers on occasion to Fisherman's Island.

Biking is a cross-border activity, with Virginia residents joining border Marylanders in the Salisbury Bicycle Club. Side roads in Virginia pass through beautiful and varied countryside, but they do not have paved shoulders and sometimes are narrow. Light traffic on most of the secondary roads permits safe bicycling.

An informal seaside route runs lateral to U.S. 13 from Route 12 at the Virginia-Maryland border through Modest Town to Accomac, then after a short segment on Highway 13 passes through Accomac on Business 13 and follows Route 605 past white frame Locustville Academy (the only surviving mid-1800 school building on the Eastern Shore, now a museum) to the fishing villages of Wachapreague (via detour on Route 180) and Quinby before moving onto state Route 600 for a run almost to the tip of the peninsula. The comparable Bayside route starts at Arcadia High School near T's Corner (also known as Massey's Corner) and follows a variety of side roads through farmlands and past historic sites at Pungoteague to Machipongo, where the route crosses U.S. 13 to go south on Route 600. These routes also can be divided into shorter segments.

An interesting circular route winds 32 miles on a number of roads from New Church to Jenkins Bridge, past handsome 1860 Emanuel Episcopal Church and sites associated with the Rev. Francis Makemie (who brought Presbyterianism to the United States), to Sanford, and then across the marsh to Saxis and back.

For round-trippers, the rule of thumb is to ride south in the morning and north in the afternoon, to take advantage of prevailing winds.

The extensive forests appeal to hunters, but most areas are privately owned.

The introduction to the Eastern Shore of Virginia starts near the Maryland border. Saxis, west along Route 695, is one of the earliest fishing villages on The Shore, with half a dozen seafood-processing houses, but its influence is far less than it was a century ago. In the nineteenth century, the community was so important that the Methodist "Parson of the Islands" founded one of his churches there. Settled in the seventeenth century and first used for grazing and farming, the island turned to fishing in the latter part of the nineteenth century and has remained true to that calling.

On the oceanside, at the end of Route 679, is the ghost town of Franklin City, breathed into life by arrival of a railroad spur that improved access to the oyster production at Chincoteague Island. A decline in the quantity of oysters and a storm drove away all the citizens, leaving a few rotting hulks to carry on the memory of the short-lived boom town.

Chincoteague Island

Never underestimate the power of a few well-publicized ponies. The annual roundup and sale of wild ponies, begun in 1924 to provide funds for equipment to fight fires, was a modest affair until the novel *Misty of Chincoteague* gave it national exposure in 1947. The formerly relaxed atmosphere on Chincoteague Island has changed drastically since then. Modern hotels and souvenir and specialty shops have replaced many of the modest homes and waterfront areas where watermen sat to talk about their catches.

In late July, when the penning and sale take place for the benefit of the volunteer fire company, thousands of people create a traffic jam on the narrow causeway to the island and crowd the small island community to watch a variety of events. On Wednesday, crowds line the banks and boats filled with photographers dot the inlet as the ponies swim across the inlet between Assateague Island, where they live, and Chincoteague. There they are herded to pens in Memorial Park, where the next few days many of them will be sold at auction. Unsold ponies are herded back to the waterfront on Friday to swim back to Assateague for another year of grazing.

The roundup and auction are only part of the festivities that have developed over the years. A carnival is held every night. Seafood dispensed from open-air grills and pots and specialties such as "pony tails" (taffy) and homemade fudge compete for crowd attention with handmade or plastic souvenirs.

Although the pony penning is Chincoteague's premier event, it is preceded by an Eastern Decoy Carver Festival in early April and the early May Seafood Festival, and followed by an Oyster Festival in early October and Waterfowl Week in late November. These attract smaller crowds.

Outside the tourist season, Chincoteague reflects a workaday existence. Livestock and farming sustain the "beautiful land across the water," as it was known to the Indians. Indeed, the first European residents were herders watching over cattle and horses owned by an absentee Maryland landlord. Today, there is even a miniature pony farm.

Fishing boats tied up in the channel near the trestle to the 7-mile-long island demonstrate Chincoteague's continuing role as a shellfish center. Its oyster and clam shoals, where the special salt oyster is raised, are famous. The Oyster Museum, opened in 1972, has live marine exhibits and an extensive library on aquatic life in addition to its primary concentration on oyster culture.

Of late, Chincoteague has developed a fondness for pleasure boating. Island Sailing Center provides instruction on the use of sailboats and sailboards. Power boats can be rented and charter and head boats fish in the backwaters of the island. Taylor's Wildlife Tours has a seven-hour bottom-fishing expedition, as well as an evening cruise aboard the vessel *Osprey,* which covers the Assateague Channel in 1½ hours. Capt. Rudy Thomas of Tangier Island makes regular runs aboard the *Steven Thomas* between Chincoteague and his home base.

The northern tip of Chincoteague Island, including Wildcat Marsh, is part of the wildlife refuge. Waterfowl hunting is permitted in this area. The Refuge Waterfowl Museum is an introduction into this side of the island community.

Chincoteague was not always so active. Indeed, permanent settlement progressed so slowly that only sixty residents were recorded in the 1800 census. The construction of a lighthouse in the 1830s, development of a seafood industry, and the improvement in social services, including a free school in 1845 and a post office, had raised the population to 1,000 by 1857. Most of today's islanders trace their roots back to those Anglo-Saxon ancestors.

The independent streak in Chincoteague Islanders showed during the Civil War, when they voted not to join the Confederacy but to remain in the Union and maintain their sea trade with the North.

Assateague Island

The route to Chincoteague National Wildlife Refuge on Assateague Island crosses Chincoteague Island, aggravating its summer traffic problems. Visitors eager to see the wild ponies should arrive early in the morning or visit during the off season. The ponies, probably descended from mustangs aboard a wrecked Spanish galleon, prefer to keep their distance when traffic on the road is heavy. A decade ago, when fewer visitors appeared, the ponies grazed close to the road.

Summer is the big season. From mid-June through Labor Day, swimmers, sun worshippers, kite flyers, and surfers crowd a quarter-mile of beachfront at Tom's Cove. Drivers along the main road catch distant glimpses of ponies and deer or closer views of a few resident egrets, herons, and Canada geese searching for food beside pools left by tidal retreat. Isolation is rare, even on the sandy trails that lead through marsh and woods. Rangers direct a wide range of group activities to supplement individual exploration: marsh and beach walks, bike tours, beach campfire programs, and audiovisual presentations and talks on wildlife, wetlands, art, surf rescue, and other subjects.

Surfcasting (no permit required, except at night) is allocated a separate section of beach spring, summer, and fall, with medium to heavy gear recommended for striped bass, bluefish, drum, and sharks. Twice a week, rangers demonstrate casting techniques and the use of bloodworms, crabs, minnows, squid, and lures as bait. Low tides bring out the clam rakers, shoreline crabbers, and oyster seekers, all seeking to reach established minimums. The best time to comb the beaches at Tom's Cove for shells is after a storm.

Wildlife viewing is a year-round activity. More than a hundred species of birds and dozens of land and aquatic animals — ponies, deer, waterfowl, shorebirds, Delmarva fox squirrel, red fox, pelicans, and dolphins among them — are regularly recorded in a log maintained at the Visitors Center. Hikers, boaters, and four-wheel-drive vehicles with permits may invade the habitat of the piping plover at Tom's Cove Hook, but rangers close the section at times during nesting season by erecting cable barriers and signs. In late autumn, the skies and waterways fill with migrating waterfowl: tundra swan, mute swan, Canada goose, snow goose, American black duck, redhead, mallard, northern pintail, northern shoveler, gadwall, bufflehead, canvasback, and scoter are common.

The terrain is typical of a barrier island. The sandy beach is backed by grassy dunes, which in turn give way to myrtle brush and loblolly pines or salt meadows broken by low-lying potholes. From spring through fall, more than eighty kinds of wildflowers bloom, berry, or leaf in the fields, marshes, and forests. Among the most common varieties are mayweed, blue-eyed grass, dog fennel, camphorweed, meadow beauty, arrow arum, salt marsh fleabane, water plantain, climbing hempweed, rose mallow, water pennywort, trumpet creeper, crested yellow orchis, Japanese honeysuckle, and rough bedstraw, the last of which filled mattresses on the beds of many settlers. Less common are astor, chickory, false heather, goldenrod, prickly pear, scarlet pimpernel, bayberry, Virginia creeper, wild grape, and marsh fern.

The wildlife walking trail, which begins near the Visitors Center, includes a boardwalk across a marshy area and a sandy path that passes a waterhole frequented by ducks and sika deer, who bound into nearby trees and underbrush when frightened. A raised platform looks across the flat open space and woods at some of the 100 to 150 ponies on the Virginia portion of Assateague Island. The same area can be viewed by automobile from 3 P.M. to dusk via a circular 13.2-mile road restricted to hikers and bikers at other times.

The 1.6-mile Pony Trail, contrary to its name, does not traverse an area frequented by ponies—except the tame ones that hang out in the parking lot. However, the trail is a pleasant walk or bike ride through a forested area, which demonstrates an environment often described as fragile but that persists despite adverse conditions and human intrusion. The Lighthouse Trail leads through woods to a symbol almost as famous as the ponies. The red and white lighthouse, visible as far away as Tom's Cove, near the southern tip of the island, towers above trees stunted by harsh conditions.

The most isolated section is a 10-mile stretch of beachfront and wash flats that extends north from the developed area of the Chincoteague Refuge into adjacent Assateague Island National Seashore in Maryland. This area is open only to hikers.

A bike trail begins at the town of Chincoteague, passes the Visitors Center, circles the Wildlife Trail, and continues to Tom's Cove. Archery and firearm sika deer hunting serve conservation purposes at Chincoteague, with the archery season in October–November followed by the firearms season through December. Hunters are assigned areas by lottery, and places are set aside for hunters in wheelchairs.

NASA and NOAA

The Wallops Island Flight Facility of the Goddard Space Flight Center has not attracted as much public attention as Cape Canaveral, Florida, and Houston, Texas, but some of the most important scientific flights launched by the National Aeronautics and Space Administration (NASA) have gone aloft from the beachfront pads of the small facility near Chincoteague. Thousands of flights have produced scientific data on the flight characteristics of aircraft, spacecraft, and rocket launchers, meteorological information to assist launches elsewhere, and studies of atmosphere and near space. The story is told Thursday through Monday from 10 A.M. to 4 P.M. at the Visitors Center, just off state Route 175 about 6 miles from U.S. 13.

The *Nike Cajun, Little Joe,* and *Scout* rockets standing in the yard of the Visitors Center have been workhorses at the Wallops facility. The *Cajun,* which can reach out about 90 miles, has been used since 1956. Manually guided flight equipment, some with monkeys on board, was tested on the *Little Joe* rocket. The *Scout,* used to place satellites in Earth orbit, is the largest missile fired from Wallops Island. A four-stage re-entry vehicle used to study phenomena associated with high-speed re-entry also stands outside the center.

The center's introduction to manually guided flight covers the dreamers and doers of aviation, including the first manned flight by the Wright Brothers at Kitty Hawk, North Carolina, on December 17, 1903; the flight of the first real helicopter in 1940; and the first use of a jet-propelled plane, the Heinkel HE178, in 1939. Space flight is represented by a moon rock, space suit, and audiovisuals on sounding rockets and launch vehicles, as well as the assistance given the United States to friendly nations. Ocean physics research produces surface maps, charts water depths and ship channels, and discovers concentrations of plankton and chlorophyll; Wallops manages the NASA balloon program, which involves balloons that expand to as many as 600 feet in diameter after being sent aloft by rocket.

Movies on topical subjects, such as upcoming launches, and scientific advances, such as living in space, are shown in the center's theater. Once each month, youthful visitors may launch model rockets.

Accomac

The town of Accomac must feel like a wallflower. It is all dressed up in its colonial finery, but not many people notice.

The compact town, whose streets present a cross-section of colonial building on the Eastern Shore, invites a walking tour, despite the absence of street signs and markers at the historic buildings. The Seymour House on Business Route 13 south of the courthouse is an excellent example of the "big house, little house, colonnade, and kitchen" style indigenous to the Eastern Shore. The first unit of the elongated, build-as-you-can frame style was erected about 1672, and subsequent enlargements resulted in a house whose segments are of various sizes and with different roof levels.

The Seymour icehouse figured in one of the town's favorite stories. During the Civil War, the Eastern Shore of Virginia was occupied early by Union troops and thus was never physically part of the Confederacy. Union Gen. Henry Lockwood set up his headquarters in Accomac and required the citizens, whose sympathies lay with the South, to take a loyalty oath. In retaliation, some youths captured Gen. Lockwood's son and demanded the son take an oath to the Confederacy. When he refused to do so, he was incarcerated in the Seymour icehouse until the approach of night convinced him that discretion was preferable to valor.

Seven Gables, the oldest remaining residence within the original 10-acre town site, and the Ailworth House also were built in sections, the former beginning in 1788 and the latter in 1795. The Bayly Mansion, sometimes identified as the Rectory, uses two kinds of bricks in its walls and is noted for its handsome interior woodwork. Among other historic buildings are Roseland (1771), The Haven (1794), Woodbridge (1700s), Rural Hill (1816), Drummond Place and The Little House (early 1800s), and The Glade (mid-1840s).

The homes are all private, but some may open during Historic Garden Week in Virginia.

The small Flemish bond brick Debtor's Prison, with one exterior and one interior chimney, is the only surviving element of a sizable walled jail complex. Alterations to the building, constructed in 1783 as a residence for the jailor and converted in 1834 to a prison, have not altered its essential character. One downstairs room is furnished to represent the 1806–1815 period when John Snead was jailor, based on the inventory of his estate. The other downstairs room shows the way debtors were incarcerated. Among the artifacts on display in the loft are a 1781 map of Chesapeake Bay, a bell from the 1756 Accomack County Courthouse, genealogical material, pictures of the walled complex, and a seventeenth-century Indian ceremonial pipe.

The nearby brick Courthouse was constructed in 1899, a worthy successor to the original raised in 1756.

Although St. James Episcopal Church dates from 1838, bricks of the predecessor church built in the 1760s were reused. The once-plain sanctuary has been painted, with columns resembling marble beside the altar.

The founder of the Presbyterian Church in the United States, the Rev. Francis Makemie, is doubly honored in Accomac. A statue of the missionary, who founded a number of congregations on the Delmarva Peninsula, stands behind white frame Makemie Presbyterian Church. The handsome building with fanlights over the door, erected in 1840, houses a congregation that is believed to date back to 1690.

A disastrous fire swept the business section of Accomac in 1921, destroying most of the earlier business buildings. One survivor is the Mercantile Building, constructed around 1816, which is said to have the most beautiful cornices in town. It now houses the Chamber of Commerce.

The town of Accomac did not just happen; it was deliberately created in 1690 because the site was equidistant between the Atlantic Ocean and Chesapeake Bay and was accessible by water via Folly Creek. It was originally named Drummondtown, in honor of Richard Drummond, on whose land the town was established.

Onancock

The patriarch of the largest communities on the Eastern Shore of Virginia, founded in 1680, Onancock puts its best foot forward right at the edge of town. Lined up along state Route 179 (Market Street) are the brown shingled Market Street United Methodist Church, white frame Naomi Makemie Presbyterian Church (named for the wife of the missionary), and light gray frame Holy Trinity Episcopal Church.

Next comes Kerr Place, a secular building that has been described as the architectural "gem" of the region. Built in 1799 for John Shepherd Kerr, a wealthy merchant and landowner, it is far and away the most impressive house on the Virginia Shore that is regularly open to the public. The large red brick Federal-style mansion, set back from the road and not as conspicuous as the churches, exudes affluence, from the superior brickwork to the ornamented interior woodwork. Although the furnishings are not original, they are authentic antiques. Owned by the Eastern Shore of Virginia Historical Society, the mansion is open from Tuesday through Saturday, March through December. Grounds are landscaped by the Garden Club of Virginia.

Not all of Onancock's attention is directed landward and heavenward. Market Street continues past monuments to Confederate General Edmund R. Bagwell (1840–1876) and World War I and II veterans and white frame Cokesbury United Methodist Church, founded in 1784, to the public dock at the head of Onancock Creek, once a terminal for steamboats.

Workboats and pleasure craft share the creek with the *Capt. Eulice,* which sails daily to Tangier Island during the warm months. The 2½-mile trip down the creek passes farmlands, plantation houses, and forests before beginning the trip across the sound to Tangier. The harbor has a boat ramp.

Hopkins & Bro. Store is both the headquarters for the boat cruise and an attraction in its own right. The 125-year-old store, owned by the Association for the Preservation of Virginia Antiquities, uses original equipment and fixtures to operate a quaint county "general store" carrying everything from food to arts and crafts. Tickets for the Tangier Island cruise are sold through the same window in the store office that issued steamboat tickets a century ago. The store's restaurant features local seafood.

Nearby Parkers Marsh Natural Area has no facilities and is so isolated that supervising rangers, located at Seashore State Park in Virginia Beach, usually inspect it from the air. It is accessible only by boat, mostly by offshore fishers.

Harborton-Pungoteague

On U.S. 13 at Keller, a faded sign directing traffic to the ferry landing at Harborton on state Route 180 practically covers the side of an unpainted frame structure on the west side of the highway. It promises access to Richmond, Yorktown, and Williamsburg via Reedville on the Northern Neck.

The sign no longer occupies the corner where it originally stood, but is located a few hundred feet north of the intersection. No matter. The ferry doesn't run anymore anyway.

Still, the short drive to Harborton on state Route 180 may be worthwhile for those who want to see it before it becomes retirement and vacation homes. The small frame tollhouse still stands beside the road, near the long wooden ramp reinforced with metal strips for automobile wheels. Among the older structures is an 1885 house now used as a bed-and-breakfast inn.

The route goes through Pungoteague, site of one of the oldest churches on The Shore. St. George's Episcopal Church dates from 1652.

Wachapreague-Quinby

Wachapreague is all set to photograph the "big ones." A hook over a signboard bearing the oceanside village's name is ready at all times to record catches of fishing parties squired by the twenty-one captains to productive sites in the ocean and sound. Boats like *Foxy Lady, Sea Fox, Nomad, AquaGem, Virnanjo, Margoa, LuLu, Seabird,* and *Scorpio,* which operate from April through November, sometimes bring back whoppers worthy of the photo station—tautog as heavy as 15 or 16 pounds, as well as smaller bass, trout, bluefish, and flounder. A favorite spot is near an underwater wreck about 10 miles offshore.

Wachapreague's waterfront reflects a diversity of interests. Commercial seafood vessels unload their cargoes at processing houses and marine railways haul vessels ashore for maintenance and repairs, including a flatboat that hauls equipment to private property on Cedar Island. Transients may use the slips at Wachapreague Seaside Marina Inc. A small amusement park draws people from the surrounding area.

Quinby, which can be reached from Wachapreague via narrow state Route 605 parallel to U.S. 13 and a bridge across the marshy Machipongo River, is another seafood and boating center. Neat but modest houses stand on roads leading to the harbor and, in another direction, to a housing development. Commercial seafood houses line the shore near the Virginia Game Commission boat-launching ramp.

Off U.S. 13 at Painter, a form of farming new to the Virginia Eastern Shore is taking place at Accomack Vineyards. The farm and vineyards, founded in 1986, may be toured.

Exmore Area

Two miles east of Exmore, a workaday market community established in 1884 by the railroad, the 1840 E. L. Willis and Co. store building still stands where the road bends to follow the waterfront in the community of Willis Wharf. Willis was a ship chandler and store operator who supplied the lifesaving station on Hog Island (one of the barrier islands) and served as postmaster.

New owners, who operate a restaurant, pub, and store, are maintaining the building as close as possible to the condition in which they found it. Much of the woodwork is original and a stage on the second floor, now used as living quarters, may have been used for vaudeville shows in the distant past.

Willis Wharf is a picturesque but thriving small waterfront community with neat houses, the inevitable hull of a sunken boat protruding from a shallow branch of the inlet, and seafood houses lining the waterfront. A large clam-processing firm whose boats dredge Atlantic waters well off the coast shares the shoreline with smaller operators who harvest clams, crabs, and oysters in the waters of the sound between the mainland and the barrier islands and a public marina with launching ramps and boat slips.

Silver Beach, on Chesapeake Bay west of Exmore, represents the kind of modest summer cottage community that preceded the era of affluence. Many of the cottages on a short bluff overlooking the Bay are small and unpretentious—the kind of place where owners can relax in jeans, shorts, and swimsuits away from the fast-paced tempo of city life.

Virginia Coast Reserve

On the south end of Hog Island, the transitory nature of humanity is evident. The site of Broadwater, a 250-resident town flattened by a 1933 storm and not rebuilt, is pocked by the holes of sand fiddler crabs, which scurry underground or into puddles of water as footsteps approach. Marsh grass, groundsel, and scrub trees wave in the perpetual breeze and grow up around fallen tree trunks and the massive iron shafts and tower left behind when a Coast Guard station was abandoned. Along the shoreline are the jumbled timbers of a collapsed lifesaving station and rotting piles that once supported piers. A mud flat, underwater at high tide, cuts across the tip of the island from the tufted sand dunes overlooking the ocean to an old docking area facing Hog Island Sound.

The isolation and dynamism are part of the sensuality of the barrier islands, productive ocean-front sentinels that have watched farmers, herders, pirates, industrial tycoons, and tourists come and go over the centuries. The islands are an important feature of the ecological interaction between Chesapeake Bay and the Atlantic Ocean. The lush salt marshes between the islands and the mainland at some point host most of the seafood harvested on the Virginia Eastern Shore.

The barrier islands have beaches and dunes, which vary in width from 15 to 550 feet, on both ocean and sound sides. Salt marshes dominated by cordgrass adjoin the upland sections of the islands; in a few instances, they are so extensive they connect the islands to the mainland. These are the primary producers of nutrients for estuarine and marine life. Many low areas are inundated at high tide. Behind the beaches are grasslands and scrub thickets and, on the larger islands, forests of loblolly pine, wax myrtle, black cherry, yaupon holly, red cedar, red maple, live oak, and other varieties of trees and bushes and freshwater marshes and ponds.

The mid-Atlantic location of the barrier islands creates an overlap in plant and animal life. They are the northern limits of many southerly occurring plants and animals and the southern limits of many northerly occurring plants and animals. Sea oats, black cherry, and live oak reach their northern limits and bayberry its southern limit on the islands.

Slowly but surely, the islands move under the relentless pounding of ocean waves, high tides, periodic storms, and a gradual sea-level rise. Geologists divide the barrier islands, which stretch the length of Virginia's Eastern Shore coastline and into Maryland, into three groups. The northernmost islands, including Assateague, are migrating westward. Parramore, Hog, and Cob islands are slowly rotating by buildup at their northern ends and shrinkage at their southern tips. Three of the four southernmost islands in the chain, like those at the north, are experiencing parallel beach retreat. Fisherman's Island, at the extreme tip of the Eastern Shore peninsula, has expanded substantially in the last 125 years.

Hog Island, one of the principal islands in the chain, illustrates the dynamic nature of the islands. The north end of the island has broadened to its present 1-mile width and hosts a rookery of egrets, herons, and ibises, while the southern end, which once had a seaside resort hotel and the town of Broadwater, has dwindled from a width of a mile to about 300 yards from soundside to oceanfront.

This island and nine others can be visited by boat on tours conducted by The Nature Conservancy or in private craft. The Conservancy, a conservation organization also involved in research on subjects as varied as piping plover and sunken ships, is the largest landowner in the islands, holding about 40,000 acres of land and productive salt marshes on thirteen islands along 45 miles of coastline. Dedicated to preserving the land and as much else as possible the way nature molds them, the Conservancy is headquartered on a historic 1,400-acre farm, Brownsville, east of Nassawaddox via state Routes 606, 600, and 608. The plantation house, a handsome Federal-style building whose brick section was constructed in 1896 and wood addition was added three years later, is used for special meetings and groups by the Conservancy and sometimes open during Historic Garden Week in Virginia.

The Nature Conservancy organizes about eight natural history and bird-watching field trips and photography workshops each spring and autumn for between 500 and 1,000 people, including some to the "crown jewel" of Parramore Island, whose 21-foot-high Italian Ridge is the highest point in the Conservancy islands; a cruise around Cape Charles to Smith Island for trawling and a walk ashore; a birding excursion to Hog and Cobb islands; and an overnight nature study on Hog Island, where the thirty-year-old former Machipongo Coast Guard Station provides modest, no-telephone, beachfront accommodations.

In addition, Tuesday evening programs at Brownsville (five in 1988) cover topics such as the geology and dynamics of the barrier islands, ground water, sea turtles, mammals, and programs of The Nature Conservancy to protect the environment on the islands and mainland. Seventeen species of reptiles and one amphibian flourish on the reserve, especially on Smith and Hog islands. Hog Island has six of the eight kinds of snakes discovered in the reserve.

The islands, way stations for migratory birds, are ideal for bird-watching. More than 250 species have been seen. In the wintertime, black duck frequent the marshes, snow goose strut on the islands, scoter rest in the surf, and oldsquaw float in the bays. Atlantic brant, pintail, mallard, teal, gadwall, hooded merganser, shoveler, and American wigeon winter on all the islands, while greater snow goose favors Parramore and Assateague. The tidal flats and channels attract scarce peregrine falcon in February and March.

Shorebirds pause in the spring to rebuild their energy by gorging on horseshoe crab eggs before flying on to the Arctic and repeat the stop in the fall, on their return to South America. Knots, dowitchers, and whimbrels have shown the largest counts, but a variety of plovers and sandpipers, including the rare Baird's and curlew, also transit.

Oystercatcher, willet, black skimmer, and seven kinds of tern are common. Large colonies of seagulls, seabirds, and shorebirds — one laughing gull colony has 18,000 birds — breed in the summertime. About a hundred pairs of the threatened piping plover nest there. Metomkin and Ship Shore islands are among the best nesting areas for these birds on the East Coast. Up to 1,500 brown pelican regularly visit. Petrel and shearwaters — offshore birds — are sometimes seen after storms.

Bird colonies should be avoided from mid-April to mid-September, especially in posted areas. Although in-season waterfowl hunting is allowed in the low salt marshes generally behind and west of the islands, the limit of one black duck a day deters many would-be hunters. Retrievers are the only domesticated animals allowed on the reserve.

Sixteen species of land mammals, eleven native, are found on the barrier islands. Despite efforts to remove them, a few feral cattle and sheep remain. Another introduced species, the California jackrabbit, is abundant on Cobb Island. Deer, raccoon, and muskrat are widely dispersed, while gray squirrel, red fox, mink, and otter are found less frequently.

Ten of the thirteen islands are open to individual visitation for nature study, hiking, picnicking, swimming, surf fishing, and photography, but knowledge of the peculiarities of the area is crucial.

The sound is a maze of cordgrass marshes, tidal flats, and twisting, often unmarked tidal creeks, with a range of about 4 feet. The largest body of water, Hog Island Bay, is half the width of Chesapeake Bay, but is so shallow in some places that oystermen harvest by hand. In summer, as many as a hundred fishing boats may be seen at one time on the sound. Stakes and floats mark privately owned oyster beds and crab pots. A few duck hunting stands, successors to the large hunting lodges that industrial tycoons constructed on the islands in the nineteenth and early twentieth centuries, are located in private marshlands. Oyster "rocks" or other impediments that can tear open a hull may lie only a few inches beneath the surface.

The dynamic nature of the area may make maps obsolete quickly. The islands have no usable docks; most landing points are inside the north or south ends of the islands. Boats should be double anchored and far enough offshore to ensure they will remain afloat at low tide.

Weather and sea conditions can change dramatically and suddenly; an otherwise clear, sunny day may produce sudden squalls, rough seas, and strong winds and tides. Boaters also must be alert to heavy rain and fog. Furthermore, there is little traffic in these waters to rescue those who get into trouble or break down.

Watermen in communities such as Wachapreague, Quinby, and Oyster can provide information and may on occasion be willing to take visitors to the islands. Boat ramps are located in those communities and in Modest Town, Gargatha, Parkers Creek, Folly Creek, and Red Bank.

Fishers find flounder, spot, croaker, and sea trout in the sound, while the islands provide good surf catches of channel bass in spring and fall, and black drum in spring. Dolphin and game fish are available in the Atlantic Ocean, while bluefish return to the ocean in the autumn. Sightings of whales, porpoises, and seals are rare.

Hog and Cobb islands, about 12 miles offshore, have former Coast Guard stations. A house on stilts stands off Little Cobb Island; when it was built in the 1920s, it was on the island. Some of the islands have forested interiors, but in general casual visitors should not venture beyond the beaches because the interiors are thickets where chiggers and ticks thrive and swarms of insects are so thick at times that they can be sucked into nostrils.

Except for conducted tours, Parramore Island is off limits to the public. So are Revel's and Ship Shore, the latter because of unexploded bombs left after former use as an Air Force bombing range. Cedar Island is mostly privately owned and is being subdivided, but the developer has donated a large tract to the Fish and Wildlife Service Foundation for a refuge that would include that land, Assawoman Island, and perhaps Metomkin Island, which The Nature Conservancy owns.

Wreck Island, a state park, also is open to day visit by boat.

All the islands were patented in the mid–1600s, principally as grazing areas. The livestock did not go unnoticed by seafarers during times of need; the British Navy took what it needed during the War of 1812. Blackbeard's Cove and Blackbeard's Creek on Smith Island and Rogue Island recall a period when pirates frequented the barrier islands to steal animals, harvest oysters and crabs, keelhaul their boats to make repairs, and, some believe, hide buried treasure. Folktales recall mysterious ships passing through the inlets, and many coastal towns have Blackbeard legends. A few records substantiate the pirate presence, including Blackbeard's use of Parramore Island as a headquarters and the capture of ships offshore. By the end of the seventeenth century, pirates had become such a problem that governors of both Virginia and Maryland stationed lookouts at strategic points such as Parramore and Smith islands.

Treasure, if ever found, has not been publicly acknowledged. Just as invisible are the hulks of numerous shipwrecked vessels that lie under the undulating shallow waters offshore.

The completion of a railroad down the Eastern Shore in the 1880s brought tourism to the islands, principally in the form of hunt clubs and resorts. Smith Island was owned by a company; a resort hotel on Cobb Island was destroyed by a hurricane in 1896. President Grover Cleveland was among those who visited the Broadwater Hotel on Hog Island to shoot shorebirds and ducks and to fish. In the year 1900, Broadwater was the second largest town on the Virginia Eastern Shore, with fifty houses, a school, church, hotel, four stores, and ice cream parlor, as well as a lighthouse and lifesaving station. Lifesaving stations also were established on Smith, Cobb, Parramore, Cedar, Metomkin, and Wallops islands around 1880. The Accomac Club was located on Parramore Island.

The Nature Conservancy also has acquired 6,000 acres of mainland property as part of an ongoing program to restrict use of the shoreline and preserve water quality, thus protecting wildlife and perpetuating the lifestyle of the watermen. The land is sold with restrictive covenants to protect the natural qualities. The organization also works with farmers to achieve the same end and prevent farms from being subdivided for homes.

It enlists volunteers to work on projects such as salvage of the façade of an 1880 lifesaving station, perhaps to be used later in a barrier islands museum, banding birds, and building trails.

Franktown-Church Neck

Nassawaddox isn't Nassawaddox — Franktown is. Well, at least what is presently Franktown was named Nassawaddox when the Quakers settled there in the 1600s. It was renamed Franktown in the late 1700s, apparently to honor the dead son of one of its pioneers, about the same time the community developed around a tavern and stagecoach stop. Nassawaddox was revived as a place name along the railroad tracks in the late 1800s.

Franktown has at least half a dozen homes that are more than a hundred years old, including the 1849 Crystal Palace (made of brick), whose owner remained a bachelor for life after his bride-to-be eloped with another man, and the Bleak House, built about the same time. The earlier nineteenth-century Fisher House was used as a store for a time.

Hungars Episcopal Church, the second oldest church building on Virginia's Eastern Shore, is appropriately located at the northern entrance to the oldest continuously inhabited place on Virginia's Eastern Shore, Bridgetown. The handsome structure, abandoned and periodically vandalized for thirty years, was reopened in 1819 and expertly restored in the 1850s.

Church Neck, where they are located, was already an important area by the 1640s.

Eastville

The county seat of Northampton County knows more about life in early America — the dirty laundry, as well as the tragedies and the historic moments — than anyplace else. Records stashed at Courthouse Square, dating back to 1632, are the longest continuous set in the United States.

Those files confirm the uneven but inexorable development from wilderness settlement to cultural sophistication. For example, the first recorded dramatic performance in the United States shows up in court accounts, when the actors of *The Bear and the Cub* were hauled before a magistrate in 1665 for criticizing the British monarchy.

Eastville is unpretentious, even by Eastern Shore standards. The historical marker in the center of town calls attention not to anything in the community, but to the long-forgotten Gingaskin Indians, whose principal camp was located 3 miles to the east. There is no hype; visitors wishing to visit the eighteenth-century buildings on Courthouse Green, maintained as museums by the Association for the Preservation of Virginia Antiquities (APVA), go to the 1899 Courthouse to obtain a key.

The 1719 Clerk's Office is furnished as it probably was in its formative years, and 1730 Old Courthouse has a small museum with period furniture and local historical artifacts. The crumbling bricks of the Debtor's Prison show its antiquity, although its exact age is in dispute. It may have been constructed in 1644, although some put the date as late as 1814. Monuments on the courthouse lawn honor Confederate soldiers and Indian Chief Debedeavon, the "laughing King of the Accomacks, Emperor of the Eastern Shoare, King of the Great Nussawattocks." Debedeavon saved English settlers by warning them of the Indian Massacre of 1622, which nearly wiped out the Virginia Colony.

Despite their antiquity, the small brick buildings facing Courthouse Green do not fully reveal Eastville's age, which goes back at least to 1677, when it was selected as the county seat.

The oldest surviving home in Eastville is Parke Hall, located next to the Post Office. The larger segment was constructed about 1784 and the smaller phase may be older. Among other historic structures that can be viewed on a walking tour are Eastville Inn (now a restaurant), which dates from 1780; Cessford, built in 1832 and used by Union Gen. Henry Lockwood as his Northampton headquarters during the Civil War; Coventon, circa 1795; and the circa 1845 Westcoat House, originally a store.

Christ Episcopal Church, at the eastern entrance to the town, was built in 1828 to house a congregation that dates back to 1635. The handsome red brick church has a plain interior and beautiful stained-glass windows above the altar and in both side walls.

A portion of the formal garden at Ingleside, built in the early 1800s, remains. This mansion is located east of U.S. 13. Elongated Holly Brook, a few miles north of Eastville on U.S. 13, is furnished with eighteenth-century antiques.

Eyre-Cheriton-Oyster

Eyre Hall, whose gate fronts on U.S. 13 three miles north of Cheriton, is privately owned but semiopen to the public. The formal gardens of boxwood, yews, magnolias, and crepe myrtle are open free of charge year round, while the mansion, built in 1759 and enlarged in 1804 and considered one of the best preserved in Virginia, is traditionally opened during Historic Garden Week. The house, which overlooks Cherrystone Creek, has a large entrance hallway, carved mantelpieces, antique wallpaper, and paintings of generations of the Eyre family. "Morningstar Bowl," among numerous family heirlooms, honors a successful racehorse so prized by his owner that he allowed the animal to drink champagne from the family silver.

Cheriton was one of the communities founded along the railroad tracks in 1884. Holmes Presbyterian Church south of town is older, dating from 1846. Cherrystone Wharf, via state Routes 680 and 663, was a principal ferry-landing point for a hotel, church, several stores, and homes prior to construction of the railroad. Unmarked Cherrystone Tavern dates from the early 1800s, while Huntington was constructed in 1888.

Oyster, on the ocean side at the end of Virginia 639, is one of the most unspoiled fishing villages on The Shore. The harbor stretches out along one side of an inlet where gulls float on the breezes and egrets wade close to shore. The view of the orderly line of piers, docks, and processing houses, with water and marsh grass dominating the opposite shore, has the quality of a fine artistic print. Oyster is primarily a waterman's community, but recreational fishing boats also operate from the harbor.

Cape Charles

The heritage of Cape Charles is simple and uncomplicated. The grid pattern of streets instantly marks the town of 1,500 people as a planned community, while frequent references in literature confirm its origin as a late nineteenth-century railroad town.

Those qualities make a visit to the town simple, but not uncomplicated. It's easy to see the twenty-seven buildings listed in a walking tour brochure, many from the late nineteenth century when farmlands overlooking Chesapeake Bay were chosen as a terminus of the New York, Philadelphia, and Norfolk Railway. Not being able to see the interiors of some of the private homes is a bit frustrating. Equally frustrating is the loss of the landing from which steamboats completed the trip to Norfolk and Old Point Comfort in Hampton.

However, Cape Charles retains the flavor of the city that grew up to service the transportation business. Almost every street has large Victorian houses and sturdy brick churches that reflect the optimism of the era. Located on Tazewell Street are white frame Sea Gate, a colonial revival house with a round-the-corner porch, now a bed-and-breakfast; an 1895 shingle and clapboard house built by a bachelor railroad superintendent but now operated as a bed-and-breakfast named Henrietta's Cottage; and turn-of-the-century Honeysuckle Lodge, built by a minister seeking a healthy climate who commuted each week to his church in New York City.

The people who settled in Cape Charles to build and operate the railroad came from various sections and varied backgrounds. They represented various religious denominations, too. The oldest church structure is St. Stephen's African Methodist Episcopal Church, built in 1885 as Bethany Methodist Church. The sanctuary of red brick St. Charles Roman Catholic Church dates back to 1888, while the rectory and former school came along a few years later. Brick and shingle Trinity United Methodist Church, originally named Centenary Methodist Episcopal Church, was built in 1893, the same year the Episcopalians built Emmanuel Church, with its square tower and flared eaves. The 1901 frame First Presbyterian Church became the Northampton County Memorial Library, honoring local men who died in World War I, when the congregation constructed its present gothic revival building in 1926. Cape Charles Baptist Church, built as a wooden church in 1902, later was veneered with brick.

A few buildings reflect the expansion that continued into the 1930s. The Cape Charles Municipal Building on Mason Avenue, most apparently the current home of the fire department, was built in 1930 in art deco style. A block away is a small colonial "domestic style" service station of the kind built in the 1930s. Another stylish service station stands at the corner of Mason and Fig streets.

Cape Charles continues to look over its shoulder at Chesapeake Bay. The town symbol is the cheery 1921 Pavilion, which stands between the Bay Avenue boardwalk and a sandy public beach. In the summer, band concerts float music over the long coastline. The self-styled drum-fishing capital sponsors an annual fishing contest in May and has two marinas and at least eight captains with charter boats.

Cape Charles celebrated its centennial in 1986, although the first lot in the 136-acre townsite was sold in 1884.

Eastern Shore of Virginia National Wildlife Refuge

More than 2 million people pass two wildlife areas at the tip of the Eastern Shore peninsula each year without paying much attention to them. While they may observe the thick, scrub vegetation, sandy beaches, and calm waters of Fisherman's Island National Wildlife Refuge as they pass over the island to enter or leave the Chesapeake Bay Bridge-Tunnel, the larger Eastern Shore National Wildlife Refuge on the mainland facing the Atlantic Ocean goes largely undetected.

Together, the two reserves occupy a large portion of the tip of the peninsula where Chesapeake Bay enters the Atlantic Ocean and add about 1,400 acres to the space where people can come face to face with wilderness.

The Eastern Shore facility, a former military base located just off Route 13 on state Route 600, is minimally developed for year-round day use. No piers or docks provide ready access to water for fishing or clamming. A small museum, housing decoys, shells, fish and reptile bones, and other representative objects, is open by appointment. An eighteenth-century cemetery is located near observation towers and concrete and steel bunkers occupied by the 16-inch coastal cannon of Fort John Custis during World War II. About two-thirds of the buildings of the Cape Charles Air Force Station, which closed in 1980, are boarded up and not open to visitors.

A half-mile walking trail follows an old road between a cultivated field and woods thick with tangled underbrush, then divides. One arm climbs wooden stairs 60 feet to the top of an old concrete bunker, where a platform looks out across pristine forest and marshes with meandering streams to the modern Cape Charles lighthouse and Magothy Bay. The other leads to an overlook on the edge of the marsh. From the divide, the main trail continues past locusts and other hardwood trees heavily hung with vines and the gaping port of one of the artillery bunkers before passing through a bunker to the roadway near the parking lot. The roads also may be used for hiking and biking.

Bird-watching is best in the autumn when the greatest concentrations of migratory waterbirds occur, especially canvasback duck, Atlantic brant, geese and swan, and shorebirds. Piping plover, peregrine falcon, brown pelican, and osprey also visit and nest on the refuges. Game watchers may spot deer and small animals such as raccoon and mink, but hunting is not permitted. A parcel of nearby county land is open during regular seasons.

Rangers conduct natural history trips to Fisherman's Island and other sites for groups of fifteen to thirty-five people. Fisherman's Island is accessible only when accompanied by refuge rangers.

The intracoastal waterway passes near the park and into Magothy Bay near the tip of the Eastern Shore.

A bird-banding station at Kiptopeke, a few miles away on the Chesapeake Bay side, is visited by more than 150 different species of passerines. As many as a hundred red-headed woodpeckers, rare for the area, have been seen in a single day. The equally rare Swainson's thrush is spotted in smaller numbers. Western birds such as the black-headed grosbeak and western kingbird occasionally stop there, perhaps 2,500 miles from their normal migratory route. About 35 warblers come through, especially the yellow-rumped warbler

(2,000 to 6,000 are banded every year), American redstart, and common yellowthroat. Counts normally include five species of thrushes, seven or eight of flycatchers, and ten or twelve of sparrows. In addition, the area is well known for peregrine falcon.

Chesapeake Bay Bridge-Tunnel

From its first settlement in 1616 to 1964, the Eastern Shore depended on water transportation for its contacts with the Virginia mainland. Private craft were replaced in the nineteenth century by steamboats. The miniature ocean voyage across the mouth of the Bay was relaxing and picturesque, but did not dissolve the mental image of separation that persisted in the minds of both Shore dwellers and mainlanders. All that ended in 1964 when the 17.6-mile Chesapeake Bay Bridge-Tunnel opened, after construction that lasted 3½ years.

The bridge was not an instant financial success, but the secondary effects were astonishing. Especially after it was widened to four lanes, Route 13 became a more desirable north–south highway for tourists. Seafood and farm products flowed south from the Shore, as well as north.

The bridge-tunnel over water ranging in depth from 25 to 100 feet itself became a celebrity. It was chosen as the "outstanding engineering achievement of 1965" by the American Society of Civil Engineers. It made headlines when ocean-going vessels broke their moorings during storms and crashed into portions of the 12 miles of trestle that connect two tunnels and two high bridges.

This is a restful drive. As vehicle tires thump rhythmically across concrete joints, a spectacular panorama unfolds. Going south, the trestle leaves Wise Point and crosses Fisherman Island, a wildlife refuge that nature continues to expand. The flat island is covered with tangled brush, a few trees, and marsh grass and has inaccessible sandy beaches in some places. Sometimes in the early morning or at dusk, deer may be seen grazing, their heads rising frequently to listen.

The first panoramic view is from the bridge over Fisherman Inlet, an important water route for fishing and pleasure boats, but the bridge over North Channel has the most spectacular outlook. Water stretches for miles on both sides and, ahead, the interrupted sweep of the bridge-tunnel moves to the uneven skyline of Virginia Beach. The view from the lower trestle is less spectacular, but not without interest. The entire ride is especially beautiful at sunset, when thin cloud layers bathe the sky and even the contrails of high-flying jets in pink.

A restaurant-gift shop and the Sea Gull Fishing Pier on the artificial island at Thimble Shoals Channel, 3½ miles off Virginia Beach, attempts to resurrect some of the relaxing atmosphere of former ferry rides. The rest area overlooks one of the world's busiest ship channels; there is a flurry of talk and a rush to the railings when a supercarrier or other large naval or merchant vessel passes. In warm months, the 625-foot pier is crowded with people dropping hooks deep into Bay waters in search of bluefish, sea trout, croaker, bass, flounder, spot, and other species. The area is also a good place to watch the undulation of the waves, the persistence of the gulls, the patience of people fishing in nearby boats, and the activity of power and sail boaters.

The facility is open year round, but is closed to traffic during severe ocean storms.

Hampton Roads

ACTUALLY, HAMPTON ROADS IS A BODY OF WATER, AN ILL-DEFINED AREA that begins at the Willoughby Spit and extends into the mouth of the broad James River. It has been called the world's greatest natural harbor. Customarily, the descriptive also is used to identify the metroplex adjacent to it, including the cities of Norfolk, Virginia Beach, Portsmouth, Chesapeake, Hampton, Newport News, and Williamsburg. Oriented toward this area is the city of Suffolk.

The region claims historical primacy, as the locale of the first permanent European settlement in the United States—the Jamestown colony on an island on the northern bank of the James River. This site is now part of the Historic Triangle, which also includes the colonial state capital of Williamsburg, an intellectual center of the national independence movement, and Yorktown, where the defeat of Lord Cornwallis confirmed independence.

The region's subsequent historical importance has been spasmodic. The world's first naval battle between ironclads occurred during the Civil War, when the *C.S.S. Virginia* and the *U.S.S. Monitor* fought

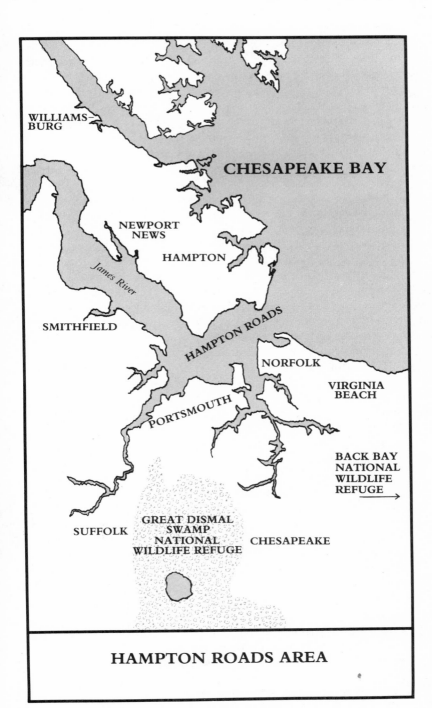

WILLIAMS-
BURG

CHESAPEAKE BAY

NEWPORT
NEWS

HAMPTON

James River

HAMPTON ROADS

SMITHFIELD

NORFOLK

VIRGINIA
BEACH

PORTSMOUTH

BACK BAY
NATIONAL
WILDLIFE
REFUGE
→

SUFFOLK

GREAT DISMAL
SWAMP
NATIONAL
WILDLIFE REFUGE

CHESAPEAKE

HAMPTON ROADS AREA

to a draw. The region nurtured early flight pioneers and demonstrated the usefulness of air power in naval warfare. The first baby steps of the U.S. space program were taken in Hampton.

Hampton Roads, which stands at the lower end of the scimitar-shaped municipal corridor fast developing along the East Coast southward from New York, is one of the two most populous areas in Virginia. Population and development in the region have been enormous since World War II. Five of the cities now cover the territories of former counties.

Hampton Roads is visibly industrial and commercial. Three of its cities have ports where vessels flying the flags of all maritime nations tie up to discharge and take on container and bulk cargo. Although operations at the coal piers in Newport News and Norfolk have slowed, not so many years ago Newport News loaded more coal than any other port in the world and Norfolk was not far behind. Shipbuilding is a major industry; the Newport News shipyard is the nation's largest privately owned shipyard and Virginia's largest single employer. The century-plus-old Norfolk Shipyard is the largest of twenty small shipyards in the area. In addition, the Norfolk Navy Yard handles major overhauls and repairs.

The nation's largest concentration of military bases is at Hampton Roads. Every major community has some facility; various branches of the U.S. Army, Navy, Air Force, and Coast Guard are represented. About 110,000 active military personnel are located within a fifty-mile radius of Hampton Roads; another 250,000 civilians, retired military personnel, and related people live in that area. The Langley Laboratory at Hampton is one of NASA's most important facilities.

It is surprising to find, in this municipal complex, some of the least developed and, consequently, least used wilderness areas in the state. False Cape State Park in the city of Virginia Beach is the most isolated mainland preserve in the Chesapeake Bay region. No highway touches it; visitors arrive only on foot or bicycle or by boat. Dismal Swamp National Wildlife Refuge, which has been commercially exploited since the 1600s, is reverting to the unusual wilderness that surprised and delighted early settlers and seamen. Old roads and canals built by loggers extend through most areas of the park, but can be used only by hikers and bikers.

It is also surprising to discover a lifestyle that is, to a considerable degree, outdoors oriented. The wilderness that challenged the first settlers continues to attract their descendents and the influx of newcomers. Boating is as much a passion as an avocation, and those who do not fish for a living do so for pleasure. People fish not only from boats, but also from bridges and shorelines. The design of minor bridges may well be influenced by whether citizens customarily fish from it, as was done in the Phoebus section of Hampton. Canoeists favor tributaries such as the James and the Chickahominy. Hunting is less common today than formerly, but still important.

Even on the hottest of weekends, bikers take to the byways on jaunts of 80 or 90 miles. While confirmed hikers sometimes head for the hills in western Virginia, others are satisfied with the trails that exist in parks and along the byways of the area.

Locally, the region is divided into two segments — the south side of Hampton Roads and the Virginia Peninsula. However, in recent years, an effort has been made to combine the principal attractions of the cities on organized tours and to promote the area as a unit. I-64 and U.S. Route 17 cut across the region and U.S. 13, via the Chesapeake Bay Bridge-Tunnel, traverses the southside section. Hampton Roads has major airports at Norfolk and Newport News and Amtrak train service.

South Side of Hampton Roads

Norfolk

Convention and Visitors Bureau, Monticello Arcade, Norfolk, VA 23510. Tel.: 804/441-5266.

NORFOLK ONCE HAD A REPUTATION AS A LUSTY, SOME MIGHT SAY BAWDY, U.S. Navy town. Novelists still search for material in the vanished houses along Fenchurch and nearby streets. Old timers remember when the windows of many stores were filled with uniforms and accessories. There is no denying the past, but there was always a gentler side to the brassy city. The old Monticello Hotel was a community center for everything from wedding and New Year's parties to conventions. The Center Theater was one of the few places in the Hampton Roads area where class entertainment could be found.

For the past two decades, Norfolk has tried hard to change its image. Not because it dislikes the U.S. Navy; it doesn't. The Norfolk Naval Station, the world's largest naval facility, and other naval bases provide a solid foundation for the local economy. Norfolk is the headquarters of the North Atlantic Treaty Organization (NATO) Atlantic Command; the Oceana Naval Air Station and Little Creek Amphibious Base are among other major installations.

Norfolk simply wants people to understand that it has a long and honorable history and personality independent of the U.S. Navy. The effort has been aided by events. The community has simply outgrown a single symbol and has invested millions in transforming whole areas, including the downtown section, into planned commercial centers where walking and shopping are a pleasure. The Waterside complex is a focal point along the city's long waterfront, where buildings are substantial, not the aluminum and glass towers that customarily populate redeveloped centers.

Norfolk's commercialization is historic and thus compatible with the overlay of history that has survived a turbulent past. The well-preserved early homes in the downtown area were constructed by prosperous merchants and seamen, who also helped finance the historic churches.

Much of the flavor that identified "old" Norfolk has gone the way of redevelopment, but vestiges have been rehabilitated. The most striking is the prestigious downtown Ghent section, once a run-down neighborhood, where many of the late nineteenth- and early twentieth-century homes have been carefully restored and renovated by young adults and people associated with the nearby medical school. Landscaping and new but compatible structures add to the days-gone-by charm of the area. Wooded Stockley Gardens is the setting for the Mother's Day weekend Ghent Arts Festival, which raises funds for the Norfolk Free Clinic. The Naro Theater shows classic movies. Dozens of trendy but mostly small restaurants for all tastes are located in a three-block section of Ghent. On weekends, people stroll the street until they find a restaurant with empty tables.

Salvage architecture also is featured at Knickerbocker Square, College Place, and Boush Street, where fascinating store fronts hide incomprehensible inventories of antiques and collectibles ranging from Victorian bric-a-brac to old park benches.

Norfolk has never received the recognition it deserves as a major educational center. Old Dominion University, sited in an upscale residential area not far from water, is one of the largest in Virginia. The largely urban university recognizes the community's long association with the water through research and study programs. Norfolk State University, the oldest in the city, has the most beautiful campus. The relatively new Eastern Virginia Medical School has achieved international status through its work on *in vitro* pregnancies. The Armed Forces Staff College also is located in Norfolk.

Norfolk is the largest transportation hub in Hampton Roads. It is the largest port in the unified Virginia port system. It is the headquarters of Norfolk Southern Railway, whose steel veins stretch almost half-way across the continent. Norfolk International Airport is the largest in Hampton Roads.

Transiting Norfolk is much easier on weekends, but driving on working days is more time consuming than frustrating. Interstate 64 cuts north–south through the city and intersects with a number of multilane east–west highways that provide access to all parts of the community and lead, via I-264, to Portsmouth and state Route 44 (toll) to Virginia Beach. These highways are heavily traveled, but need be avoided only during weekday rush hours or when an accident occurs on one of them. State Highway Department radio signals are weak, but warn wary motorists of traffic jams. Local radio stations also perform the same service.

A number of parking lots and the downtown attractions are linked by a free shuttle bus, easily identified because it resembles an old-fashioned trolley on wheels, and efforts are made to accommodate short-term parkers. The parking garage at Scope Convention Center is usable when conventions and entertainment programs are not going on.

Visitors who listen to local radio sometimes are confused by frequent references to "corners" and "circles" — Ward's Corner, Military Circle (neither a circle nor military), and Landsdale Circle (once a traffic circle, but no more). These local reference points have no significant meaning for visitors.

Norfolk Tour: Designed as a circular driving tour of ten principal historic and esthetic attractions that can be started at any point, the Norfolk Tour is best approached by a combination of walking, public transportation, and driving.

Four of the attractions — the Douglas MacArthur Memorial, St. Paul's Episcopal Church, and the Moses Myers and Willoughby-Baylor houses — are within walking distance of each other in the downtown area. An easy way to approach the downtown segment from April through October is to park at The Waterside parking garage and take the Trolley Tour, which passes each downtown attraction about every 45 minutes. Riders can get on and off at will.

Outlying attractions—Chrysler Museum, Norfolk Botanical Gardens (better known as the Azalea Gardens, because more than 200,000 azaleas are planted there), the Adam Thoroughgood House (actually in Virginia Beach), Hermitage Foundation Museum, Lafayette Zoological Park, and Norfolk Naval Station (usually referred to as a "base" rather than a station and sometimes just by the obsolete acronym NOB) are best reached by driving, and each has parking facilities.

General of the Army Douglas MacArthur, World War II Pacific and Korean War commander, would have been born in Norfolk had he not arrived prematurely. That makes the city an appropriate site for the multifaceted memorial that stands on City Hall Avenue. Four buildings face the fountains and flowers on MacArthur Square, across from a parking lot that can be used when walking the downtown area. In the theater, a 22-minute compilation of newsreel clips from his life and era and a few displays provide an introduction to the memorial building, the neoclassical 1847 former City Hall.

General MacArthur is entombed under the dome, surrounded by standards of the units he commanded, the names of the battles in which he participated, some of his famous sayings, and a chronology of his life. In a nearby room are the slouched khaki hat, sunglasses, and corncob pipe that were part of his public image and the numerous medals he received from the United States and other grateful nations around the world.

Uniforms and his five-star limousine also are on display in the eleven galleries devoted to his life. Striking photographs, murals, and beautiful and exotic relics vividly depict his long military career, from West Point through the trench warfare of World War I to the island-hopping strategy of World War II and the heartbreak of the Korean War. Gifts from world leaders include samurai armor suits, a lacquer desk from the emperor of Japan, a pair of huge cloisonné vases from the people of Japan, and silver items. Salt and pepper shaker sets collected by his wife also are on display.

The separate Library and Archives houses more than 2 million documents and books, including war records, correspondence, and reports. The memorial is open from 10 A.M. to 5 P.M. Monday–Saturday, 11 A.M. to 5 P.M. Sunday, except on major holidays. The library and archives are open weekdays from 8:30 A.M. to 5 P.M., except holidays.

A two-block walk on City Hall Avenue leads to St. Paul's Church for a look at the cannonball embedded in the east wall. The 1739 church, which survived the destruction of the city during the Revolutionary War, opens at 11 A.M. on Tuesdays, 10 A.M. Wednesday–Saturday, 2 P.M. Sunday (except holidays), and closes at 4:30 P.M. each day. From noon to 2 P.M. weekdays, mid-June through the first week in July, the historic walls of the church resound to the music of rock bands, string quartets, and folk musicians as part of the Festival in the Churchyard.

Cumberland Street, adjacent to the church parking lot, leads to the modest 1794 Willoughby-Baylor House, built by a sea captain, and the 1792 Moses Myers House, a block away at the corner of East Freemason and Bank streets. The Willoughby-Baylor House, built by Capt. William Willoughby, is distinguished by an English herb garden and eighteenth-century antique furnishings. The Myers House, a superior example of Federal architecture, was built by one of America's first millionaire merchants and has spacious rooms with high ceilings. Most of the furnishings owned by Moses Myers when he hosted President James Monroe, including an eighteenth-century pianoforte and a volume of eighteenth-century music, are still in the house, along with other antiques that show the lifestyle of wealthy Americans after the Revolution.

These houses open at 10 A.M. Tuesday–Saturday and noon on Sunday, and close at 5 P.M., April through November; noon to 5 P.M. on the same days the rest of the year, except major holidays.

Bank Street continues north to Chrysler Theatre and Scope, a modern, gently sloping domed structure with buttresses that can be viewed up close from its esplanade. Four blocks west on Bute Street and one south on Duke Street is the Hunter House/Victorian Museum on the edge of Freemason Historic Neighborhood and the 1791 Taylor-Whittle House at Duke and West Freemason streets, which now houses the Norfolk Academy of Medicine.

Duke Street curves into Boush Street, which runs to Town Point Park and Waterside, a shopping and entertainment complex of more than 120 shops, restaurants, kiosks, and pushcarts. The brick promenade that follows the curve of the Elizabethan River is a good vantage point for watching activity on the river. Waterside Drive and Commercial Place, with modern high-rise buildings on both sides, return to the MacArthur Memorial.

The Chrysler Museum, at Olney Road and Virginia Beach Boulevard on the fringe of the downtown area and facing an inlet known as The Hague, is one of Virginia's most outstanding art museums, with 30,000 pieces from Egyptian artifacts to contemporary painting and photography in its permanent collection. Started in 1933, it was chosen in 1971 by Walter P. Chrysler, Jr., to house his extensive art collection.

Paintings and sculptures are arranged chronologically. Major European and American artists, ranging from Tintoretto and Rubens to Pablo Picasso and Roy Lichtenstein, are represented. Ancient Persian and Roman vessels and examples of Greek and Asian art are among the artifacts from ancient cultures. Pre-Columbian votives and household relics also are on display. The museum has one of the most comprehensive glass collections in the United States, with works by Tiffany, Sandwich, and French Art Glass included. The museum is open daily from 10 A.M. to 4 P.M. Tuesday through Saturday, 11 A.M. to 5 P.M. Sunday. Lectures, movies, and concerts are held periodically.

Drive next along Hampton Boulevard to the Naval Tour Office outside Gate 2 of the Norfolk Naval Base (buses also leave from Waterside daily April–October) to take a 55-minute guided bus tour that passes docked vessels being rested and resupplied. The station is home port to 135 vessels of the Atlantic and Mediterranean fleets and to 38 shipboard aircraft squadrons, and the supply center for sixty-five shore-based facilities. The tour runs daily from 10:30 A.M. to 2:30 P.M. from mid-April through October. Two ships are open for visits from 1 P.M. to 4 P.M. on weekends year round.

The Hampton Roads Naval Museum, which uses ship models, art, photographs, and artifacts to relate the Hampton Roads naval history, occupies the Pennsylvania Building on the base. Enter through the tour office between 9 A.M. and 5 P.M. Monday–Friday, 9 A.M. to 4 P.M. Saturday, and 10 A.M. to 4 P.M. Sunday.

The spacious, landscaped lawn of the Hermitage Foundation Museum at 7637 North Shore Boulevard overlooks the Lafayette River, a major recreational boatway in the city. The paneled interior of the elegant mansion is noted for its collection of Asian art, including T'ang Dynasty tomb figures, jade, cloisonné, and ceramics, but also has excellent examples of antique furnishings, sculptures in ivory, wood, and bronze, and valuable paintings and tapestries. Open 10 A.M. to 5 P.M., Monday–Saturday, 1 to 5 P.M. Sunday, except Thanksgiving and Christmas and New Year's days.

Both the 55-acre zoo and the 175-acre botanical gardens are centrally located, near the airport.

The zoo is a hands-on, hands-off affair, where children can pet farm animals such as sheep and admire from a distance white rhinos and other wild animals in simulated natural surroundings. The park is open daily year round, and early arrivals get a break — from 10 A.M., the opening hour, to 11 A.M. entry is free. The park, which overlooks the Lafayette River, closes at 5 P.M., except on weekends and holidays May 1–October 1 when it remains open until 6 P.M.

The botanical gardens, begun in 1936 as a WPA project, provide only partial aural relief because jetway noises from the adjacent airport float over the grounds. However, the 200 varieties of azaleas, 700 varieties of camellias, 250 varieties of roses, dogwood, laurel, holly, tulips, and rhododendron, and the greenery of bushes and evergreens and the changing colors of the trees compensate for the pressure on the eardrums. The entrance road passes an island fishing area and crosses Lake Whitehurst on a causeway, then transits a forested area to the information center. Tours leave from that point.

The most romantic way to see the gardens is in a slow-moving canal boat, which during the warm months passes many of the large flower beds and natural areas. Walking the meandering paths, resting occasionally on benches, is the way to commune closely with nature and to climb the observation tower for a bluebird's view of the nearby section of the park. A fragrance and sunken garden has braille markers for the blind and facilities for other handicapped people.

During the warm months, a trackless train makes a 30-minute narrated journey past units featuring specific plants, starting with camellias and hollies. The International Azalea Festival queen, chosen each year from a different NATO country, is crowned in late April among the azalea blossoms and flowering dogwood of the Renaissance Garden. Among other theme areas are rose, Japanese, lone pine, desert, and colonial plots. Eleven sculptures in Carrera marble by Sir Moses Ezekiel, a native of Virginia, are featured in the Statuary Vista, which is bordered by tulip magnolia, windmill palm, Kwazan cherry trees, and photinia shrubs. The drive also passes a 200-year-old statue of an American eagle; a 45-year-old redwood; Japanese red maple; the cattails, iris, pickerel weed, and duckweed of the Bog Garden, a Civil War prisoner of war camp; a 200-year-old white oak, the oldest tree in the gardens; more than 17 acres of flowering trees; and a wildflower garden.

There are always some plants in bloom, regardless of the time of year. In the autumn, the park provides a safe and convenient way to watch the rich yellows, reds, and bronzes of hickory, oaks, dog-woods, and other trees.

Paths through the woods lead to the shoreline of Lake White-hurst, where a pier for viewing and fishing extends over the marsh grasses. The gardens are open from 8:30 A.M. to sunset daily year round.

The Norfolk Tour cannot include everything, of course. The city's most prized possession, the Norfolk Mace, is on display in the lobby of Sovran Center on Main Street during regular banking hours. The elaborately adorned, silver mace was given to the city in 1763 by Governor Robert Dinwiddie on behalf of the king as a symbol of authority as a city. Fort Norfolk overlooking the Elizabeth River at the foot of Colley Avenue, now an Army Corps of Engineers headquarters, is best seen from the Harbor Tour.

All the downtown buildings, including historic homes, are lighted during the Christmas season and the ships at the naval base compete for the best decorations. The Myers House decorates for Hannukah. A special tour of the holiday lights operates at 6 nightly from December 15 through New Year's Eve.

The 10,000-meter Elizabeth River Run is held in early May.

Signed bike routes are nonexistent, but knowledgeable riders still use a former 13.6-mile trail known as Ghent Way.

Norfolk-by-the-Sea: The easiest and cheapest way to take a water trip is to catch the ferry that shuttles back and forth across the Elizabeth River between Norfolk's Waterside complex and Ports-mouth's Portside. Both esplanades have exceptional views of the heavy commercial and lighter recreational use of the waterway. The short crossing aboard an ersatz paddlewheel steamboat is a pleasant diversion, which many locals take just for the ride and to visit Ports-mouth's delightful waterfront area.

Longer harbor and sunset cruises of the river and Hampton Roads are available during the warm months. A 90-minute cruise aboard the *Carrie B.*, a small replica of a nineteenth-century Mississippi river-boat, sails upriver past the large vessels undergoing repairs and renovation in the Norfolk Shipyard and naval vessels being worked on at the Norfolk Naval Yard, then turns to pass in close proximity to moored nuclear submarines, aircraft carriers, and other vessels at the Norfolk Naval Yard and the home of the Cousteau Society's ocean-exploring vessel *Calypso*. The vessel departs the historic Dun-more Docks at noon and 2 P.M. daily from April 15 through May 31 and after Labor Day through October; 10 A.M. (except Saturday and Sunday), 12:15 P.M., 2:15 P.M., and 4:15 P.M. daily from June 1 through Labor Day.

The larger *New Spirit* makes a more thorough, 2½-hour tour of the river and nearby Hampton Roads. It departs daily at 1 P.M. Memorial Day through Labor Day, except on Monday.

The *American Rover,* a handsome three-masted sailing ship modeled after nineteenth-century Chesapeake Bay schooners, is a way to experience authentic Bay sailing. The 135-foot schooner moves past ocean-going vessels anchored off Norfolk to pass over the tunnel and pick up the wind as it enters the Bay. It then sails past historic Fort Monroe and Fort Wool and isolated Grandview (see section on Hampton, below) before returning. The tan sails that have become a trademark of the vessel were an accident; the Hong Kong company from which white sails were ordered sent the tan sheets instead. The vessel departs from Waterside twice daily from Memorial Day through Labor Day.

Skills of the kind that built the *Rover* still may be observed at the Norfolk School of Boatbuilding. Sailboats, sea chests, and half models are on display from 9 A.M. to 3:30 P.M. Monday–Friday.

The Ocean View area was until a few years ago a separate city. It faces both Chesapeake and Willoughby bays, and each side has its own personality.

Ocean View's most famous Bayside attraction, a roller coaster at the intersection of East Ocean View Avenue and Tidewater Drive, is gone. When it became too old to be repaired, it was dynamited in making the movie *Roller Coaster.* The site currently is a public beach, but various other uses have been discussed. Sarah Constant Shrine Beach, near the intersection of I–64 and U.S. 60, has a cluster of trees shading picnic tables on the approach to the sandy beach. Offshore, the future of naval aviation was confirmed by the first successful flight from a flat-decked ship. Elsewhere, private cottages and motels provide access to a long, sandy beach whose modest waves attract swimmers, casual surfers, fishers, sailboaters, and motorboaters.

Willoughby Bay's shoreline is popular with sunfish sailers and small boaters. Deep-sea fishing parties leave from a marina that rents slips to transients and has one of the three fishing piers at Ocean View. The Norfolk Parks and Recreation Department maintains five boat ramps—on Willoughby Bay at the end of 13th Street, at Lafayette City Park, on Delaware Avenue at the Lafayette Boat Club, at the end of Merrimac Avenue on the eastern branch of the Elizabeth River, and on 44th Street.

Just off U.S. Route 13, two miles south of the Chesapeake Bay Bridge-Tunnel, Lakes Whitehurst and Smith together provide more than 420 acres of freshwater fishing.

Harborfest in mid-June differs markedly from the sedate Azalea and Ghent festivals. It is purely and simply an opportunity to have waterfront fun. Tall ships welcome visitors on board, while sailboats race, motorboats parade, "pirate" ships engage in mock battles, and waterskiers show off their skills. Spectators consume thousands of pounds of steamed crabs, clams, shrimp, lobster, corn on the cob, and hushpuppies; dance; and listen to entertainers before a fireworks display climaxes the four-day event. An international in-the-water boat show occurs in late September.

Portsmouth

Visitor Information Center, Portside 23704. Tel.: 804/393-5111.

The Elizabeth River, which separates Portsmouth from Norfolk, is a commercial river. The sound of hammers ringing on metal and the voices that float across the river from the Naval Yard reinforce the impression created by moving tugs and anchored naval vessels.

The impression is diffused by other sights and sounds. A motor-powered rubber launch, puny compared to the vessels being worked on, emerges from the Portside harbor. Speedboats create long wakes as they race past both the plodding tugs and the anchored ships. In the distance, the ferry boat leaves Norfolk's Waterside and, minute by minute, grows perceptibly larger as it drives toward Portside. When it docks in the harbor, it disgorges dozens of passengers in shorts onto a tastefully redeveloped waterfront that features a Visitors Center, Olde Harbour Market filled mostly with food places, motel and new apartments, waterside promenades, and two museums. On weekends, musical and dance groups perform on the outdoor stage.

These contradictory impressions are historically appropriate. The diverse Olde Towne historic area, which occupies more than a dozen blocks adjacent to Portside, confirms the many changes that have taken place since the city was founded in 1752 by Col. William Crawford. This historic area claims more houses on the National Register of Historic Places than any other Virginia city and more old houses (most are private residences) than any city between Alexandria, across the Potomac River from the nation's capital, and Charleston, South Carolina.

Hampton Roads tour boat Carrie B, *docked at Portsmouth, Virginia.* PHOTO
BY JOHN BOWEN.

A 45-minute narrated trackless trolley tour titillates passengers
with colorful tales associated with the old buildings — ghost stories
that include a pair of pit bull terriers and the personal idiosyncrasies
of the owners among them. The Murder (Pass) House got its name
from the Murdaugh family, not a killing. A cockfighting pit was
discovered during restoration of the house at 218–220 London Street,
which was originally a tavern catering to sailors. A number of structures were pressed into military service during the Civil War, including the 1846 home at 423 London Boulevard, which was a
hospital, and the 1859 classic revival home at 315 Court Street,
designed by Pierre L'Enfant, which was used as headquarters by
Union Gen. Benjamin Butler during the occupation of Portsmouth.

Even those who take the tour will want to return on foot for a
closer look at some of the forty-four buildings listed on a self-guided
tour and to visit buildings open to the public. The area can be easily
walked in an hour or two, starting with the Lafayette Arch on
Crawford Street, a Bicentennial reconstruction of one erected in 1824
when the marquis visited the city.

The Portsmouth Historical Society shows the original antique furnishings of the Hill family on conducted tours of the four-story Hill
House on North Street, built in the early 1800s, Tuesday through

Saturday afternoons. The circa 1790 Hartt House on Court Street may be the oldest home in Portsmouth still in its original state, while the corner 1841 Pass House has identical porches fronting on both Crawford Street and London Boulevard. The late eighteenth-century Brown-McMurran House on Washington Street originally was a farmhouse, while the politically prominent Watts family, whose 1799 Federal-style home now stands at the intersection of North and Dinwiddie, hosted both President Andrew Jackson and Sauk Indian warrior Black Hawk.

The Victorian era also is present in the area. The romanesque revival house at 329 North Street, built in 1892, recalls the flamboyance of an era that added turrets and ornate façades, some with gold ornamentation, to residences.

Trinity Episcopal Church, built in 1762, is the only surviving structure on Towne Square, the center of the original city. The 1846 Doric-columned Courthouse contains the Portsmouth Fine Arts Gallery and Children's Museum, where hands-on exhibits range from a simulated ride on a police motorcycle to mirrors that change the shapes of objects. Next door is the Virginia Sports Hall of Fame, where Virginians from pro football stars to local heroes are recognized by memorials and artifacts, such as Green Bay Packer Star Henry Jordan's game jersey and medals won by horsewoman Jean McLean Davis.

Two additional museums are adjacent to Portside. The landlocked lightship Charles, which guided passing ships at five sites for 48 years after its commissioning in 1915, is now a museum demonstrating the lifestyle of those who served on board, as well as their equipment. The nearby Portsmouth Naval Shipyard Museum details the progress of naval ship construction from the nation's inception to modern times and houses an extensive collection of ship models (including the *C.S.S. Virginia,* which engaged in the first duel of ironclads), uniforms, flags, weapons, and a model of the city in 1767.

Portsmouth's largest park is physically located in the adjacent city of Suffolk. The Sleepy Hole complex, off Route 17 on Bennett Pasture Road (state Route 627), includes a golf course, the Victorian-style home of the founder of the Planters Peanut Company, Amadeo Obici, and a city-operated park with twenty campsites, pond for fishing stocked with bream, largemouth bass, and catfish, and nature trails through the tidal marsh around the park, including one for handicapped people.

Virginia Beach

Visitors Center, 1000-19th Street, Virginia Beach, VA 23451.
Tel.: 804/428-8000.

Virginia Beach has a split personality. This results from the merger of the resort city with adjacent and rapidly developing Princess Anne County. The consolidation did not remove the differences of style and substance. The free-wheeling ocean-front section, although more mellow now than in the decades immediately following World War II, contrasts with the rest of the city, part of which fronts on Chesapeake Bay and where year-round inhabitants live a more settled life.

The city has 29 miles of shoreline, divided more or less equally between the Atlantic Ocean and Chesapeake Bay and including both public and private beaches. The Atlantic coastline, which includes the primary public resort area usually identified as The Oceanfront, has crashing waves at times and the undertow customary at ocean shores. Parts of the shoreline are fully developed for residential use, full or part time, but stretches are set aside as nature preserves. The Bay coastline and its several large inlets, including Lynnhaven Bay, which has given its name to a succulent oyster raised on nearby bottom, is one of the oldest settled areas in the United States and retains some of its traditional character as a seafood center.

The oceanfront section, a premier resort that occupies a strip of sand that was semi-isolated and littered with shipwrecks little more than a century ago, is hyperactive in summer, when sunbathers under varicolored umbrellas and swimmers pack a 40-block-long white sand beach under the watchful eyes of lifeguards. The Norwegian Lady statue, a reminder of the ocean-going vessels that have come to grief on these shores, impassively watches the sightseeing boat paralleling the shoreline and a small airplane towing messages overhead that range from restaurant ads to Happy Birthday personals. Vacationers in beachfront hotels take in a scene that has been appropriately described as "happy hubbub."

The oceanfront also has growing appeal in the shoulder seasons, starting in April and ending in early October, and concentrates on conventions and meetings at other times of the year.

Strollers and bikers are heavy users of separate lanes on the boardwalk, which extends from First Street to 39th Street. A sightseeing tram operates on the boardwalk. The bike trail continues along shoulder lanes on Pacific and Atlantic avenues as far as Seashore State

Youngsters discover many objects of interest at The Narrows in Virginia Beach, Virginia. PHOTO BY JOHN BOWEN.

Park and the North Beach area. In all, the city has about 45 miles of bike trails. An average of 2,000 runners take part each March in the Shamrock Marathon, whose course includes the boardwalk.

A former Coast Guard lifesaving station on the boardwalk at 24th Street, built in 1903, has been converted into the Virginia Beach Maritime Historical Museum. Displays include scrimshaw and other maritime memorabilia, as well as numerous photographs of ship-wrecks and rescues. One exhibit tells the story of the Norwegian Lady statue, presented by the people of Voss, Norway, in apprecia-tion of rescue efforts when the Norwegian bark *Dictator* ran aground.

The blocks immediately back of the beach are just as active, with an extensive selection of off-beach diversions. Visitors can play miniature golf in a jungle setting, absorb culture at the art center and visit an annual Boardwalk Art Show in June, plunge down watery chutes, eat seafood in quiet settings, or gyrate in discos, wander through a haunted house, ride on old-fashioned trams, and indulge the senses numerous other ways. A trolley runs up and down Atlantic Avenue between Rudee Inlet and 42nd Street until 2 A.M.

Between March 1 and sometime in autumn, depending on weather, charter and head boats leave marinas at Rudee and Lynnhaven inlets on full- and half-day fishing expeditions in both the Atlantic Ocean and Chesapeake Bay. Catches include bluefish, tuna, marlin, swordfish, trout, sea bass, tautog, mackerel, and dolphin. Public boat ramps are located at Owl Creek, Seashore State Park, Lynnhaven Waterway, Munden Point, and Shore Drive. Landlubbers use fishing piers at 15th Street and Oceanfront, Lynnhaven Inlet, and Little Island in Sandbridge, and a shoreside angling site at Rudee Inlet.

Sailing gets a lot of attention at Virginia Beach. Rope-strung masts stand in close order at marinas along the shoreline. The World 1000 race from Florida to Virginia Beach in late May attracts international multihulled vessels. The dangerous 122-mile stretch between Jacksonville and Tybee Island, Georgia, and daily starts directly from beaches, are severe tests of boating skills that many crews flunk. Hobies and catamarans compete in the 27-mile Chesapeake Challenge and other races. Surfing is permitted during the day near Rudee Inlet (lifeguards are on duty at the north section of Croatan Beach) and in other places after 5 P.M. The city has hosted the August East Coast Surfing Championships for more than a quarter-century. Other summer sports activities include snorkeling and scuba diving, parasailing, skateboarding, roller skating, golf (seven courses), and tennis.

Even novice canoeists can negotiate the West Neck Creek segment of the Virginia Beach Scenic Waterway System, which can be entered from parking areas where Princess Anne and Ware Neck roads cross Ware Neck Creek. Wilderness E.A.S.T. conducts daylong canoe, kayak, and bike trips during August.

The Virginia Beach commercial waterfront is only a fraction of the city's 29 miles of coastline. A combination of private and public property stands on both flanks, with cottages of various sizes for rent, particularly in the North Beach and Sandbridge areas. The stilt beach homes at Sandbridge, south of the commercial oceanfront, are convenient to a combination of city, federal, and state parks that complement each other. Some of the oldest homes in the country, survivors of colonial, revolutionary, and civil struggles and the ravages of nature, are located in Virginia Beach.

The Adam Thoroughgood House, 2 miles off U.S. Route 13 on Thoroughgood Drive, recalls the early struggle to settle the wilderness by the exercise of personal initiative. The builder went to Virginia as an indentured servant, served his time, and returned to England, where he married the daughter of a wealthy British merchant. He returned to Virginia with his bride and amassed 5,358 acres by sponsoring the immigration of indentured servants. The four-room and hallway house, built between 1638 and 1680, is probably the oldest surviving brick structure in the United States.

The kitchen has a large fireplace for cooking — separate kitchens became standard later, in the wake of many house fires — and original large ceiling beams. A cutaway section in the hallway shows the original plaster, while dog tracks in exterior chimney bricks suggest they were unprotected while drying. Furnishings, which include Tudor-style windows in the parlor, cupboard with ivory and walnut inlays, Bible box, rush lamp used for everyday lighting because candles were expensive, and rope-slatted beds, are complete down to "beasties," small animal figures supposed to ward off the "uglies," or unfortunate occurrences. Among other unusual furnishings are two leather ale mugs in the shape of barmaids, presented by Queen Anne to John Ashford in 1729, and a puzzle pitcher with holes in the sides, which made pouring tricky.

The gentleman's pleasure garden, so-called because it was designed for viewing, recreates a popular home adjunct of the seventeenth century. Shrubs and flowers mingle in the small formal plot overlooking the Lynnhaven River. The property is open Tuesday through Sunday year round, except holidays.

Lynnhaven House at 4405 Wishart Road, owned by the Association for the Preservation of Virginia Antiquities, illustrates a typical floor plan of the eighteenth century, but it's just as well known for its demonstration of arts and crafts during its mid-April through November season. The Dutch gambrel-roofed Francis Land House at 3131 Virginia Beach Boulevard, built in 1732, is part of a recently established historic district encompassing mostly private homes. The Land House is open Wednesday through Sunday.

Virginia Beach has its share of ghosts and legends. Upper Wolfsnare at 2040 Potters Road, open Wednesdays and Thursdays from May through October, was reported to be haunted by the son of the builder long before historical societies began restoring the 1759 house and making archeological digs on the grounds. You are not allowed to dig in search of gold supposedly hidden by the pirate Blackbeard at Seashore State Park. Witchduck Road, a key intersection on the Norfolk–Virginia Beach Expressway (state Route 44), memorializes Grace Sherwood, an early eighteenth-century farmer's wife who survived a ducking in the Lynnhaven River, the standard test for witches at the time. One of her supposed feats was to sail to England at midnight in an eggshell to bring back seeds of wild lupine and rosemary. Curiously, rosemary grows wild in only that section of Virginia Beach.

While tourism dominates the warm months at the oceanfront and historical centers, the remainder of the city is a "bedroom" community that hosts military bases and a lively commerce year round. A large cross at Cape Henry, now part of Fort Story Army base, marks the landfall of the first permanent settlers in the new world on April 26, 1607. A statue of French Admiral Comte de Grasse commemorates his victory off the Virginia Capes, which prevented help from reaching the beleaguered British at Yorktown. Nearby is the first lighthouse authorized by the Congress of the new nation, a handsome hilltop rock structure built in 1791. It can be viewed from ground level year round, and is opened to visitors from Memorial Day to Labor Day by the Association for the Preservation of Virginia Antiquities. Its successor, a taller 1881 structure, is across the road.

Virginia Beach's structural attractions are not all historic. The Association for Research and Enlightenment Inc., headquartered in hillside buildings just off Atlantic Avenue at 67th Street, uses an ESP-testing program, exhibits, audiovisuals, and lectures to illustrate its activities in the field of psychic phenomena and dreams. The center is often known by the name of founder Edgar Cayce, a former salesman whose psychic ability was widely recognized. The center's lotus garden is a tranquil rest area.

The Virginia Marine Science Museum, at 717 General Booth Boulevard south of the beachfront, includes a 50,000-gallon aquarium filled with regional and exotic species and hands-on exhibits where visitors can duplicate natural phenomena such as waves and storms, tong for oysters, view water snakes and turtles, learn about marine environment, and follow an outdoor boardwalk through a salt marsh populated with waterfowl and other animals. The planetarium operated by the city's schools sponsors free public programs on Tuesday and Sunday evenings every month except July. Topics vary from UFOs to the possibilities of life on other planets.

A number of recreation centers, including the YMCA and city-operated facilities, provide an opportunity for indoor sports, including bowling. The huge Farmer's Market at 1989 Landstown Road is open year round, except when weather prevents. Guided tours of the television studios of the Christian Broadcasting Network and CBN University are conducted daily.

The city's combination of parks is one of its best features. These range from inland Mount Trashmore, a 60-foot-high converted landfill with two artificial, stocked lakes for fishing and boating, a soap box derby track, and two skateboard bowls, to a string of complementary national, state, and local reserves—Seashore State Park on the Bay side, and Little Island City Park (a surfing area), Back Bay National Wildlife Refuge, and False Cape State Park facing the Atlantic.

Seashore State Park

Seashore State Park, one of the oldest in Virginia dating from the 1930s, has a freshness about it that comes from periodic upgrading of its facilities. The park, which lies astride U.S. 60, occupies the land bridge between Chesapeake Bay and small Broad and Linkhorn bays. It is divided into two elements: the Chesapeake Bayfront camping area and the day park across the highway, which breaks down into two segments with separate motor vehicle entrances but linked internally by hiking and biking trails.

The main entrance to the day park—the first reached entering Virginia Beach along U.S. 60—leads to the Visitor Center and the head of the hiking and biking trails. Displays and three short audiovisuals in the Visitor Center provide an excellent introduction to the park's progression of natural features from the shoreline to upland lifeforms—sand beach, tufted dunes, tidal marsh, and forest. Rangers conduct programs for children Tuesday, Thursday, and Saturday and nature walks for adults and older children on Wednesday and Saturday during the peak season.

The park is a naturalist's delight, with cicadas chirping on hot summer days from several varieties of grass and wildflowers and such bushes as yellow jasmine, partridge berry, yellow orchis, foxglove, blueberry, and bush strawberry adding color from spring through autumn. Mole and "ghost" crabs hide in the earth, while small animals such as squirrels, muskrat, mink, and periwinkle snails inhabit the forests and the bird population fluctuates as seasonal changes bring in ducks, osprey, and herons.

Nine color-coded, interconnecting hiking trails, ranging in length from a quarter-mile to 5 miles, and a 6-mile hike-or-bike path reach all areas of the park. The Main Trail extends the length of the park, skirting marshes dominated by bald cypress and Spanish moss, a lake and creek, and the shoreline of Linkhorn and Broad bays, and passing through forests of tall oak, maple, loblolly pine, black and sweet

Spanish moss on bald cypress at Seashore State Park, Virginia. PHOTO BY
JOHN BOWEN.

gum, beech, hickory, dogwood, and holly. It intersects with four other trails, which in turn lead to the remaining trails. The principal feature along the short High Dunes Trail is, indeed, a mound covered with small trees and underbrush.

The 1.5-mile Bald Cypress Nature Trail is a combination of board-walk and stabilized soil and sand path, whose numbered signs start with historical references to the "white hilly sand" backed by "faire meadows" and "goodly tall trees" and Chesapean and Kecoughtan Indian settlements encountered by the first settlers. Other numbered points identify plant life capable of existing in sandy soil; 100-foot-tall bald cypress trees hung with Spanish moss; the dark-colored swamp water, which the Indians drank; loblolly pines probably 200 years old with serrated or "bug" bark, sometimes scarred with horizontal rows of pits made by sapsuckers; the colonies of small animals and plants that thrive in rotting wood and forest debris; the Indian remedies derived from berries, roots, and leaves, particularly the partridge berry; and the development of ferns and mushrooms.

The shaded entrance road to the other section of the park, an extension of 64th Street, is a favorite track for joggers during the hot months because overhanging trees moderate the temperatures and because it intersects with the main park hiking and biking trail. It is also a beautiful drive with two stops. The first is a small sandy beach where sunbathers (swimming is forbidden because of tricky currents) in brief, brightly colored bathing suits soak up sun and ignore the drone of passing jet skis launched at the ramp for small boats. The second is at the end of the road, where a boat ramp for standard and larger boats is located.

A high sand dune between the two provides a vantage point for watching all these activities, as well as children strolling the water's edge and wading in pools left by a receding tide. A plateau at The Narrows, the point where Linkhorn and Broad Bay meet, provides a lower but closer view of boat launches and offshore fishers.

Back Bay National Wildlife Refuge

Back Bay Refuge, a 4-mile–long coastal area set aside in 1938, is a typical Atlantic Ocean barrier area. A sandy beach gives way to dunes, then to marsh and woodlands. Along the shoreline, the twice daily flow of the tide creates a changing habitat, where ghost crabs hide, shorebirds dodge the waves to peck at bits of food washed ashore, and osprey and tern fish in shallow water. The substantial dunes provide sustenance for a few hardy plants, particularly beach grass and sea oats, which in turn help stabilize the dunes against tides and storms. The marshes, including the soggy islands in the Bay, are set aside for the protection of migrating birds, especially the abundant snow and Canada goose, northern pintail, mallard, and black duck. Waterfowl and southward-migrating shorebirds begin to appear in large numbers in September, while swallows and other songbirds depart. Waterfowl landings increase in October and reach peak levels in November and December. By the end of March, most of the ducks and geese will have flown north, to be replaced by songbirds and northward-moving shorebirds. Osprey arrive in April.

Other bird species commonly seen in the park include pied-billed grebe, brown pelican, great blue and green-backed herons, great and snowy egrets, turkey vulture, northern bobwhite, black-bellied plover, lesser yellowlegs, semipalmated sandpiper, king and Virginia rails, Eastern screech and great horned owls, Carolina wren, European starling, prairie warbler, and eastern meadowlark. A section of the beach is closed during the nesting season to protect the piping plover, now believed to number only 700 pair on the Atlantic coast.

Back Bay is alive with wild animals, including ferocious feral hogs descended from swine that reverted when left to fend for themselves, white-tailed deer, gray fox, raccoon, muskrat, opossum, nutria, and small rodents. Once a year, from the end of October to mid-November, bow and shotgun hunters selected by lottery are allowed to take white-tailed deer and feral hogs.

The 4,589-acre refuge attracts about 100,000 humans each year during its daylight opening hours. A blind overlooking the bay puts photographers close to migratory waterfowl. Three miles of beach are dedicated to wildlife-oriented activities, including observation, photography, and surfcasting, and to walking. Anglers also may hook bass, crappie, catfish, and perch from small boats in the shallow bay. Hiking trails, the shortest a quarter-mile boardwalk to the beach, cover all the major features of the park, including dunes and the bayside. Trails along dikes erected to maintain water levels that attract waterfowl provide the only land access to False Cape State Park to the south.

False Cape State Park

False Cape State Park is similar in terrain to the Back Bay Refuge, but is preserved in a near-natural state by its isolation. Public access is limited primarily to the 4.2-mile-long paths through Back Bay Refuge used by hikers and wide-tire bikers and a boat landing at Barbours Hill in the northern end of the park. Canoes may be floated across from Little Island Recreation Area just north of the Back Bay Refuge and power boats can be launched along the west shore of Back Bay. A few buses are allowed to pass through the Back Bay Refuge to carry participants to maritime environmental study programs at the Wash Woods Center, located in a Back Bay marshy area.

The scenery at False Cape is reminiscent of that which the first settlers saw on arrival. Restless ocean waves have created parabolic dunes 75 feet across, now partially stabilized by vegetation. The inland marsh and maritime forests, dominated by loblolly pine, hollies, and live oaks once used to construct seagoing vessels, teem with deer, horse, boar, great blue heron, osprey, raccoon, opossum, and other wildlife.

The remnants of the town of Wash Woods, reduced by storms in the 1930s and abandoned in the 1960s, and six hunt clubs sit unobtrusively on the site. Volunteers and the Methodist Historical Society have helped park officials create a memorial at the remains of the Wash Woods Methodist Church, constructed of shipwreck materials more than a hundred years ago and destroyed by a storm during the 1930s. State interest in restoring properties like the old Newport News Hunt Club as part of a historical trail and expanding access to the park is not shared by federal officials at the Back Bay Refuge, who do not want additional traffic in the refuge.

False Cape Park is open year round for day use and has primitive facilities, including nonpotable water, for overnight camping in two designated areas. Overnight parking is allowed at Little Island Park.

Chesapeake

Office of Public Information, P.O. Box 15225,
Chesapeake, VA 23320. Tel.: 804/547-6323.

The alleged sighting of a "Big Foot" in Northwest River Park in 1980 brought national attention to this 353-square-mile city, which extends from the vicinity of Hampton Roads to the North Carolina line. Chesapeake's "Big Foot" was a shadowy figure, which lumbered across a road one dark night when strange odors wafted across the park. Just what was seen is not clear. Ranger Gary Williamson, who has been at the park more than twelve years, says he has never seen anything he could not easily explain, but he keeps an open mind.

"Big Foot" or not, the 763-acre park along the Northwest River, with Indian and South creeks on its flanks, has plenty to offer canoeists, hikers, bikers, horseback riders, and others.

Canoeists can use the forested, basically lowland park with two boat ramps in a variety of ways. A mile-long lake can be extended by portaging a short distance to the river, which can be paddled in either direction along about 16 miles of waterway in Virginia before the stream enters North Carolina. In addition, about 1½ miles of both Indian and Smith creeks can be paddled. These routes cross a largely undisturbed southern swamp, with water darkened by tannic acid from bald cypress, water tupelo, and other trees.

About 7 miles of nature and hiking trails follow old roads through forests dominated by swamp chestnut oak, red maple, shagbush hickory, and loblolly pine and an extensive list of wildflowers rare for the region, including spring beauty, trout lily, dwarf ginseng, wood anemone, twayblade orchid, and green adders mouth, and blooming bushes such as silky camellia, wild azaleas, and bigleaf snowbill. Animals and birds most likely to be seen include turtles, squirrels, raccoon, gray fox, and great blue heron, but bald eagle, deer, and even bobcat have been spotted occasionally. More than 160 species in all have been identified.

Bikers may use about 3 miles of wooded trails, while equestrians also have about 3 miles of bridle path.

The park, open all year, has 103 campsites, about half of them with electric hookups. It also has day-use facilities.

Founded in 1963 by the consolidation of the former city of South Norfolk and Norfolk County, Chesapeake has a split personality. The dense and fast-growing industrial section adjacent to Portsmouth and Norfolk contrasts sharply with the remainder of the city, which is largely rural in character and sparsely populated. Farming of corn, soybeans, and wheat continues on more than 58,000 acres in the rural southern section of the city. One of Virginia's largest horticulture industries uses another 1,000 acres to produce tree seedlings and bushes.

Northwest River Park is only one of many places for recreation. A substantial portion of the city is devoted to outdoors activities. The Great Dismal Swamp (see section on Suffolk, below) straddles the boundary between Chesapeake and Suffolk. The largest feature of the national wildlife refuge, Lake Drummond, is located in Chesapeake.

An old logging ditch off the Dismal Swamp Canal provides the best water approach to the swamp. The Intracoastal Waterway for pleasure boats, which extends from New York to Florida, passes through the city along the historic Albemarle and Chesapeake Canal connecting Chesapeake Bay and Albemarle Sound in North Carolina. Locks are located at Great Bridge, also the site of an important Revolutionary War battle, and Deep Creek. The latter has day-use facilities.

Canoeists also paddle on the Southern Branch of the Elizabeth River, Dismal Swamp Canal, a feeder canal to Lake Drummond, scenic Pocaty Creek (which connects with the North Landing River in Virginia Beach), and Deep Creek. In all, Chesapeake has at least 30 miles of canoe trails.

Suffolk

Suffolk Council, Hampton Roads Chamber of Commerce, 1001 Washington Avenue, Suffolk, VA 23434. Tel.: 804/539-2111.

Suffolk's association with peanut farming and processing is so complete that residents of neighboring cities tend to forget its other good qualities—long history, water-related assets, and wilderness areas.

As presently constituted, Suffolk dates only to 1970 when the former city of Suffolk and Nansemond County consolidated. That youthful appearance is misleading: Nansemond County was settled by a trader, John Constant, just prior to the Indian massacre of 1622, and Suffolk received a town charter in 1742. The wharfs at the head of the Nansemond River and at South Quay on the Blackwater River, the latter accessible from North Carolina sounds, made it a popular port for the export of tobacco, lumber, and grain and importation of linen, sugar, salt, pig iron, and manufactured products.

Suffolk endured the British flames during the Revolutionary War, but fire was a danger in peacetime, too. Most of the community was destroyed by fires in 1837 and 1889.

Peanut farming began during the Revolutionary War and expanded after the Civil War, but early attempts at local processing failed. The first successful processing plant was the Suffolk Peanut Company in 1898. Perhaps the most famous was Planters Peanut Company, founded in 1912 by Amedeo Obici. The peanut connection is clearly visible. Despite considerable residential growth in recent years, the

430-square-mile city is still substantially rural in nature. Peanut farms, storage silos, and packing houses are prominent features of rural Suffolk and nearby Isle of Wight and Southampton counties.

Historical relics are concentrated in the old city of Suffolk, reached via U.S. 58 from Norfolk and state Route 10–32 from Newport News. Suffolk has an airport for light planes.

The periodic burning of the old city of Suffolk eliminated many historic structures. However, four buildings are on the Register of National Historic Places, including Riddick's Folly at 510 North Main Street, whose name reflects local ridicule because of its size. The four-story, 21-room mansion in Greek revival style, erected in 1837 by Mills Riddick, is now a museum and cultural center. Among other historic structures are a two-story clapboard house at Main and Mahan streets, built shortly after the Revolutionary War; 1830 Whitehall on West Washington Street; and 2½-story, Second Empire-style Holland House, constructed in 1875. The twin towers of the 1890–1891 Victorian-style City Hall, which has a farmers' and seafood market on the first floor, are the city's most distinctive architectural landmark.

The Suffolk Museum on Bosley Avenue operates a cultural and educational program, with displays on local history (10 A.M.–5 P.M. Tuesday–Friday, and 1–5 P.M. Sunday).

The northern tip of Suffolk borders on Hampton Roads, but the city is better known for its freshwater lakes, which are stocked with largemouth bass, bluegill, bream, pike, crappie, and other fish species. The nineteen reservoirs, most of which have boat ramps, together cover about 8,000 acres and are open for day use.

The Lone Star Lakes system in the Chuckatuck region, created when groundwater filled borrow pits, includes 500 acres of water in twelve lakes and 569 acres of wooded countryside. Among the most important are tidal Crystal Lake and tree-bordered Crane Lake. Canoeists paddle down Cedar Creek to the Nansemond River. Unmarked nature trails pass a variety of trees and flowers; the soil contains fossilized sea animals.

Bennett's Creek Park on state Route 757, a former U.S. Army Nike installation, is another multipurpose park, with a boat ramp and fishing and crabbing pier on the tributary of the Nansemond River. A 1.25-mile nature trail winds along the creek and through a stand of Florida maple trees (rare this far north), and crosses bridges over a marshy area.

Boats with motors up to 12 horsepower are permitted at 1,579–acre Lake Western Branch near Chuckatuck and 777-acre Lake Prince, on Route 604 two miles off U.S. 460. Boat rentals are available at 510-acre Lake Cohoon, 222-acre Lake Kilby, and 512-acre Lake Meade, while 600-acre Lake Burnt Mills and 197-acre Lake Speight's Run rent motors and batteries. Shore fishing is permitted at Cohoon, Kilby, Meade, Prince, and Western Branch.

Suffolk also provides the best land access to the Great Dismal Swamp National Wildlife Refuge.

Great Dismal Swamp National Wildlife Refuge

Despite its name, the Dismal Swamp is a pleasant and rewarding experience. It has been generous to resident and visitor alike since the first aboriginals searched the soggy forests more than 13,000 years ago. It has been explored, surveyed, cut over, fished, hunted, and enjoyed — and even used to fill freshwater casks of sailing ships in the colonial era.

The 106,000-acre national wildlife refuge, which straddles the Virginia–North Carolina border drawn in 1728 by a survey party led by a redoubtable Virginian, William Byrd II, is minimally developed, which means that relatively few people (approximately 15,000) use the park each year. Most of the access comes from the canals and 140 miles of unpaved roads constructed to remove trees cut from the thick forests over a period of more than two hundred years. George Washington, among the first to recognize the potential of the Dismal Swamp, surveyed it in 1763.

The logging roads, especially those alongside the Washington and Railroad ditches off state Route 642 (White Marsh Road) south of Suffolk, can be hiked their entire 5-mile lengths, ending at the principal natural feature of the refuge, Lake Drummond. Yellow flies and mosquitoes are a problem during warm months. The road that parallels the Washington Ditch also is suitable for biking.

Both trails extend through thick forests with occasional wildflowers, including the abundant orange jewelweed. Spring bloomers include orchids, coral honeysuckle, yellow jessamine trumpet, passion vines, and yellow poplar. But the swamp hides one of its most beautiful secrets: the dwarf trillium, which blooms in mid–March, is located primarily in the inaccessible northwest corner of the refuge. Autumn colors peak in late October and November, the same time that wild fruits, including paw-paw, black gum, and grapes, attract flocks of blackbird and robin. The red maple flowers in February.

Dismal Swamp reportedly has more Swainson's and Wayne's warblers than any other preserve on the East Coast. Altogether, it hosts 213 species of birds, 93 of which nest there. The best time for bird-watching is during the spring migration, from April to June, when up to 34 species of warblers arrive. Bird watchers prefer the Jericho Ditch in the northwestern corner of the refuge.

Bobcat and perhaps 350 black bear, who roam most widely in early June, live in the park but are seldom seen. Regular sightings include white-tailed deer in the forest and river otter and mink around the lake. Numerous small animals, including rabbits, chipmunk, southern flying squirrel, beaver, vole, and weasel, live in the refuge, along with about sixty species of turtles, lizards, salamanders, frogs, and toads.

The easiest trail is the Boardwalk Trail at the start of the Washington Ditch. The raised, plank walkway meanders through a dense forest primarily of pine, cedar, cypress, and maple with considerable underbrush. The ¾-mile loop, with side paths, ends at the site of the first lumber camp, Dismal Town, which was built by Washington's Dismal Swamp Land Company.

Lake Drummond is a natural, 3,100-acre, freshwater body named for William Drummond, the North Carolina governor acknowledged as the first European to discover it in 1665. The lake, about 6 feet deep, is open year round during daylight hours for boating and fishing. Boaters are attracted by the unusual color of the water; by the isolation and primitive condition of the lake, with river otter and other water lovers dodging rotting stumps along a shoreline bordered by dense forest; and by the canal trip through the forest. The rare log fern is found in abundance around the lake. The water is dark brown because of the tannic acid from cypress and gum trees, but is so pure that early sailors filled casks there to sustain them on the long voyages across the Atlantic Ocean.

Fishers are rewarded by 26 species of fish, including longnose gar, largemouth bass, crappie, perch, sunfish, bluegill, swampfish, bullhead, pickerel, bowfin, and warmouth. Boats reach the lake from the eastern side of the park via the Feeder Ditch, which extends from the Dismal Swamp Canal along Route 17. A public boat ramp is located near the entrance to the ditch and a marine railway operates from 8 A.M. to 4 P.M. daily to transport boats across the Army Corps of Engineers spillway on the Feeder Ditch.

An ongoing conservation program, similar to that in other preserves, helps retain the natural uniqueness of the park through habitat and water conservation and burning of underbrush. Repopulation of the cypress and Atlantic white cedar and habitats for deer, quail, rabbits, shrew, and woodpeckers are a major concern. One white-tailed deer hunt is held every fall, during which several hundred are bagged.

Smithfield

Isle of Wight/Smithfield Chamber of Commerce, P.O. Box 38, Smithfield, VA 23430. Tel.: 804/357-3502.

The visitors from Sweden were amused. Accustomed to ham with a milder taste, they marveled at the tangy flavor of Smithfield ham. Their host offered the standard explanation—the use of peanuts as feed and the special curing process. Satisfied, they settled down to enjoy their lunch.

This incident illustrates one side of this small town on the Pagan River. Mention Smithfield and countless numbers think of the ham products that flow in a steady stream from the city's large meat-packing plants. The city's economy is based on these plants, although residential development of nearby areas has given it a greater boost than anything since the invention of the steamboat.

The dependence on a single industry is not unusual. The history of Smithfield is one of boom and bust. Founded in 1750 on land near the confluence of the Pagan River and Little Creek that was part of an original grant by the King of England to the third son of Arthur Smith of Essex, England, it received its first boost from port activities and construction of the courthouse. It had another period of growth during the nineteenth-century steamboat era, and then settled back lazily until recent decades brought an influx of population from the neighboring cities of Hampton Roads.

As a result, farmers—it is surrounded by peanut and truck farms—are often seen on Smithfield streets. Young adults from the farms hitch rides with neighbors and then walk the remainder of the way home. In short, the way of life is in many ways a throwback to an era when life was more moderate.

Smithfield's traditional water orientation survives in the pleasure craft that plow the Pagan River, past the thin wooden docks of homes on the banks and the Smithfield Station, a new motel and restaurant whose marina is the weighing station for the annual Smithfield Kiwanis Club Fishing Tournament in late August.

The substantial architectural assets of Smithfield lay fertile until recent years, when an organized effort was made to include sixty-five historic buildings from the early 1700s to the Victorian era in a walking tour. Smithfield's small-town atmosphere — residents recognize visitors instantly and often offer a friendly greeting — makes strolling the narrow, uncrowded streets of the historic area a pleasant experience. Ample parking is provided along Cedar Street and, although some of the lots are commercial, there are no signs to warn away noncustomers.

The historic area is compact, with most of the structures located on Church, Main, Cedar, Grace, and a few intersecting streets, and can be explored on foot in an hour. Church Street (Route 10–158) is the main entrance from the east. Most of the buildings are not grandiose expressions of the rich, but the homes of hard-working citizens of modest means. This ordinariness increases their charm. Since nearly all the buildings are private residences, they can be viewed only from the outside, except when some are opened during Historic Garden Week.

Most impressive among the eighteenth-century homes is The Grove at 220 Grace Street, constructed in the final decade of that century by Thomas Pierce in a grove of trees. The handsome red brick structure had a spotty history — the trees were cut down and sold to the Russian navy during the Crimean War, and the building served as a boardinghouse and hotel — before it was restored by a former lieutenant governor of the state. The nearby Oak Grove Academy building, built in 1836, was used by three institutions of learning.

A dozen pre-Civil War structures and slightly more late nineteenth-century buildings on Church Street are anchored by 1830 Christ Episcopal Church. Among them are the brick 1752 Wentworth-Barrett House, one of the first structures erected in Smithfield; the King-Atkinson House, built about 1798, whose principal occupants were heroes in the Revolutionary War and the War of 1812; the 1756 Eason-Whitley House, the home of the Whitley family from its construction until 1913; the Wilson-Morrison House, whose wings date from 1775 and 1788; the 1796 Andrew Mackle House, with a formal colonial garden on the sloping banks of Little Creek; the circa 1820 Watson P. Jordan House, home in the mid-1800s for a congressman, Archibald Atkinson; and the Delk House, built in 1877 for the captain of one of the steamboats using the port on the Pagan River.

Leading structures on Main Street are the 1750 Old Courthouse and Clerk's Office, currently a Visitors Center and headquarters of the Chamber of Commerce, and 1752 Smithfield Inn and Tavern, whose restaurant continues a tradition dating from 1759 but interrupted in the mid-nineteenth century when it served as a church rectory. Also on this street are the Todd House, built about 1753; the small Gaming House, whose name describes its early function; the circa 1837 Hillyer House; and the Valentine House, built in the first half of the nineteenth century.

The former Smithfield Academy, a red brick structure on South Mason Street dating from 1826, currently is used by nearby Trinity United Methodist Church, whose 1898 gothic brick structure replaced an earlier frame building.

Two worthy structures are a short distance from the historic area — Windsor Castle, a stucco-covered brick home erected in 1750 by Arthur Smith IV, founder of Smithfield, and Pierceville, built about 1730 by merchant Thomas Pierce, who later became a leader in the fight for American independence.

The Isle of Wight County Museum occupies a wing of the former Bank of Smithfield, which was erected in 1913 using imported stone. Local historical artifacts are displayed under a large dome skylight. It is open Wednesday, Saturday, and Sunday afternoons.

Along state Route 10, which parallels the south shore of the James River west of Smithfield, history, modern technology, and nature coexist comfortably. Historic manor houses, built on plantations established soon after Jamestown was settled, retain important architectural features and priceless antiques. New technology is represented at the Visitors Center on state Route 650 at the Surry Nuclear Power plant operated by Virginia Power.

Nearby Hog Island State Waterfowl Refuge is a natural overlook of the wide James River. Farther west, the high banks provide spectacular views of one of the most beautiful stretches of the broad river, where ocean-going ships occasionally appear among the billowing sails and wakes of boats out for pleasure. The state has established a park on state Route 673 (alternate 674 to 673), open Wednesday through Sunday, where the Civil War earth fortifications known as Fort Boykin are located. Signs conduct visitors on a walking tour of the remnants of the fort, which stood on a bluff overlooking the James River.

The lightly used side roads, which lead to both the major historic relics and waterfront sites, are a pleasant respite from the heavily traveled throughways of the region. The absence of traffic makes them a favorite of bikers.

Bacon's Castle, built in 1665 by Arthur Allen, is the oldest documented brick house in English North America and a National Historic Landmark. Its unusual name derives from its role during Bacon's Rebellion against tyrannical Royal Governor William Berkeley a hundred years before the American Revolution created a new country. The house was seized by a lieutenant of Nathaniel Bacon, leader of the revolt, and became the strong point from which the revolters controlled the county for four months before the rebellion was put down.

Now owned by the Association for the Preservation of Virginia Antiquities, the handsome structure on state Route 617 is open Tuesdays, Fridays, Saturdays, and Sundays. Guided tours cover three centuries of architectural and economic development. The original structure with Flemish gables and triple chimney stacks, now the left wing of the house, reveals the original paneling and floors, as well as antique furnishings. The brick right wing was added in the 1850s.

America's oldest known formal garden, planted in 1680 on a grid plan with six large and two small beds, is being reconstructed with the assistance of the Garden Clubs of Virginia. Archeologist Nicholas M. Lucchetti described it as "the largest, earliest, best preserved, most sophisticated garden that has come to light in North America." Remnants of eighteenth- and nineteenth-century gardens, differing slightly in size, also were discovered on the same site. A Civil War graveyard is located on the lawn.

Hog Island State Wildlife Refuge, which juts into the James River, is so quiet the visitor can hear the lapping of waves on the shoreline and the humming of small motorboats near the opposite shore of the river. Minimally developed for public use from 8 A.M. to 6 P.M. daily, the refuge has a 1.8-mile gravel road that provides twin views of the river. Flat island hammocks and inlets sustain clumps of trees and marsh plants that host waterfowl in winter and small populations of songbirds and migratory herons during the warm months. The refuge is especially known for bald eagle, great blue heron, and killdeer, but more than 240 species have been sighted there, although many are rare. Among the more common birds are Canada goose, double-crested cormorant, mallard, northern pintail, sandpipers, snipes, gulls, mourning dove, barn swallow, crows, Carolina chickadee, brown-headed nuthatch, yellow-rumped and pine warblers, song and white-throated sparrows, dark-eyed junco, red-winged blackbird, common grackle, brown-headed cowbird, and American goldfinch.

Finfishing requires a permit, and shellfish harvesting is illegal. The refuge is a managed hunting area, with bow hunting during a special season.

About 600 acres of tidal marsh, diked and fitted with water control devices, are drained each spring and planted in millet, then flooded in the fall. Another 400 acres of tidal marsh remains untouched as a feeding area for migratory waterfowl. Approximately 200 acres of farmland are cultivated to provide winter food and grazing.

Chippokes

Another pleasant side road is state Route 634, which leads to one of the oldest continuously farmed plantations in the country, now Chippokes Plantation State Park. Founded in 1619 and named for friendly Chickahominy Indian Chief Choupoke, the plantation was a pioneer in the planter commerce that quickly developed on the James River. Old mulberry trees, remnants of past attempts in the Hampton Roads area to establish a silk industry, grow in the park.

Chippokes is the complete day-use facility. It retains several historic structures and functions as an observable farm and forest-replanting area, while providing numerous public recreational opportunities, including a swimming pool, in a handsome riverside setting.

The Visitors Center on a bluff overlooking the river provides an introduction to all these aspects. Its walls are lined with antique farm implements, while exhibits and an audiovisual presentation highlight Indian culture and important moments in the life of the plantation. A second audiovisual describes the progress of early commerce along the James River.

The park has five trails, four of them connecting and traversing a combination of upland and lowland featuring pine, oak, tupelo, cypress, and wildflowers, including columbine. The 1.3-mile hiking and biking College Run Trail, which starts at the center, parallels the park road as it follows the forested bluff where bluebird and indigo bunting gather. It passes the unrestored River House and ends at the 1854 mansion, now a museum depicting the lifestyles of former residents. Guided tours of the manor houses are held three times daily Wednesday through Sunday from Memorial Day to Labor Day. Eight rooms in the mansion are decorated in the Victorian style for special pre-Christmas tours. Guided tours of the gardens are held on specific dates from late June through August.

Three connecting paths leave the College Run Trail or park road near the mansion. A mile-long hiking and biking trail skirts both woods and open fields to reach a marshy area at the mouth of Lower Chippokes Creek. Birds are abundant in this area, with herons, egrets, and warblers and other songbirds abundant in summer and water-fowl, dominated by Canada goose, prevalent in late autumn and winter. Eagles sometimes nest in the area. A mile-long trek through cultivated fields ends farther up Lower Chippokes Creek, while a 1.3-mile circular offshoot takes hikers through a heavily wooded area to the shoreline of the James River. A separate, half-mile forest path extends off Cedar Lane, the farm road.

Rangers lead evening strolls on the trails and Chippokes beach on specified days during June, July, and August.

The self-guided driving farm tour begins along the entrance with a reforestation project of loblolly pines, planted in 1971, and includes examples of crops, livestock, and farm equipment on two other roads. Fields are planted in historically important crops such as corn, pea-nuts, wheat, soybeans, and tobacco, while a cotton demonstration plot shows the six-month cycle, ending with October cutting, of the plant. Antique implements of husbandry are displayed in a mu-seum and corn crib. Angus and Devon cattle graze year round on timothy, clover, fescue, and orchard grass in pastures where the first cattle were loosed in 1611. Beehives visible from the road also repre-sent one of the oldest farm activities in Virginia.

Nature tours for children are held on Wednesdays and Fridays, while planned family activities on specific summer days include fishing, Indian lore, and "mystery" events. Games, historical and otherwise, are emphasized on the Fourth of July and Labor Day. The annual Port, Peanut, and Pine Festival on the plantation grounds highlights the three main industries of Surry County, in which the park is located.

A number of privately owned manor houses west of Surry, in-cluding Upper Brandon, are sometimes open during Historic Garden Week. Archeological excavation at Flowerdew Hundred, about 20 miles upriver on the fringe of the Piedmont region, has uncovered more than sixty-five sites, including a complex of seventeenth-century English-style houses. Thousands of artifacts dating from 9000 B.C. to the Civil War have been recovered, many of which are on display in a museum. A replica of an eighteenth-century windmill has been constructed.

Smith's Fort Plantation on state Route 31 north of Surry Court House gets its name from a fort constructed by Capt. John Smith in 1609 to protect settlers at Jamestown from attack, but is more famous as the dowry of the Indian princess Pocahontas when she married John Rolfe in 1614. The much-copied, dormer-windowed, brick Rolfe-Warren House dates from the mid-seventeenth century and retains almost all its original woodwork. It is furnished in antiques from the sixteenth to early eighteenth centuries, including a William and Mary lacquered mirror and 1717 pewter chandelier. A footpath leads to ruins on the original fort site. Owned by the Association for the Preservation of Virginia Antiquities, it is open daily during Historic Garden Week and Tuesday through Sunday from April to September.

The car ferry on state Route 31 between Surry County and Jamestown occupies almost the exact site where a ferry has operated since colonial days.

Isle of Wight County is the headquarters of the Tidewater Soaring Club, which operates from privately owned Garner Airport. The expanses of water in the Hampton Roads area — as well as elsewhere around the Bay — are not conducive to gliding, but gliders can reach altitudes of 5,000 to 8,000 feet and distances up to 60 miles by using the thermal lift provided by open fields and large asphalt areas. The buoyancy in the area is erratic and can dissipate quickly, however. The record altitude in the area is 12,000 feet, low by gliding standards.

Virginia Peninsula

Virginia Peninsula Tourism & Conference Bureau,
Patrick Henry International Airport,
Newport News, VA 23602. Tel: 804/881-9777.

Hampton Department of Conventions & Tourism,
710 Settlers Landing Road, Hampton, VA 23669.
Tel.: 804/727-6108.

THE SHORELINE OF VIRGINIA IS DOMINATED BY A SERIES OF PENINSULAS divided by the broad James, York, and Rappahannock rivers. In this situation, it is strange, but true, that one of them is identified as the Virginia Peninsula or simply The Peninsula—generally, with a capital "T." The Peninsula, which lies between the navigable James and York rivers, claims its title by virtue of being the first area in the United States to receive a permanent English colony and its major contribution to the creation of the United States.

Jamestown, where the first fragile colony was established, is there. So is Williamsburg, the colonial capital of Virginia and the seat of early Constitutional law. So is Yorktown, where the decisive defeat of Lord Cornwallis's British army confirmed American independence. The area was an important battleground and staging area during the Civil War.

These national monuments are supplemented by modern cities that build many of the warships in the U.S. Navy, participate in the U.S. space program, and unload and process a large portion of the Bay seafood.

The James and York have served the dual purposes of social and commercial intercourse since the founding of the first colony. They were the primary means of travel for the early settlers, when virtually every plantation had its own transportation. Crops were moved from the plantation to waiting vessels from Europe. Boats were

235

used for fishing and hunting, and even social visits to nearby farms. A ferry system across the James River developed quickly, using dugout canoes. By 1704, three ferries provided transportation across the James River — one near the site of the present Jamestown-Scotland Ferry on state Route 31.

The geographical Peninsula extends inland almost to Richmond. The area generally referred to as the Lower Peninsula — the cities of Newport News and Hampton, town of Poquoson, and urbanized county of York — and the city of Williamsburg and James City county are within the Bay sphere.

The first impression that most visitors will get of The Peninsula is that it is a single unit. Economically and physically, that is true. Urban areas have grown together so that it is difficult to detect when one passes from one community to the next. The second impression will be that of spaciousness; the political subdivisions spread out over more than 200 square miles of land and water areas. Older buildings tend to be only a few stories in height; the modern towers of ten or more stories have risen in the last two decades.

Interstate 64 crosses the Hampton Roads Bridge-Tunnel from Norfolk and cuts across The Peninsula on its westward journey. I-64 connects with I-664, which when completed in 1991 will complete a beltway around Hampton Roads. Mercury Boulevard — named after the Mercury space program, which was first headquartered in Hampton — and U.S. Route 17 are the major intersecting roads.

While the terrain is relatively flat, going from sea level to 50 feet at the highest point, the attractions are too scattered to make walking between them attractive. Bike trails pass many of them and also open up the numerous parks and significant areas of vegetation that lie in the northwestern area of Newport News and around Williamsburg.

Hampton and Newport News have marked self-driving tours that overlap to some degree but reach all the major attractions.

Hampton

Hampton's character is a curious mixture of past and future. A tendency to dote on its exciting history has never impeded its interest in visionary projects. Apparently, the present takes care of itself.

The oldest continuous English-speaking city in the United States has continued to make history since Fort Algernon was established in 1610 to guard the approaches to the settlement at Jamestown. A replica of the kind of Indian village visited by Capt. John Smith stands on West Mercury Boulevard beside the small museum honoring Thomas Eaton and Benjamin Syms, who in 1635 set aside land to sustain the first free school in the United States.

Hampton developed first as a colonial port and was important enough to interest Blackbeard, alive and dead, and other pirates, as well as commercial and naval vessels. According to local legend, one of Blackbeard's favorite hideouts lay along the banks of Sunset Creek. For sure, he was in Hampton after he was caught off the North Carolina coast. His severed head was stuck on a stake near the entrance to Hampton River, as a warning to others inclined to ravage the Bay and Middle Atlantic coast.

Ivy-fringed St. John's Episcopal Church, a handsome 1726 brick structure housing a congregation that dates back to 1610, survived the burning of the city during the War of 1812 and the Civil War. Its communion service, made in London in 1618 and in use since 1627, is the oldest in continuous service in the United States.

Moated, star-shaped Fort Monroe, completed in 1834 as part of America's coastal defenses, is the largest stone fort ever built in the United States. It retains most of its early nineteenth-century appearance, with narrow firing ports and large casemates, despite additions over the years and the presence of an active military command. The Casemate Museum, which includes the cell in which Confederate President Jefferson Davis was imprisoned after the Civil War, occupies several casemates. Other displays extend from the increasing range of coastal artillery over the years to housekeeping and uniforms of the mid-nineteenth century. The museum is open 10:30 A.M. to 5 P.M. year round.

President Lincoln stayed at Quarters 1, a white frame structure, during a visit in 1862. The housing used by Robert E. Lee as a young engineering officer directing completion of the fort is not far away. A 49,000-pound Rodman cannon, used in the Civil War, overlooks the parade ground flanked by nineteenth-century barracks.

Waterside concerts by the Continental Army Command Band are presented at 7:30 every Thursday evening during warm months at Continental Park. An Easter sunrise service is held at the same site.

Big Bethel Monument Park, on Big Bethel Road in the northern part of the city, marks the area where the first major ground battle and the first combat casualty of the Civil War occurred.

Hampton remains as water oriented as ever, but the emphasis has shifted from international trade to seafood and pleasure boating. More than three hundred slips along Hampton River and smaller streams secure the sleek hulls of sailboats and power boats. Recreational fishers try their luck in the James River, Mill Creek, Chesapeake Bay, and the pond at Big Bethel Monument Park. In July, Hampton River is the terminus of the Virginia Cruise Cup race, which starts in Annapolis, Maryland. A few weeks earlier, in late June, the Hampton Cup Regatta attracts scores of inboard and outboard racers. A brand new downtown esplanade featuring a Visitors Center in the shape of a nineteenth-century Bay lighthouse emphasizes the change.

Seafood harvesting and processing is one of the city's major industries, although it is decreasing in relative importance as small high-tech and research industries grow up around the Langley Laboratory of the National Aeronautics and Space Administration. Nevertheless, the seafood plants in the downtown and Phoebus areas continue to justify the "Crabbers" name of Hampton High School teams.

A 2½-hour narrated boat tour, which leaves from the downtown Visitors Center, descends Hampton River past the late nineteenth-century buildings of Hampton University and the point where Blackbeard's severed head hung ingloriously, and crosses Hampton Roads to pass the Norfolk Naval Yard. During a stop at Fort Wool, which has been open to the public only a few years, rangers pinpoint changes in fort design and construction over the last 150 years — some of the original 1826 casemates, five major 1901–1908 batteries, and one constructed during World War II. The *Miss Hampton* cruises daily from May 1 to the end of September.

In recent years, Hampton has become almost as devoted to entertainment events as to history. A "party at the point" brings music and feasting to a downtown waterfront area each Friday during the summer. Free luncheon concerts are held on weekdays during the same period. For three days in mid-September, Hampton Bay Days produce free concerts, traditional seafood feasts, tall ships, a yacht race, sporting events, waterskiing shows, a 10K run, and a fireworks display.

An annual June jazz festival is co-sponsored by the city and Hampton University, a prestigious school that has grown to 4,000 students from the still-standing Emancipation Oak under which freed slaves were taught. The university's cultural program also includes a museum emphasizing African, American, and American Indian art and artifacts and a continuing program of plays, musicals, and visiting lecturers. Hampton University's original buildings, including Victorian-style

Virginia Hall and the Romanesque revival Memorial Church with a 150-foot-high tower, date from the 1870s and 1880s.

The Visitors Center at the NASA Langley Laboratory emphasizes the facility's dual function as a primary aircraft research station and as headquarters of space programs. The more than 40 exhibits include a moon rock, Apollo 12 capsule that went to the moon, space suit, Viking Mars automated laboratory, and scale models tracing the evolution of airplanes from cloth-covered wooden planes to the supersonic transport and multi-Mach fighters. Open every day except major holidays: 8:30 A.M.–4:30 P.M. Monday–Saturday, noon to 4:30 P.M. Sunday.

Langley exhibits are scheduled to become part of the Virginia Air and Space Center and Hampton Roads History Center when they open in 1990 in downtown Hampton. The multifaceted museum will cover Hampton's long and intimate relationship with settlement, seafood, boating, aeronautics, and space.

A few of Langley's thirty-five wind tunnels are open to the public during an annual open house in late October. Adjacent Langley Air Force Base, the Air Force's largest tactical command, puts its sleek fighter planes on display at the same time.

Modern warplanes and missiles are on permanent display at Air Power Park at 413 West Mercury Boulevard, across from the Syms-Eaton Museum. Bluebird Gap Farm is a 15-acre recreational farm where children may see and pet small farm animals from 9 A.M. to 5 P.M. Wednesday–Sunday, except Thanksgiving and Christmas days.

More than any other Hampton Roads city, Hampton remains a community of sections with strong local identification. This results from the existence of small communities such as Buckroe Beach, Phoebus, Fox Hill, and Grandview before the present 55-square-mile city took shape.

Buckroe Beach, until a few decades ago a summer resort attracting visitors from Richmond and other inland cities, retains a sizable public beach although most of the area has been converted to private use. A fishing pier operates during the warm months, and the city is creating a 10-acre park adjacent to the boardwalk in the area once occupied by an amusement park.

The more isolated beach at Grandview has a long history of recreational use by local residents. A fishing pier and campground lie south of the 578-acre Grandview Nature Reserve, open daily and favored by bird-watchers. The beach on the reserve stretches all the way to

Factory Point, where Back River enters Chesapeake Bay, but has no parking lot. Parking in nearby residential areas leaves at least a mile walk to the beach, which sunbathers and surfcasters share with shorebirds, including nesting piping plover, egrets, and terns. Another frequent visitor is the snow bunting, which normally prefers to navigate along the Atlantic coastline.

At Old Point Comfort, traditionally Hampton's most prestigious resort area, the Chamberlin Hotel carries on a tradition that dates back to the early nineteenth century. The handsome brick structure, noted for large lobby columns, has a roof garden that overlooks the water and nearby Fort Monroe.

Newport News

A mural in the downtown branch of the Newport News Public Library depicts Capt. Christopher Newport refilling his water casks at a spring a short distance from where the library now stands. The mural illustrates a curious fact about Newport News: it was a recognized place name almost three centuries before it became a city. The city developed in the 1890s after Collis P. Huntington chose the site as the deep-water terminus of the Chesapeake and Ohio Railway and of a shipyard to build ocean-going vessels.

The stringbean city, which stretches 25 miles along the James River and is 4 miles wide at its broadest point, has remained true to that calling. The Newport News shipyard, where the tug *Dorothy,* its first construction job, is on public display, is now the largest privately owned shipbuilding company in the United States. The C&O tracks, now part of CSX Corporation, carry bulk and break bulk cargoes to the major port.

These aspects have shaped the history of the city in other ways. During World War I and II, millions of U.S. soldiers marched to war through the port. A Victory Arch stands on the since-vanished street down which most of them marched to and from troopships. Large outdoor paintings depict the events, while memorials on the arch honor those who have died in combat since World War I.

Christopher Newport Park, on the banks of the James River, preserves the site of the spring that helps explain the city's unusual name. In all probability, starving colonists ready to abandon Jamestown sighted the tardy supply vessels commanded by one-armed Capt. Newport and proclaimed the good news. Outdoor paintings and a statue of Huntington stand among the flowers and fountains of the attractive park.

Huntington Park, between Warwick Boulevard and the James River, is more than a rose garden escape from the traffic and bustle of the city. Nestled among the trees and flower beds is the War Memorial Museum of Virginia, which traces American conflicts from the Revolutionary War to the present, with emphasis on the twentieth century. A French "40 & 8," the train car used to transport U.S. soldiers in France during World War I, is one of five remaining *merci* cars sent to the United States as expressions of gratitude by France. Machine guns, tanks, cannon, medals, uniforms, wartime posters, a silver service used in Hitler's Reich Chancery, and other artifacts are among more than 16,000 items on display. Each December, reactivated Civil War units establish a winter camp on the grounds, not far from an old railway steam engine. The museum is open 9 A.M. to 5 P.M. Monday–Saturday and 2 to 5 P.M. Sunday, year round. A fishing pier juts into the river.

The Mariners Museum, which has its own park at the intersection of Warwick and J. Clyde Morris boulevards, recently opened a new 16,000-square-foot gallery devoted to the ecology and history of Chesapeake Bay. The 3,200-pound golden eagle figurehead from the steam frigate *U.S. Lancaster* hovers over the entrance to the gallery, which uses hundreds of artifacts, maps, photographs, and computer games to cover subjects ranging from Indian methods of fishing and canoe building to the traditions of the Bay oysterman and crabbers. A 30-foot dead rise power boat, circa 1630 log canoe, 35-foot menhaden purse seine boat, and menhaden striker boat stand near a working Cape Charles Lighthouse lens, examples of three shipbuilding traditions (wood, riveted metal, and welded steel and aluminum) and displays on the Bay's economic importance, recreational use, and military presence.

In other galleries are miniature vessels, hand-carved by August Crabtree, that have received international acclaim, relics from the Union ironclad *Monitor* recovered from the bottom of the Atlantic, dozens of ship ornaments, detailed scale models of ocean-going ships, and artifacts that range from scrimshaw on whalebone and maritime art to a one-man submarine. The Hampton One, a racing sloop designed by two Peninsula men, continued the long-standing Bay tradition of creating new boats to meet particular needs. The *Jaysto,* the first Hampton One racing sloop ever built, in 1935, sailed in many races before it was donated to the museum in 1976.

A Christmas at Sea display, which depicts the life of a nineteenth-century seaman at that time of year, opens every mid-December. Visitors also may watch classes at work in the boatbuilding shed. The museum also has a major maritime library.

The Peninsula Fine Arts Museum on the grounds of the museum houses permanent and changing exhibits.

A two-hour tour of the Hampton Roads is provided by cruise ships *Ocean Patriot, American Patriot,* and *Virginia Patriot,* which depart from the Small Boat Harbor at the end of Jefferson Avenue one to four times a day from April 1 to the end of October. The double-deck vessel passes close to the CSX coal-loading piers and the nuclear submarines and carriers under construction in the Newport News shipyard, then turns to follow the south shore of Hampton Roads past commercial terminals and the naval vessels tied up at the Norfolk Naval Base. It returns to port along the Hampton shoreline.

Longer night cruises run Friday–Sunday from June through September. An 8-hour trip across Hampton Roads, up the Elizabeth River, through the Great Bridge locks on the Intracoastal Waterway and along the eastern edge of the Dismal Swamp sails Thursday–Saturday mid-April until the end of May and late August to the end of October.

The U.S. Army's Transportation School is located at Fort Eustis, in the northern part of the city. Its museum, open from 9 A.M. to 4:30 P.M. every day except federal holidays, traces the development of army transportation from the colonial era to the present experimental vehicles. On display in outside pavilions are watercraft such as a tugboat and amphibious vehicle DUKW, helicopters and planes, railroad equipment, including a full-size steam engine, and tanks and armored vehicles. A "Super Day," which includes helicopter demonstrations, train rides for the kids, and a display of active military vehicles, is held annually in early August. Although one of The Peninsula's oldest homes, Matthew Jones House, is located on the base, the site generally is not open to the public.

The 10-acre forested Virginia Living Museum on J. Clyde Morris Boulevard between Warwick Boulevard and Jefferson Avenue provides in-city observation of wild animals on the shore of Deer Park Lake. Animal life at the water's edge, including beaver, otter, and wild birds, is viewed from a lakeshore boardwalk, which leads back into the native forest inhabited by turkey, foxes, bobcat, eagle, and deer. Signs and interpreters provide information about the interrelation of animals and their habitats, starting at 9 A.M. Monday–

Saturday year round, closing at 6 P.M. from Memorial Day to Labor Day and at 5 P.M. the rest of the time. Sunday hours are 10 A.M. to 6 P.M. during the warm months and 1 P.M. to 5 P.M. at other times. Also open every Thursday evening from 7 to 9 P.M., but closed Thanksgiving Day, Christmas Eve and Day, and New Year's Day.

Indoor displays include a walk-through, two-tier aviary, four 15-foot aquariums, and displays on wildlife survival, Chesapeake Bay, and the James River. Planetarium programs are presented one or more times daily.

The annual two-day January Hampton Roads Waterfowl and Wildlife Festival at the Hellenic Community Center on Route 17 near I-64 features art and crafts and benefits the Virginia Living Museum.

Each year, in August, an air show is held at Patrick Henry International Airport.

Newport News' historic affinity for the outdoors shows best at Newport News Park, located on Jefferson Avenue (Route 143) just north of Fort Eustis Boulevard. The park provides opportunities for a variety of activities on about a third of a reservoir system, which includes two impounded lakes. The park has three coordinated areas with separate entrances: a day-use portion with playgrounds, picnic tables, ranger station, and interpretive center, camping area, and Deer Run Golf Course, an 18-hole championship course.

The park has a number of interconnected hiking trails, starting at either the interpretive center or the campground, which frequently attract hiking clubs for walks of up to several hours. The basic route is the 2.8-mile white oak nature trail, which starts at the center and passes the fringe of the golf course to cross the head of Lee Hall Reservoir before plunging into the dense forest on the opposite shore of the lake. Additional loops lead off this main path, including a 1.2-mile windmill loop and a 0.7-mile twin forks loop, which passes a number of Civil War earthworks. A footbridge across the reservoir returns to the interpretive center. A short nature trail for handicapped people visits old homesites in a forested area.

Hikers also may use fire roads in the park and, with proper precaution, may enter the larger section of the watershed area, which is undeveloped. A 5.6-mile bike trail, which starts at the camping area, loops through the same forest as the hiking trails. Horseback riding also is permitted.

These trails wend through the park forest, which features conifers and flowering trees, including eastern red cedar, pine, ash, beech, dogwood, elm, hickory, holly, and oak. Underbrush includes a variety of ferns, including the royal, cut-leaf grape, cinnamon, bracken, and marsh fern, and shrubs and vines such as blackberry, elderberry, huckleberry, scotch broom, honeysuckles, and Virginia creeper. Mushrooms also grow in the forest. Wildflowers brighten the trails from spring into October. Among them are bugle, dwarf iris, grape hyacinth, ground ivy, periwinkle, violets, pink lady's slipper, showy and southern yellow orchis, buttercups, Japanese honeysuckle, bloodroot, yellow wood sorrel, strawberry, bull thistle, New York ironweed, purple gerardia, scarlet pimpernel, swamp rose, closed gentian, nodding lady tresses, small woodland orchid, black-eyed Susan, evening primrose, winged monkey flower, and passion flower.

Deer and small animals, including foxes, weasel, river otter, and raccoon, are frequently seen. Numerous species of bats have been identified, as have a variety of snakes and reptiles, including turtles. Bobcat is not unknown, although no recent sightings have been reported. Resident birds include great blue heron, black duck, wood duck, mallard, killdeer, rock and mourning doves, owls, belted kingfisher, eastern bluebird, mockingbird, eastern meadowlark, and red-winged blackbird. The population explodes in winter with the arrival of whistling swan, Canada goose, gadwell, pintail, green-winged teal, canvasback, ring-necked duck, bufflehead, merganser, scoter, scaup, and ruddy duck. Spring and summer visitors and migrants include thrushes; green-backed, Louisiana, and little blue herons; common and snowy egrets, glossy and white ibises, sandpipers, terns, yellow-billed cuckoo, yellow-bellied sapsucker, purple martin, warblers, and vireos.

A ramp for small boats gives fishers access to the reservoir, which is stocked from a spawning pond on the edge of the golf course. Catches include widemouth bass, yellow and white perch, crappie, pickerel, northern pike, catfish, sunfish, bluegill, and warmouth.

A Confederate defensive line, which stretched 12 miles across The Peninsula, passed through the current park. On April 16, 1862, during Gen. George B. McClellan's Peninsula Campaign to take the Confederate capital at Richmond, elements of the 1st, 3rd, 4th, and 7th Vermont Infantry attacked units of the 15th North Carolina, 7th Georgia, and 2nd Louisiana Infantry, but were repulsed with heavy losses. Although the Confederates later abandoned the defensive line, the Battle of Dam No. 1, which was part of the Confederate fortifications, delayed the Union advance for a month. Ten miles of original earthworks, some as high as 20 feet, are preserved and portions are visible from hiking trails. The dam, now under water, can be seen from the footbridge across the lake. A display of Civil War relics, including artillery projectiles and bullets and a photo of the original dam, supplements the butterfly, snake, and aquatic life exhibits in the Interpretive Center. A Civil War cannon and limber stand beside the entrance to the center.

The long, lean contour of Newport News is ideal for bike trails and the city has responded by marking ten that follow byways, some of them scenic, through various parts of the city. The longest stretches 18.4 miles from Route 60 near Fort Eustis in the west to City Hall, near the tip of The Peninsula. It traverses a number of waterfront and inland residential areas, including World War I–era Hilton Village, the first planned government housing development, and parks. Several shorter paths project fom this trail. The road through the grounds of the Mariners Museum is a 1.3-mile scenic route, while a 4.2-mile path connects Warwick High School and U.S. Route 17 at the York County line. Trails also are marked in the East End section of the city near the Hampton Roads shoreline.

Just across the James River Bridge from Newport News, off Route 17, is Ragged Island Wildlife Management Area. The flow of traffic on the highway is so constant that it can be heard on the marshy refuge, but the natural area demonstrates the diversity of the wetlands at Hampton Roads. A short trail wends through tall pines and then skirts the edge of the marsh before dividing, with one branch extending on a boardwalk over the marsh. The boardwalk not only provides a close encounter with the movements of marshland, from wind-blown grass to the peregrinations of the birds, but also looks across the river to the residential and industrial skyline of Newport News.

York River State Park

The natural beauty of 2,505-acre York River State Park northwest of Williamsburg is inspiring. The park, opened to year-round use in 1980, permits easy access to all activities with a minimal disturbance of natural surroundings. The experience begins on the paved entrance road, which traverses a rolling forested area, and continues on foot trails through woodlands, past a pond, and to sandy beaches with dead tree stumps at the water's edge.

Canoe excursions led by the park naturalist are a major activity from mid-July to early September. Two-hour trips on Saturdays and

A canoeing expedition paddles up Taskinas Creek in York State Park, Virginia. PHOTO BY JOHN BOWEN.

Sundays explore Taskinas Creek, which meanders through a tidal marsh intrusion into the forest. Twilight canoe trips on Fridays expose the creek at a time when animals are moving about. Four-hour floats, which explore both saltwater marsh and freshwater swamp or the park's York River shoreline, are held on specific days. The organized program for children also includes instruction on plant and animal life and nature, and on art. Programs for adults range from demonstrations on how to catch and cook blue crab to discussions of the habits of marsh creatures.

Eleven hiking trails and connecting segments, some of which use short bridges to cross difficult areas, cover all sections of the pine and hardwood forest, which is the habitat of deer and smaller animals and numerous species of birds, especially hawks and songbirds. Paths range in length from the 0.2-mile Spur Trail, actually a connection between other trails, to the 1.9-mile Backbone Trail. A 1.3-mile bike and fitness trail skirts Woodland Pond and extends into the nearby forest, where it intersects with the 1.4-mile Mattaponi hiking way. The circular 1.6-mile Taskinas Creek Trail, marked with interpretive signs, parallels the entrance road through a forested area and past a meadow where goldenrod, daisy, lespedeza, and berry bushes grow in the shadow of pine, tulip poplar, and sweet gum. The flowering underbrush and ferns under oaks, black walnuts, and maples help provide sustenance for white-tailed deer, rabbits, woodchuck, snakes, frogs, lizards, bees, butterflies, ticks, chiggers, thrushes, vireos, warblers, and woodpeckers. The tidal marsh has two faces, depending on the run of the tide, but the abundant salt marsh cordgrass thrives on the ebb and flow of water. In this changing habitat live muskrat, rails, marsh and fiddler crabs, mink, raccoon, mosquitoes, gnats, and wildfowl. Both the Pamunkey and Majestic Oak trails lead to overlooks on the banks of the York River.

Fishing lines may be dropped in either salt or fresh water. Steps near Picnic Shelter No. 3 lead to a small beach, where surfcasters may try to hook spot, croaker, bluefish, catfish, and other varieties in the York River. Perch, catfish, and eel frequent Taskinas Creek, and bass and bluegill are among the inhabitants of freshwater Woodland Pond.

York River State Park is only a few miles off Interstate 64, via state Routes 607 and 606. A separate section of the park, reached by continuing along state Routes 607 and 605, has twin ramps and piers to launch boats into the York River, but use of these facilities is recommended only at high tide.

Historic Triangle

STARTING A NEW COUNTRY WAS NOT EASY. THE FIRST PERMANENT ENGLISH colony at Jamestown, founded in 1607, lost so many citizens during the winter of 1609 that the period was known as the Starving Time. Those who survived were preparing to abandon the adventure when relief ships arrived. Nor was keeping it going easy, even after the capital of Virginia was moved to more amenable climate in Williamsburg. Nationhood had to be won on the battlefield at Yorktown.

This three-act drama of early America is conveniently lined up along a 23.8-mile arc named the Colonial National Parkway, one of the most scenic roadways in America. The parkway, Jamestown, and Yorktown are united in the Colonial National Historical Park, covering about 10,000 acres, while Colonial Williamsburg is preserved by a private foundation.

The parkway, an extra-wide two-lane road, is an ideal bike route from Jamestown National Historical Park at one end to Yorktown National Historical Park at the other. Williamsburg lies near the center, and is a good place to start on either leg. A variety of natural perspectives along the mostly flat terrain make the parkway interesting year round—hikers and bikers are out even on relatively warm days in winter—but it is particularly beautiful in the spring when the dogwoods bloom. Parking overlooks and grassy plots, where people picnic, sunbathe, toss Frisbees, and walk their dogs, are just as convenient for bikers as they are for automobile drivers.

At the Jamestown end, the parkway passes a marshy area and extends for several miles along the banks of the James River, broken in places by sandy beaches. It then turns inland through forested areas, past fields, and over streams and ponds to Williamsburg. A more circuitous off-parkway route explores rural roads 612, 511, 633, and 614 west and south of the city en route to Williamsburg.

The 13-mile leg between Williamsburg and Yorktown is the most popular for nature viewing. Leaving the Colonial Williamsburg Visitors Center, the roadway passes through a lane of tall pine trees and under graceful brick arches handling cross traffic. The first scenic turnout is at Jones Mill Pond, whose dam is now covered by the parkway. The pond may have existed in the colonial era, since it is carefully marked on Civil War maps. A path leads from the parking site through the woods to the edge of the pond. In the summer, visitors will not be aware of the narrowness of the parkway land at this point because foliage will block off the houses and military bases, which in winter, when many trees are barren, occasionally are visible just outside the boundaries.

Passing over Kings Creek, much of which is covered with marsh grass, the visitor enters an area where Indian villages were replaced by colonial farms. On the grounds of Ringfield Plantation, granted to Capt. Robert Felgate in 1630, are turnouts revealing historical associations with Col. Nathaniel Bacon (not "the Rebel Nathaniel Bacon who led the 1676 uprising against royal authority") and overlooking the piers and buildings of the U.S. Navy's Cheatham Annex supply center. A little farther on are the graveyard and ruins of Bellfield Plantation, which was the home of two colonial governors. One of them, Edward Digges, produced superior tobacco and experimented with developing a silk industry. The site was farmed until after World War I, but for the most part has reverted to nature.

A low shoreline bordered by trees and marsh grass identifies Indian Field Creek, once the home of the Chiskiack Indians, a small tribe whose "werowance" or leader was a subordinate to the powerful Chief Powhatan. Powhatan's village, Werowocomoco, was located on the Gloucester County shore of the York River. For some distance from this point, the relative lack of foliage permits clear views of the broad York River and the neatly spaced white houses on the far shore. English colonists named the river, whose tidal waters flow over the deepest natural channel in the Chesapeake Bay area, after the Duke of York. The river was known to the Indians as the Pamunkey, a name now associated with a smaller Virginia river.

Just before the road passes over Brackens Pond, a turnout provides a clear view of the piers of the Naval Weapons Station, founded in 1918 as a mine depot and still an important supply base. Past a sandy beach in a cove and other natural sights, where unfortunately no turnout exists, are exits to the Victory Center, Route 17, and the Yorktown Battlefield at the end of the parkway.

The Historic Virginia Triangle, which this scenic road connects, represents more history than any area of comparable size in the country. The easiest way to tour it is to progress chronologically.

Jamestown

Cooperation between state and federal governments enhances the presentation at Jamestown. Remains of the early colony are preserved at Jamestown National Historical Park, while the state has reconstructed at nearby Jamestown Settlement the three small ships that brought the first settlers to these shores and the log fortress that protected them.

A visit to the Jamestown National Historical Park is as much an outdoors as a historical experience, beginning with a turnout on the entrance road that introduces the visitor to the topography confronting the first settlers. In 1607, a sandy isthmus stood where the road now crosses to the island, making Jamestown Island in effect a semi-island and, consequently, more vulnerable to attack. The land bridge was washed away in the 1700s. This vantage point also provides a good view of the Jamestown-Scotland Neck ferry across the river and the replicas of the three vessels on which the first settlers sailed.

Displays at the Visitors Center, ranging from weapons and a silver ornament owned by Chief Powhatan's daughter Pocahontas to a model of the second James Fort constructed in June 1607, provide a short course in the significance of the park. An introduction to the lifestyle includes models of early homes and information on animals. Horses and dogs were prized by early settlers, but were so susceptible to disease, wolves, and hostile Indians that only one horse was shown in the census of 1625.

The national park has two principal trails — a walking path to excavated sites and memorials near the Visitors Center, and a circular drive through the woods, over the marshes and creeks, and along the shoreline of the eastern end of the island.

The walk from the Visitors Center and obelisk memorializing the colony and its achievements involves two loops. One diverts past the excavated foundations of early homes and building sites, a few supplemented by paintings showing the appearance of the homes. The other winds past monuments, the foundations of the first statehouses, markers, and statues of the two most colorful figures associated with the early years of the colony — Pocahontas and Virginia's first governor, the talented and charismatic Capt. John Smith, who believed Pocahontas saved his life on two separate occasions. Appropriately, the statue of the peripatetic Smith looks down the river, while the Indian maiden ambles along a wooded trail. Rangers conduct historical tours of the excavations on a regular schedule in summer, or people can make the circuit at their own pace.

The Indians, members of the Algonkin group, belonged to a confederation extending from the James River to the Potomac River that had been organized by Pamunkey Chief Powhatan shortly before the English landed. While each of the thirty-five tribes retained its own chief, they paid tribute to Powhatan and provided warriors to fight his enemies north and west of the confederacy. Powhatan's relations with the settlers fluctuated. The settlers learned to plant corn, now recognized as the "great gift" of the Indians to the settlers, and to exploit the natural riches of the land and water. But at times the Indians massacred individual settlers and isolated groups, and threatened the existence of the colony. Powhatan's decision to kill Capt. John Smith produced the most romantic and enduring legend of the colonial period — Powhatan's daughter Pocahontas offering her own life to save Smith.

Markers indicate the probable sites of the first landing and initial forts, both now under water because the bank has been naturally eroded over the centuries. These sites have not been excavated, but offer interesting potential for underwater archeology. Indeed, only 24 of the 60 acres of "James Citty" have been thoroughly explored.

The significance of religion to the colony is represented by a huge wooden cross, a memorial to the Rev. Robert Hunt, the first Anglican minister, and the brick church tower, raised about 1649 as the successor to several wooden churches destroyed by fire. The tower, the entrance to a Memorial Church donated by the National Society of Colonial Dames of America, is the only above-ground seventeenth-century structure to survive the ruin that eventually followed relocation of the capital to Williamsburg in 1699. In the wooden building erected in 1617 on the same site met the first representative government in the New World. A live oak, planted June 15, 1965, commemorates the 750th anniversary of the signing of the Magna Carta, the basis of representative government in the English-speaking world.

The foundation of the third statehouse stands near the probable gravesite of many who died during the Starving Time of 1609, partly an Indian attempt to destroy the colony. A narrative board explains the incident as follows: in October 1609, when John Smith sailed for England, 490 settlers remained behind. Forty were at Point Comfort and survived the winter; 30 were killed while trying to trade with Powhatan; 30 stole a boat, the *Swallow,* and sailed for England.

Of the remaining 390, only 60 survived to the following May because the Indians killed most of the settlement's 600 hogs, drove the deer away, refused to trade corn, and killed settlers who strayed from the fort. Many settlers died of dysentery and typhoid from drinking the brackish well water, while others died of starvation and famine.

The marriage of Pocahontas, Powhatan's favorite daughter, and planter John Rolfe helped establish peace with the Indians for a time. She was accepted at the English court as Princess of Pamunkey and died while preparing to return home.

· The driving loop, also an excellent route for bikers, is laid out in two segments. The shorter is a 3-mile circuit that takes about 25 minutes; the complete loop covers 5 miles and takes about 45 minutes, plus whatever time one wants to spend walking a short foot trail to Black Point, the first point seen by the settlers as they sailed up the river. The view from Black Point covers both shores of the James.

The driving trail several times crosses the marshy areas that cover more than half of Jamestown Island. The Pitch and Tar Swamp, which has flowing water, was the northern boundary of "James Citty," as the colony was originally named. The name of the swamp apparently derives from the use of pines along its banks to make pitch and tar. The route also skirts Orchard Run, another marshy inlet, which formed the eastern boundary of "James Citty" and Goose Hill Marsh on Passmore Creek. The tall marsh grass was used as roof thatch by early settlers, and by muskrat to build their beehive-shaped houses. The habitat also is attractive to red-winged blackbirds.

Thirty pullouts along the long route provide an introduction into the historical significance of a number of places and the lifestyle of the initial settlers. Large paintings at eleven of the stops portray the homes and activities of the colonists, including construction of small boats for transportation, fishing, and trade; the art of brick making (three kiln sites have been identified), a necessary talent for the new settlement; making potash and soap ashes from the forest, so important to the colony that artisans were especially recruited in England; manufacture of glazed earthenware, under way within 25 years after the first landing; wine making, from the vines described by Capt. John Smith as being in "great abundance in many parts that climbe the toppes of the highest trees"; settlers visiting an Indian village on a trading expedition; the first planting of crops within weeks after arrival and development of tobacco farming, which became the "economic cornerstone" of the colony; home weaving; fashioning of lumber and wood products; the cooper at work about

1625; and the interior of a comfortable Jamestown home of 1650, with a few luxuries added to the necessities.

Signs without paintings point out nearly a score of important features, including the remnants of a Civil War earthen fort; migrating wildfowl in such numbers that colonist William Strachey reported, "no country in the world may have more"; trade between the colonists and the Indians, who prized copper and white bread and offered furs and wild meat in exchange; the value of the oak, walnut, cypress, cedar, and pine trees to settlers in making "staves, clap-board, yards and masts"; the grant of three acres of land to each settler to encourage agriculture; the massacre of a family by Indians while the father was attending church; sightings of herds of 50, 100, and 200 deer, according to a letter written in 1611 by a settler; the site of the Island House, built in 1619 by Richard Kingsmill, an ancestor of the explorer Meriwether Lewis; and the property owned by Sir George Yeardley, who carried the "Great Charter" to Jamestown in 1619 and served two terms as governor.

Multifaceted Jamestown Settlement, built as part of the celebration of the 350th anniversary of the founding of Jamestown, complements the national park by exploring the reasons for settlement, the means of transportation, and the lifestyle of the settlers. A museum enlarged in 1989 cites the inducements, including tales of semiprecious stones strewn on the beaches, which encouraged settlers to leave England for the New World, and the growth and development of the colony.

Reconstructions of the first fort and the three ships that brought the initial settlers depict the difficult life of the colonists. In the log fort, costumed guides explain the details of the daub-and-wattle houses and the homelife of the settlers. Replicas of the *Susan Constant, Godspeed,* and *Discovery,* docked on the James River waterfront, seem much too small for journeys across the Atlantic Ocean. On board, visitors may look at decks where the settlers lived during the crossing. They were so small the passengers could not stand up on them. The *Godspeed* sails occasionally on ambassadorial missions.

Colonial Williamsburg

The historic city of Williamsburg not only looks like a colonial capital, it acts like one. Duke of Gloucester Street, the heart of the 173-acre historical district, is one of the most romantic streets in America. During the daytime, there is no vehicular traffic. Visitors

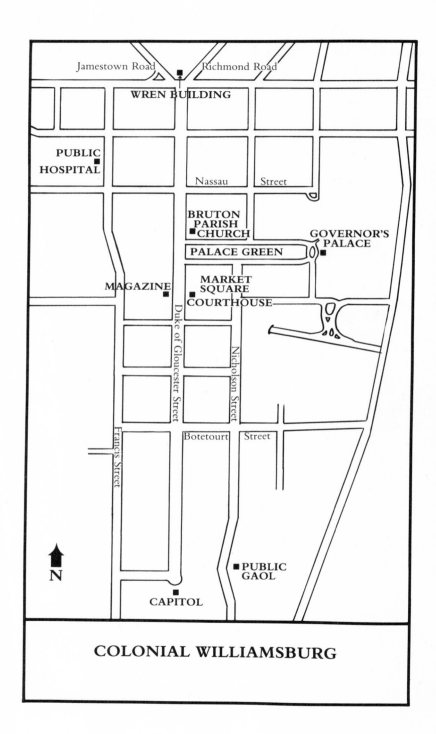

COLONIAL WILLIAMSBURG

stroll about the area the way their ancestors did; college dandies, men in knee breeches and buckled shoes, and women in long dresses performing daily tasks mingle with visitors. Horsedrawn carriages roll slowly along in a scene reminiscent of 200 years ago, sometimes carrying youngsters in tricorn hats.

Artisans use 200-year-old methods in authentic surroundings to create eighteenth-century silverware, boots, barrels, and other items complete to the last detail. Wigmakers, milliners, bookbinders, and apothecaries perform their daily tasks. Costumed interpreters relive both the comforts and the conflicts of the period when American political doctrine was being formulated within the walls of handsome brick and frame buildings. Eighteenth-century fare is served by costumed waiters and waitresses in authentic surroundings at King's Arms, Chownings, Christiana Campbell's, and Joseph Shields taverns. Walking tours pinpoint the places where George Washington, Thomas Jefferson, and Patrick Henry pitted their wills and talents against royal officials.

Events typical of those that took place when Williamsburg was the eighteenth-century capital of Virginia occur daily year round. Among more than 1,000 planned events in the 173-acre historic area are musket firing and militia drills, fife and drum corps parades, candlelight tours and concerts, eighteenth-century plays, witch trials, fairs, decorating workshops, lectures, folk art exhibitions, architectural scavenger hunts, and seasonal events, especially the Grand Illumination for the Christmas season and the fifty-day Prelude to Independence before July Fourth, which salutes the original thirteen colonies.

Many of the exhibit buildings, including the Governor's Palace, are used for after-hours programs. The soft light of candles deepens the colors of the ballroom at the Governor's Palace as it did when seven colonial governors and the first two executives of the Commonwealth of Virginia, Patrick Henry and Thomas Jefferson, listened to the high-pitched tones of the harpsichord.

The Governor's Palace, which fronts a long green off Duke of Gloucester Street, is impressive at any time, however. From the Chinese vases in the entrance hall to the 200-year-old rag wallpaper in the supper room, it is furnished according to records kept by early governors. The opulence of the Georgian-style "governor's house" so dismayed taxpayers that they derided it as a "palace," a name that stuck.

The 10 acres of grounds are just as impressive as the mansion.

Visitors exit to the ballroom and holly gardens, a harmonious mixture of flowers, shrubs, and trees including golden-rain, dogwood, dwarf boxwood, jonquils, and tulips. A formal box garden and terraces overlook an old canal seeded with aquatic plants and the graveyard of 156 unidentified Revolutionary War casualties, now marked by a single stone and weeping willow trees. At the rear of the property, past a fruit garden, is a popular eighteenth-century diversion, a boxwood maze.

The circa 1755 George Wythe House, also noted for its garden, fronts on the west side of the Palace Green. The garden combines productive and ornamental plants around a bowling green hedged with boxwood. In this setting, law professor Wythe ruminated about the law and political philosophy he imparted to Thomas Jefferson, John Marshall, and Henry Clay. George Washington stayed at the house before the siege of Yorktown. Interpreters today make yarn and cloth and handle kitchen chores beside the herb garden, fruit orchard, crepe myrtle, paw-paw, chinaberry, fig, sycamore, and locust.

The frame Brush-Everard House, built in 1717 by a gunsmith and first keeper of the town armory, is an example of an early middle-class home. The Geddy House and foundry and house also represent a well-to-do craftsman of the era.

Bruton Parish Church, at the southwest corner of the Palace Green and Duke of Gloucester Street, has two distinctions. It has been in continuous use as an Episcopal Church since 1715 and has a bell, used regularly on Sundays, that has announced important community events since 1761. The story of how the rector, the late Rev. W. A. R. Goodwyn, conceived the idea in the 1920s of restoring Williamsburg and enlisted the assistance of John D. Rockefeller, Jr., has entered the national folklore. Less recognized is the chain reaction, touching every section of the country and every period of American history, that the project initiated. About three hundred such restoration projects have been developed in the intervening years.

A walk along the shaded brick sidewalks of Duke of Gloucester Street progresses, "warts and all," through the early history of the town and reveals the melding of preserved and reconstructed buildings that recreate an authentic eighteenth-century city. The Wren Building of the College of William and Mary, at one end, is the oldest academic structure in the United States in continuous use. In 1775, the royal governor's surreptitious moonlight removal of the town gunpowder from the octagonal red brick Magazine brought armed citizens out into the streets. The polished muskets, bayonets, and other relics in the racks of the reconstructed Magazine probably are in better condition than those that caused the ruckus. A number of craftsmen's houses show how early communities mixed residential and business uses. Among them is the Anderson House and Blacksmith Shop, where an archeological exhibit shows the careful restoration work done in the colonial area.

Duke of Gloucester Street ends at the Capitol, where every four years the Virginia legislature holds a memorial session in recognition of the important events that took place there. The reconstructed, H-shaped building reflects the composition of Virginia's colonial government — one wing holds the first-floor chamber and second-floor committee rooms of the House of Burgesses, while the other is divided between the General Courtroom and the Chamber where the Royal Council met. The interpretation in this building, including re-enactments of political debate, court drama, and conversations with ordinary people, is among the best in Colonial Williamsburg.

Along Nicholson Street, which parallels Duke of Gloucester Street, are the public Gaol, complete with stocks where visitors temporarily confine themselves for photographs, and the Peyton Randolph House, constructed early in the eighteenth century and later the home of the first president of the Continental Congress. The Comte de Rochambeau stayed there before leaving for the siege of Yorktown and Lafayette was a visitor during his triumphant return to America in 1824.

Colonial Williamsburg is not all idealized history. One of the newest reconstructions is the Public Hospital of 1773 on Francis Street, whose exhibits portray crude eighteenth-century methods of treating insane and mentally disturbed patients. The underground DeWitt Wallace Decorative Arts Gallery, entered through the hospital, houses more than 8,000 pieces of furniture, ceramics, prints, maps, and costumes. More than 1,500 pieces of folk art are displayed in eighteenth-century room settings at the Abby Aldrich Rockefeller Folk Art Center near the Williamsburg Inn and Craft House. Metalcrafts, paintings on wood, canvas, and paper, drawings, glassware, and other pieces are changed frequently. In Bassett Hall, off Francis Street at the eastern end of the historic area, the antiques and American folk art collected by the John D. Rockefeller, Jr., family are preserved.

No ticket is required to walk the historic area and visit the crafts shops, stores, and period restaurants (reservations), but tickets are required to enter the exhibit buildings, which are open from 8:30 A.M. to 8 P.M. March 1–December 31, 8:30 A.M.–6 P.M. the rest of the year. Tourists should start by viewing movies and reviewing printed material at the Visitors Center, on Route 132 away from the historic area. A bus system, free for those holding admission tickets, connects the historic area and Visitors Center.

Williamsburg was a pioneer in developing in-town and countryside biking paths. Bicycles are fairly common on the streets of Williamsburg, many of them used by students when the College of William and Mary is in session. In-town trails include Lafayette and Hunt streets and Newport Avenue, as well as the roadways on the grounds of the College of William and Mary. The Visitors Center stands on the fringe of Colonial National Historical Parkway. In the other direction, a macadamized highway shoulder lane extends along Route 132 and Route 60, then follows state Route 646 and 696 to the York River State Park, one of the most beautiful in Virginia. A challenging 6-mile route, with steep climbs and sharp curves, follows South England Street and the Country Road to Carter's Grove mansion, built in the 1750s by Carter Burwell, and the excavated seventeenth-century settlement, Wollenstenholme, which was destroyed by warring Indians in 1622. A Route 60 return option follows a heavily used highway past Busch Gardens-The Old Country.

The Carter's Grove Country Road also is a driving route with numbered markers keyed to a guidebook identifying major sights and explaining the use of the land from the colonial period to the modern era. Although built in 1979 — Route 60 more closely follows the colonial roadway — it recreates scenes that farmhands experienced in the 1700s when they drove wooden carts loaded with meat, grain, cider, and firewood into Williamsburg. The 20-minute drive of today — past mature beech and white oak, fast-growing gum and tulip poplar, loblolly pine, locust, bayberry, rare umbrella magnolia, sycamore, and mountain laurel in the woodlands, ravines, meadows, and marshland — was almost an all-day trip for colonials. Drivers or bikers also will see wildflowers such as Queen Anne's lace, rose pink, yarrow, trumpet creeper, and butterfly weed, and cattails, sedges, and marsh mallow. Mud turtle, muskrat, raccoon, and a variety of birds live along Tutter's Neck Creek and in the flatlands, which the Indians cleared to plant corn, beans, squash, and melons. Zig-zag split-rail fences have been reconstructed. Later periods are represented by farm sites abandoned as recently as 30 years ago and by the modern homes and condominiums of Kingsmill development.

Carters Grove stands on land that was patented in 1619 as Martin's Hundred, an 80,000-acre tract that extended across the present U.S. Route 60. The mansion, built by a grandson of the original plantation owner, the wealthy Robert "King" Carter, is one of the most handsome homes in Chesapeake Bay country. It is open daily from March through November and at Christmas.

Wollenstenholme Towne, on the shores of the James River a short distance from the mansion, may have been the first planned British town in North America. The foundations of other ancient structures have been located and examined. Based on excavations, replicas of the log walls and early buildings have been reconstructed to show what it looked like.

Busch Gardens-The Old Country, a theme park off U.S. Route 60 adjacent to one of the company's breweries, is a newcomer to the Historic Triangle. It tastefully recreates European atmosphere in England, France, Germany, and Italy with more than a hundred rides, shows, and attractions. Key elements are the Globe Theatre with regular musical performances, train, and riverboat rides, a Munich-style festhaus, and a serpentine roller coaster named the Loch Ness Monster. The world-famous Anheuser-Busch Clydesdales perform, and the park has a collection of deer and other wild animals for viewing.

The Old Country is open daily from Memorial Day to Labor Day, weekends starting in May and ending in October.

Guided tours of the brewery start at a separate Hospitality Center.

The city of Williamsburg operates two areas of outdoor interest. Waller Mill Park, off Old Airport Road (state Route 645), surrounds a 343-acre reservoir well supplied with stripers, bass, yellow perch, catfish, crappie, bluegill, and brim. A launching ramp is supplemented by concessions renting fishing boats, canoes, and pedal boats. Three circular trails cover various areas of the 2,300-acre park. The 3½-mile Dogwood Trail on the upper end of the lake follows a bank with stands of bayberry and circles back through a forest of dogwoods, oaks, holly, and underbrush. The 3-mile Lookout Tower Trail on the lower lake covers the same kind of ground but has an observation platform on the lake. A 1½-mile self-guided nature trail has seventy-two numbered stakes, keyed to a guidebook, which identify major tree groups such as scarlet oak, northern red oak, and bayberry, shrubs, blueberry, ground cover such as Virginia creeper, and relics such as an old split-rail fence and pumphouse. College Landing Park on South English Street has a boat ramp and boardwalk over the marsh where people can relax and fish.

Yorktown

A sign on U.S. Route 17 at the entrance to York County identifies the community as the place "where American independence was won." It is justified pride. The colony born at Jamestown and nurtured at Williamsburg was confirmed as a nation on the field of battle at Yorktown.

In 1776, British Gen. Charles Lord Cornwallis led his army into Yorktown, then an important port on the York River, in the belief that British vessels would guard the sea lanes and evacuate his forces if need be. Gen. George Washington, commanding the American forces, and the Comte de Rochambeau, general of his French allies, recognized an opportunity to trap Cornwallis, if the French fleet could prevent the British linkup. After engaging the French in the Battle of Virginia Capes, the British fleet returned to New York, leaving Cornwallis to his fate. The successful American-French siege of Yorktown, which ended with Cornwallis's surender, was the last major battle of the Revolutionary War.

The battlefield is preserved at the Yorktown National Historical Park, while the related state-operated Victory Center and the historic structures in the town of Yorktown help place the momentous event in the context of the life of the period.

National Historical Park: A below-deck walk-through of a Revolutionary warship and other innovative exhibits supplement audio-visuals on the battle and surrender of Cornwallis in the Visitors Center. The "Lafayette cannon" was identified by the Revolutionary War hero as one that had been surrendered at Yorktown when he visited the country again in 1824. A platform atop the center overlooks portions of the battlefield, the Victory Monument erected to commemorate the winning of independence on the site, and the York River.

The Visitors Center opens at 8:30 A.M. daily year round, closes at 5 P.M. during the winter, 5:30 P.M. in spring and autumn, and 6 P.M. during the summer.

A walk along the ramparts of the British inner defense line, which stretched for 1½ miles around Yorktown, shows the strength of Cornwallis's position as long as the British controlled the York River. Revolutionary War cannon and hornworks typify the methods used to defend the position. Rangers lead guided tours of the fortifications and demonstrate operation of period cannon. "Don't stand in front of the cannon," the ranger warns a visitor who has volunteered to help in the nonfiring demonstration.

A tour of the battlefield combines walking and driving along a 6-mile route. A taped commentary can be used, but narrative boards are located at principal stops. A 9-mile extension visits sites involved in the Allied encampment, including Washington's headquarters.

Redoubt No. 10, which Americans led by Col. Alexander Hamilton stormed with fixed bayonets, was part of the British outer defense line. At Surrender Field, on October 19, 1781, a sullen British army laid down its arms to a tune named "The World Turned Upside Down." Cornwallis claimed illness and sent Gen. Charles O'Hara to surrender. George Washington, commander-in-chief, designated Gen. Benjamin Lincoln, who had been treated badly by the British when he surrendered Charleston, South Carolina, to accept it.

Other key points are the reconstructed site of the Grand French Battery, the largest gun emplacement in the initial siege line; the second Allied siege line; the site of Redoubt No. 9, stormed by the French at the same time Americans took No. 10; and the Moore House, built about 1725 and restored to the appearance it had when surrender negotiations took place there. The house is open from 1 P.M. to 5 P.M. on weekends during spring and fall, from 10 A.M. to 5 P.M. seven days a week in summertime.

The stabilized earth portion of the Battlefield Tour (identified also as the Historical Trail) is a favorite biking route during the summer months because much of it is shaded, frequent stops are possible, the route can be cut short at intersecting highways, and occasionally deer graze at dusk or dawn in open fields.

The trail starts in open fields and passes through a heavily forested area before crossing Wormley Creek on a road that has been in use for more than 300 years. A short uphill run leads to a level forested area, with historical markers identifying the campsite of Gen. Lincoln and his regulars and the camp of Virginia militia under Gen. Thomas Nelson, Jr., of Yorktown. Light infantrymen from New England, New York, and Canada, under Lafayette, camped in a nearby open field. The path continues to the positions of the American and French field hospitals; Surrender Field; the section held by Baron von Steuben's 2,000-man division, primarily composed of Virginians, Marylanders, and Pennsylvanians; American and French artillery parks, with a few cannon symbolizing the scores that stood there during the siege; narrow, sluggish Beaver Dam Creek, which was the general dividing line between the French and American forces; various headquarters sites; and the French cemetery, where fifty unknown soldiers are buried. A reconstructed redoubt, part of the outer line that the British built to cover the approach to Yorktown, and the remnant of one of the original redoubts, which the British abandoned on September 30, 1781, stand near the end of the route. **Victory Center:** On the lawn outside this modern building, dedicated in 1976 as part of the national Bicentennial celebration in Virginia, the Revolutionary War goes on at an annual summer encampment. Interpreters dressed as soldiers drill and fire muskets, while their wives prepare food, sharpen knives, and repair clothing.

The living history program is part of the attempt to place the fighting at Yorktown in the context of the period. This theme is carried out inside the museum, where the thoughts and reactions of people to the war are recreated along Liberty Street, a late eighteenth-century street. A 25-minute movie and other exhibits explore "The Road to Yorktown." The center, whose entry court off state Route 238 near the Colonial Parkway and Route 17 flies the flags of the original thirteen colonies, is open from 9 A.M. to 5 P.M. daily year round except Christmas and New Year's days, with later closing in the summer months.

Yorktown: So much attention centers on the battlefield that the historic relics in the town of Yorktown often do not get the attention they deserve. Nine buildings that survived the intense bombardment of the British fortifications and Civil War activity and the Victory Monument can be visited on a 45-minute walking tour from the battlefield Visitors Center.

A footbridge crosses a slope down which colonial hogsheads of tobacco were rolled to the harbor and ends at the Victory Monument on a bluff overlooking the York River, about a mile from the actual surrender site. The erection of the 80-foot column, topped by a statue, Goddess of Liberty, took a long time even by governmental standards. Authorized by Congress in 1781, it was not actually raised until a century later as part of the centennial celebration.

Six historic structures, most of which are privately owned and not open to the public, stand along Main Street within a few blocks of the monument: the Dudley-Diggs, Sessions, Nelson, Pate, and Somerwell houses and the Customhouses. The Swan Tavern and Medical Shop are reconstructions.

The circa 1711 Nelson House, a large Georgian brick structure, is architecturally the most impressive. According to legend, Gen.

Nelson directed fire against his own home. The cannonballs on the Nelson Street side were placed there later, however. The house, furnished with antiques, is open 10 A.M. to 5 P.M. daily mid-June to Labor Day. Two additional eighteenth-century homes, the Edmund Smith and Ballard houses, face Nelson Street. The Customshouse, built about 1721 by the collector of customs, is owned by the Comte de Grasse Chapter of the Daughters of the American Revolution.

Although the native marl exterior of Grace Episcopal Church on Church Street is not impressive architecturally, its strength and solidity have survived many adversities. Built about 1697, the church was used by the British as a powder magazine during the siege, partly burned in 1814, and damaged by a nearby explosion during the Civil War. The communion silver dates from 1649. Gen. Nelson is buried in the graveyard. The building is open from 9 A.M. to 5 P.M. daily.

A diversion from the historic walk follows a path down the bluff to the riverfront, near a cave reputedly used by Cornwallis as headquarters during the Allied bombardment and a pier to the developing museum preserving underway hulks of wrecked British warships. Before the war, merchant vessels anchored nearby while waiting to discharge tea, spices, slaves, and manufactured goods from England and take on tobacco, corn, lumber, furs, and tar for the return voyage.

The waterfront area is as active as the battlefield during the warm months. Crowds assemble on the small beach to sunbathe and swim, while fishers and crabbers use the dock behind the Post Office.

Middle Peninsula

VIRGINIA'S MIDDLE PENINSULA IS A STUDY IN CONTRASTS. THE PICTURE presented by U.S. Route 17, the major highway through the area, is different from that which occurs only a few miles off this beaten path.

Divided, four-lane Route 17 is basically a land route. It bustles with through traffic and commercial and residential activity, with only an occasional historic structure to break the monotony. The hodgepodge of offices, stores, restaurants, signs, and motels is especially noticeable near Gloucester Point, and diminishes toward

Gloucester Courthouse. North of that, houses, stores, and abandoned or operating gasoline stations spaced at intervals prevent the driver from achieving complete identification with the countryside. Only an occasional boat outlet, plant nursery, or fiberglass sailboat manufacturer provides a clue to the real nature of the region.

Route 17 is a dividing line. In general, farming predominates west of the highway; east of the route, the lifestyle is oriented toward the water. Almost all side roads lead to waterfront of some type, although some twist and turn and change numbers so that they sometimes present a bewildering network. Tree-lined, two-lane state roads lead to small county seats, fishing communities, and docks where watermen unload their catches near 30-foot yachts. Villages reflect the more placid way of life lived by watermen and farmers, despite the incursion of residential development.

The region long has been a favorite summer nesting place for a few wealthy outsiders, but an influx of permanent residents has occurred over the past three decades. The recent passion for waterfront land has increased to such an extent the region often is described as the "platinum coast." Said a recent newspaper article, "Sleepy, rural Mathews County is waking up—even if it doesn't like it." Other places are undergoing the same process.

Fishers and summer residents are well aware of the sports potential of Deltaville, Gwynn's Island, and Mobjack Bay. Other coves support clusters of private homes with piers where personal or workboats tie up. Public "landings" vary considerably in accessibility and quality, the best frequently being identified by state markers along U.S. Route 17. One of the most pristine streams in the Chesapeake Bay area, Dragon Run, flows through.

The flat terrain of the region is amenable to biking, but there are no established trails. Hunters are active, but are confined mostly to private land and forests that industries open to a limited number of shooters.

The Middle Peninsula gets its name from its location—between the two other peninsulas on the western shore of Chesapeake Bay in Virginia. It lies between two broad, navigable rivers—the York to the south and the Rappahannock to the north—and covers five counties—Gloucester, Mathews, Middlesex, Essex, and King and Queen—and part of King William County. The Middle Peninsula in turn is divided into three small peninsulas that jut into Chesapeake Bay, two of them adjoining sizable Mobjack Bay.

There are no cities, save West Point, which is located at the head of the York River at the western boundary of Chesapeake Bay country and reflects its principal industry, a paper mill. Two small Indian reservations also stand on the fringe of the region — the Pamunkey on a bend in the York River and the Mattaponi on its namesake river, but these resemble country villages more than reservations. The tribes nowadays are known chiefly for the tradition of presenting a deer to the governor each year, but Chief Custalow operates a small museum at the Mattaponi Reservation.

Despite sharp internal divisions, the Middle Peninsula generally is regarded as a unit by outsiders; even those living on adjoining peninsulas use the Middle Peninsula descriptive more frequently than the names of individual counties.

The Middle Peninsula is one of the oldest settled places in the United States. Plantations began to sprout along the 100-mile-long shoreline of Gloucester County in 1644, only thirty-seven years after the first settlement was founded at Jamestown. Agriculture, serviced by strategic river ports, dominated the early life of the region.

Many historic buildings survive at Gloucester Courthouse, Urbanna, Tappahannock, and on individual sites. Most of the historic homes, many of them dating back to the earliest days of settlement, are privately owned and not open to the public. During Historic Garden Week, sponsored by the Garden Clubs of Virginia, a changing list of private homes, both old and new, are made available for public viewing.

Gloucester-Mathews

Geography dictates a close association between Gloucester and Mathews; the only land approach to Mathews is through Gloucester. They also have close historical ties — Mathews originally was part of Gloucester County.

Geographical proximity was all the two had in common, however. In its early years, Gloucester was dominated by great landowners, whose fortunes were built on tobacco and who regarded the coast primarily as an outlet for their harvests. Mathews had few farms and was closely identified with the water. The two people in one body did not last long, and Mathews became a separate county in 1793. It chose shipbuilding as the theme of its new seal.

The distinctions remain to a certain degree, although Gloucester now has a considerable maritime presence along its 100 miles of shoreline. Seven marinas operate from sheltered coves, and the Abingdon Ruritan Club sponsors a seafood festival at Bena every May.

Gloucester Point, in recent years one of the fastest-growing areas of Virginia, reflects the creeping urbanization along Route 17 and the expanding residential development. However, a waterfront atmosphere remains at the Virginia Institute of Marine Science (VIMS), whose signs bear unfamiliar names such as crustaceology and ichthyology. Now part of the College of William and Mary, VIMS conducts one of the nation's foremost marine science research programs from piers that jut into the York River. Its boats conduct continuing evaluation of all phases of marine life. A limited interpretive program includes a small aquarium stocked with representative Bay life, including fish, horseshoe crab and starfish, and life-size models of deep-sea swimmers such as whales and sharks. The aquarium in Waterman's Hall is open from 10 A.M. to 4 P.M. weekdays.

Nearby is the county's only public beach and fishing pier, a joint project of the state-federal Virginia Outdoor Fund. On the opposite side of Route 17, at Tyndall Point, a small park preserves the remains of Revolutionary War and Civil War earthworks. Colonists

This former ferry pier at Gloucester Point, Virginia, is now a laboratory for the Virginia Institute of Marine Science. PHOTO BY JOHN BOWEN.

built a fort at Tyndall Point as early as 1667, but violence did not arrive until the British occupied the site in October 1781, just prior to their surrender at Yorktown. Confederates again fortified the point in 1861, but evacuated it in 1862 and it was thereafter fortified by Union troops.

Side roads west of Route 17 near Gloucester Point serve mainly waterfront cottages and residential areas. However, state Route 614 leads to several historic sites. A small white frame house with two chimneys at Belroi was the birthplace in 1851 of Dr. Walter Reed, conqueror of the dreaded yellow fever. The site, presented by the Medical Society of Virginia to the Society for the Preservation of Virginia Antiquities, acknowledges Reed's work in Cuba in 1900, which demonstrated that mosquitoes cause yellow fever. A few miles away, down state Route 618 on the banks of the York River, is Cappahosic, a since-modified early eighteenth-century home with eight unique corner fireplaces. It stands near the landing of an early eighteenth-century ferry, now a public boat ramp, and good examples of the kinds of summer cottages and riverfront houses erected in the early part of this century. A modern Bellamy United Methodist Church, off Route 614 via state Routes 606 and 615, continues the work of Dr. Reed's father, who was minister of a congregation that dates back to 1795.

The Virginia Game Commission maintains a boat ramp on the marshy Porpotank River, via state Routes 610 and 617 (Tanyard Landing Road) off Route 614.

The most distinctive area of Gloucester, known as Guinea, does not appear on maps. Despite the dilution that has occurred since World War II, it remains a distinctive section in the minds of the residents, who traditionally have mistrusted outsiders and depended on themselves. "This is Guinea," said the young watermen standing on a dock on the south shore of the Severn River. "Over there is Glass." Even the young adults are proud of their heritage and perpetuate the name.

Gloucester, more than the other counties in the region, presents a bewildering network of state roads, many of them short and intersecting with other short roads. All of them are well maintained and sooner or later lead to water.

Gloucester has a variety of recreational opportunities, including fishing, boating, and camping, concentrated around Mobjack Bay and the shoreline of the York River. In addition to seven marinas, it has a number of strategically located public landings suitable for launching from boat trailers, as well as docks used primarily for commercial fishing. Reaching Cook's Landing Marina at Perrin, which has grown in the last 40 years from 15 rustic slips to more than 300 slips with a marine railway and swimming pool, is easy (right off 649 and down 1101 and 1102) because signs have been placed showing the way. An honor system charge is made for using the ramp.

Canoes and other small boats can be carried into the water at many undeveloped landing sites, like the one at Maryus, which is used by local residents for personal crabbing and boating. A number of boats tie up near the undeveloped public landing on Monday Creek, which is reached as follows: turn off Route 17 onto state Route 216 to Achilles, then right onto 649, then take Route 1104 and turn right at the T-intersection onto 646 and follow it a considerable distance to the end.

The agricultural side of Gloucester County that will interest most visitors will be its berries and flowers. Pick-your-own signs are tacked to trees along roadways every spring and summer, identifying farms where people can, for a fee, pick as many pints of strawberries or blueberries as they like. The Virginia Department of Agriculture compiles a list of farms that welcome pickers. Wildflowers, including some daffodils, grow along some roadsides, and an organized effort is being made to beautify the historic district of Gloucester Courthouse with plantings.

The daffodil, an ideal companion to many perennials and annuals, has long been part of the Gloucester image. Brought to the county by English settlers, daffodils thrived even when left in a semiwild state and were marketed by Gloucester farmers in an informal way before George Heath, a retired consular official who had observed flower growing in Europe, created a scientific industry. Noticing the way the flower thrived, Health imported new varieties from England and Holland to organize a daffodil industry that at one time was foremost in the nation.

His grandson, Brent, carries on the family tradition at the Daffodil Mart. In April, the fields cultivated by Brent and his wife, Becky, ripple with the golden color of daffodils and produce bulbs that are shipped across the United States. In their hothouse, they strive to create new colors (they are close to all-green and all-orange daffodils), fragrances, and shapes. The Daffodil Mart opens its gardens to prearranged bus tours, including nonaffinity groups put together by the county (usually leaves from Botetourt Elementary School) during the annual Daffodil Festival and Show the first weekend in April.

The official center of the county is Gloucester Courthouse, which stands just off Route 17 (the highway went through town until a bypass was built). Long Bridge Ordinary, a colonial watering hole for weary travelers, is preserved as the headquarters of the Gloucester Woman's Club. Courthouse Circle has been a quiet, sylvan focus of governmental life for more than two hundred years. Among its historic structures are the 1766 courthouse, sometimes described as one of Virginia's architecturally most sophisticated early courthouses; the 1823 Clayton Building, which stands on the foundations of an eighteenth-century structure that later burned; the 1873 Jail, which replaced a prison on the site burned by Union troops during the Civil War; and the 1896 Roane Building. The 1810 Debtor's Prison, used as an arsenal during the Civil War, houses the Gloucester Historical Committee.

The green and a number of nearby structures, including those on Lawyers Row, constitute the Gloucester Courthouse Historic District.

Gloucester County's historic homes are almost all private. Among them are Elmington, Toddsbury, Little England, Airville, Lisburne, and White Marsh. Overlooking the York River are the ruins of Rosewell, one of the most prestigious eighteenth-century homes in the county until it burned in 1916.

Historic Abingdon Church is located on Route 17 at White Marsh. The present church was consecrated in 1755 and is the third in the parish. The first, built about 1650, was located on the waterfront. Ware Episcopal Church, just off Route 14–3 east of Gloucester Courthouse, is even older. It was constructed in 1690.

Dragon Run, a swampy waterway that forms the border between Gloucester and Middlesex County and continues west into King and Queen County, is an underdeveloped natural resource that Heath and others are trying to conserve. Conservationists have banded together as the Friends of the Dragon to purchase land and lobby both state and owners to give conservation easements along the banks to protect one of the purest tributaries of Chesapeake Bay.

The Dragon is available for canoeing, especially from Route 17 eastward; bird-watching; and similar activities. Public access is limited to points where bridges cross, such as Church View and Mascot; the Route 17 crossing is unmarked, as is the small access road just north of the bridge. Narrow in most places, Dragon Run has many sections where the stream flows under a natural arch of trees and other vegetation. The isolated swampy area has no amenities, and rotting trees and stumps in the water present natural hazards. It is not the kind of place for a person to visit alone. Wilderness camping along the banks is possible, provided the landowners give permission.

Motorboats can penetrate the lower reaches of Dragon Run from the Piankatank River, a practice that Friends of the Dragon would like to stop.

Mathews County was relatively isolated until recent times and thus is just now beginning to develop commercially and residentially along the lines of neighboring Gloucester County. It is not as well organized as most places in Virginia to direct visitors to recreational facilities or historic attractions. For information, locate someone who is involved in the annual festival or the historical society or Chamber of Commerce. Maps that show public facilities sometimes can be found in gun and tackle shops.

Although it was settled early in the colonial period, the modest homes of fishers and farmers were more susceptible to the elements and did not survive the test of time as well as more solid plantation manor houses. Courthouse Square, a registered National Historic Landmark, has the largest collection of historic structures. At one end is the Tompkins House, a frame structure built about 1818 and preserved as the headquarters of the Mathews Historical Society. The nearby handsome red brick structures date from the early 1850s. Near the tall Confederate Monument is a marker honoring Capt. Sally Thompson, a county native whose service to wounded soldiers earned the only commission given a woman by the Confederacy.

Haven Beach is public, b .t has no turnaround or parking area. Surfcasting is as customary there in late May as swimming, although booms have been placed close inshore to identify a protected swimming area.

Gwynn's Island, where colonial Governor Lord Dunmore took refuge from the patriots at the start of the American Revolution, is a recreational area where marinas serve both watermen and pleasure boaters and many houses have their own docks. The scene at Milford Haven, which separates the island and the mainland, is a typical Bay tableau. Small, unpainted buildings stand near a short pier piled high with crab pots. The land curves eastward in a long arc that creates a cove. Boats move in and out of a larger docking area in the distance. A small, white motorboat moves slowly landward and docks at the end of the nearest pier. The waterman glances at those watching him, then silently places a half-empty bushel basket of gleaming blue crabs on the pier and begins unloading empty pots.

He is more talkative than most watermen. In response to a question, he explains his half-empty basket. This conservation-minded waterman has thrown back the "white" or papershell crabs and kept only full-grown blues. He blames — regretfully not accusatively — fellow watermen for helping cause a decline in the crab population. Why are crabs declining? Others are taking too many "cushion" crabs — the crabs with the big orange pouch of eggs on their stomachs. No hatching, no crabs, he says matter-of-factly.

Middlesex

Middlesex County is a minipeninsula within the larger Middle Peninsula. The tip of slender Middlesex County touches Chesapeake Bay, but most of the county's shoreline lies on the Rappahannock and Piankatank rivers. U.S. Route 17 and state Route 33 cross at Saluda, with Route 17 continuing north and Route 33 extending eastward to end on the shores of Chesapeake Bay.

Saluda, a quiet county seat near the center of a slender county that is developing a fondness for antique shops, is dominated by Courthouse Square. The main part of the courthouse dates only to 1852 but copies a style of arcaded architecture popular in the colonial period. A museum in the two rooms of the Old Clerk's Office features Indian artifacts, farm implements, books, clothing, and other items from the county's past. Forest Chapel of the United Methodist Church at Warner, a few miles north of Saluda, dates from 1840, while Glebe Landing Baptist Church at Jamaica is a year older.

The earliest port in Middlesex, Urbanna, is one of two principal population centers in a county where place names often represent a few houses. It became one of the first planned communities in the nation when 50 acres were purchased in 1680 by the Virginia legislature for the express purpose of laying out a town on the main route between the capital at Williamsburg and the settlements on the Northern Neck. Growth was so slow the community did not even have a name until 1705, when "ye towne lands" were officially renamed for the reigning British queen. Urbanna is literally the "city of Anne." In time, Urbanna became one of Virginia's most important colonial ports and was threatened frequently by pirates, savaged by the British during the Revolutionary War and the War of 1812, and shelled by Union artillery during the Civil War.

The town's most important structures survived such violent intrusions into its sedate life. The small brick tobacco warehouse on a bluff overlooking Urbanna Creek, the sole survivor of twenty such structures around the state authorized in 1680 by the Virginia legislature, now houses a branch of the county library. Nearby is the 1695 brick Customs House, a private residence. The 1763 Lansdowne Mansion, located on the main thoroughfare (Route 227), is being restored to reflect the period when Arthur Lee, who purchased it in 1791, made it a center of gracious living and lively debate. It is named for William Fitzmaurice, the earl of Shelburne and marquess of Lansdowne, a British statesman and friend of Lee, who was prime minister when the treaty recognizing American independence was signed. The Old Court House, in use before the court moved to Saluda, now houses the Middlesex Woman's Club. The fiery orator, Patrick Henry, is believed to have delivered one of his moving orations from the porch of the 1742 Old Tavern on Prince George Street.

Urbanna's waterfront is undergoing a revival, too. Marinas with as many as 110 slips and 30-ton travel lifts, new waterfront restaurants, and upscale condos and summer homes occupy the shore and bluff overlooking the creek, sites that small summer cottages and watermen's homes previously dominated.

The two-day annual Oyster Festival at the beginning of November, the town's principal event since its inauguration in 1958, was designated as the "official" state oyster festival by a 1988 resolution of the Virginia General Assembly. The reality is less formal: oysters are served raw, roasted, stewed, fried, and frittered; oyster boats are opened to public inspection; an oyster-shucking contest picks a winner to represent the state in national competition; and parades, a carnival, arts and crafts exhibits, and an Oyster Queen contest are held.

Standing in the countryside near Urbanna are two excellent examples of colonial manor houses, now private homes. The builder of 1675 Rosegill suffered from both sides during the Revolutionary War — from the patriots because he was a Tory and from the British, who plundered his house in spite of his loyalty to the crown. Urbanna's elite frequently gathered at 1675 Hewick. Christ Church School is one of the state's most prestigious college preparatory schools. Wilton (circa 1763), Grymesby (circa 1700), and Deerchase (circa 1740) are off Routes 3 and 629 on the Piankatank shore. Early nineteenth-century Belle Aire (circa 1841) is at Hardyville on Route 33, and North End Plantation is off Route 631 at Amberg.

The Grey's Point Bridge on state Route 3 spans one of the most scenic stretches of the lower Rappahannock River and, in summer, overlooks a steady stream of sail and power boats. A small public beach is located at the southern end of the bridge, near a 312-site campground on a bluff overlooking the river. Nearby Hummel Air Field handles small planes.

Deltaville, the other population center, was a quiet fishing village a half-century ago when Richmonders in search of summer residences began moving in, partly because of its proximity. Since then, the character of the town has changed drastically, as the watermen, one by one, have sold property at what they considered excellent prices.

This has been their downfall. "Playboats drive out the workboats," says one long-time resident. "The recreational boatsmen don't want the smelly fishing boats around. In addition, large numbers of boats churning up the water drive the fish away."

The nature of the change is apparent along almost every side road and fishing bay and the five large creeks. Pleasure boats, lifts, ramps, and service facilities populate a dozen marinas. Supporting them are marine railways and a dry dock capable of handling vessels 100 feet long and up to 600 tons. Although many vintage Deltaville-built boats still drop nets, haul crab pots, or tong for oysters, most of the twenty boatbuilders whose skills were recognized the length of the Bay are gone. Some of the families who pioneered in the area have accepted the inevitability of change and now hire out their boats.

The few remaining practicing watermen take their boats out before dawn, come back near mid-day, and sort their catch of spot, sea trout, and other varieties, depending on what is running at the time. These are quiet folk who talk freely about the things that interest them, especially the quantity of fish available and the prices they can get for them.

A visitor watches a fisherman toss his catch of spot and sea trout into separate baskets, preparing to take them to a wholesaler. "Are prices good?" he asks.

"Good for trout," the young waterman says with a smile, "not for spot."

Deltaville, which is tied to U.S. 17 by state Routes 3 and 33, traditionally has been a settled resort, populated by full- or part-time landowning residents. Infrastructure required to serve transients, such as a motel, has been added in recent years but is by no means dominant. Although most marinas accept transient boats, they normally have only five or six slips available for that purpose.

Route 33 runs in a straight line through Deltaville. Large, colored roadside signs identify marinas and a privately owned boat ramp on the East Branch of Broad Creek. One of the longest side roads, state Route 636, parallels the western shore of the creek. Along this route are a number of marinas; the dock used by brothers John and Ulman Miller to take fishing parties to grounds between Windmill Point and Wolf Trap, including Hole-in-Wall; one of the few surviving boatbuilders; and a public dock at the end.

Route 33 ends where the peninsula meets the Bay at Stingray Point, visited as early as 1608. A small parking area permits sunbathing and shoreline fishing at a sandy beach bordered on both sides by private property. From Memorial Day through Labor Day, Zoar Baptist Church sponsors an interdenominational Worship on the Beach at 8:30 A.M. each Sunday. The Stingray Yacht Club stands at the end of state Route 688.

Other events in Deltaville are equally water oriented. The Deltaville Fishing and Conservation Club is one of the hosts for the annual Governors Cup Fishing Tournament in August. An annual bluefish tournament is held the Saturday before Labor Day.

Although Deltaville dominates the eastern end of the county, both the Rappahannock and Piankatank river shorelines are active farther inland. A state boat ramp and pier are located on Mill Creek at the end of state Route 626. Another faces Parrotts Creek near Water View. A public beach is maintained at McKans Bay at the end of state Route 605. State Route 3 crosses both rivers.

Essex

Bay inflence begins to wane west of Middlesex, especially in the inland areas where farming predominates. However, the water exerts strong influences on isolated communities as far as Fredericksburg on the upper reaches of the Rappahannock River.

Tappahannock in Essex County, whose bridge exits to the Northern Neck, shows its worst side — along busy Route 17 — to passersthrough. A gentler and more genteel side off the highway includes new high-rise condos and St. Margaret's School on the riverfront and a historic district centered on the Old Jail. Other historic structures include the old clerk's office, Courthouse, and unheralded buildings such as the white brick house at the corner of Prince and Cross streets where Thomas Ritchie, founder and editor of the noted nineteenth-century newspaper, the *Richmond Inquirer,* was born.

Pretty, frame St. John's Episcopal Church on Duke Street is successor to the South Farnham Parish, founded in 1683. The town office on Duke Street also is a historical landmark. A Confederate monument stands on a center island on Prince Street.

The *Capt. Thomas,* which made the run to Tangier until replaced by a larger boat, leaves from a dock on Hoskins Creek, just off U.S. Route 17, to cruise approximately 20 miles up the Rappahannock River. The vessel docks at Leedstown on the Northern Neck for a wine-tasting bus trip to Ingleside Plantation. A second stop is made at Saunders Wharf, perhaps the only original steamboat dock left on the river. The nearby clapboard 1810 mansion, Wheatland, and its boxwood gardens can be toured. The *Capt. Thomas* leaves at 10 A.M. and returns at 5 P.M. daily May through October.

North of Tappahannock, Route 17 parallels the Rappahannock through the eastern edge of Caroline County, which once was river oriented, but now is occupied primarily with farming and the Army's Fort A. P. Hill.

Approximately 35 eighteenth and early nineteenth-century structures in Port Royal serve as a reminder that ocean-going ships once sailed far up the Rappahannock River. Port Royal was established by royal decree in 1744 to serve the persistent movement into the hinterland of Virginia. The community has retained much of its early atmosphere without protection or sponsored restoration.

Fredericksburg

Fredericksburg Tourism, 706 Caroline Street, Fredericksburg, VA 22401. Tel.: 703/373-1776.

NOT LONG AGO, EVERY SPRING, THE YOUNG MEN OF FREDERICKSBURG used to line up on the banks of the Rappahannock River to repeat a bit of early American folklore — Washington throwing a "dollar" across the river. The event no longer occurs, but it was appropriate. If Washington ever attempted such a feat, which is disputed, it happened here and not on the Potomac, as alleged.

The Washington family connection began when Fredericksburg was young. The falls of the Rappahannock had intimidated even the inquisitive Capt. John Smith, but little more than a century later a substantial number of people had moved overland into the interior and more were on the way. Fredericksburg was created in 1728 by the Virginia legislature as a transshipment point for people and goods. George Washington spent ten boyhood years at Ferry Farm, in Stafford County across the river from Fredericksburg, and attended school in the city.

Memories about George are not as strong as those about his mother, who lived the last seventeen years of her life in Fredericksburg, and about his brother-in-law, Fielding Lewis, who was one of the pillars of the community. The home and garden of Mary Washington at 1200 Charles Street, purchased for her by son George, reflects the simple family lifestyle that occupied her last years. The house is furnished in eighteenth-century antiques, including some of Mary's personal possessions. Some of the original boxwoods she planted separate the formal flower garden from the vegetable garden. A tall obelisk a few blocks away, at a spot where she often went to meditate and pray, marks the site where at her own request she is buried. Although President Jackson laid the cornerstone in 1833, the monument was not completed until 1894. Her will is on display in the gothic-style 1852 courthouse.

Kenmore, built in 1752 by Fielding Lewis, husband of George Washington's sister, is regarded as an outstanding example of colonial Virginia architecture. The simple exterior of the brick mansion on Washington Avenue East gives way inside to beautiful decorative plaster ceilings. The Great Room was cited by one author among the hundred most beautiful rooms in the nation. Tours of Kenmore include an opportunity to sample gingerbread made from Mary Washington's recipe. Lewis was a superpatriot during the Revolutionary War, supplying at great financial sacrifice many of the cannon used by Washington's army. Overwork and financial strain took a toll and he died in 1781. Nearby houses are more modern, many from the Victorian era.

Fredericksburg relives its history well. At Rising Sun Tavern on Caroline Street, costumed "wenches" help recreate the convivial atmosphere of early taverns, where citizens often met to discuss political and economic affairs. The frame structure was built about 1760 as a residence by Charles Washington, younger brother of the first president, and did not become a tavern until 1792. Docents at Hugh

Mercer's Apothecary Shop discuss eighteenth- and early nineteenth-century medical treatment in a setting that includes doctor's instruments and medicines.

Another president, James Monroe, maintained a law office in Fredericksburg for three years. The brick structure, now a museum and library, exhibits memorabilia from Monroe's career as ambassador to France and fifth president, including the Louis XVI desk on which the Monroe Doctrine was signed in 1823, china, silver, jewelry, and clothing. Many of the documents, manuscripts, maps, books, and newspapers in the library date to the seventeenth and eighteenth centuries. A cannonball imbedded in a wall recalls the destruction caused by Civil War fighting. A bronze bust of the president adorns the walled old-fashioned garden.

These buildings are open from 9 A.M. to 5 P.M. daily, except Christmas and New Year's.

In all, Fredericksburg's historic area covers 40 blocks of mostly private homes and can involve about 4 miles of walking. A shorter, self-guided walking tour of lower Caroline Street passes almost thirty homes of historic interest. Two homes in particular reveal the original appearance of the street. The elegant Georgian brick house at 213 Caroline Street, built in 1764 as a prototype of what the land developer hoped would follow, is the oldest remaining original structure, but the porch is a twentieth-century addition. No. 301, the home of a prominent attorney of the Revolutionary War period, has been restored to its original appearance. Other styles range from the Georgian wooden home at No. 211, built circa 1789 with an unusual combination of interior and exterior chimneys, and the circa 1813 Federal-style law office at No. 300 to the 1855 Greek revival townhouses at Nos. 132–38 and the turn-of-the-century houses at Nos. 204 and 201, which combine Queen Anne Victorian and colonial revival styles. The Christian Church was erected in 1833.

Some of the houses usually are open during Historic Garden Week in Virginia, including gambrel-roofed St. James House, built about 1768 and now owned by the Association for the Preservation of Virginia Antiquities. St. James, whose seventeenth- and eighteenth-century appointments include a grandfather clock that belonged to Daniel Webster, also is open the first week in October and by appointment.

Parallel blocks of Princess Anne and Sophia streets hold a number of interesting buildings. Gardens and dependencies of Caroline Street homes originally stood on Princess Anne Street, but the street gradually came to house artisans and shopkeepers. The house at 300 Princess Anne Street is a converted stable, while Nos. 314–20 are early brick row houses. Along Sophia Street, which started with waterfront warehouses and docks and turned to milling and other industrial activities in the nineteenth century, are the building that according to local legend was the ferry toll collector's house (No. 208); an 1876 warehouse known as the Commission House; the Old Stone Warehouse built at the beginning of the War of 1812; and the late eighteenth-century Silversmith House (No. 813), which houses the Fredericksburg Center for the Creative Arts.

Brompton, home of the president of Mary Washington College, looks down on the city from Marye's Heights. The Roman revival central portion dates from 1740 and the wings were added by 1840. The Georgian-style railroad station, constructed in 1910, reflects the city's importance as a rail hub after the Civil War. The Presbyterian Church is one of the oldest church structures in Fredericksburg. Erected in 1833, the Greek revival building supports a bell tower trimmed with mask designs. The church was used twice as a hospital during the Civil War, but the antebellum appearance has been restored. The box pews in 1849 St. George's Episcopal Church survived the war, as did the town clock installed in the tower in 1850. St. George's has three Tiffany windows.

At the Fredericksburg Area Museum and Cultural Center in the 1814 Town Hall and Market on Princess Anne Street, audiovisuals, antique guns, furniture, and other artifacts relate the history of the city from Indian times to the twentieth century. A reception for Lafayette was held at this site when he toured the United States in 1824. The Information Center at 706 Caroline Street is a former confectioner's shop and residence built in 1824.

The Thomas Jefferson Religious Freedom Monument on Washington Street recalls that the Virginia Statute of Religious Freedom, the basis for the first ten amendments to the U. S. Constitution, was formed in Fredericksburg. A commemorative ceremony is held at the site on January 13 every year.

In the years before and after the Civil War, Fredericksburg was a mill town, using the falls, a dam, and canals to generate power. Old Mill Park and a few ruins and foundations remain.

Fredericksburg has laid out three bike routes past the main historical attractions. A 3-mile trail loops through the downtown area, while a 7-mile route extends past the Civil War battlefield park to

Mary Washington College. A 20-mile course also includes Lee Hill, with well-preserved Civil War positions, outside the city.

The Civil War had a devastating effect on Fredericksburg. Union troops bombarded the town for hours before moving through its streets to attack Confederate positions on Marye's Heights. Intense Confederate artillery fired from the hilltop did additional damage.

At the Confederate Cemetery on Washington Avenue, where one of the earliest Memorial Day services was held, a life-size statue of a Confederate soldier stands guard over more than two thousand soldiers and Lucy Ann Cox, who was made an honorary veteran for accompanying her soldier husband through four years of warfare.

Some essential features of the December 13, 1862, battlefield are preserved as a national park and cemetery, although Fredericksburg has expanded around the area. A walking tour from the battlefield Visitors Center along the base of Marye's Heights passes the stone wall at the Sunken Road, which Confederates used as a barricade from which to mow down Union soldiers attacking across open fields; the ruined home of the "heroine of the battle of Fredericksburg," Martha Stevens, who stayed in her house to tend the wounded; the Innis House, which survived the shooting and bombardment; and a monument to "The Angel of Marye's Heights," Richard Rowland Kirkland, the South Carolina soldier who risked his life repeatedly to give water to the thirsty wounded of both sides.

Fifteen thousand Union troops are buried in the terraced national cemetery on Marye's Heights amid period cannon and memorials to many of their units. The view from the cemetery shows how the heights so dominated the surrounding terrain that an exultant Confederate artillery commander boasted "a chicken could not live on that field."

An 8-mile driving tour through wooded terrain, which begins at the base of Lee Hill, 4 miles from the Visitors Center, covers the vantage point from which the Confederate commander watched the battle; a well-preserved section of Confederate infantry trench; the point where Maj. Gen. George G. Meade's Federals briefly pierced the Confederate line; and Prospect Hill and Maj. John Pelham's position, Confederate artillery strongpoints, still fortified with period cannon.

The Union was more successful in attacking the thinly held heights the following spring, but the culmination at Salem Church, now restored as part of the battlefield park, was subsidiary to the fighting around Chancellorsville, 10 miles away. Relics of that battle are strung out along state Route 3 (the Orange Turnpike) and a circular driving tour in the national park. The 12-minute slide presentation and the excellent museum at the Visitors Center explain the master strokes that achieved another Confederate victory against superior Union forces holding strong positions. Period cannon at Hazel Grove point toward Union batteries at Fairview with which they dueled.

The brilliant flanking maneuver of Confederate Gen. Thomas J. "Stonewall" Jackson, which achieved victory, can be traced by following the Furnace Road and Jackson Trail, part of it unpaved, to state Routes 613 and 3.

The battle was costly to the Confederacy: Jackson was fatally wounded. Taken 27 miles to T. C. Chandler's Fairfield Plantation at Guiney (now Guinea) Station, a key supply center on the Richmond, Fredericksburg, and Potomac Railway line, he died in a small frame building used as a plantation office. The building is the main feature of the Jackson Shrine, 5 miles off Interstate 95 via state Routes 606 and 607. The bed and blanket and the clock (which still works) on the mantel are original. Another room is outfitted as the doctor's room.

Only the foundations of the brick manor house, which already was so filled with wounded that Jackson had to rest in the frame office, remain. A painting, with a recorded commentary, at the entrance to the small park depicts the plantation at the time of Jackson's death. It also recalls the words of British statesman David Lloyd George on a later visit: "In this little house the Confederacy also died."

The victory was the last the Confederates would achieve along this line. The nearby Wilderness Battlefield shows the dense thickets and tangled overgrowth where Union Gen. Ulysses S. Grant began the costly campaign of attrition that would end the war. A drive around the national park, which lies roughly south of state Route 20, passes remnants of Confederate trenches dug for the May 5–6, 1864, battle; landmark farms; and monuments to units that took part. The Exhibit Center has paintings and written commentaries on the battle.

Union soldiers did not pull back after this battle, but attempted to outflank Lee. Brock Road (state Route 613) follows the route they took to Spotsylvania Court House. A 7-mile walking tour of the battlefield and the drive through the park reach the principal features, including the Bloody Angle, a salient where heavy firing severed the trunk of a tree 22 inches in diameter. A walking trail over the salient passes monuments to New Jersey, New York, and Ohio troops who assaulted the Confederate fortifications.

Once again, Grant attempted to outflank Lee, who finally retreated to prepared positions around Richmond and Petersburg. The final phase of the war had begun.

The gardens at Belmont, on state Route 1001 a few miles west of Falmouth, include a walkway lined with English boxwood, 200-year-old oak and elm trees and informal plantings of azaleas, wisteria, and other flowers. The 1761 house, which was enlarged in 1843, stands on 27 acres of rolling farmland overlooking the Rappahannock River.

The mansion is furnished in antiques, including paintings by such European masters as Pieter Breughel, Auguste Rodin, and Berthe Morisot. More than 50 works by Gari Melchers, one of America's most renowned turn-of-the-century artists, are displayed in the studio where he worked the last sixteen years of his life. His workbench, easels, brushes, paint, and model's platform also are on display.

Falmouth, an old port and trading center established in 1727, seldom advertises its sizable number of eighteenth- and nineteenth-century private homes, but even the novice can distinguish them from the modern buildings.

King George County

As the closest city of any size near the Northern Neck peninsula, Fredericksburg naturally has special ties with that region. King George County, while not considered part of the Northern Neck, lies between the two places.

The county is an actual, as well as a geographical, transition. Virginia Route 3 passes through King George Courthouse, with handsome red brick county buildings and four churches, and heads straight down the Northern Neck. However, large forests press against side roads, sometimes used by giant farm combines, which lead to such recreation areas as Fairview Beach and Caledon Natural Area.

Fairview Beach, 11 miles from Fredericksburg along state Routes 218 and 696, is a small resort community on a beautiful stretch of the Potomac River. Scores of power boats from the national capital area around Washington anchor off the pier during weekends from the middle of March to the middle of October, but the area is as laid back as a resort can be. The campground is used year round. Fairview

Beach Yacht Club, which is open to the public, has twenty-eight slips and a double boat ramp.

St. Paul's Episcopal Church, near the intersection of SR 218 and 206, is a registered Virginia Historic Landmark. The present Flemish bond brick structure, in the form of a Greek cross, was raised in 1766, but the congregation dates back at least to 1667. The church declined in the early years of American nationhood and the interior was altered to accommodate an academy. The church was re-established in 1831, and the structure has changed little since then.

Caledon Natural Area

Caledon, 2,579 acres of wilderness and open land between Route 218 and the banks of the Potomac River a dozen or so miles east of Fredericksburg, is one of the most significant summering places for eagles on the East Coast. As many as 60 have been seen at one time, and the soaring birds receive preference in any plans for development.

The state park is divided into three zones — the recreational section; the eagle wildlife area, which is a buffer zone; and the eagle impact tract, where the eagles nest. The park currently permits passive recreation, nature education, and research.

Eagle observation tours operate almost every day from mid-June to the end of September. On these tours, a maximum of fifteen people are bused along a forest trail to a cleared site in the woods, where participants are shown an artificial eagle's nest and given information on the eagle's vision and its comparison with other birds. The bus then proceeds to the riverbank, where binoculars and a telescope are provided for eagle watching. Rangers provide information on the eagle's nesting habits and river ecology. Trips are canceled when protection of the eagles requires it.

Park naturalists also lead wildflower and night vision walks, lecture on animal camouflage and construction of bird feeders, conduct orienteering trips, demonstrate bird sounds, and show how to use pinecones in crafts.

Four self-guided loop trails, each about a mile long, traverse sections of a 2,300-acre hardwood forest, which has one 800-acre stand of trees from 80 to 150 years old. The Fern Hollow Trail, which begins at the Visitors Center, passes through a hollow filled with Christmas ferns. It connects with the Poplar Grove Trail deep in a forest frequented by more than 120 types of birds, including uncommon migrants such as the gray-cheeked thrush and the Canada warbler, and by gray fox, small animals, and 39 species of reptiles and amphibians. Mountain laurel, ground pine, and creeping cedar are featured along the Laurel Glen Trail and the fourth trail, opened in 1989 and named for a surveyor's marker along the route. Trails are open daily from dawn to dusk.

The Visitors Center, a turn-of-the-century frame home, is open from 9 A.M. to 5 P.M. daily during the summer, Saturday and Sunday the rest of the year. Exhibits illustrate the types of vegetation found in the park.

Caledon was established in the early 1980s after the site was donated by descendants of the original owner, Capt. John Alexander, who purchased it in 1659. The park shoreline was one of the sites where the fugitive John Wilkes Booth tried to land after assassinating President Lincoln.

Northern Neck

Northern Neck Planning District Commission, Drawer H, Callao, VA 22435. Tel.: 804/529-7400.

THE SIGN ON THE DESK OF ONE NORTHERN NECK REAL ESTATE AGENT reads, "One day I traveled to the Northern Neck and it was closed." It is intended as humor, but there is a lesson in it.

The Northern Neck is the uppermost of the three Virginia peninsulas that jut into Chesapeake Bay and, thus, traditionally the most isolated. Contact with nearby areas across the Potomac and Rappahannock rivers was limited to river traffic until bridges were constructed in the 1920s. Fredericksburg, the nearest city, is oriented in a north-south direction.

Geographical isolation did not prevent the area from achieving historic importance. In this regard, the Northern Neck compares favorably with almost any area of Virginia. The peripatetic Capt. John Smith was the first Englishman to venture there, and he was impressed by the beauty and natural wealth of the area. One of colonial Virginia's most prestigious leaders, Robert "King" Carter had his seat in Lancaster County. The Washington family put down its roots in Westmoreland, and George was born there at a time when it was regarded as a planters' paradise. Three of the first five American presidents were born in this small area.

Isolation saved it from wartime destruction. All the wars in which Americans have participated, including the Civil War, virtually bypassed the region, leaving it unscarred.

A colonial subculture, commercial fishing, took a firm hold on the shoreline as the great plantations declined after the Revolutionary War. Other users sought the long shoreline, too. The appeal of isolation made the region popular with vacationers, and the Potomac River steamboats made regular stops in their heyday. In this century, retirees, occasional fishers, and vacationers have transformed Reedville from a sleepy fishing village into a popular boating resort and have prompted the creation of a prestigious resort, Tides Inn, at Irvington. The forests from which paper mills draw lumber also host thousands of hunters each year.

Long and narrow, measuring 20 miles in width at its widest point, the Northern Neck is divided into four counties—Westmoreland, Richmond, Lancaster, and Northumberland. The peninsula always has been thinly populated. Westmoreland, with 15,000 inhabitants, is the largest and most populous county. There are no cities. The largest town, Warsaw, is a farmers' market. Colonial Beach, a recreation center, counts about 2,500 people. Lancaster County's biggest town, Kilmarnock, counts around 1,000.

The counties are topographically similar, but differ to some degree in land use. Forty percent of Westmoreland's land is devoted to the production of corn, soybeans, and grain, while 70 percent of Richmond County is covered by forests. The primary industry in Northumberland County is the harvesting and processing of seafood, especially menhaden, followed by farming and tourism. In Lancaster County, which has followed the sea one way or another since its founding in 1651, water-oriented recreation is fast overtaking seafood processing and farming as a means of livelihood. Farming and commercial seafood occupy perhaps a quarter of the residents.

The lifestyle shaped by farmers and fishers is changing as "waterfront for sale" signs move deeper and deeper into the peninsula, offering sites on the high bluffs to purchasers from Washington, D.C., and other population centers. While a few outsiders have maintained summer homes in Reedville and other communities for many years, population increases in some areas now are entirely due to the arrival of retirees.

The steamboat era is long since passed, but individual boaters still make the Northern Neck a primary destination. Every cove along the serrated coastline has some form of docking facility. On weekends during the summer, hundreds may be seen anchored at Colonial Beach and other places.

Boaters experience the peninsula the way Capt. John Smith did, exploring the attractive Coan River and short bays, and standing off bluffs studded with prehistoric fossils. Land rovers travel the routes of the great planters along state Routes 3 and 202 east from Fredericksburg to the tip of the peninsula. Or they use a more modern route north from Richmond via U.S. 360 to Reedville, or SR 3 paralleling the Rappahannock to White Stone. Travelers from Hampton Roads along U.S. Route 17 can divert via state Routes 33 and 3 to the tip of the peninsula at White Stone or connect with U.S. 360 at Tappahannock.

Colonial and Potomac Beaches

The resorts on the south shore of the Potomac River came into their own in the 1880s as Washingtonians sought new places to recreate and recuperate. Colonial Beach, until then a somnolent fishing village, became one of the most fashionable stops on the Potomac steamboat runs from the nation's capital. Colonial Beach also was at the southern end of a string of "watering places" that people visited for their healthful drinking water. The white sand in the vicinity of Colonial and Potomac beaches was so prized that landscape architect Frederick Olmstead moved entire shiploads to parks in Washington, New York City, Boston, and Philadelphia.

The rise of the train, and later the automobile, changed the situation. As the steamboats declined, land transportation bypassed these areas and created new destinations. Colonial and Potomac beaches settled down to a peaceful period as havens for retired government officials and commercial fishing. A short revival of prosperity occurred in the post-World War II period when proprietors on the Virginia shoreline built piers into the river, which lies in Maryland, and installed slot machines. Hoping to pacify Virginia sensibilities, some of them went so far as to cut a small break in the piers and erect border signs. Likewise, vessels loaded with slot machines anchored offshore. Among them was the *S.S. Freestone,* the renamed former excursion steamer *S.S. Tolchester,* which had 200 slots, a restaurant deck, and a dancing and bar deck. The business was perceived as a festering sore in Virginia, which did not allow gambling, but it continued to expand. By 1963, eight gambling piers and two ships stood along the shoreline in Westmoreland and King George counties, all serviced by boats from the Maryland shore.

The contrived good times did not last long. In 1958, the Maryland legislature acceded to perennial requests from Virginia and passed a law that permitted gambling only in places that could be reached on foot from the Maryland shore. Existing nonconforming gambling halls were to be phased out between 1963 and 1968. Colonial Beach reverted to the kind of resort it had been before its flirtation with gambling.

The community has an unusually long, 2.8-mile shoreline along the Potomac and Monroe Bay, part of it paralleled by a boardwalk. Private cottages, small motels, and restaurants on Irving Avenue, some with private fishing piers, face a river shoreline divided between sandy beaches and riprap to protect the land from erosion. A public boat ramp and the Bay Yacht Center, a town-owned marina with covered and uncovered slips, occupy the point where the river and bay meet. Monroe Bay Avenue follows the bay shoreline through a residential area, where wild ducks have become so tame they walk across the roadway, and enters a mixed area of residence and water-oriented businesses.

Outside the town, off state Route 605, is another area on Monroe Bay for fishing, boating, crabbing, and swimming. The birthplace of President James Monroe, Monrovia, is identified by a historial marker, but undeveloped.

Festivals include the annual Potomac River Festival in mid-June, a boardwalk craft show in July, a boardwalk art show in August, and the Classic Marathon in late October.

Ingleside Plantation Vineyards: On the opposite side of Route 3, about 2½ miles south of Oak Grove along state Route 638, Ingleside winery occupies a 2,500-acre site similar in character to the Bordeaux region of France. The site previously had been used for a school, a Civil War camp for Union soldiers, and a dairy.

A free conducted tour begins with an 8-minute audiovisual covering the viniculture on the Northern Neck and the history of the company, which was started by the Carl Flemer family in 1980, and includes visits to large metal fermentation vats, bottling machine, and warehouse. The visit ends with wine tasting. Tours are conducted from 10 A.M. to 5 P.M. Monday–Saturday and noon to 5 P.M. Sunday year round, except on major holidays.

Westmoreland Berry Farm and Orchard: Anyone who has ever lived on a farm will remember that harvest time makes the taste buds a little keener, the step a little quicker. These year-to-year sensations may be largely a thing of the past for urbanites, but opportunities still exist to recapture the feeling on a short-term basis and to taste the special sweetness of fruit and berries that ripen naturally.

Although quite a few places in Chesapeake Bay country allow vacationers to "pick your own," few are as organized as this farm on state Route 637 about 2½ miles from Oak Grove via SR 634. From mid-May, when the strawberries begin to ripen, to late October, when pumpkins and gourds reach maturity and apples hang heavily on the trees, this farm is open every day for self-harvesting activities. Seasons overlap as, in turn, black and purple raspberries, blueberries, apricots, peaches, blackberries, plums, and grapes precede the apple and pumpkin finale.

Harvest time hours are 8 A.M. to 6 P.M. Monday–Thursday, 8 A.M. to 8 P.M. Friday–Saturday, and 10 A.M. to 6 P.M. Sunday. Reduced rates for senior citizens on Tuesday, groups of five or more on Sunday.

Leedstown: A one-time Pissaseck Indian settlement and colonial port, Leedstown is overshadowed by its neighbors and often overlooked. It is a resort with a boat ramp.

George Washington Birthplace National Monument

When George Washington was a boy, the latchstring on the door of the plantation house was an accepted method of signaling to prospective visitors. When it was out, visitors were welcome. Such folktales abound at this monument, also known as Wakefield, which recreates the self-sufficient farm and lifestyle where the Father of the Country was born. George lived on this farm, which overlooks Pope's Creek in Westmoreland County, for the first 3½ years of his life.

A visit to the site begins with a view of a memorial obelisk at the entrance to the park, about 2 miles off state Route 3 and 38 miles east of Fredericksburg. A 14-minute movie in the Visitors Center relates the planter's dependence on good weather and defenses against predators to obtain the essentials to survive harsh winters. A corn-planting rhyme — "One for the blackbird, one for the crow, one for the cut-worm, and one to grow"—illustrates the problems confronting the farmer. Graphic exhibits in the center cover the Washington family history in America, which began in 1657 when George's great-grandfather, John, decided not to return to England on his ship.

A creek overlook provides an introduction to the natural and artificial attractions of the site. Wildflowers, trees, and underbrush decorate the path along the shoreline, past signboards identifying points of historic interest. Young George no doubt looked out from this vantage point at vessels tied up at the farm's landing. The path goes directly to the house and dependencies, but a short detour through a thin stand of trees over a grass and clover carpet takes the visitor to Burnt House Point for a panoramic view of the creek.

The site of the original plantation home, which burned in 1779, lies on the approach to the reconstructed farmstead. The excavated foundations have been recovered to protect them, but oyster shells create an outline of the U-shaped home, with at least nine rooms, in which George was born.

A guided tour of the buildings begins in the separate kitchen, rebuilt on its original site and outfitted to represent a typical eighteenth-century kitchen, including the usual herbs and produce that hung from the mantel and rafters. Costumed guides explain the recovery of artifacts probably used in the kitchen, use of the large fireplace, and methods of cooking, and relate some of the fancies of the era, including the fable that the rubbing of rosemary on one's head twice a week produced total instant recall.

A nearly 200-year-old hackberry tree stands near the entrance to the Memorial Building, where the latchstring is out daily year round except on Christmas and New Year's days. The house is a typical upper-class home of the colonial period, with a wide central hallway opening both front and back. Large hallways were popular because they were not taxed, as rooms were, and could serve several functions. They helped cool the house in summer and they could be used for dancing, parties, and the like.

Each of the two floors has four rooms—the main rooms and the master bedchamber downstairs and four bedrooms upstairs. A few of the antiques, including a small tea table, are original.

The fields of the farm are worked as they were in Washington's day. At certain times, visitors may see men in kee-breeches and tricorn hats guiding yoked oxen in fields or tending to other chores, such as hoeing or harvesting. Costumed workers demonstrate everyday farm crafts, including leatherworking, blacksmithing, and weaving.

A colonial herb and flower garden near the mansion recreates an eighteenth-century fixture of colonial plantations and recalls the various legends associated with the medicinal powers of herbs.

Interpretive programs are held during the warm months. These include daily archeology walks, Sunday nature strolls, and Tuesday and Thursday herb garden walks; musical programs using a spinet and other instruments every Sunday, Monday, and Tuesday; colonial clothing demonstrations on Friday and Saturday; and occasional programs on sheep shearing, the importance of wool and flax, children's games, and other subjects. Black Heritage-History Day is observed in July.

The section of the farm across Dancing Creek shows another side of the colonial lifestyle. A circular walking trail, which leaves from a picnic area overlooking Popes Creek, covers the kind of countryside in which young George played, rode, and hunted. Narrative boards along the trail note the value of horses in travel and hunting and of dogs in serving as farm watchdogs. Horses were turned loose to forage in woods such as these, and the dogs were sent to locate them when they were needed or to find the colts foaled in the forest.

The trail, which skirts marshy Dancing Creek, crosses the roadway to the picnic area and traverses a dense forest, with thickets of raspberry, gooseberry, and huckleberry and fruit-bearers such as grape and fig among walnut, hickory, chestnut, red oak, willow, white oak, gum, mulberry, locust, poplar, dogwood, cedar, maple, and cypress trees. Blooms include flowering maple, magnolia, yellow jasmine, mayapple, and redbud.

On the Potomac side of the farm, past the burial ground where many early Washingtons lie, is a small, sandy beach for sunbathing and surf fishing. The site is not without historical interest; in colonial days, the Potomac was a major waterway, where the billowing sails of pinnaces brought welcoming boats scurrying from shore.

Westmoreland State Park

The message here is loud and clear: "Marshes and swamps are important to wildlife, adjacent lands, waterways and man. Wetlands provide food for birds and mammals; their stems and roots help hold shoreline soil in place; and they help trap and neutralize some pollutants."

This indirect appeal for conservation occupies a prominent place in the small Visitors Center at 1,295-acre Westmoreland State Park,

8 miles east of the George Washington Birthplace off state Route 3. Exhibits on caring for the resources of the Potomac River and Chesapeake Bay reinforce the message. So do displays of fossilized shark teeth, whale bones, and shells, relics of a period when twenty different kinds of sharks lived in the river. Such fossils are found in abundance in Westmoreland County.

Even the entrance roadway of the park sets a favorable tone by winding through a heavily forested area before dividing at the bluff overlooking the river. One leg goes to the campground, cabins, and Visitors Center, all well hidden among the trees, and the other descends to the sandy beach at the foot of Horsehead Cliffs.

The beach is one of the focal points of the park. In the warm months, it is crowded with sunbathers, but swimming is restricted to a pool just back of the beach. Water skiers, boaters, and windsurfers cast off from an adjacent boat ramp, while other visitors surf fish or stroll along the shore to view Miocene-era fossils that are embedded in the bank or occasionally are washed ashore from natural erosion.

Six color-coded hiking trails, the longest about 3 miles in length, explore various habitats. The Turkey Neck Trail meanders through forests, marshes, and swamps where white-tailed deer, wild turkeys, and small animals such as raccoons live in an environment similar to that at Wakefield. It intersects with the half-mile Rock Spring Pond Trail, which traverses a forested area to a small pond before connecting to the 1.3-mile Laurel Point Trail, which hooks to the riverfront. The 0.6-mile Big Meadow Interpretive Trail passes Yellow Swamp to reach an observation tower on the edge between the swamp and the riverbank.

Stratford Hall

Stratford Hall, the ancestral home of the Lee family, is one of the most impressive early eighteenth-century homes in America. Its red brick eminence dominates the scene, even in the presence of massive competition from nature—a thick forest background and a broad, meticulously mowed meadow that slopes gently to the Potomac riverbank.

The symmetry of the structure is striking. Each wing is perfectly balanced and topped by four connected central chimneys. Windows are matched and even the varied use of bricks on different levels is identical. Dependencies, including a kitchen and schoolhouse, stand

Stratford Hall Plantation, birth place of two signers of the Declaration of Independence as well as Robert E. Lee, commander of the Confederate forces during the Civil War.

at each of the corners. Of the eighteen rooms in the mansion, only two do not have fireplaces.

A guided tour begins in a dependency, lightly decorated with historic relics and information about Clifts, an earlier plantation on the site, and kitchen, where a docent explains the functions of the large fireplace and heavy kitchen utensils.

The interior of the mansion, built in the late 1720s or early 1730s, depicts all sides of plantation living. On the first floor, past leather buckets filled with sand to combat the ever-present danger of fire, is an accounting office, which kept records of tobacco harvests and sales in an era when as many as 15 vessels a month might anchor offshore. Among the antique furnishings in four bedrooms on that floor are such personal items as a shaving stand, a traveling chest that belonged to Hannah Ludwell Lee, the wife of the builder, Thomas Lee, and a cradle, one of seven Lee pieces in the house. A governess's room has a small antechamber where the children could study.

The formal rooms on the second floor have ceilings 13 feet high. The Great Hall, the centerpiece of the house with double doors front and back, was used for formal entertaining, weddings, christenings, and other activities. A harpsichord similar to that now in the 29-foot-square room no doubt played for dances. The family often preferred a small adjunct dining room to the formal one, which is furnished with a large table and hung with family portraits. The library and card rooms also were frequently used, and almost every visitor stopped to refresh in the receiving rooms, one of which now holds a field desk owned by Light-Horse Harry Lee.

The bedroom where Robert E. Lee was born is the only exception to the eighteenth-century character of the mansion. It represents the period around 1807, when he was born. Tours are conducted daily, except Christmas Day, from 9:30 A.M. to 4:30 P.M. Special garden and furniture tours are made for groups. The grounds close at 5 P.M.

The vegetable garden and boxwood-enclosed formal garden beside the house contrast with wildflowers and the nearby woods, which hide the spring that supplied water to residents for more than eighty years. In the period when the mansion was built, the existence of a good spring was so essential that it determined the location of a house. The short circular, signed path to the spring enters a forest, which, as in the eighteenth century, provides sustenance for 135 species of birds (including bald eagle), white-tailed deer, beaver, opossum, raccoon, chipmunk, rabbit, and squirrel, some of which may be seen along five longer forest and waterfront trails. Other common inhabitants are pileated woodpecker, thrushes, flycatchers, cardinal, bluebird, mourning dove, great blue heron, bufflehead, ruddy duck, turkey vulture, northern bobwhite, gulls, crows, gray catbird, northern mockingbird, pine warbler, and eastern meadowlark.

The Little Meadow Trail, at 0.8 mile the longest and most difficult, leaves the Spring Trail and cuts directly through the forest to cross Little Meadow Run and connect with the 0.5-mile Silver Beech Trail along the waterfront, also rated difficult but ending at a Potomac River overlook, which also can be reached by vehicle. The easy 0.4-mile Vault trail is connected by a short stretch of roadway to the 0.6-mile Mill Pond Trail, which winds through a forest of flowering dogwood, gum, hickory, locust, oak, maple, loblolly pine, tulip poplar, sycamore, black walnut, sassafras, paw-paw, *Magnolia virginiana* (sweetbay), American holly, and mountain laurel to a stone and frame mill rebuilt on the original foundations. The "rolling road," along which huge hogsheads of tobacco once were rolled to as many as fifteen ships a month waiting at the riverbank, also goes to the mill.

Montross

This seat of Westmoreland County has not always been as sleepy as it appears today. In the courthouse, part of which dates back to 1717, Richard Henry Lee presented a resolution to assist Boston, whose port had been closed because of the Boston Tea Party. The story is related among the memorials on the lawn of the brick structure.

Others are told in the Westmoreland County Museum across Route 3, which covers the history of the county from the Indian villages mapped by Capt. John Smith through the nineteenth century. The tragic fates of Lee Hall, home of Henry Lee, and Chantilly, owned by Richard Henry Lee, are depicted in exhibits. Relics include a chest from the Nelson home in Yorktown thought to have been used by Lafayette and a painting of William Pitt by Charles Wilson Peale.

A small Virginia Presidents Garden beside the museum enshrines busts of Washington, Madison, and Monroe among shrubs and beds of flowers. The museum is open from 10 A.M. to 4:30 P.M. Tuesday, Thursday, and Saturday.

A number of other historic buildings stand in Montross, including the six-room Inn at Montross, which carries on a tradition dating back to 1683 when an "ordinary" was opened. The original handwritten authority is on display in the inn, reconstructed in 1800 on the original foundations.

Hunters for wild turkey and deer are active in the forests south of Montross.

Route 3 Continued

East of Montross, at Templeman's Crossroads, the highway divides. Route 3 turns toward the Rappahannock shoreline, crosses U.S. Route 301 at Warsaw and continues to the southern tip of the peninsula. State Route 202 parallels the Potomac shoreline, then unites with Route 301 at Callao and continues to the northern tip of the peninsula. This creates the opportunity for a circular trip, which, with short detours along side roads, visits all the principal attractions.

Warsaw, the seat of Richmond County since 1730, is a market center surrounded by privately owned historic homes. Sabine Hall, built in 1720 by Robert "King" Carter, sometimes is open during

Historic Garden Week. Belle Ville, constructed 1826–1830, can be seen from the Route 3–360 bypass. The courthouse dates from 1816. At St. John's Episcopal Church, located on Route 3–360 at the eastern edge of town, a monument donated by the people of the Philippines honors the late Congressman William Atkins Jones, author of the 1916 bill to grant independence to the island nation. The church building was erected in 1835.

East of Warsaw, a short detour on Route 692 reaches North Farnham Episcopal Church, a handsome red brick church in the shape of a Latin cross. Built about 1737, the church still bears bullet scars from a skirmish fought in 1814 between Virginia militia and raiders from British Admiral Cockburn's fleet in Chesapeake Bay. Union soldiers used the church as a stable during the Civil War, necessitating restoration of the plain interior in 1872. It was again restored after a fire in 1877 destroyed the interior.

Several side roads lead to Rappahannock River landings with marinas and boat ramps, including those at Simonson and on Totusky Creek. Chinn's Mill Pond straddles the border between Richmond County, carved out of the old Rappahannock County in 1692 and named for a favorite at the court of William and Mary, and Lancaster County, formed in 1651.

St. Mary's White Chapel, apparently named after a church in London, England, sits in a grove of trees at the intersection of Routes 201 and 354 about 4 miles from Lively. A church has existed on the site since 1669, but the present rectangular structure with a side pulpit and rear choir loft basically dates from 1741. Tombs of the Ball family, maternal ancestors of George Washington, stand in the graveyard.

The side roads in this area are rewarding in other ways. Historic homes that are now private residences, like circa 1760 Belle Isle, whose paneling was removed to the Winterthur Museum in Delaware in the 1930s, dot the shoreline and traditional market routes. Many can be seen from afar, some are open during Historic Garden Week, and a few are open on a more regular basis.

Seventeenth-century Epping Forest, the birthplace of George Washington's mother, Mary Ball, stands on a rise in the shade of large tulip poplars and sycamores. Four original dependencies and the house, noted for handcrafted mantels and attractive staircase, are open from 9 A.M. to 5 P.M. from April 1 to December 1. The garden at Fox Hill, an L-shaped plantation house whose original wing was built in 1761, has been carefully restored along the lines of the original garden, with boxwood, holly, crepe myrtle, dogwood, tulip, iris, and peony. The house is off state Route 201 south of Lively.

Lancaster Court House

The Chesapeake Nature Trail, a half-mile west of Lancaster Court House on Route 3, passes through a portion of a 1,000-acre forest owned by the Chesapeake Corporation, a paper manufacturer in West Point, Virginia. The site is untended, but a box at the parking lot beside the highway dispenses printed guides to the 1.6-mile loop trail, which can be divided into two segments. A leisurely trip can be accomplished in an hour and a half, including stops at rustic wooden benches along the way.

A loop segment of about half a mile begins with a warning about poison ivy, then passes examples of mountain laurel, *Liriodendron tulipifera*, sweet gum, sycamore, red maple, and yellow poplar growing along a stream bottom and a variety of ferns, including the Christmas fern. An old sawmill site, thought to have operated around the turn of the century, still has evidences of logging operations. Nearby is a large black walnut, commercially the single most valuable tree in American forests and sometimes "rustled" by thieves with chain saws. The rings of a white oak, blown down by a storm, show that it sprouted soon after the first English settlers arrived in the area. The settlers used the roots and bark of the sassafras tree to make a spring tonic.

A wooden observation deck stands on a marshy site once used to load logs onto barges for transport to sawmills downriver. It looks across the narrow Western Branch of the Corrotoman River, which is trimmed with large areas of cordgrass, pickerel weed, arrowhead, cattail, and arrow arum. Farther away from the noise of the highway is a lookout point, with an open vista down the river and a marsh dominated by cattail. Nearby are paw-paw, holly, alder, and spice-bush, whose strong odor resembles sassafras. The trail can be shortened by cutting back across the rising terrain to the point of origin.

Those continuing the full distance will see the vegetation change perceptibly as they climb from the riverbank to the higher elevation at Echo Point, overlooking a bend in the river where steamboats tied up in the nineteenth century. Pine trees stand among oaks whose nuts are eaten by animals, beech whose trunks may show beaver tooth marks, flowering dogwood, red cedar, and black cherry. Headwater Point provides a clear view of the navigable portion of the river, underlaid by rich oyster beds and visited by ducks, blue heron, osprey, egrets, and red-winged blackbird. The river also is favored by duck hunters.

The trail, a reminder that lumbering joins agriculture and fishing as one of the principal industries of Lancaster County, is open during daylight hours year round.

The historic district of Lancaster Court House, one of the best in the Northern Neck, is lined up along Highway 3.

The oldest structure is the small Old Clerk's Office, whose ancestry can be read in the slightly varying colors of its red bricks. The original building, which dates from about 1797, was enlarged in 1833. The structure is part of the Mary Ball Memorial Museum and Library, which also includes the 1821 Old Jail and the circa 1798 frame Lancaster House. On display in the Lancaster House are items owned by the Washington family and others, antique furniture, period ladies' dresses, and old prints, as well as items of local interest. The museum and library, named for the mother of George Washington, is open from 9 A.M. to 5 P.M. Tuesday–Friday, 10 A.M. to 3 P.M. Saturday.

Among other historic structures are 1790 Lancaster Tavern, for many years the home of the clerk of court, and several turn-of-the-century structures, including a former general store now housing the Lancaster Woman's Club.

Lancaster was a latecomer as county seat. Court sessions were first held in homes along the Corrotoman River after the county was created in 1651, then at Queenstown at the mouth of the river in 1698. The court was moved to its present site in 1742; the courthouse has since undergone a number of renovations.

Levelfields, an 1857–1858 mansion about 2 miles east of Lancaster Court House, has a handsome setting. The 300-yard, tree-lined entrance road frames a house with handsome double-tiered portico and four massive chimneys. Boxwoods border the walkway on the expansive lawns, which overlook 12 acres of cultivated fields and 40 acres of timberland bordered by a stream.

State Route 604 winds through rolling countryside and descends the riverbank to a small beach on the Corrotoman River, where the unpretentious Merry Point automobile ferry operates when needed between 7 A.M. and 7 P.M. The river at this point is photogenic, with sail and motorboats crossing the bow or stern as the ferry chugs to Ottoman on the opposite shore. The sights are vaguely reminiscent of what existed in the colonial era, when sailing ships anchored to discharge new settlers and take on the hogsheads of tobacco rolled down the hill road to the plantation dock.

On the ferry approach road stand historic homes such as Verville, built about 1690 and essentially unchanged from its eighteenth-century appearance, and 1767 Merry Point, a modest clapboard structure with four chimneys raised by the Rev. James Waddell, a Presbyterian minister. Both are now privately owned. On the opposite side of the river is Payne's Shop at Ottoman, built about 1803 as an "ordinary" or tavern and now a private residence.

Weems, a fishing village at the end of state Route 222 with a handsome view of Carters Creek, was a popular excursion port during the steamboat era, when boats from Baltimore made 34 stops along the Rappahannock River. Nearby Wharton Grove, a popular religious camp meeting ground from 1893 to 1927, vaguely recalls the era when the smoke of steamboats and the white sails of individual boats filled the river off the longest pier on Chesapeake Bay.

Kilmarnock-Irvington-White Stone

Although these communities at the southeastern tip of the Northern Neck are separate, they are closely bunched and often hyphenated in the minds of residents and visitors alike. Kilmarnock, the largest town with a population of around 1,000, is the commercial center of Lancaster County. Local legend insists the original name was Crossroads and that it was renamed Kilmarnock by Scottish immigrants. Irvington, once known as Carter's Creek Wharf, takes full advantage of its favorable creekfront site to mix commercial seafood and resort atmosphere. White Stone's name is the oldest of the three, and probably derives from the stone of a grist mill that once stood on the site.

Traditionally, this is watermen's country, where the migration of the crabs and finfish was as important as the weather. Although diluted by an influx of retirees and vacationers after the Downing Bridge at Warsaw opened in 1929, this aspect is still important. A majority of the residents of the county still look to the water for their livelihood, as the large number of plants processing oysters and menhaden along Carter's Creek suggests.

The natural beauty of Carter's Creek inspired the development of a prestigious resort named Tides Inn, which has become the symbol of the tri-town area.

Tides Inn: "Quiet quality" is an appropriate description for this resort, which has a dedicated clientele addicted to its water-oriented activities, world class golf, and relaxed ambience. Tides Inn stands on a scenic point of land jutting out into the creek, a tributary of the Rappahannock, that was farmland and unmolested wilderness until the late 1940s. When Ennolls A. Stephens and his wife, Ann, started the complex, underbrush in the woods was so thick that walking was well-nigh impossible and the farmland was reverting to wilderness. He acquired the site for its beauty, with no thought of building a resort.

Once the vision began to take shape, Stephens paid careful attention to detail. Cypress for the dining room and view room was cut from a swamp about 20 miles away. Carpets were purchased from Brussels and Sheffield silver and Chippendale furniture imported from England. The eagle hanging in the Chesapeake Club, now used as the resort logo, was salvaged from an old house on the site. Tides Inn opened on a small scale in 1947 and has been growing ever since. It now is comprised of two separate lodging facilities, two 18-hole golf courses, and assorted boating facilities, including its own yachts.

The yachts cruise the Rappahannock River and Chesapeake Bay. Luncheons are served on Monday and Friday aboard the 124-foot *Miss Ann,* which on Wednesday anchors off Windmill Point for a bayshore fish fry. On Tuesday, Thursday, and Sunday, narrated cove cruises explain the crabbing, oyster, and fishing industries spotted along the creek, as well as some of the historic homes on the bank. That leaves Saturday for the traditional trip to Urbanna on the south shore of the Rappahannock, once known as the "whiskey run" when Irvington was dry but now devoted to historical sites and shopping.

The *Miss Ann,* built in 1926 at Wilmington, Delaware, is an attraction in itself. A familiar sight in American yachting centers in the late 1920s under the names *Siele* and *Sea Wolf,* she was used by the Navy as an experimental sonar ship named *Aquamarine* during World War II. Stephens purchased the vessel after the war and had it reconverted for use at the resort.

Tides Inn also has docking facilities, including twenty-one slips, sailboats, and small power boats, as well as a saltwater swimming pool. Inn personnel will arrange for local captains to take fishing parties into the Bay. A boating rendezvous in mid-September benefits Chesapeake Academy.

Land-oriented visitors have adequate opportunities for diversion, too. The Golden Eagle Course, about 2.5 miles from the inn, covers

6,960 yards. The older 6,600-foot Tartan Course adjoins Tides Lodge, across the creek from the inn. A 1,150-yard par 3 course is located on the grounds of the inn. Tournaments include Sir Guy Campbell's in early April, the American Cancer Society contest in early August, and the Fall Tartan in late November.

Ponds on the golf course are stocked with bass for fishers. Four paved tennis courts are available. Bikers may use any of the roads near the resort, which provides cycles for guests. Hunters use nearby private lands to bag ducks, geese, quail, and doves.

Individuals make their own way to most of the historic sites in the area, but the inn arranges visits to privately owned Ditchley on Dividing Creek, a Georgian brick mansion built in 1762, and to Muskettoe Pointe. The 2½-story clapboard Muskettoe Pointe is shaded by paper mulberry trees and has a formal garden and an herb garden.

Tides Inn operates from late March to after New Year's Day.

Christ Church: "Historic" properly is used as an integral part of the name of Christ Church, one of the nation's greatest architectural and historical monuments. Except for minimal repairs, the structure is virtually unchanged from the way it "came from the hands of the builders" in 1732.

Volunteer guides identify special features of the church during tours, which are conducted daily on a regular basis. The church has a plain interior, covered with plaster made of oyster shells. The stones used in the floor were imported from England as ballast aboard commercial vessels. The box pews and rare triple-decker pulpit, with a lower level for the clerk, were handmade of native pine and walnut. The imported marble baptismal font has carved angels' heads and the acanthus leaf motif used on Carter's tomb. The original communion silver dates from the late seventeenth and early eighteenth centuries. The 3-foot-thick Flemish bond brick exterior walls of the cruciform building use color variations to avoid monotony. The doors are highlighted by using a lighter color of brick in the frames.

Tombs of Robert Carter and two wives, with carefully duplicated slabs replacing the deteriorated originals, stand behind the church.

Relics and pictorials in a separate museum building place the church and its builder, Robert "King" Carter, in the context of the colonial era. Carter's wealth and political and commercial influence earned his nickname. His forty-four plantations covering 300,000 acres, and his 2,000 cattle and 1,000 slaves made him the second largest farming, importing, and exporting business in the colony.

He served on the King's Council and, for a time, was acting governor. His descendants included three signers of the Declaration of Independence, two presidents, eight Virginia governors, and Confederate Gen. Robert E. Lee.

A gold watch that Carter gave to his oldest daughter, Elizabeth, is on display. Other relics include the original key to the church, architectural hardware from the construction period, fireplace tiles, a brass candlestick, Rhenish jug, and an angel from the original "King" Carter tomb. Photographs of the excavation of the foundations of Corrotoman, Carter's mansion that burned in 1729, indicate it was the largest built in America to that time, with a frontage twice that of the Governor's Palace in Williamsburg. Although no description survives, a conjectural drawing of the mansion based on archeological research hangs in the museum.

Christ Church is open from 9 A.M. to 5 P.M. daily, except Christmas Day. Episcopal religious services are held once a month during the warm period.

Bayside Northern Neck

The Northern Neck does not taper as it approaches Chesapeake Bay, but ends abruptly with a flat end interrupted by numerous fingers. Most of them are devoted to private pursuits, but two have substantial public diversions—the finger that ends at Windmill Point, the easternmost point on the Northern Neck peninsula, and the one where Reedville dispenses aquatic diversions.

Windmill Point: The drive to Windmill Point along state Route 695 passes a succession of farmhouses and coves whose shores are lined with marsh grass and the entrance to the private Windmill Point Yacht Club. The lightly traveled road, an excellent biking or hiking highway, ends about 6 miles from White Stone at a small public beach, used by crabbers and surfcasters.

The nearby Windmill Point Marine Resort has 135 open and covered slips for sail and power boats alongside a modern motel and restaurant and a long sandy beach. Other recreational activities and facilities include the Windjammer golf course, three tennis courts, and the annual Rappahannock Seafood and Arts Festival in late April, which features working boats, seafood served outdoors, and arts and crafts.

Charter boat captains from Hartfield and Achilles on the Middle Peninsula take out fishing parties from the resort. The 80-foot MV

Miss Gloucester handles scenic charters, as well as fishing parties. Windmill Point Resort is within easy driving distance of tour boats that depart Reedville for Tangier and Smith islands in the center of the Bay.

The place has not always been so peaceful. During the War of 1812, the British put troops ashore and attacked a small garrison, only to be driven off by Virginia militia arriving from across the Rappahannock River.

Reedville: Fishing has always been important to Reedville, but the rise of the menhaden brought it heretofore unknown prosperity. Some say that, for a time, Reedville had the highest per capita income on the East Coast. Be that as it may, the community's position at the end of U.S. Route 360 made it a popular summer retreat for residents of Richmond. Their judgment has been justified by the passage of time.

Reedville is still one of Virginia's busiest fishing ports, with solid Victorian watermen's houses mingling with summer homes. Route 360 moves right through the village to the waterfront, where an active seafood-processing house stands near a dilapidated pier.

Most outside interest in Reedville is more transitory these days. For the time being, it centers on day cruises to Tangier and Smith islands and charter fishing trips. Both embarkation points are away from the village.

The *Chesapeake Breeze* leaves at 10 A.M. daily May through mid-October from Buzzard Point Marina, on state Route 656 via state Route 646. The 5¾-hour narrated cruise leaves busy Cockrell's Creek and crosses about 12 miles of water to the island, where passengers spend 2½ hours ashore. The cruise to Smith Island in Maryland aboard the 150-passenger *Capt. Evans* begins at the KOA Campground at Smith's Point, reached from U.S. 301 via SR 652, 644, and 650. The 6¼-hour trip begins with a slow journey past the private homes, some of them historic, overlooking Sloop Creek and the Little Wicomico River. The 13-mile cruise narrated by Capt. Gordon Evans, a native of Smith Island, is capped by passage through inland waterways and a visit ashore for lunch and/or a walk around Ewell. The vessel leaves at 10 A.M. daily from May through the end of September (see Chapter 3, Islands in the Bay).

Charter boats cast for the rockfish, spot, and croaker offshore between the mouth of the Great Wicomico River and Smith Point, bluefish near Buoy 48, and drum near wrecks southwest of Tangier Island. On state Route 644 at Sunnybank, a ferry operates in the manner that once was common in the region. It sails as needed from

7 A.M. to 7 P.M. Monday through Saturday. Drivers honk for service if the flat vessel is tied up on the opposite shore of the Little Wicomico River.

Routes 360–220

A westward run along these highways completes the journey around the Northern Neck. Almost all side roads lead to picturesque fishing villages, many with marinas, along a shoreline once inhabited by Indians and first visited by Europeans in 1608.

A few historic structures stand along the route. At inland Heathsville, named for the founder of Phi Beta Kappa, John Heath, the small, white frame church building with narrow stained-glass windows is relatively young, but St. Stephen's Parish was founded in 1653 as Chickacove Parish. The courthouse, seat of Northumberland County, contains valuable records. Old Hughlet's Tavern, now an apartment building, was built in the early 1700s.

Lewisetta, at the end of SR 624, is straight out of an early twentieth-century engraving. It sits in splendid isolation on a flat, marshy point overlooking the Coan River, whose beauty impressed Capt. John Smith. A country store looks beyond a T-shaped pier, boat ramp, and marina across the wide river to the forested shore beyond. The marina rents slips to transients. Olverson's Marina off SR 624 has both covered and open slips.

The one-time deep-water port of Kinsale, at the end of SR 203, is another pleasure boating center. Many of the attractions on the Potomac River shorelines of Virginia and Maryland, as well as Tangier and Smith islands, are within easy reach of Kinsale's three marinas. White Point Marina hosts the Westmoreland Ruritan's annual Lower Potomac Bluefish Tournament in early September.

Founded in 1705, Kinsale is the oldest town on the Potomac in Virginia, but has few signs of it. From the private circa 1800 Great House on the bank overlooking the creek, it is easier to imagine Kinsale as a quiet lumber mill town than a lusty port. But Kinsale was established as a port and attracted hundreds of shipwrights, chandlers, riggers, coopers, and merchants to the area. Tobacco and grain passed through, but Kinsale became best known for the lumber cut in nearby forests. It also was the home of many Potomac River pilots because it gave them easy access to vessels entering the river.

A base for small naval vessels during the War of 1812, it was burned by British Adm. Cockburn, but afterward revived as a stop on the steamships operating from Baltimore. Two-way smuggling was a major occupation during the Civil War. Later, Kinsale was a major canning center, and Maryland farmers, irate because Kinsale tomatoes were holding prices down, rowed across the river one night to burn it. They missed the mark and mistakenly burned canneries at and near Lewisetta.

State Route 202 passes through country familiar to George Washington's mother, Mary Ball, who lived in her youth in the home of her guardian, Col. George Estridge, at Sandy Point. One of the few relics remaining from the period is Yeocomico Church, about 4 miles off Route 202 along SR 604 and 606. The present church, whose 1705 construction date is certified by markings on one of its exterior bricks, has an unusual, handsomely decorated, covered entrance porch. Although the windows were modified during maintenance and restoration in the eighteenth and twentieth centuries, the 1705 structure is essentially intact. The walnut Holy Table and interior arrangement also are original.

Many of the most historic homes in this area burned before the modern era. One was Machotick, where Richard Henry Lee, signer of the Declaration of Independence, is buried. It was located on state Route 612, north of Route 202.

Farther along the roadway is Coles Point, a fishing village with the nostalgic oyster shell mound near a processing plant. Small homes and sheds also interrupt the flatness of the low-lying terrain near a boat ramp and private pier.

The plain white brick façade of Nomini Episcopal Church on a peaceful, shaded bluff above Nomini Creek provides little indication of the stormy history of the church. The first building (sometimes spelled Nominy) was built in 1704 and replaced in 1755 by a brick structure. That church was burned by the British in 1814, but was reconstructed in 1852.

PART FIVE

The National Capital Area

Overview

BY OCTOBER, YOU MIGHT EXPECT THE CROWDS AT THE GREAT FALLS Park in Maryland northwest of Washington, D.C., to be gone. Not so, if it is a warm, sunny Sunday. As a matter of fact, the drive off the Beltway to the end of MacArthur Boulevard can be pointless at such times. Like as not, a sign at the entrance to the national park will signify that the quota already has been reached and vehicles will be parked bumper to bumper for hundreds of yards outside the entrance, despite the presence of "No Parking" signs.

Washington has a justly deserved reputation for traffic jams. During the morning and afternoon rush hours, entering or leaving the city on interstates, the Beltway, or any through highway is slow, tedious, and frustrating, because so many people who work in the city live in the Virginia or Maryland suburban areas.

The crowded condition at Great Falls Park proves that people jams also occur frequently. As a matter of fact, the impression of crowds is almost unavoidable in the national capital area. This crowding does not mean that you should avoid the area. Indeed, Washington has attractions, cultural as well as governmental, that cannot be found anywhere else. Suburban areas not only witnessed a fair amount of history, but also are becoming repositories of governmental activities that cannot be accommodated in the capital itself. A surprising amount of greenery exists, ranging from The Mall and other open spaces inside Washington, which are the result of almost three centuries of conscious planning and monument raising, to a variety of parks and other recreational facilities in the suburban areas.

Because of the volumes of traffic, a good rule of thumb in approaching Washington is "suburbs during the week, city on the weekends." That will at least avoid some of the heaviest traffic volumes.

"National capital area" is not just a convenient way to describe the national capital and suburbs. The language becomes more factual with each passing year as governments of Washington and the suburban communities try to coordinate their problems. The District of Columbia is a member of the Chesapeake Bay consortium, which unites Virginia, Maryland, Pennsylvania, and the District in a compact to clean up the Bay.

Northern Virginia

THIS SECTION OF THE STATE IS KNOWN IN THE VERNACULAR AS NORTHERN Virginia. For the 1.3 million people living in the region, the terminology is simply descriptive. For people elsewhere in the state, it carries certain unfavorable connotations. Northern Virginia is more liberal than the rest of the state and is oriented more toward the functions and attitudes of the national capital than the rest of the state. It has problems peculiar to the region, especially regarding transportation, most of which cost more money than the rest of the state wants to pay.

On the other hand, the entire state benefits from the rapid development of Northern Virginia. Things happen quickly and grandly. The growth rate of the area is astounding. The meanings of many traditional names have been transformed almost overnight; Tyson's Corner — a mere geographical reference little more than a decade ago — is a major new commercial and residential center. Other crossroads corners made the transition to high-rise hotels, multistoried organizational offices, and high-tech businesses even earlier. And the urban area continues to expand like ripples in a pond.

George Mason University has quickly become one of the state's largest institutions of higher learning — with an international reputation and an extensive cultural program.

Northern Virginia consists of a number of cities, towns, and counties (cities and counties are separate jurisdictions in Virginia). It includes the cities of Alexandria, Falls Church, Manassas and Manassas Park, county and city of Fairfax, urban Arlington County, part of Prince William County, and a number of townships whose populations spill out into land beyond the Chesapeake Bay region, especially along the Dulles International Airport–Leesburg axis. Governmental distinctions need not bother the visitor; indeed, many residents themselves are not confident of boundary locations.

Fairfax County, which begins above the Great Falls of the Potomac and wraps around Arlington County and the city of Alexandria, has changed from a rural to an urban atmosphere in little more than three decades. The city of 20,000-plus residents with the same name sits in the heart of that mass. Yet without highway signs few could tell where one begins and the other leaves off. Falls Church, Vienna, and Herndon, which not so long ago were urbanized islands, have been absorbed by the onrush of development.

Fairfax County is, first of all, a bedroom community for the national capital, but it also is rapidly becoming a locus of corporate headquarters and high-tech development. Reston is a prototype of the modern planned community designed to eliminate commuting, integrate work and home life, and save energy, with a variety of walkways and bikeways. The first buildings, erected in 1964, surround Lake Anne. The nation's first earth-sheltered school, Terraset, was constructed there.

Despite such intensive development, this county retains considerable greenery. The Fairfax County Park Authority manages more than thirty parks covering 14,000 acres, with extensive wilderness, sports facilities, and even some historic structures. Fairfax city hides a number of historical features on its overworked streets. The original wills of George and Martha Washington are preserved in the Courthouse records. Earp's Ordinary on Main Street, built 1805–1813, was a stagecoach stop and post office in the 1820s.

Arlington County (usually referred to simply as Arlington) has become in fact what it was intended to be geographically—a part of the District of Columbia. Land ceded by Virginia for the national capital was returned after most of the development occurred on the north side of the Potomac River. Since World War II especially, it has absorbed much of the population overflow from the national capital. The urban county is characterized by major throughways and roads that once handled local traffic but now conduct solid streams of cars.

The heavy volume of traffic detracts from a beautiful shoreline with an outstanding view of the Lincoln Memorial and the surrounding waterfront park in Washington. President Lyndon B. Johnson and his wife, Lady Bird, are honored by a park where the George Washington Parkway crosses Columbia Island south of Memorial

Bridge. Quotations from Johnson are inscribed on stones at the LBJ Memorial Grove. The profusion of flowers in the park recalls Lady Bird's beautification campaign. The principal attractions on the shoreline facing Washington are the Pentagon and Arlington National Cemetery. The Arlington Historical Society's Ball-Sellers House is a log cabin built by John Balls in the mid-eighteenth century.

The complexity of the region has spawned an advanced regional concept. Although each community has its own facilities, they share many others. There are regional authorities for transportation, parks, and other activities.

Northern Virginia is shaped by Interstates 95 and 495 (the Beltway) and through streets that intersect with these. Many of the secondary routes follow historic trails; Route 29 or Frying Pan Road, for example, was established in 1792 by Robert "King" Carter to transport copper from Bull Run Valley to the city of Fairfax.

The actual southern boundary of Northern Virginia is indefinite because it keeps moving. However, the suburban area reaches at least 25 miles to Woodbridge and the picturesque village of Occoquan, whose small frame structures now primarily house specialty shops and restaurants. Quantico Marine Base, with the Marine Corps Museum, only a few years ago was isolated in countryside; now it is on the fringe of the national capital area.

Prince William Forest Park

The temperate climate of the Chesapeake Bay area provides few opportunities for skiers to unlimber, but Prince William Forest Park near Triangle is one of them. About 35 miles of trails and fire roads that admit hikers and bikers to pristine wilderness during the warm months beckon cross-country skiers when snow is on the ground. Snowfall normally is not heavy and lasts for only a few days at a time, but a cold winter improves the chances of extended skiing activity within 35 miles of Washington.

The 18,571-acre Prince William Park, a deciduous forest of beech, oak, hickory, and tulip poplar alongside stands of pine that have recaptured former farm fields, has considerable beaver activity along its creeks and drainage areas. Other animals include white-tailed deer, opossum, raccoon, flying squirrel, wild turkey, and both predatory and song birds. About 150 species of birds have been identified.

A variety of wildflowers, especially violets, mountain laurel, and rhododendron, also may be seen along about 35 miles of trails, many of which interconnect. The longest stretch of trail, presently named T-8, meanders more than 8 miles along the South Branch of Quantico Creek from the vicinity of Oak Ridge Campground on the western side of the park to the North Branch of the creek on the eastern side. The parts of the park along the streams are extremely beautiful.

Two self-guided nature trails, each of which takes about 45 minutes, introduce walkers to the history of the park, which was a Civilian Conservation Corps camp in the 1930s, and to the way the forest has recovered former farmland by stages. Posts along the routes are keyed to guidebooks distributed at the park Visitors Center. The mile-long Farms-to-Forest loop passes old cemeteries, including a few dating from the Civil War, and wagon roads and winds through a forest in various stages of recovery, from Indian pipe, reindeer moss, and wild blueberry and blackberry to older trees on steep banks that were never cut by farmers. The route can be extended another 2½ miles to Quantico Creek via a connecting trail. The Crossing, a 0.8-mile loop with some 150-year-old tulip poplars, relates the wilderness to historical periods — to geologic history, to Indian use of sassafras and other plants for medicinal purposes and of beech for food and construction, to the young and tender plants preferred by deer, to the use of dogwood and oaks by settlers to make furniture and implements such as spinning spools, and to any visitor's need to avoid poison ivy.

The paved Pine Grove Forest Trail, accessible to handicapped and people with strollers, has signs and informative audiotapes in push-button boxes. Located near the park entrance on state Route 619 a short distance west of I-95, it can be completed in 15 minutes. Bikes are permitted on roads and fire roads, but not on the foot trails.

About 15 miles of park streams and two impoundment areas are open year round to fishing for largemouth bass, crappie, chain pickerel, brown bullhead, bluegill, pumpkinseed, and redbreast sunfish. The park is open from dawn to dusk for day use.

The park has a family campground, a group tenting area at Turkey Run Ridge, and an RV concession village with hookups. Five cabin camps, which date back to CCC days, are rented to groups and organizations. Year-round weekend guided hikes, presentations, and talks at the Visitors Center emphasize beaver activity, with visits to worksites, as well as the importance of snakes in the ecosystem. Evening campfire programs are held at the campground during the summer months. Hands-on exhibits, including animal games and discovery boxes, are to be moved from the Turkey Run Nature Center to the Visitors Center when expansion is completed.

The 400-acre Chopawamsic backcountry area has primitive campsites within a mile of parking areas. A limited number of cross-country backpacking permits are issued, but the area is closed during the hunting season because of its proximity to Quantico Marine Corps Base, where hunting is allowed.

Leesylvania State Park

The newest park in Northern Virginia occupies a tip of a peninsula south of Occoquan Bay. The 500-acre site, still in the early development stage, has basic day-use facilities, including ramps for launching sailboats and motorboats and a beach for swimming. Nature and bicycle trails, overlooks, and observation decks will be added to expose the hardwood forest, dominated by oaks, holly, and hickory, an extensive waterfowl population, and archeological sites. A swimming pool and amphitheater will be built.

The park is located about 2 miles off U.S. Route 1 along state Route 610.

Mason Neck

Mason Neck, a boot-shaped peninsula jutting into the Potomac River about 11 miles south of Alexandria, illustrates how important a few miles can be. The calm that prevails on Gunston Road (state Route 242) contrasts sharply with the rush on U.S. Route 1, once the primary southern approach to the national capital and still heavily traveled despite the existence of parallel I-95. The restful change in atmosphere has been enhanced by the preservation of historic Gunston Hall, home of George Mason, and the existence of three large areas devoted to recreational and wildlife uses. Bald eagles are responsible for one of them.

In the Algonkin Indian language, *pohick* meant "the water place." Pohick Bay Park, 1,000 acres on the northern side of the peninsula facing Pohick Bay, justifies its name with a long, scenic waterfront, and facilities for boating, fishing, sailing, swimming, 300 campsites (100 with electrical outlets), and picnicking. Its marina has twin extrawide boat ramps and piers. In the warm months, concessions rent sailboats and pedal boats.

A 1.6-mile nature trail past inlets carpeted with water lilies and through woods with laurel and holly begins near the boat ramp. A 1.4-mile woods trail starts near the minigolf course. The park also has 4 miles of horse trails. An 18-hole, par 72 golf course has a separate entrance.

Half-day guided canoe trips into a tidal freshwater marsh are led by naturalists on weekends from early April through October, plus one winter trip in early December. While paddling through the area, the naturalist interprets various flora and fauna and their relationship to the environment. The marsh presents a different perspective at different times of year. Warblers and wildflowers are most evident in the spring, and resting ducks and fruit-bearing paw-paw in autumn. Great blue heron and osprey also are frequently seen. Bald cypresses, oaks, hickories, mulberries, and tulip poplars change throughout the year. The trip passes an old beaver lodge, where the hard-working animals are often seen. Muskrats and even an occasional deer pose for the canoeists.

The park and campground are open all year; concessions and swimming pool operate from Memorial Day to Labor Day. The park is part of the Northern Virginia Regional Parks Authority system described below.

Mason Neck National Wildlife Refuge and Mason Neck State Park occupy the toe of the boot, stretching along the shores of the Potomac River and Occoquan and Belmont bays not far from historic Gunston Hall manor house. They complement each other well.

The wildlife refuge, through which visitors drive to reach the state park, devotes 2,200 acres of upland forest, grassland, and marsh primarily to saving the bald eagle. Established in 1969, Mason Neck is one of the largest eagle wintering areas in the Chesapeake Bay area, with as many as sixty eagles feeding and nesting on the refuge. More than 300 species of other birds, mammals, reptiles, and amphibians share the site with them.

The 3-mile Woodmarsh Hiking Trail, open from April 1 to November 30 during daylight hours, loops through a forest dominated by hickory, oak, and maple and skirts the 285-acre freshwater Great Marsh, features that sustain many animals rarely seen in an urbanized area, including beaver, muskrat, otter, and great blue heron, as well as a few deer. Songbirds also frequent the forest. A blind for photographers is located away from the public path. The 0.75-mile Great Marsh Trail on Gunston Road, open from December 1 through March 31 or by special permit, meanders through the forest to an overlook at Great Marsh. The best opportunity to see bald eagle woodpeckers, and migratory waterfowl, which rest and feed in the park, is along this trail.

The refuge's riverfront, marsh, pond, swamp, meadow, and pine and hardwood forests also are used for environmental study. Fishing, hunting, camping, and picnicking are not allowed.

The animal population at adjacent Mason Neck State Park, 1,800 acres of woodlands and wetlands fronting on Belmont Bay, is just as large. More than 600 great blue herons nest in the park, which also hosts large populations of bluebird, wood duck, hawks, owls, and white-tailed deer. Eagles also are among the 145 species of birds regularly seen, more than 25 of which may be viewed in one season. Terrestrial animals also include groundhogs, turtles, otter, and beaver.

Rangers conduct an extensive interpretive program, including bird and nature walks, canoe trips, and children's programs, such as pond studies. Wildlife lectures, especially on turkeys and deer, are given once a month. Although the ruins of Lexington, an old plantation house, are generally off limits because bald eagles roost nearby, several times a year rangers take groups to the site.

Two circular hiking trails, and a short link, provide access to various types of landscape and lifeforms. The mile-long Bay View Trail circles a freshwater pond, parallels the shore of the bay, and crosses three boardwalks over marsh and wetlands before entering the forest. Kane's Creek Trail, also a mile long, tours a level forested area past the edge of the creek. A short diversion leads to an observation blind for eagle surveys, which also can be used for general observation and photography. The Wilson Spring Trail that connects them explores woodlands and passes a spring.

Although fishing is not allowed, the beaches may be walked. Horses are allowed only on the paved roads.

The Visitors Center, which overlooks Belmont Bay, completes the lessons in history and nature science. History exhibits cover George Mason, a framer of the U.S. Constitution whose home is near the park, and agricultural methods of the eighteenth century. Scientific exhibits include those on wildlife within the park.

Gunston Hall

Many of the ideas for the American Bill of Rights germinated in the elegant rooms of Gunston Hall, a bright Georgian mansion built in 1754–1758 by George Mason. Mason's concept of individual rights, unusual for the period, made him the Father of the Bill of Rights.

The simple, 1½-story brick mansion with four interior chimneys looks much as it did when Mason ruminated about rights and entertained George Washington at Sunday dinner. It is especially noted for the delicate wood carvings and red silk damask wallcovering in the Palladian room, the "Chinese-style" formal dining room carefully executed by an indentured servant, William Buckland, and furnishings that belonged to the Mason family, much of it made before 1792. In the study is the table on which he wrote the Virginia Declaration of Rights of 1776, forerunner of the national Bill of Rights, the first ten amendments to the Constitution.

Ancillary buildings, including a schoolhouse with desks and instructional materials, kitchen furnished with the solid wooden and metal implements of the period, laundry, dairy, and smokehouse, have been reconstructed. An unusual semioctagonal porch opens onto the formal gardens between the mansion and the Potomac River. The original boxwood walkway planted by Mason is about 12 feet high and has been supplemented by plants typical of the colonial period by the Garden Club of Virginia, with parterres of different patterns.

A guided tour of the mansion and grounds begins with an audio-visual orientation. Gunston Hall is open from 9 A.M. to 5 P.M. daily, except Christmas. A favorite colonial pastime, kite flying, is enjoyed during a May festival. Other key events include Historic Garden Week in Virginia the last week in April, George Mason Day in May, and a mid-December display of Christmas decorations.

Both George Mason and George Washington were vestrymen at 1774 Pohick Church, built in 1774. Washington selected the site, now on U.S. 1 just north of Mason Neck, and worshipped there for twenty-three years. The building was damaged by Union troops during the Civil War, but was restored. Concerts featuring old string instruments sometimes are held there.

Northern Virginia Regional Parks

The multijurisdictional Northern Virginia Regional Park Authority, created in 1959 with what many considered a visionary plan to preserve 25 miles of shoreline along the Occoquan River, is now one of the region's biggest landholders, with more than 8,600 acres under its control. A green strip along and near the northern shore of the river and tributary Bull Run is supplemented by more than half a dozen outdoors and historical attractions elsewhere, some on the shores of the Potomac River.

An abandoned railway right of way has been turned into a 100-foot-wide park that stretches 44 miles from Alexandria to Purcellville, near the Blue Ridge Mountains. The Washington & Old Dominion (W&OD) Railroad Regional Park, paved from Shirlington Road in Arlington to west of Leesburg, has some uphill areas and is not well marked. It takes hikers, bikers, joggers, and horse riders from the heavily populated commercial and bedroom area past Wolf Trap Farm Park, historic structures, a distillery, Dulles International Airport, forests and neat fields hosting 450 kinds of wildflowers, birds, and wildlife, and horse farms, to within sight of the Blue Ridge Mountains. A separate bridle path covers the western section of the park, from Vienna to Purcellville. The regional authority publishes a trail guide.

Plans call for construction of strategic way stations and extension of the park to the Blue Ridge Mountains so that it will connect with the Appalachian Trail at Bluemont. Ultimately, W&OD Park is supposed to be part of a 700-mile Potomac Heritage National Scenic Trail from Mount Vernon (or perhaps Southern Maryland) to the tributaries of the Ohio River. It is to be formed by new links to connect some existing trails, including Pennsylvania's Laurel Highlands Hiking Trail, and is to incorporate the towpath of the upper end of the Chesapeake and Ohio (C&O) Canal.

Seven connected regional parks — Bull Run, Hemlock, Fountainhead, Sandy Run, Occoquan, and Bull Run Marina — begin just southeast of the preserved Manassas (Bull Run) Civil War Battlefield and stretch along bluffs covered by mature forests of hemlock, pine, and cedar. Numerous small streams descend through the parks to enter Bull Run and Occoquan River, creating a water-rich area alive in season with songbirds, waterfowl, and wildflowers. The up-and-down forested trails are some of the most challenging in the Chesapeake Bay area.

A 20-mile streamside Blue Trail through four parks exposes especially beautiful groves of mature hemlocks, small streams, wildflowers, rock outcroppings, and stream islands. It begins at the north end of the park strip just off I-66 amid the bluebells and forest of Bull Run Park and continues past the 300-year-old hemlocks of Hemlock Overlook Park through the varied terrain of Bull Run Marina Park and drops down to end in a forest enlivened by rhododendron, lady's slipper, and other wildflowers at Fountainhead Park.

All these connected parks have short trails and other attractions, as well.

Bull Run Park's 1,800 acres of relatively flat woods and meadows provide both recreational facilities and a sanctuary for small animals and birds, including wild turkey, quail, doves, and pileated woodpecker. The park has three interconnected blazed trails. The 1-mile Yellow Trail and 1.8-mile White Trail circle through woods and follow the soggy banks of the creek, where bevies of bluebells and other wildflowers bloom in spring. The Blue Trail overlays parts of these trails as it begins its southward journey along the streambanks. Facilities also include 5 miles of bridle paths; 150 tree-shaded campsites for tents and vehicles; swimming pool (open Memorial Day through Labor Day); miniature golf; skeet and trap shooting center; indoor archery range; and playgrounds.

Interpretive events include re-enactment of the first major battle of the Civil War in 1861; the largest dog show in the United States; a late-March evening swamp hike to listen to the frogs croaking and hopping; and the mid-April Bluebell Walk, led by naturalists through the largest stand of bluebells on the East Coast.

The park is open during daylight hours (except for campers) from the second week in March through November.

Hemlock Overlook, atop a steep embankment, looks out over forested hillside to a bend in the stream and hills on the opposite shore of Bull Run. Open year round during daylight hours, the park also hosts an environmental center.

Bull Run Marina has both water and land facilities. Its boat-launching ramp is used by fishers and pleasure boaters. In addition to the transient Blue Trail, two short loop trails explore slopes and ridges thick with hemlock. The park is open Friday–Sunday from the first week in April to Labor Day.

The hills at Fountainhead Park also provide popular panoramas. The 1-mile Yellow Trail, which traverses a high ridge above a small cove, has short spurs that end at overlooks. The 2-mile White Trail meanders through high ground set back from Lake Occoquan. A campground for backpackers, accessible only on foot, is located in the southern extreme of the park. A boat-launching ramp, miniature golf, and rowboat rentals are near the Visitors Center. Fountainhead is open during daylight hours (except for campers) from the second week of March through November.

The placid water of Occoquan Lake off Sandy Run Park, which anchors the southeastern end of the riverfront green strip, is well known to crew rowers, scullers, kayakers, and canoeists. A number of crew rowing contests, including the 1984 Olympics trials, have been held there. A 1-mile walking path along the shoreline connects a boathouse and crew race course open for boat storage and a limited number of regattas.

Tiny Occoquan Regional Park uses the 8-foot-wide abandoned track of a railroad spur to accommodate walkers, bikers, and horseback riders. Ultimately, this short link will be part of a hiker-biker trail that will extend to the city of Fairfax. The park also has a boat-launching ramp and storage area.

Scattered throughout Northern Virginia are 50-acre Cameron Run Park inside the Beltway in Alexandria, with recreational facilities that include a wave pool, fishing and boating on its lake, and a short path around the lake; 100-acre, wooded Potomac Overlook Park in Arlington, whose panorama extends downstream as far as the Washington Monument and which has 2 miles of easy walking trail and a nature center that features wildlife and archeological displays; and 26.5-acre Upton Hill Park, where swimming, miniature golf, and picnicking are balanced by a mile of wooded footpaths, waterfalls, and reflecting pools.

At Meadowlark Gardens Park, planted trees, shrubs, flowers, and herbs enhance the natural foliage on 95 acres of woods and meadows 3 miles west of the towering hotels and office buildings at Tyson's Corner and not far from Wolf Trap Farm. Azaleas, daffodils, rhododendrons, flowering cherry tree, and dogwoods bloom around ponds created by damming Little Difficult Run. The park also has trails and scenic overlooks, and ultimately may connect with the Washington & Old Dominion Railroad Trail 2 miles away.

In Loudoun County, one step removed from Chesapeake Bay country, are Algonkian Park, a 511-acre tract with 1½ miles of Potomac riverfront, an 18-hole golf course, conference center, and rental chalets; 67-acre, heavily wooded Red Rock Wilderness Overlook Park, with 3 miles of trails; Balls Bluff Park, whose 173 acres preserve the site of an important but not-well-known Civil War battle; and Temple Hall Park, a historic and still operating farm on 286 acres. Primitive trails on authority-owned wilderness south of Algonkian Park lead hikers and equestrians past the Seneca Rapids, remnants of the Patowmack Canal and over steep hills.

The Northern Virginia Regional Park Authority also administers two historic buildings in Alexandria — 1752 Carlyle House and the Bank of Alexandria Building (see Alexandria).

The final element in the regional group is Pohick Bay Regional Park, which is part of the local-state-federal triptych on Mason Neck.

Manassas (Bull Run)

Two psychologically important vocal developments occurred in the forested hills southwest of Bull Run during the first major battle of the Civil War—the Rebel Yell was born and Maj. Gen. Thomas J. Jackson received the nickname Stonewall, by which he is universally known.

A combination of trails and signs, memorials, reconstructions, and strategically placed period cannon at Manassas (Bull Run) National Battlefield Park create a mental picture of the progress of the battle, the first in history between two civilian armies. The battle was, in a way, an object lesson in the changes taking place in warfare—the emerging dominance of firepower and maneuver. Three trails cover the two distinct phases of the Battle of First Manassas on July 21, 1861, the largest ever fought to that time in the Western Hemisphere.

A mile-long, self-guided walking tour of Henry Hill, which starts behind the Visitors Center, covers the final phase of the battle, in which federal troops made five partially successful assaults only to be driven back each time by rallying Confederates. The trail also visits the Warrenton Turnpike and the Robinson House, owned by a freed slave at the time of the fighting, which has a spectacular view over Bull Run and to the mountains to the west. The final leg crosses the eastern edge of Henry Hill, where a stern-faced equestrian statue of Jackson stands on ground where he received the nickname "Stonewall" for his stubborn defense.

Two paths meander through much of the ground involved in the morning phase, which basically involved a Union flanking movement. A 1.4-mile loop starts at the Stone Bridge across Bull Run, which Confederates defended, follows Bull Run northward to Farm Ford, and then proceeds to Matthews Hill, the scene of the principal morning fighting that pushed Confederate forces back to Henry Hill. A second trail passes Sudley Ford, the principal crossing point for Union forces, the unfinished railroad grade of the Manassas Gap Independent Line, Sudley Road, Sudley Church, and the ruins of Sudley Spring. The Stone Bridge, destroyed several times, and the houses around which the fighting swirled have been reconstructed. Adjacent to the new Henry House are the 1865 monument to the "patriots who fell at Bull Run" and the grave of Mrs. Judith Carter Henry, the only civilian casualty of the battle, an elderly woman killed by Union shrapnel after she refused to leave her home.

Acquisitions in recent years have saved additional land on which the Battle of Second Manassas was fought from August 29 to September 1, 1862. It was larger and the fighting was more intense than the first. More than 100,000 troops were involved and 19,514 were killed or wounded — four times the number of the first battle. About 3,600 of the 4,500 acres involved had already been included in the national park when Congress decided, in 1988, to acquire additional land, including the site of Lee's headquarters during the battle.

A number of places along the Warrenton Turnpike (U.S. Route 29) and state Routes 234 and 622 identify key features of the battle. Trails lead to others, including the unfinished railroad grade, still partly visible, which Jackson defended until the arrival of Gen. Robert E. Lee's forces. Other features include the Stone House, used as a hospital; Groveton Confederate Cemetery, where only 40 of 200 casualties are identified; Chinn Ridge; and Henry Hill, which this time was defended by Union forces.

The battlefields are open 8 A.M. to dark and the Visitors Center is open 8:30 A.M.–6 P.M. June 15 to September 1, closing at 5 P.M. the remainder of the year. The Stone House admits visitors from 10 A.M. to 5 P.M. during the peak period.

Sully Plantation

Richard Henry Lee, Northern Virginia's first delegate to Congress, found more than political inspiration in Philadelphia. His admiration for the architecture of that city is reflected in the mansion he built in 1794.

The 2½-story Federal-style house on state Route 28 off U.S. Route 50 looks much as it did at the end of the eighteenth century. It is modest by tidewater plantation standards because it has no ballroom, game room, or library and has a clapboard exterior with mortared bricks set between studs in the frame.

The 12-foot-wide asymmetrical hallway, with front and back doors and an 11-foot-high ceiling, is the most striking interior feature. Lee apparently intended to double the size of the house at a later time, but added only a small wing. Sitting rooms and living quarters, which are furnished with antiques from the late eighteenth and early nineteenth centuries, open onto the hallway. The dining room is the largest and most elaborate, with fine woodwork. The north room, which has a separate entrance, may have been used as a plantation office. The master bedroom, directly above the dining room, has the most elaborate mantel in the mansion. Georgian influences are apparent in the doors and window frames throughout the house.

Dependencies include a kitchen–laundry (with huge fireplace, rafters hung with meat, herbs, and utensils, and typical wooden furniture of the period) that may antedate the mansion and that was connected to the dining room by a 60-foot covered walkway; a dairy with fieldstone walls 2 feet thick at the base and a second-floor apartment; and a 12-foot-square frame smokehouse.

An eighteenth-century–style garden features boxwood, juniper, hollies, and rhododendrons, dogwood and redbud, perennials and annuals, especially iris, poppies, roses, columbines, and candytuft.

Forty-five minute guided tours are held from 11 A.M. to 5 P.M. Wednesday–Monday from March 15 to December 31 and on Saturday and Sunday from 11 A.M. to 4 P.M. the rest of the year, except on Thanksgiving, Christmas, and New Year's Day.

Some Other Parks

More localized parks include three lakes not far from the Beltway. Lake Fairfax Park, which covers 475 acres 7 miles from the Beltway via state Route 7 and county Route 606, accommodates cross-country skiers in the wintertime and also has athletic fields, miniature golf, and rides. Burke Lake Park, 6 miles off the Beltway via state Route 28, has a golf course and rides on 888 acres; the 218-acre lake is stocked with largemouth bass, chain pickerel, bluegill, crappie, channel catfish, muskie, walleye, and pumpkinseed. Canoeing is among the activities at 470-acre Lake Accotink Park, 3 miles from the Beltway via Route 620 and Heming Avenue.

Mount Vernon and Neighbors

The place that George Washington loved above all others may be the most beautiful homesite in America. Mount Vernon sits majestically on a knoll that slopes gently toward the broad Potomac River. The vista covers fields and clumps of trees and miles of tree-lined banks on both sides of the river.

George did not pick the site, but he played there as a youngster before his father moved the family to Ferry Farm near Fredericksburg. He purchased title to the plantation in 1754, two years after the death of his brother. One of the ironies of his life was that duty

Mount Vernon, home of George Washington. PHOTO COURTESY OF THE WASHINGTON CONVENTION & VISITORS ASSOCIATION.

would keep him away so much; he was absent the first five years for service in the French and Indian War, and the Revolutionary War took additional years, as did service with the Continental Congress and two terms as president.

Mount Vernon stands much as the Father of the Country planned it prior to the Revolutionary War, thanks to the Mount Vernon Ladies' Association of the Union. After acquiring it in 1858, the organization has worked continuously over the intervening years to restore it and retrieve original furniture bit by bit. Today, the mansion is one of the best-known houses in the country.

Both the mansion and the orderly grounds reflect Washington's preoccupation with enlarging and improving them. The original house was only 1½ stories high, with a central hallway and four first-floor rooms, but Washington added another floor before 1759 and, with the aid of a kinsman, enlarged both ends and added dependencies during the Revolutionary War. After the war, he added a bowling green and planted trees along the driveway, a few of which are still standing.

The appearance is more pleasing than impressive, but it is attractive from all angles. The building may look as if it were made of stone, but that illusion is created by sanding the frame siding. A long, colonnaded porch overlooks the river and slopes, while the side facing the circular courtyard has a simple entrance set off by dependencies connected to the house by colonnades. One was the detached kitchen and the other was used for various purposes, including an office.

The interior of the mansion is more ornate than the exterior would indicate, but reflects the tastes of the era. As improvements progressed year by year, Washington is known to have had some reservations about the cost. He described the mantel in the New Room or banquet hall, completed in 1786, as "too elegant and costly by far." The mantel in the west parlor dates from before 1775, while the library was ready sometime after 1775. Most of the furnishings on the first floor and in the master bedroom, where Washington died on December 14, 1799, are original. The remainder are period pieces similar to those present when Washington lived there.

Among the ancillary buildings that have been reconstructed, and can be visited, are the greenhouse and quarters, icehouse, spinning house and quarters (where at least a dozen people worked on textiles), storehouse, gardener's house, storehouse and overseers' quarters, smokehouse, washhouse, coach house, and stable. A museum building, added in 1928 to hold additional memorabilia, fits inconspicuously into the complex.

The grounds are just as attractive, and as well designed, as the mansion. The gardens Washington planted and diligently supervised have been restored on the original sites. The boxwoods around the flower garden are believed to have been planted in 1798, while the large kitchen garden is enclosed by the original brick walls. A greenhouse grows tropical plants.

A walk to the river is a pleasant diversion. Paths that begin at the stable lead in two directions, one passing the vault where Washington is buried in a marble sarcophagus that was provided in 1837.

Mount Vernon is open daily year round: 9 A.M. to 5 P.M. from March 1 to October 1; it closes an hour earlier the rest of the year.

The George Washington Grist Mill State Historical Park, 3 miles from Mount Vernon along state Route 235, is a reconstruction on the original foundations of the 3½-story stone mill that Washington operated for his own use and for neighboring farmers. An audiovisual presentation explains the gradual shift on tidewater plantations from tobacco to grain. A tour of the building follows the grain through the milling process. The park is open daily from 9 A.M. to 5 P.M. Memorial Day to Labor Day and on weekends from Labor Day to October 1 and April 1 to Memorial Day.

The Collingwood Library and Museum on Americanism overlooks the Potomac River 4 miles north of Mount Vernon on property once owned by Washington. Part of the house, which was enlarged in 1932, dates from 1785. American history is emphasized in both the library and museum, with the latter exhibiting Indian artifacts, a Bowie knife, the lantern used to signal Paul Revere from the tower of the Old North Church in Boston, and presidential china. Collingwood is open Monday through Wednesday from 10 A.M. to 4 P.M. and on Sundays from 1 to 4 P.M., except from December 20 to January 3.

River Farm, one of Washington's five farms, now is the home of the American Horticultural Society. The 27 acres, about 5 miles from Mount Vernon off the George Washington Parkway, contain a rose garden with 300 All-America selections, perennials, wildflower meadow, ballroom yard with pear and osage orange trees, shade garden, water garden, and dwarf fruit tree orchard. A ha-ha wall, the type used in the eighteenth century to keep livestock in pastures, stands near the house, part of which dates from 1757.

The most unusual feature of Green Spring Farm Park and Horticultural Center, on Route 236 (Green Spring Road), is a plot devoted to blue flowering plants. It also has other flowers, forty varieties of fruit trees, vines and berries, two vegetable gardens, a medieval herb garden, rock garden, and a plot to attract birds and pollinating insects. The mansion on the 27-acre estate, which dates from 1740, is now a museum. The Fairfax County Council of the Arts Art Society sponsors art shows and special events year round.

Woodlawn

Woodlawn Mansion is an ideal complement to Mount Vernon. Constructed in the first years of the nineteenth century, on land George Washington bequeathed to his adopted daughter and nephew as a wedding present, it represents the gracious living of succeeding generations of gentry in Northern Virginia.

The Gray's Hill site overlooking Dogue Creek and the Potomac River, selected by George Washington, is almost as impressive as that of Mount Vernon. Washington also chose the architect, Dr. William Thornton, the first architect for the U.S. Capitol, but died before construction began. The result was a superior example of Georgian proportion and balance, with a wide central hall and handsome fireplace mantels, including a carved Italian marble mantel in the formal drawing room.

The furnishings span the period when Washington descendants lived in the house. Much of the furniture was brought to Woodlawn from Mount Vernon by the daughter, Nelly Lewis. Later additions include excellent examples of black and gilt Federal chairs and footstool. Portraits of George and Martha Washington painted by Edward Savage before 1789 and a Hiram Powers bust of the general-president, which was owned by his daughter, survey the hallway. Porcelain vases believed to have been a gift to Washington from Lafayette and silhouettes, in paper over black cloth, by painter Charles Wilson Peale are among the artifacts in the parlor. Examples of Nelly's needlework, including the unfinished pattern she was working on at the time of her death, are located in several rooms. Appropriately, Woodlawn hosts an annual three-week needlework contest in March and needlework seminars in the summer and fall.

The interest of the last family owner of the estate, Lorenzo Lewis, in taxidermy is represented by specimens from his extensive collection.

Two nature trails lead from the mansion. One meanders through the woods and the other circles an open field past profusions of wildflowers — Queen Anne's lace, black-eyed Susan, aster, butterfly weed, and goldenrod.

The formal garden has been recreated, but incorporates early nineteenth-century practices and the interests of the Lewises. Two parterres, bordered in dwarf English boxwood, are planted in roses that bloom from summer through fall around crepe myrtle. Golden-rain trees and perennials such as hyacinths, peonies, and chrysanthemums line the wide walkway to a gazebo with coral honeysuckle at the corners.

Fragrant bushes and trees, such as lilac, crabapple, Carolina allspice, and magnolias, grow along the entrance drive, while oaks and holly are among the trees on the lawn. Bordering the serpentine are *Ilex opaca,* spiraea, Scotch briar, tulip poplar, hemlock, mountain laurel, firethorn, *Nandina domestica* or heavenly bamboo, eastern red cedar, and scilla. Kitchen and cutting gardens and an orchard with apple, peach, plum, pear, and cherry trees also are located on the property.

The 1940 Pope-Leighey House, architect Frank Lloyd Wright's

response to the need for "moderate cost" housing, was moved to the Woodlawn estate to prevent its destruction during construction of a highway in 1964. Many features of the cypress, brick, and glass house, including its flat roof, carport, heated concrete slab floors, and windows that are an integral part of the wall, greatly influenced the design of subsequent housing in America.

Owned by the National Trust for Historic Preservation, Woodlawn and the Pope-Leighey House are open daily from 9:30 A.M. to 4:30 P.M. except Thanksgiving, Christmas, and New Year's Day.

Alexandria

Visitors Center, 221 King St., Alexandria, VA 22314.
Tel.: 703/838–4200.

Somehow, despite the overpowering proximity of the national capital and the sharp swings in its fortunes, Alexandria has retained its individual character.

It has always exhibited a balance of lustiness and refinement. The city's favorable geographical location made it an ideal place to warehouse tobacco for shipment abroad. The shipyards and port, which as late as the middle of the nineteenth century was the third largest in the Chesapeake Bay area, had the roisterous qualities generally associated with eighteenth- and nineteenth-century harbors. Furthermore, its "ark" community of houseboat dwellers, which stretched from Roslyn to Jones Point, was as notorious as the one across the river in the national capital until both disappeared after World War II.

Yet Alexandria is also a model of historical respect. This was George Washington's hometown, and much of the present city would be familiar to him. The club he frequented is still there. So is the Friendship Veterans Fire Company, which he organized, and the hand-pumped, bucket-fed engine, which he donated. He served on the vestry of 1723 Christ Church, whose brick exterior and bright Georgian interior have changed little since his day. He would recognize the Old Presbyterian Meeting Hall, too, which was carefully restored after an early eighteenth-century fire. In the graveyard is the Tomb of the Unknown Soldier of the American Revolution and the surgeon general of Washington's army, Dr. James Craik.

An annual Birthnight Ball was held at Gadsby's Tavern during Washington's lifetime, a tradition that is now re-enacted as part of a series of February programs honoring the Father of the Country. Today's Gadsby's actually incorporates the eighteenth-century Gadsby's and City Taverns, and houses a reconstructed Revolutionary bar, ballroom, and bedrooms, including the one in which a mysterious unknown lady guest died. Captain's Row on South Fairfax Street, in the Old Port section near the river, is so authentic that the street is still surfaced with cobblestones and houses bear the symbols of the fire associations that protected them.

The surfeit of historic structures also includes the Visitors Center in the pre-1749 Ramsay House at 221 King Street, the oldest building in the city. One-hour guided walking tours, which start there, cover the principal historic structures of the downtown area.

Those who saw Carlyle House, built in 1752 by Scottish merchant John Carlyle, in its dilapidated condition in the early 1970s will be amazed at what restoration can accomplish. Those who did not see it at that stage can get an insight into the painstaking research and loving work that went into the project by visiting an unplastered room in the house that illustrates the construction and restoration techniques.

The gray stone manor house is undoubtedly one of the most handsome in the area. Details inside and out, like the carved woodwork in the formal parlor and the stone cornice on the façade, reveal an attention to impressive detail that appealed to the wealthy of the era. The "grandest mansion" in Alexandria fitted Carlyle, who married into one of Virginia's most powerful families and held various public offices, in addition to his business activities. A succession of important men rode up to his door, including British Gen. Edward Braddock, who summoned the five colonial governors to a council there to discuss strategy in the French and Indian War.

The house is now located in a commercial area, but is isolated by trees and gardens with shrubs, blooming bushes, and flowers. One-hour guided tours are conducted Tuesday through Saturday from 10 A.M. to 5 P.M. and Sunday from noon to 5 P.M. except on Thanksgiving, Christmas, and New Year's Day. Costumed attendants also recreate scenes from early American life at evening interpretive programs. Each April, the Carlyle House Garden Guild holds a sale of pot plants, annuals, herbs, and perennials grown in the gardens of the house.

The Bank of Alexandria building on the corner of the property was built in 1801 by Carlyle's son-in-law and housed the first chartered bank in the city. The exterior has been restored, and the building is leased for commercial uses.

The Boyhood Home of Robert E. Lee is a 1795 brick structure on Oronoco Street. Lee lived in the house from 1812 to 1816 and from 1821 to 1825. Tours daily with entertainment and refreshment on significant anniversaries.

Alexandria preserves its antique appearance by desire and design. By law, new buildings in the downtown area must reflect the colonial heritage. Archeological digs to uncover colonial or Civil War sites occur on a regular basis. Archeology Alexandria, which accepts volunteers for one- to ten-day study programs, works with artifacts from sites such as the Stabler-Leadbeater Apothecary Shop. In addition, diggers from James Madison University recently excavated buildings associated with a Civil War stockade.

A modern monument to Washington, a 330-foot-tall building on Shooter's Hill at the west end of King Street, is visible for miles. The George Washington Masonic National Shrine has a small museum, which includes the original furnishings of the lodge where Washington was "Worshipful Master" and a lookout platform reached by elevator. The building is open daily from 9 A.M. to 5 P.M.

Numerous other buildings have architectural or historical interest, including Lyceum. Alexandria is also the home of prestigious Mary Washington College.

Alexandria was occupied by the Union throughout the Civil War and was part of the defense ring around the national capital. Ford Ward Museum and Park preserves one of a chain of earthen fortifications built to protect the national capital against Confederate incursions. Each year, reactivated Civil War units recreate the only serious Confederate attack against the Washington fortifications.

Although Alexandria remains a port, the city is no longer the important export-import center it once was. A 22-foot channel admits ocean-going vessels to two terminals. The Robinson Terminal, owned by the Washington Post Company, handles mainly newsprint, plywood, and steel. The port area is mainly a mixture of heavy business and light recreation. The two warehouses of Robinson Terminal are separated by a number of blocks devoted to a city marina, trendy shops, and parks. A World War I torpedo plant has been converted into an art center where more than 200 artists and craftspeople work under the watchful eyes of visitors.

Mount Vernon Trail

The breezes that blow off the Potomac River along the Mount Vernon Trail always seem fresher than anywhere else near the national capital. The bike trail begins among the moderately rolling countryside at Mount Vernon, parallels the bank of the river through Old Town Alexandria, and skirts noisy Washington National Airport and beds of flowers planted as part of Lady Bird Johnson's beautification program in the 1950s. The northern terminus is the Memorial Bridge, with the marble Lincoln Memorial on the Washington side and Arlington National Cemetery on the Virginia side.

The 17-mile route has enough diversions—historic structures, forested picnic areas at Fort Hunt and Riverside parks, marshy wildlife sanctuaries, memorials, historic Alexandria structures, the skyline of Washington, and a mixture of pleasure boats in the Potomac River—to justify frequent stops. It parallels part of the route of the George Washington Parkway, a scenic highway that starts at Mount Vernon and extends to Cabin John Bridge north of Washington.

In addition, Fairfax and Arlington counties have created gravel and asphalt bikeways in a number of county parks. Six miles of gravel trail abut Burke Lake, while a 5-mile route is laid out from the north side of Wakefield Park to Highland Street, just south of the park. The 1-mile Long Branch Stream Valley Trail runs from Braddock Road at Wakefield Chapel Road to Queen Elizabeth Boulevard, while the 1.3-mile gravel and asphalt Holmes Run Trail goes from Annandale Road at the end of Hockett Street to Sprucedale Drive.

Arlington has a new I-66/Custis Bikeway.

Pentagon: The massive walls of the Pentagon, military headquarters of the nation, dominate the southern approach to Washington. One of the world's largest office buildings, it has an open-door policy—of sorts. Guides lead 1¼-hour tours Monday through Friday from 9:30 A.M. to 4:30 P.M. year round, except on holidays.

Pentagon, as the name implies, is a five-sided structure with a 5-acre central courtyard. It was constructed at the start of World War II.

Arlington National Cemetery: Around the clock, ramrod straight soldiers in spotless dress uniforms march slowly back and forth in front of the marble monument where Unknown Soldiers since World War I rest, a memorial to the sacrifice of all who gave their lives in war. The guard is changed, in a sober, precision movement, every half-hour from April to September and every hour the rest of the year during the day, every two hours at night.

The white marble amphitheater, where Memorial Day services and other programs are held, complements the tomb. Tributes from a number of nations to the Unknown Dead are displayed in an amphitheater building.

Even without the Tomb of the Unknown Soldier, this is no ordinary cemetery. Situated on slopes glistening with white headstones are 175,000 graves, including an assassinated president, soldiers from the Revolutionary War to the present, statesmen, Astronaut Virgil Grissom, and boxer Joe Louis. On Saturdays during the warm months, music produced by the forty-nine bells of the Netherlands Carillon Tower soars over Civil War and Marine Corps memorials and other areas of the cemetery.

An eternal flame burns over the grave of assassinated President Kennedy. Thousands annually visit the hillside site overlooking Washington and the nearby smaller memorial for his assassinated brother, Senator Robert F. Kennedy. President William Howard Taft is buried in another area of the cemetery.

Arlington House, which sits on a bluff overlooking the national capital, was the home of Robert E. Lee when he resigned his federal commission to join the Confederacy. Begun in 1802 and completed in 1818, it features heavy, forceful Doric stucco-on-brick porch columns. The interior, more Federal than Greek revival, is lighter, with attractive woodwork. The mansion, which opens daily at 9 A.M. year round and closes at 6 P.M. April–September and 4:30 P.M. October–March, is furnished in period antiques, including some owned by the families of Lee and his wife.

The cemetery opens at 8 A.M. year round, closes at 7 P.M. April–September and at 5 P.M. the rest of the year. Vehicular traffic is restricted, but a narrated tour leaves from the Visitors Center.

Fort Myer, an active Army base since the Civil War, occupies part of the Arlington estate.

Falls Church: Most people know only that there is a town by this name, but the name comes from a church founded as Truro Parish in the mid-1700s. The present Falls Church building dates from 1769, when George Washington was one of the vestrymen, and has been restored on a number of occasions. The interior is not original. The church is open daily from 9 A.M. to 5 P.M.

The Fountain of Faith at National Memorial Park combines bronze figures and many jets of water to create one of the most impressive fountains in the national capital area. Sculpted by Swedish artist Carl Milles, it is dedicated to the four chaplains — two Protestants, one Roman Catholic, and one Jewish — who lost their lives after giving their lifejackets to soldiers on the torpedoed troop transport *Dorchester* during World War II. The park is open daily from 8 A.M. to sunset.

Wolf Trap and Vicinity: Wolf Trap Farm Park for the Performing Arts is as unusual as it is famous. First of all, it is a joint public-private operation. As a center for the performing arts, it features both world-famous performers and promising novices. Among the most attractive features of this Virginia farm, just off the Dulles Airport Highway, are two eighteenth-century barns imported from upstate New York and used as theaters.

The center conducts an extensive program for adults and youth, even preschool children, in an informal setting. Visitors to the national capital area each year join thousands of local residents at performances in the barns and open-air theater. Picnicking on the lawn during performances has been a practice since Wolf Trap opened in 1971. The Filene Center, a fir and pine structure, has a seating capacity of 6,866, including 3,100 on the lawn.

The Wolf Trap Opera Company attempts to discover and foster talents among young adults through training and performing experience alongside established professionals. The Wolf Trap Institute for Early Learning through the Arts hosts teacher training workshops, one- to seven-week residencies in preschool classrooms, and field trips by school groups that attend live performances.

Cooperative programs with Fairfax County schools include annual festivals at which students perform short plays and sections of Shakespeare's plays. Internships and workshops provide opportunities in other aspects of the arts. Officially, the name is Wolf Trap Farm Park for the Performing Arts, but it is universally known as Wolf Trap. The 100-acre site and many improvements were donated to the National Park Service by Catherine Filene Shouse.

Dranesville Tavern on Leesburg Pike has an early November basketry festival and late November Christmas Boutique, at which handmade crafts are sold.

Claude Moore Colonial Farm at Turkey Run: Most historic recreations depict the prosperous side of an era. This one represents the majority of 1770s early settlers, the small-scale, low-income farmer struggling to make a living. Costumed attendants, including many volunteers, work 12 of the 100 acres on the farm just as Farmer Owens would have done, planting corn, tobacco, and wheat in the spring, hoeing in summer, harvesting and picking the orchard in autumn, and shutting down in the depths of winter. His "wife" tends the chickens and turkeys, milks the cows, picks the vegetable garden, cooks and performs household chores, and takes care of the children.

Split rail fences keep animals away from crops and the vegetable garden. The "family" operates from a one-room log house, where only simple implements and furniture are available and meals are prepared at an open hearth. This authentic scene is recreated from 10 A.M. to 4:30 P.M. Wednesday through Sunday, April 1 through December 31. Like the farmer, the staff stays indoors on rainy days. Visitors walk past fenced corn and tobacco fields and a pond to reach the farmhouse, root cellar, and steep-roofed barn, then may follow other paths to visit the spring, wheatfield, fallow field, bee hives, pig pen, large kitchen garden, orchard, and field where a quarter horse and red Devon cattle are kept.

Typical eighteenth-century communal events, held each month the farm is open, include market fairs on the third weekends of May, July, and September. Visitors may help bind wheat on the third Sunday in June, watch the tobacco being cut and stored in August, and participate in end-of-harvest games, music, and country dancing. Caroling and dancing are featured at the late-December Christmas Wassail. Eighteenth-century skills courses are offered and groups of forty-five or more may spend three days in an eighteenth-century encampment.

Local approval of the farm was so strong that, when federal budget cutbacks in 1980 threatened to close it, a foundation was created to save it. The National Park Service leases it to the Friends of the Claude Moore Colonial Farm at Turkey Run.

Great Falls Park

The Great Falls of the Potomac River are among the most beautiful natural phenomena in the national capital area. Fifteen miles north of Washington, the water is compressed into an area about 200 feet wide, increasing the speed of the water as it rushes past rocky islands and cascades over a series of low falls. The falls are visible from the Virginia side of the river at Great Falls Park, opposite the Chesapeake & Ohio Canal National Historical Park on the Maryland shore. The beauty of the turbulent water is deceptive; an average of seven people a year drown near the Great Falls and downstream Little Falls, despite constant warnings by rangers and others.

Two overlooks on the bluff above the falls provide a panoramic view of the choppy river and rocky shoreline. Those who are not mesmerized by the falls may inspect Patowmack Canal and the remains of the town of Matildaville; follow prepared trails through the woods and along the riverbank; fish for bass, carp, catfish, and other species; and climb rocky cliffs — a rare activity in the usually flat Chesapeake Bay area.

The Patowmack Canal at Great Falls was one of five designed to make the river navigable between Georgetown and Cumberland, Maryland. George Washington regarded the waterway as the "door" to the West and was largely responsible for it being built in the final decades of the eighteenth century. The difficulty of bypassing the Great Falls with locks was one of the factors that extended the construction period, led to the insolvency of the company, and resulted in later construction of the C&O Canal on the Maryland side of the river.

Five frequently intersecting, color-coded hiking trails that explore various facets of the park may be subdivided a number of ways. Historic interest is highest along the 1¼-mile Canal Trail, which follows the canal locks, and the 2.8-mile Old Carriage Road, which was the route to Matildaville. The Swamp/Nature Trail, a loop off the Old Carriage Road, is an easy 1.8-mile journey through violets, bluebells, and other wildflowers and an abundance of birds. The moderately strenuous Great Falls Park Circuit Trail links the River, Ridge, and Swamp/Nature trails in a 4.5-mile, 2½-hour hike that requires some climbing over rocks. It begins in the picnic area and moves through the woods to the river bluff, then follows the cliff above Mather Gorge to Cow Hoof Rock, turns inland on a generally flat path through a lightly visited forest dominated by oaks and maples, and returns via the Swamp/Nature Trail. The River Trail does not stop at the northern boundary of the park, but continues into adjacent Riverbend Park operated by Fairfax County, which has a marina, Visitors Center, and nature center.

Cyclists may use the Old Carriage Road and Difficult Run paths and fire roads. A bridle trail, which incorporates sections of the Old Carriage Road and Ridge trails, crosses the park in a north–south direction.

Great Falls Park has a hyperactive interpretive program, partly conducted by volunteers from the National Wildflower Society and other organizations. They include 1- to 2-hour narrated Saturday walks along the ruins and foundations of a dry lock or trails on the cliffs overlooking the falls and Sunday strolls through the natural vegetation and to "breakfast with the birds." In addition, rangers give lectures on the Potomac and its features, horseback riding, and the basics of kayaking.

Mile-long Mather Gorge is whitewater country (Class I–III) and boating is best left to experts. Putting boats into the water above the falls in the park is prohibited. Unsupervised kayakers, canoers, and whitewater trippers must qualify under Maryland law, which requires a degree of proficiency and equipment meeting certain specifications. River levels of 4 feet and higher are considered dangerous for canoes, rafts, and other open boats, while 5 feet and above is dangerous for all boating. Information on levels is available at 703/898-7378. Rafting trips and boating classes are conducted by several outfits.

The annual Patowmack Canal Days in mid-May features exhibits on the history of the canal, music of the period when the canal was dug, boating, and arts and crafts. The park is open from dawn to dusk every day except Christmas Day; the Visitors Center is open from 9 A.M. to 5 P.M. daily.

Nearby Colvin Run Mill Historic site hosts an annual Autumn Traditions program, which features nineteenth-century fall activities and music and a Country Christmas in mid-December.

Fraser Preserve

The Nature Conservancy owns a 220-acre Potomac River site off state Route 603 north of the Great Falls, which has steep, rocky bluffs, a floodplain, streams, a cold spring swamp, open meadows, and a mature hardwood forest with thickets. Indian arrowheads, pieces of pottery, and remnants of stone weirs have been found in the bottomland beside the river.

An unusual variety of wildflowers, including rare species like purple cress, purple fringeless orchis, and white false hellebore, grow in the preserve. The diverse habitat also sustains more than 110 species of birds, including bald eagle, red-shouldered hawk, scarlet tanager, ruby-throated hummingbird, downy woodpecker, and blue-gray gnatcatcher, as well as white-tailed deer, beaver, foxes, turtles, frogs, toads, and salamanders.

About 2¼ miles of paths cross the preserve from east to west and follow the shoreline for 0.4 mile. They connect with trails owned by the Northern Virginia Regional Park Authority.

District of Columbia

Tourist Information Center, 14th and Pennsylvania, Washington, DC 20036. Tel.: 202/789-7000.

WHEN KATHARINE LEE BATES WROTE ABOUT AMERICA'S "ALABASTER cities" gleaming, she must have had more than one community in mind. However, Washington, with its white marble buildings and monuments, certainly qualifies as one of them.

Thousands of people troop through the White House each year, admire the dome and paintings in the Capitol, gorge themselves on the riches of the Smithsonian and art galleries, inspect the Declaration of Independence and Constitution at the National Archives, ride the elevator to the top of the Washington Monument for a panoramic view of the city and Virginia suburbs across the Potomac River, climb the steps of the Lincoln Memorial, and walk among the cherry trees around the basin of the Jefferson Memorial.

The L'Enfant design, which discarded the grid for streets radiating from the Capitol and a series of other circles and squares, provided Washington with an exceptional opportunity to remain attractive. Until recently, it had not lived up to that promise because whole areas became blighted over the years. Redevelopment and renovation gradually is changing the appearance of seedy areas and dilapidated buildings, especially the section east of 15th Street. L'Enfant Plaza, a commercial center at D Street near the Southwest Freeway, was designed as a model of urban renewal. Office buildings are complemented by a paved square with a central landscaped garden. It was opened in 1968.

Washington is not "national" in the sense that it is representative. Indeed, it is just the reverse; it marches to its own drummer. Washington society is highly structured. Many of the most powerful people are temporary residents, but some of the social lions are permanent residents who have seen many administrations come and go. One

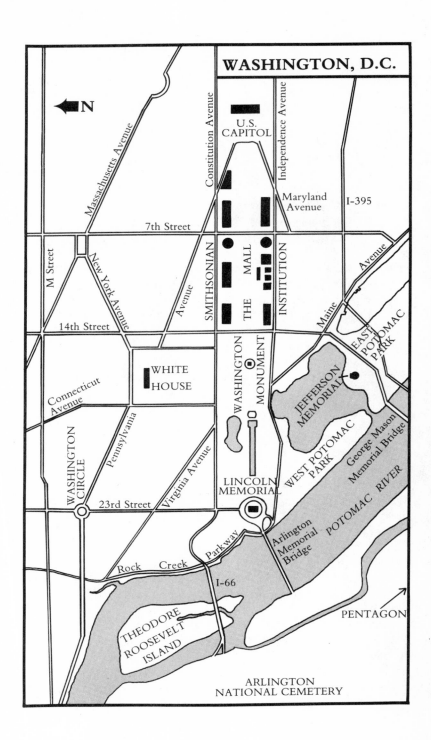

has only to see the lavishly decorated reception rooms of the State Department to recognize that haute monde is an aspect of life in the national capital. Congressional representatives and senators are feared and courted, but shiver when a delegation from home arrives. On the other hand, the U.S. government is the most open in the world — even the public rooms of the White House, the president's residence, are open.

Distinctions are just as important, though in a different way, for the visitor as they are for residents. The first is that two separate jurisdictions, the city and the federal government, control the attractions. While each has basic information about the other, the best information is available from the government involved. Long lines are a way of life for the tourist; the longest lines naturally occur at the things everyone wants to see, such as the White House and Washington Monument.

However, in Washington, taxpayers get something back for a change. Much of the sightseeing and entertainment is free, including the most attractive government structures. Free concerts are held periodically. Military bands play at the Washington Monument or U.S. Capitol. Foreign and domestic performers entertain at the FBI Building, Washington National Cathedral, and Washington Harbour, while sunset serenades are heard at the zoo. The famous Wolf Trap Farm Park performers also present free shows at the Sylvan Theater near the Washington Monument.

The national capital is also, in a sense, the cultural capital. Its centers of performing arts — the Kennedy Center is the newest trend setter, while the National Theatre is the oldest still in continuous operation — are among a long list of entertainment media. The Washington Ballet and the National Symphony Orchestra have international reputations. More than twenty stage theaters are prospering. In many instances, tickets can be purchased on the day of the performance for half-price by those willing to take potluck.

Washington is a festive place, as well, with festivals taking place almost every month. Among the most popular are those that use large open spaces. The Smithsonian Kite Festival in late March makes use of the winds that whirl around the Washington Monument. William Shakespeare's birthday is observed in late April with music, exhibits, and theater at the Folger Shakespeare Library. Friendship House Market Day is May 1. Potomac Riverfest, which occurs in early June, emphasizes water events, including a boat parade, and crafts. The Festival of American Folklife on the Mall at the end of that month draws representatives of many ethnic groups, with concerts, programs, and daily events. Mid-July brings boat races on the Potomac River. The Adams Morgan neighborhood sponsors a Hispanic-American Cultural Festival in late July.

Visitors may have to abandon some of their preconceived notions, for things are not always as they seem. The Smithsonian Institution, for example, is not confined to the handsome buildings fronting on The Mall. It has branches in many parts of Washington, and it never stops growing. Its administrative structure need not concern the visitor, who will be more interested in location than who's in charge.

Washington is less one city than a collection of sections. People speak of "The Mall," "the government area," and Georgetown as though they were separate units, and in a way they are. Exploring the city is easier and more profitable when those distinctions are observed. Outside the government area, the "neighborhoods" provide the clearest divisions. The best known are Georgetown, Chinatown, Embassy Row, and the Adams-Morgan section.

A commercial center in colonial times, Georgetown retains a flavor of the period as it goes on being brazenly commercial. It is a lively place, with chic shops and trendy restaurants and nightclubs housed in historic buildings and compatible new developments, complete with fountains and columned ornamentation. Washington Harbour on K Street is a waterfront complex combining residences, restaurants, hotels, offices, and shops.

This "neighborhood" reveals its other side to visitors during mid-April, when a number of exceptional private gardens are put on view for the benefit of the Georgetown Children's House. For five hours, walkers may enter private gardens for a narrated visit, which often includes tea. Later in the same month, a tour of Georgetown homes includes tea at St. John's Georgetown Parish Church. Georgetown University also is the scene of many cultural and intellectual events. The Old Stone House at 3051 M Street NW, built in 1765, is the oldest house in Washington. The first floor of the modest five-room structure, furnished in period furniture, is open from 8:45 A.M. to 5:15 P.M. Wednesday–Sunday, except Thanksgiving, Christmas, and New Year's Day.

A China Friendship Archway creates a formal entrance to Washington's small Chinatown, an eight-block area bounded by G, H, 6th, and 8th streets NW. Chinese New Year is celebrated in the streets, restaurants, and shops. A facelift is reinforcing the ethnic imprint by adding Chinese-style streetlamps and other symbols.

Massachusetts Avenue between Sheridan and Observatory circles is known as Embassy Row because many, but not all, of the 150 foreign embassies in the city are located there. The embassies range from massive structures to simple row houses, but all are identified by an escutcheon on the façade. Aside from comparing the relative wealth (or expenditure) of nations on the embassies, most of the time the only attraction is the varied architecture of the buildings. However, in mid-May, many embassies open their doors to public tours to benefit Davis Memorial Goodwill Industries. Participating embassies do not treat the occasion lightly; diplomats of various rank greet the public and mingle with visitors at tea.

Adams-Morgan is a multiethnic neighborhood where Latin, African, and Caribbean flavors predominate in the restaurants, shops, and news stands. The "neighborhood" centers on 18th Street, Columbia Road, Adams Mill Road, Biltmore Street, and Calvert Street.

The circles and squares will pose some problems for visiting drivers unfamiliar with traffic patterns, but they also demonstrate the capital's affection for heroes, dead as well as living. Many of the circles are named for their equestrian statues, especially of Civil War generals. Some of the most interesting statues go largely unnoticed in heavily traveled places.

Transportation is the key to seeing the national capital in relative comfort. The 14 percent of Americans unfamiliar with traffic congestion in an American Automobile Association survey will quickly learn in the national capital what the other 86 percent already know. The city's official brochure recommends "the use of public transportation and other alternatives to driving." It's good advice.

The city operates an integrated subway-bus system, which covers more areas than the average tourist will visit, operates on time, and is clean. The Metro currently has sixty-four stations along 70 miles of suburban surface track and inner-city underground. It extends into the Virginia and Maryland suburbs and can be used to reach Arlington National Cemetery, The Mall, Capitol, and other places. The Metro consists of four lines that intersect at the Metro Center, Farragut West, L'Enfant Plaza, and Gallery Place. The red line starts at Silver Spring, Maryland, in the northeast and runs to the government area, then curves to the northwest past Rock Creek Park. The orange and blue lines run from New Carrollton and Addison Road, Maryland, through southwest Washington across The Mall and turn west north of the White House to enter Virginia, the former proceeding to Vienna and the latter to National Airport. The yellow line runs from Gallery Place in downtown Washington to Crystal City, Alexandria, and Fairfax, Virginia. When the system is completed, it will have eighty-seven stations along 183 miles of track. A weekend pass is available, in addition to single trips.

The city also has an extensive bus system operating on nearly 1,600 routes. A Metro hotline (202/637-7000) provides information on service and bus connections.

Narrated bus tours are operated by several companies. Sightseeing trams, which riders may get off and on at will, make circular trips that cover most of the key attractions in the city.

The Tourmobile®, a concessioner authorized by the National Park Service, makes continuous circular runs from the Capitol to the entrance to Arlington Cemetery, with eighteen stops conducive to sightseeing. For one fare, visitors may get on and off all day at any of eighteen stops, including several stops along The Mall, the White House, Washington Monument, Jefferson and Lincoln memorials, and Kennedy Center. A connecting tram (additional fare) circles through Arlington, with stops at the mansion, Tomb of the Unknown Soldier, and Kennedy gravesite. The Tourmobile® operates daily from 9 A.M.–6:30 P.M. June 15 to Labor Day, 9:30 A.M.–4:30 P.M. the remainder of the year. The circuit takes a minimum of 1½ hours. The lines of the tram and the Metro cross at The Mall and Union Station.

The Old Town Trolley Tours stops at fifteen motels and hotels, several of which are near The Mall and Arlington. The route also extends northwest as far as the National Cathedral and includes a stop near Rock Creek Park. Riders may catch the red and black trolley at any stop and stay aboard for a full 2-hour tour or get on and off for sightseeing. The trolleys run daily year round from 9 A.M. to 4 P.M.

Those who insist on driving their own cars will have to adjust to traffic and parking problems. Wherever possible, Washington should be visited on a weekend, when federal employees remain at home in the suburbs. Traffic on both the approach roads and city streets is lighter then. Other days require more planning. Parking? Forget it, unless you want to arrive so early the museums and public buildings are not open or spend a lot of money financing parking lots and garages. Check all parking signs carefully; the city is notorious for hauling away offending vehicles and holding them for expensive ransom.

Washington has a surprising 8,559 acres of parkland, including the circles, which have plantings and benches in addition to statues. The open parkland between the Capitol and the Potomac River creates beautiful vistas from many vantage points. Washington also has made a conscious effort to beautify with massive displays of flowers that bloom at various times of year. Lafayette Square, in front of the White House, Pershing Square, Fountain Four at the entrance to East Basin Park, and Kenilworth Gardens at Anacostia Avenue and Douglas Street NE also have large plantings. The Floral Library at Independence Avenue and East Basin Drive was created in 1969.

Visitors on their own should divide Washington into walking segments linked by public transportation, starting perhaps with The Mall, Tidal Basin, and Capitol. Most of the buildings fronting on The Mall belong to the Smithsonian Institution, started with a bequest by James Smithson, a British scientist, "to found . . . an establishment for the increase and diffusion of knowledge."

The rectangular Mall is so simple to walk that no directions are necessary. Around-The-Mall walks can start at any point, but convenience suggests beginning at the Metro or Tourmobile® stops. The Smithsonian station of the Metro, located on The Mall at 12th Street near the "Castle," the turreted original 1855 building, is a good place to start. The Capitol, which is as near the Capitol South Metro station and on the Tourmobile® route, is an alternative launching pad. Detour to Constitution Avenue to see the Declaration of Independence, Constitution, and Bill of Rights at the National Archives.

Visits to the buildings are time consuming because of the enormous numbers of sights and the volumes of visitors. Only a few places can be visited adequately in a single day, and interests will largely determine the length of even a "quickie" highlight trip.

The Mall

THIS 2-MILE-LONG PARK, WHICH EXTENDS FROM THE FRONT OF THE hilltop Capitol to the Potomac River, is one of the unique features of Washington. Near the Capitol are a memorial to Senator Robert A. Taft, the Ulysses S. Grant Memorial (one of the world's largest equestrian statues), and the Capitol Reflecting Pool. The botanical gardens seem out of place in this setting, but are worth a visit. The east section of The Mall, generally flat and uncluttered, hosts buildings of the Smithsonian, and ends at the rise on which the Washington Monument is located.

From the monument, the ground slopes unevenly down to the riverbank and hosts a variety of plantings and monuments. Constitution Gardens include 50 acres of tree-shaded lawns and a 6-acre lake with an island on which stands a monument to the signers of the Declaration of Independence. Nearby is the Vietnam War Memorial, where almost every visitor to the city stops to check for the name of a friend or relative. Across the street is a statue of a seated Albert Einstein, whose theory of relativity opened the door to many modern developments. The long, narrow reflecting pool points directly to the Lincoln Memorial near the river. The memorial, shaped like a classical Greek temple with a 16-foot-high seated statue of the martyred president, surrounded by wall engravings showing some of his most famous remarks, is as much an outlook as a monument. The views of The Mall from the steps, and of East Basin Park and the Virginia side of the Potomac from the colonnade, are spectacular.

Another detour provides a self-guided tour of the Bureau of Engraving and Printing, which includes presses that turn out more than 7,000 sheets of currency per hour. Stamps are also printed in this building.

Like other Washington natural attractions, The Mall is not a showplace, but is used widely by residents and visitors alike. Strollers and joggers use the paths and rest on the grass, sit by the reflecting pool to read or eat, and enjoy the plantings. The Washington Monument and the Lincoln and Jefferson memorials are lighted at night.

Smithsonian On-The-Mall

Displays at the Freer Art Gallery, African Art Gallery, and Hirshhorn Museum and Sculpture Garden range from Asian and African art and artifacts to the modern art of Degas, Matisse, and Picasso. At the National Gallery, the new I. M. Pei-designed East Building contrasts sharply in architectural design with the classical West Building, but the two are connected by an underground concourse and a paved plaza. Guided and self-guided recorded tours of European masters and American art are available. The Natural History Museum also is chock-a-block with exhibits; few can resist the lure of the gem collection, which includes such massive stones as the Hope

Diamond. Skeletons of dinosaurs and reconstructions of an African bull elephant and blue whale are among other impressive displays. The Air and Space Museum is especially noted for its historic airplanes, including the craft used by the Wright Brothers for the first successful powered flight, Charles A. Lindbergh's history-making *Spirit of St. Louis,* and recent space equipment.

The Museum of American History is really the part of the Smithsonian that qualifies as the nation's attic. It holds relics as varied as a War of 1812 warboat, George Washington's false teeth, the gowns of the first Ladies, and the flag over Fort McHenry that inspired "The Star-Spangled Banner." A recently installed permanent exhibit explores everyday life in the United States after the Revolutionary War and includes a log cabin built in Delaware in 1793, room interiors, household items such as furniture and cooking utensils, musical instruments, books, and clothing. The building has a cafeteria.

Smithsonian buildings are open 10 A.M. to 7:30 P.M. daily.

The Capitol

When Congress makes decisions, the entire world watches and listens. Members of Congress, in turn, are usually looking over their shoulders toward their home districts. Although members of Congress do not advertise their availability, they can be useful on occasion. At the least, visitors to Washington may take advantage of their voting power to peek at the federal government in action. Obtaining a pass to the visitors' gallery when the Senate and House of Representatives are in session is one way to get a look. Admission to the gallery does not promise an exciting time, however, because many sessions are routine. Frequently visitors are surprised by the small number of representatives and senators present (the others may be in committee meetings, subject to call) and puzzled by how business can be conducted in such a fashion. But when important committees meet, the subjects are usually interesting.

Unless the visitor happens to hit at an exciting moment, the experience may well be an anticlimax to a tour of the Capitol building. Inside the 10-ton bronze doors on the East Side, fashioned by Randolph Rogers, is an eclectic assortment of art and architectural influences that mirrors American political history. The recently restored fresco by Constantino Brumidi on the 180-foot Rotunda dome is called "The Apotheosis of George Washington." In the painting, Washington is flanked by Liberty and Victory; other figures represent the original thirteen states and allegories on the sea, art and science, war, mechanics, commerce, and agriculture. Paintings of historic themes are located on the main level of the Rotunda.

The Statuary Hall has two figures from each state, selected by the states. These include political, religious, military, and sports heroes.

Free half-hour guided tours also include a peek at the Senate or House Chamber, usually from the gallery, and the Crypt, the original Supreme Court Chamber. The Capitol opens daily at 9:30 A.M. and closes at 10 P.M. Easter to Labor Day, 3:45 P.M. the rest of the year. It is closed on Thanksgiving, Christmas, and New Year's Day.

The White House

The people standing in long lines outside the White House usually are not protestors, but visitors waiting to tour the state rooms of the executive mansion of every president except George Washington. The White House is democratic about the one million visitors it receives per year — tickets are issued on a first-come, first-served basis.

Visitors approach the White House through the East Colonnade, from which the perennials of the Jacqueline Kennedy Garden are

The White House, oldest public building in Washington. PHOTO COURTESY OF THE WASHINGTON CONVENTION & VISITORS ASSOCIATION.

visible on the left, and enter the ground floor of the White House. Passing the Vermeil Room, which houses an extensive collection of gilded silver often used for state functions, and the Library, with 2,700 volumes on American life, Federal-period furniture, and portraits of five Indian chiefs, visitors then climb the stairs to begin an inspection of five of the 132 rooms in the mansion.

The painting of George Washington that was saved by Dolley Madison before the White House was burned in 1814 now hangs in the East Room. The largest room in the White House, where state balls, receptions, and other events are held, has white paneled walls installed by Theodore Roosevelt, large cut-glass chandeliers, an elaborately decorated ceiling, and a floor of oak parquetry. The Green Room is furnished as a Federal parlor of the 1810 period, with furniture made by Duncan Phyfe and his contemporaries, a silver coffee urn owned by John Adams, a pair of candlesticks used by Dolley Madison, and a cut-glass and gilded bronze chandelier fashioned in 1810.

Many consider the elliptical Blue Room, which still has many pieces of furniture purchased by President James Monroe after the fire of 1814, the most beautiful. Standing on the white marble mantel are a pair of French porcelain vases acquired in 1817, while paintings of Thomas Jefferson by Rembrandt Peale and John Adams by John Trumbull are among those on the walls. The Red Room, which gets its name from wall coverings of red twill satin fabric with gold scroll borders and matching furniture, represents an American Empire-period parlor of 1815–1830. A nineteenth-century musical clock stands on a marble mantel identical to the one in the Blue Room.

The State Dining Room, which can seat 140 people, features English oak paneling installed by Theodore Roosevelt, an elaborately decorated stucco ceiling, gilded chandelier, a portrait of President Abraham Lincoln by G. P. A. Healy, and the Monroe Plateau on the table. A walk down the North Entrance Hall passes portraits of the most recent presidents. Visitors then leave and follow the walkway to the East Colonnade to leave the grounds.

Tours, conducted Tuesday through Saturday from 10 A.M. to noon except on holidays and state occasions, begin at the East Gate on East Executive Avenue. Between Memorial Day and Labor Day, distribution booths on the Ellipse at Constitution Avenue open at 8 A.M. to issue tickets for tours at specific times. At other times, visitors wait at the East Gate for tickets.

Gardens of flowers and shrubs, including the Rose Garden where many ceremonies are held, border the building. The north lawn extends to Pennsylvania Avenue, and an extensive greensward looks southward to the Washington Monument and the Potomac River beyond. An American elm planted by John Quincy Adams and some of the twenty-five magnolias, oaks, maples, beeches, and other trees planted by his successors can be seen from outside the fences around the property. President Lyndon B. Johnson left a Children's Garden, while Presidents Andrew Johnson and Ulysses S. Grant built fountains.

Only glimpses of the landscaped grounds, which are one of the best features of the White House, are possible on the regular tour. However, special tours of the gardens, including the Jacqueline Kennedy Garden and the West Lawn, are conducted in mid- to late-April. An easter egg hunt for children under eight years of age, accompanied by one adult, has been held annually on the grounds since the time of President Rutherford B. Hayes.

Nature in the District

Potomac Park: This riverfront extension of the Mall has two sections. West Potomac Park, closest to the Mall, has a shoreline promenade from which the activities on the river and Virginia shoreline are clearly visible. Along the walkway are clusters of trees and plants and handsome memorials to such people as John Ericsson, designer of the Civil War ironclad ship *Monitor,* who are not exactly household words today. This section of the park also surrounds the Tidal Basin, where the pink and white Yoshino and Akebono cherry trees bloom brightly in the spring and provide the rationale for the week-long National Cherry Blossom Festival in early April, when the beauty of the blossoms is enhanced by Japanese lanterns and supplemented by fireworks, a parade with princesses and floats, music, a fashion show, and even a marathon run.

The classical white marble dome of the Thomas Jefferson Memorial completes a tableau that has few equals in Washington. Inside the memorial is a 19-foot-high statue of the author of the Declaration of Independence and third president, as well as numerous quotes. His birthday observance is a formal occasion, with military drilling and wreath laying at the memorial.

East Potomac Park, on the other side of the highways, is devoted largely to a public golf course and a giant statue titled "Awakening at Hains Point."

National Aquarium: Located in the Department of Commerce Building at 14th Street and Constitution Avenue NW, the aquarium holds more than 1,000 living examples of freshwater and saltwater life. A touch tank allows visitors to feel a number of crustaceans, including crabs, conches, and sea urchins. Glass windows permit visitors to watch the feeding of sharks at 2 P.M. on Monday, Wednesday, and Saturday and of piranha at the same hour on Tuesday, Thursday, and Sunday. Movies on aquatic life are shown continuously. Open daily from 9 A.M. to 5 P.M.

Kenilworth Aquatic Gardens: The only national park devoted exclusively to water plants is a 12-acre oblong island of nature in the bustling urban vastness of northeast Washington. Pathways divide more than forty cattail-lined ponds of various sizes, formed by diking marshland on the Anacostia River. These hold thousands of water lilies, lotuses, lavender water hyacinths, water primrose, and bamboo trees. The floral and frequently aromatic display begins in late April or early May, but the best time to visit the park is June through August, when most of the flowers bloom. Park rangers conduct narrated tours for organized groups. Tropical lilies are stored in greenhouses, which also may be visited, during the winter.

The park and an adjacent marsh constitute an active wildlife sanctuary. Osprey, egrets, great blue heron, ducks, hawks, coots, ibises, owls, red-winged blackbird, ruby-throated hummingbird, and kingfisher are among more than 250 species of birds that visit the ponds and 44-acre marsh. Along a 1½-mile nature trail that follows the bank of the Anacostia River, turtles bask in the sun, bullfrogs groan, raccoons and muskrats hunt, and beavers work.

The gardens are more than a century old. In 1880, a Civil War veteran purchased a tract of land on the banks of the Anacostia River and imported some lilies from his home state of Maine. Walter B. Shaw's nostalgia soon became a passion, as he dredged more pools and, with the help of a daughter, imported aquatic plants from all over the world. In the 1920s, the gardens were a favorite rendezvous for capital residents, including President and Mrs. Calvin Coolidge, who liked to stroll along the paths. The gardens, incorporated into the National Park Service system in 1938, are open daily from 7 A.M. to sundown, except on federal holidays during the school year.

U.S. National Arboretum: If the Smithsonian is the nation's attic, the 444-acre National Arboretum is certainly its backyard. Trees, shrubs, and flowering plants from all parts of the world grow there. The arboretum, across the Anacostia River from the Kenilworth

Gardens, has plantings in generic or botanical groupings along 9 miles of paved roads, with parking areas for picnicking and walking along forested and flowered paths. Single-genus groupings include azaleas, hollies, crabapples, irises, daylilies, peonies, viburnums, rhododendrons, magnolias, boxwoods, cherries, and maples. It also has ten specialty sections. A relatively recent addition is the American garden, which includes various ornamental grasses, woody plants, and perennials. Other sections include a 5-acre garden of evergreens and holly, magnolia, and boxwood collections. Fern Valley, sponsored by the National Capital Area Federation of Garden Clubs and other organizations, grows native trees, shrubs, ferns, and wildflowers. The Indian garden has plants that American Indians used for food, fiber, and implements, including birch, whose bark was chewed as a medicine, and buttonbush. The Oriental influence is apparent at the National Bonsai Collection of potted dwarf trees and a section of Chinese penjing, which range in age from 50 to 200 years. Other key areas are a 2-acre National Herb Garden, a historic rose garden, and gardens growing plants used for medicine, beverages, fragrants, and dying fabrics.

Some plants are in bloom or fruit at any time of year, starting with witchhazels, conifers, winter jasmine, and pussywillows during the first three months of the year. In late March to early April, camellias, magnolias, and winterhazels initiate a warm-weather blooming period that soon brings out rhododendrons, daffodils, azaleas, dogwood, peonies, and mountain laurel. Crepe myrtle, hibiscus, lilies, and roses precede the fall mixture, extending through October, of berried shrubs, holly, crabapple fruit clusters, and fall foliage changes. Interest in November and December centers on pinecones, conifers, and viburnum and holly in fruit. The Gotelli dwarf and slow-growing conifers, Bonsai, boxwoods, Holly Walk, and herb garden are spectacular year round.

Walks, lectures, workshops, and demonstrations, held on an irregular schedule, deal with such topics as landscape uses of holly, Bonsai, Japanese maples, plant propagation, and holiday arrangements. Horticulture lovers could easily spend a day in the gardens, while others cruising on their own will need an hour or more. The arboretum is open every day except Christmas Day: 8 A.M.–5 P.M. Monday through Friday, 10 A.M.–5 P.M. on weekends. Groups can arrange a 2-hour narrated guided tour.

Lafayette Park: This handsome park across Pennsylvania Avenue from the White House holds a unique place in Washington lore. In a city where "big" thinking is routine, it is surprising to find a small park with so much appeal. The late financier and presidential adviser Bernard Baruch went there on a regular basis to get away from the pressures of the city. A plaque identifies the bench he frequently used.

Named for the Marquis de Lafayette after his triumphant return visit to the United States in 1824, the square has a series of tastefully arranged statues amid beds of flowers and a few trees. The equestrian statue of President Andrew Jackson in the center is surrounded by tulips, which bloom in the spring.

The surroundings add to the attractiveness. The park provides the most picturesque view of the White House. A number of other historic buildings, including Federal-style Decatur House and St. John's Episcopal Church, are spotted among the compatible architecture of later construction. Decatur House, designed by Benjamin Latrobe and built for naval hero Commodore Stephen Decatur in 1819, admits visitors 10 A.M.–2 P.M. Tuesday–Friday, noon to 4 P.M. Saturday and Sunday. Often called the "church of presidents" because every American president since James Madison has sat at one time in Pew 54, St. John's is open from 8 A.M. to 4 P.M. Monday–Saturday; guided tours can be requested after the 11 A.M. Sunday service or at other times.

Roosevelt Memorial: The Roosevelt honored by this island in the Potomac River between the Key and Roosevelt bridges is conservation-minded Theodore Roosevelt. Appropriately, it is preserved in a near-natural state, which includes an upland ridge bordered by swamp and marsh.

Although the Theodore Roosevelt Bridge crosses the southern tip of the island, the island is accessible only by a footbridge across what is known as Little River from the parking lot just off the George Washington Memorial Parkway in Virginia. A path at the end of the footbridge crosses one of the trails and footbridges over a moat to reach the terraced memorial to the twenty-sixth president. Four 21-foot-high granite tablets on that level are inscribed with Teddy Roosevelt's words on nature, manhood, youth, and the state. One quote expresses his love of the outdoors: "There are no words that can tell the hidden spirit of the wilderness, that can reveal its mystery, its melancholy and its charm." On the next level, a 17-foot-tall bronze statue of the outdoors-minded president stands in front of a 30-foot-high shaft of granite.

About 2½ miles of interconnecting loop trails explore the varied terrain of the island—the upland forest of oaks, elms, red maple, and tulips frequented by gray and red fox, rabbits, chipmunk, downy woodpecker, and wood thrushes; the mud flats where raccoons hunt for crayfish under the shade of willow, ash, and maple trees; and the swamp, where red-winged blackbird, kingfisher, marsh wren, frogs, turtles, and muskrat live in the cattails, arrow arum, and pickerel weed.

The Woodland Trail, which parallels the western shoreline, and the Upland Trail down the center of the island can be entered near the monument. The Swamp Trail starts at the ends of these paths and follows along the soggy eastern coastline. The Swamp Trail is impassable after a rain.

The island park, which has been both a farm and boating center during its varied history, is open daily from 8 A.M. to dusk. George Mason and Lord Baltimore are among former owners. It has been known as Anacostian, My Lord's Island, Barbadoes, and Mason's Island at various times.

Rock Creek Park: It is almost possible to cross Washington without entering the urban area—almost, but not quite. The reason is string-bean Rock Creek Park, set aside by Congress in 1890 to preserve the "timber, animals and curiosities . . . in their natural condition" and since enlarged. One of the world's largest urban parks and dissected often by highways, it vaguely lives up to the congressional mandate.

The 1,754-acre tract runs north–south from Georgetown into suburban Maryland, following the course of a natural depression called Rock Creek Valley. It incorporates land along Rock Creek and some of its tributaries and connects with other reserves, including Dumbarton Oaks and Montross parks, Scapstone Valley Park, and, via the C&O Canal in Georgetown or a series of streets from Hazen Park, 183-acre Glover-Archbold Park.

Rock Creek ripples in places through a forest inhabited mostly by small animals, such as squirrels and skunks, and an occasional white-tailed deer. The trees and shrubs, especially in the wooded northern section of the park, range from alder and ash to walnut and willow, and include a large number of oaks, hickory, and beech. Flowering plants include pink azalea, dogwood, gingko, Japanese honeysuckle, magnolia, mountain laurel, paw-paw, rhododendron, and rose.

The park's facilities and activities—nature center and planetarium, hiking, biking, horse riding, tennis, sledding, and skiing at Battery

Kemble when snow falls, zoo, art barn, golf course, 4,000-seat amphitheater in the woods, history, picnic areas, and scenic drives — are among the favorite escape valves of Washington residents. Exhibits in the Nature Center and Planetarium introduce animal and plant life, as well as the appearance of night skies over the national capital.

Rock Creek Park has 29 miles of hiking trails. The Potomac Appalachian Trail Club has color-coded paths along the creek and the more difficult western ridge of the park, as well as connections. Two self-guided loop nature trails expose the park's natural variety. A 1.5-mile exercise course begins near Calvert Street and Connecticut Avenue. Rangers conduct guided nature walks and ecology programs.

Eleven miles of bridle trails extend from the Horse Center in a number of intersecting loops that combine to form black and white trails, each nearly 4.5 miles long. One crosses the Maryland line to the Meadowbrook Riding Stable.

Signs identifying the paved, 7.5-mile Bike Trail begin near the Lincoln Memorial and mark the route through the reserve and into Maryland. At the southern end, it can be combined with the Mount Vernon Trail via Memorial Bridge to complete a 24-mile journey. Weekends and holidays are the best times because Beech Road, which cars also use, is closed to vehicular traffic on those days. The bike route passes a number of premier historical attractions, including the Godey Lime Kilns, Pierce Mill, and (on one of two alternative routes north of Military Road) the log cabin where the poet Joaquin Miller ("Song of the Sierras") lived, as well as the exercise course, zoo, and Art Barn.

Pierce Mill, the last of eight early nineteenth-century mills along Rock Creek, has been back in operation since 1985 — as a living museum. Attendants operate the water-powered machinery and grind flour and cornmeal, while visitors pass through four levels of the blue granite building erected in the 1820s by Isaac Pierce. The mill is open from 8:30 A.M. to 4:30 P.M. Wednesday through Sunday, except on holidays.

The Art Barn, formerly the mill carriage house, exhibits local art and offers free drawing lessons at times. The barn has the same hours as the mill. Sites of four earthen forts constructed to defend Washington during the Civil War are within the park. The remains of Fort DeRussey are located at Oregon Avenue and Military Road.

More than 2,000 animals are housed in natural environments at the National Zoological Park, but none attracts as much attention as the two giant pandas, Ling-Ling and Hsing-Hsing, donated by the People's Republic of China in 1972.

The zoo, open daily, except December 25, is spread out along an axis named Olmstead Walk. Six color-coded routes, each marked with symbols of the animal groups living along that route, leave that central walkway. Signboards provide information on the animals and their behavior. The longest trail, which is almost a mile long and requires about 45 minutes to walk, passes small hooved animals and two bird stations, dominated by waterfowl but also including everything from Andean condors and East African crowned cranes to flamingoes, cassowaries, and bald eagles. Larger hooved wildlife — zebras and gazelles among them — and the giant pandas and kangaroos are located nearby. A quarter-mile trail past the Elephant House, giraffes, and hippos is followed by a ½-mile walk past aquatic animals such as seals, otters, and sea lions, as well as bears and wolves. Next, short trails feature lions and tigers in a moated, terraced, circular indoor-outdoor complex on one side of the main path and bobcats, pumas, jaguars, porcupines, tayras, and coatis on the other. Small animal, ape, reptile (including crocodile pools), invertebrate, and monkey exhibits front on Olmstead Walk.

Free outdoor sunset concerts are held at Lion-Tiger Hill at 6:30 P.M. during July and August. Complementary movies are shown once a month (1 P.M. second Sunday) from November through March in the Education Building near the Connecticut Avenue entrance.

An 18-hole, par-65 golf course with narrow fairways is laid out among the undulating hills and ravines of the area near 16th Street and Rittenhouse. The course is open daily. An easy 3.6-mile hiking trail runs through the woods of Glover-Archbold Park from Van Ness Street to the C&O Canal.

Dumbarton Oaks is famous as the site where major nations agreed to establish fixed currency exchange rates, thus fueling the post-World War II world economic recovery. Visitors may follow paths past wildflowers and forest that diplomats used during the complex negotiations.

Near the Mall

Archives and Library of Congress: Although the National Archives and Library of Congress are separate institutions, and located a good distance apart, their operations are similar. Both are primarily sources for researchers, but each has some attraction for the casual visitor.

The Archives are the repository of the original Declaration of Independence, Constitution, and Bill of Rights, which are on public display in guarded protective cases. Visitors also may research their family history or eyeball "Rosie the Riveter," a World War II poster, among a variety of documentary relics. Open 10 A.M. to 5:30 P.M. year round, till 9 P.M. April 1 to Labor Day.

The main attraction at the Library of Congress at 10 First Street SE, at least for patrons not interested in using stacks burdened with every book printed, is the ornate lobby of the 1879 Jefferson building. The Italian renaissance style is dominated by columns and lavish murals. Tours are offered from 9 A.M. to 4 P.M. Monday through Friday. Exhibit halls open at 8:30 A.M., close at 9:30 P.M. Monday–Friday, 6 P.M. on Saturday. Concerts, poetry readings, and lectures are held on a regular schedule.

Interior Department: A museum on C Street between 18th and 19th streets emphasizes the history and activities of the National Park Service through display of lifelike dioramas, stuffed animals, and geological samples.

D.A.R. Museum and Constitution Hall: Thirty-four period rooms demonstrate American crafts before the Industrial Revolution. Paintings, furniture, glassware, silverware, costumes, and ceramics are included. Concerts, lectures, and meetings are held in Constitution Hall. The Daughters of the American Revolution (DAR) also maintain a genealogical library. Tours from 9 A.M. to 4 P.M. Monday–Friday, 1–5 P.M. Sunday.

Churches: New York Avenue Presbyterian Church at 1313 New York Avenue retains relics, including a draft of the Emancipation Proclamation, of President Abraham Lincoln's attendance during the Civil War. The contemporary stained-glass windows are unusual. Open daily, with guided tours after Sunday morning services. National City Christian Church on Thomas Circle NW, which President Lyndon B. Johnson attended, is an impressive contemporary structure, designed in 1929 by the architect of the Jefferson Memorial. It is open daily from 9 A.M. to 4 P.M. for guided tours and noontime concerts.

Old Post Office Building: The "clock tower" of this structure at 1100 Pennsylvania Avenue, completed in 1899 and recently renovated for commercial use, is the second tallest structure in Washington. An elevator to the top of the tower provides an alternative platform to that in the Washington Monument.

Folger Shakespeare Library: Best known for its Elizabethan theater, the library at 201 East Capitol Street SW also houses original Shakespeare portfolios and quartos, as well as a substantial collection of

Renaissance books and manuscripts. Open from 10 A.M. to 4 P.M. Monday–Saturday year round and on Sundays from April 15 to Labor Day, except federal holidays. Tours from 11 A.M. to 1 P.M. Monday through Friday.

Columbia Historical Society: An 1894 landmark building at 1307 New Hampshire Avenue NW that features hand-carved woodwork, stenciled wallpaper, mahogany and onyx fireplace mantels, and antique furniture. Guided tours from noon to 4 P.M. Wednesday–Saturday except federal holidays.

Corcoran Art Gallery: A comprehensive collection of American paintings and sculpture, plus a small European collection. Open at 9 A.M. Tuesday–Sunday, closed at 9 P.M. on Thursdays, 4:30 P.M. other days. The oldest and largest private museum in the city, it is free.

Federal Bureau of Investigation Building: One-hour guided tours of crime laboratories, photos of most wanted criminals and FBI activities, and a live gun-firing demonstration Monday–Friday from 8:45 A.M. to 4:15 P.M., except on federal holidays. Located on E Street, between 9th and 10th streets.

State Department: The "foggy bottom" references to the site of this function of government are meteorological, not descriptive. Indeed, a tour of the beautifully appointed Diplomatic Reception Rooms on the eighth floor of the building at 22nd and C streets will help dispel such thoughts. Tours of the rooms where foreign diplomats are received and entertained are held three times a day Monday through Friday for those making reservations.

John F. Kennedy Center for the Performing Arts: The most impressive recent structure in Washington, with major art gifts from many countries, is located on New Hampshire Avenue at Rock Creek Parkway. Attendance at a performance in one of six theaters for music, dance, drama, and film can be combined with viewing its elegant architecture and works of art. In addition, tours are conducted daily from 10 A.M. to 4 P.M.

Ford's Theatre and Lincoln Museum: The theater at 511-10th Street NW where President Abraham Lincoln was assassinated has been carefully restored to its 1865 appearance and is once again an active theater, with family-oriented entertainment. Rescued from destruction a few years ago, the building also houses a museum of relics associated with the president and John Wilkes Booth, the actor-assassin. The Peterson House across the street, where the president died, also is restored to reflect that event. Tours are conducted from 9 A.M. to 5 P.M. daily year round.

Farther South of The Mall

Navy Yard: A World War II destroyer, the *U.S.S. Barry,* can be boarded by visitors to the Navy Museum, which also includes nineteenth- and twentieth-century naval guns and thousands of medals, paintings, uniforms, and equipment from vessels, including a submarine room with operating telescope. Dioramas recreate famous naval battles and the exploits of early heroes. The Navy Yard is the oldest naval facility in the United States. The museum at 9th and M streets SE is open from 9 A.M. to 5 P.M. Monday–Friday during the summer, until 4 P.M. on those days the rest of the year; from 10 A.M. to 5 P.M. Saturday and Sunday, except on Thanksgiving, Christmas, and New Year's Day. The Marine Corps Museum uses weapons, uniforms, and other relics to portray the 200-year-old history of the corps.

Frederick Douglass Home: The last home of the black civil rights leader during the Civil War and postwar eras, located at 1411 W Street SW, documents his life through exhibits and movies. Many of the antique furnishings are original.

Farther North of The Mall

Octagon House: A small museum of historical archeology and other subjects is located in this unusual house, built in the last years of the eighteenth century and used by President James Madison as the executive mansion after Washington was burned by the British during the War of 1812. Located at the corner of 18th Street and New York Avenue NW, it is open from 10 A.M. to 4 P.M. Tuesday–Friday and noon to 4 P.M. weekends, except major holidays.

Ansel Adams Collection: Landscape photographs at the Wilderness Society, 1400 Eye Street NW, printed by the photographer in the early 1980s. Open Monday–Friday 10 A.M.–5 P.M. except national holidays and Friday after Thanksgiving.

B'Nai B'Rith Klutznik Museum: A permanent collection of Jewish ceremonial art and special exhibits, at 1640 Rhode Island Avenue NW. Open 10 A.M.–5 P.M. except on Saturdays and Jewish holidays.

Martin Luther King Library: The main outlet of the city's public library system at 901 G Street NW houses an extensive collection of photographs and clippings about the nation's capital, a black studies division, and an Oral History Research Center, as well as regular shelves. Gallery exhibits and free movie and concert programs also are held. Open 9 A.M.–9 P.M. Monday–Thursday, 9 A.M.–5:30 P.M. Friday–Saturday, 1–5 P.M. Sunday, except federal and district holidays.

National Geographic Society: The entrance hall at 17th and M streets holds artifacts and pictorial displays on famous exploration, archeological, and scientific expeditions. A globe 11 feet in diameter was installed in 1988 for the society's hundredth anniversary. Open 9 A.M.–5 P.M. Monday–Saturday and holidays, 10 A.M.–5 P.M. Sunday.

Washington Cathedral: A gilded equestrian statue of George Washington stands near the entrance to this striking, gothic-style Episcopal Cathedral Church of St. Peter and St. Paul. Decorative rose windows, a statue of President Lincoln, and stone carvings are among the features of one of the largest cathedrals in the world. Its tower is the highest point in Washington. Guided tours are offered from 10 A.M. to 3:15 P.M. Monday–Saturday and at 12:30 and 2 P.M. Sunday. Midday recitals are held most of the year: organ on most Wednesdays, bells on Sunday, and carillon on Saturday November–March (5 P.M. rest of year). The London Brass Rubbing Center, where paper copies of London carvings can be made, is open from 9:30 A.M. to 5 P.M. daily.

National Shrine of the Immaculate Conception: The largest Roman Catholic church in the United States has a collection of art that includes works by Murillo and Titian and a large mosaic called "Christ in Majesty," by John de Rosen. Guided tours of the Neo-Byzantine structure are held from 9 A.M. to 4 P.M. Monday–Saturday. Organ recitals are at 6 P.M. June through August, bells at 2:30 P.M. Sunday.

Suburban Maryland

MARYLAND DONATED THE LAND ON WHICH THE DISTRICT OF COLUMBIA sits (Virginia gave some, too, but got it back). At the time, no one could anticipate the megapolis that government would sire, which now reaches farther and farther into the Maryland countryside with each passing year. Towns and once independent community developments in Montgomery and Prince Georges counties have grown together around interstate, state, or local highways radiating out from the national capital.

The heavy traffic is somewhat intimidating, especially to those not accustomed to it, but can be handled by avoiding the morning and afternoon rush hours and by following the "city on weekends, suburbs on weekdays" rule. The Baltimore-Washington Expressway, intended as a scenic drive between the two cities, is still a limited access roadway, but the volume of traffic takes all the pleasure out of driving through a lane of trees. The later construction of I-95 along a parallel route merely helped keep pace with the traffic. The Beltway, a combination of I-495 and I-95, circles Washington and connects with Interstate 270, which siphons off the traffic heading northward into Pennsylvania. Some routes heavily used by local traffic emanate from downtown Washington, including U.S. 50 to Annapolis and the Eastern Shore, which is jammed on summer weekends; Routes 6, 4, and 210 into southern Maryland; U.S. 1 and 29 toward Baltimore; and D.C.-Maryland 355 and 185 into the northern suburbs.

The Maryland suburban zone is not as green as northern Virginia, but it is not devoid of parks and open spaces, either. The Chesapeake & Ohio Canal National Park stretches for miles along the Maryland shore of the Potomac River. Huge, popular Greenbelt Park straddles the Baltimore-Washington Parkway just inside the Beltway. The federal Agricultural Research Center is located at Beltsville. The Maryland suburbs have compensating diversions, including the Goddard Space Flight Center of the National Aeronautics and Space Administration and the huge campus of the University of Maryland at College Park. Andrews Air Force Base is the home of *Air Force One,* the presidential plane.

Bethesda, Silver Spring, and Rockville are perhaps the best-known Maryland townships in the national capital area. Although they are essentially bedroom communities, they do have an active social and cultural life. For example, in late March, the Chevy Chase Presbyterian Church hosts an annual Bach Marathon in honor of the composer's birthday, during which soloists perform on the church's huge pipe organ.

Rockville-Bethesda

The name of the Civic Center at Rockville does not indicate the attractiveness of the complex, which has a 100-acre park and large antebellum (1833–1840) mansion, art gallery, and formal outdoor gardens. The F. Scott Fitzgerald Theatre honors one of America's foremost interpreters of the Roaring Twenties. The author and his wife, Zelda, are buried in the cemetery of St. Mary's Roman Catholic Church, Rockville Pike and Vets Mill Road.

More than a hundred homes of architectural and historic interest, most of them Victorian in style, stand in Rockville's West Montgomery Avenue Historic District. The area also has brick sidewalks. A huge abstract mural combining historical and contemporary features of Rockville covers the south exterior wall of the Metropolitan Federal Savings and Loan Building at 232 North Washington Street. It was painted by Spanish-born Gerardo Gomez Morena.

At nearby Bethesda, the Visitors Center of the National Institute of Health shows movies and slide shows and a model laboratory Monday–Friday between 10 A.M. and 4 P.M. The National Capital Trolley Museum at Wheaton offers rides on Saturdays and Sundays and major holidays from noon to 4 P.M. during the summer months and from noon to 4 P.M. on Wednesdays during July and August.

C&O Canal National Historical Park

The Chesapeake & Ohio Canal was one of a number dug in the Washington area, but it is the only one that still attracts attention. Indeed, it has more users now, as a park, than it possibly could have had at its peak as a commercial waterway in the 1870s when more than 540 barges and boats used it regularly.

The towpath of the 1828 canal, which rises 604 feet along its 184.5-mile journey to Cumberland, Maryland, is used extensively for hiking, biking, and jogging.

Hikers were largely responsible for the pathway being preserved. In 1954, Supreme Court Justice William O. Douglas and officers of The Wilderness Society hiked the length of the canal to dramatize its potential, but it was not proclaimed a national monument until 1961 and another decade passed before it became a national historical park. Hiking, still an important activity the entire length of the park, uses the elevated towpath, along which mules once pulled canalboats. The trail is nearly level its entire length. Primitive overnight campsites are located about every 5 miles from Horsebend Branch, at the McKee Besher Wildlife Management Area, to Evitts Creek near Cumberland. Primitive camping also is permitted in the Marsden Tract south of Great Falls if a permit is obtained from park rangers.

The C&O pathway is a key link in the 704-mile Potomac Heritage National Scenic Trail, created recently by chaining together a number of paths. It also includes the Mount Vernon Trail and the Washington and Old Dominion Railway Trail in Northern Virginia, and connects with the Appalachian Trail at Bluemont, Virginia.

For less committed walkers, a short walk along the towpath south of the Great Falls Visitors Center leads to Mather Gorge, cut by the falls. In addition, a loop trail leads through the upland forest to an old gold mine site near the end of Falls Road (Maryland Route 189).

Biking is another favorite activity on the canal path, which cuts through dense forest as it parallels the course of the Potomac. A bikeway begins in Georgetown, once the terminal for transshipment of coal, building stone, lumber, whiskey, furs, and farm products from the West and manufactured goods, ice, fish, and other products from the East, and rolls the entire distance of the park, although some rough spots may require dismounting. MacArthur Boulevard also is a bike trail, which continues on Maryland Route 189 past the Great Falls entrance to the park.

Horse riding is permitted north of Swain's Lock.

Trail information is available at the Visitors Center at the end of MacArthur Boulevard, about 15 miles off the Beltway. The center is housed in the Great Falls Tavern, built between 1828 and 1830 as a lockhouse and located on one of the most beautiful sections of the river. A 15-minute audiovisual presentation is supplemented by historical exhibits, including a model of a canalboat, lock horns, bottles, and other artifacts. Most of the locks in the Palisades area, or the southern end of the park, have been restored to show the step-by-step method of raising barges to higher levels of the river.

From mid-April to mid-October, mule-drawn canalboats recreate the experience of this form of transportation popular in the first half of the nineteenth century. During a mile-long upstream tow, costumed members discuss the construction of the canal and the lifestyle of those running and using it when it was in commercial operation.

Canoeing and rowing are so popular that rental boats are available at Georgetown and north of the Great Falls at Swain's Lock. Canal canoeing is easy on the watered levels between Georgetown and Violettes Lock near Pennyfield, although some portage is necessary. The irregular river, not in the park and under Maryland jurisdiction, is best left to experienced canoeists; the Great Falls, Little Falls Dam, and Little Falls areas are considered hazardous even for experts.

Fishers use both rowboats and the banks to catch bass, catfish, and other species in the canal.

A second Visitors Center is maintained at the Foundry Mall between 30th and Thomas Jefferson streets in Georgetown. Canalboat tours also operate from this site.

In addition to the Great Falls entrance, access is possible at other points along MacArthur Boulevard by walking down the wooded slopes to the towpath. The park service has parking lots at circa 1860 Old Anglers Inn, a commercial restaurant on the highway, and at Carderock, which is about 4 miles south of the Great Falls tavern off the George Washington Memorial Parkway on the Maryland side. People visiting the park mainly to relax and enjoy the outdoors frequently use those entrances.

Similar sights and activities exist along the northwestern section of the canal park, which is outside the Chesapeake Bay region. Another Visitors Center in Hancock, Maryland, covers the western section of the canal.

Historic Sidelights

The historical significance of the area has been largely lost in the rush to urbanization, but a few significant relics remain.

Glen Echo, near the canal park, set the standard for many amusement parks in the early twentieth century as thousands of Washingtonians climbed aboard the Washington and Great Falls Electrical Railway for a ride along the Potomac riverbank in search of cotton candy delights. The open-air streetcars continued to roll from Georgetown to Glen Echo and Cabin John until 1960, providing a leisurely view of the countryside and river. Hand-carved wooden animals are now the main attraction at Glen Echo Park, whose more than 50-year-old carousel is open daily except Friday from April through October.

Glen Echo also was the home of Clara Barton, whose experiences as a Union nurse during the Civil War led her to establish the American Red Cross. Her home is open Thursday through Sunday from 10 A.M. to 5 P.M.

The historic community of Poolesville still has a ferry operating across the Potomac River, starting at 6 A.M. and continuing to 11 P.M. March 22 to December 21 and until 8 P.M. the rest of the year. Historic structures include the 1793 John Poole House at 19923

Fisher Avenue and the 1866 one-room schoolhouse built of Seneca sandstone.

Bladensburg, established in 1742 at the head of tidewater on the Eastern Branch of the Potomac River, quickly became a bustling tobacco export port with more than a hundred houses, a dozen stores, including the first chain store on the river, a spa, and manufacturing plants ranging from a rope walk and flour mills to a herring-salting and -packing plant. Silting closed the river so tight that the port site now is a commercial center. Historic structures include the circa 1732 Indian Queen Tavern, the 1750 Market Master's House, and Bostwick, built in 1746 by merchant Christopher Lowndes and later owned by the first U.S. Secretary of the Navy, Benjamin Stoddert (private residence).

Montpelier near Laurel, built in the 1740s, is open April–June and September–November on Saturday and Sunday from noon to 4 P.M. Riverdale, built 1801–1807, was the home of the founder of Maryland Agriculture College, now the University of Maryland. Open Sunday from noon to 4 P.M.

Greenbelt Park

Many metropolitan areas recognize the need for relief from brick and concrete landscapes by providing one or two large parks. Greenbelt Park serves that function for the nation's capital. It is large enough to block out the noise and rush of the network of nearby highways and the press of an enclosing urban area. Furthermore, it is not a manicured outdoors, but the real thing, where posters warning of poison ivy, copperhead snakes, wasps, yellowjackets, ticks, and chiggers are balanced by the spectacular colors of azalea, dogwood, and mountain laurel in the spring and the autumnal shades of red, gold, and green.

Walking trails through sloping forests put the visitor in proximity of more amenable plants such as blueberries; animals such as red fox, raccoon, and squirrel; and birds such as the blue jay, bobwhite, and cardinal. The 1.2-mile Azalea Loop Trail, which connects three picnic areas, is especially beautiful in spring when the woods comes alive with new underbrush and blooming wildflowers and wildlife stirs on the banks of Still Creek. The 1.9-mile Blueberry Trail, which begins at the entrance to the campgrounds, explores a mature forest of oak, tulip poplar, sweet gum, and sassafras, abandoned farmland,

and the marshy stream bottom. The Dogwood Nature Trail, a 1.4-mile loop near the central parking lot, illustrates the relationship between humankind and ecology.

A 6-mile hiking and bridle trail circles the western area of the park, while a fire road cuts through the area east of the parkway. Walkers and joggers also use the edges of paved roads, and the half-mile physical fitness course has twenty stations.

Bike races engage novices and professionals at 6 P.M. every Wednesday from Memorial Day to Labor Day. Novices do five laps (about 10 miles) on the main road, while licensees of the American Biking Association pedal twenty laps.

Rangers point out various aspects of the urban woodland on nature walks at 10 A.M. each Saturday from April to November and on Sunday from Memorial Day to Labor Day. Forty-five–minute campfire programs are held at 9 P.M. daily, except Wednesday, during the warm months, at 7 in the evening when the days shorten. A police station is located near the entrance; the ranger station is near the campground, which has 178 sites for tents, RVs, and trailers up to 30 feet in length, but no utility connections.

The year-round park is reached by Exit 28 (Kenilworth Avenue–Maryland 201) and Greenbelt Road (Maryland 193) from the Beltway or via Greenbelt Road from the Baltimore-Washington Parkway.

Goddard Space Flight Center

Check the contents of food packages that sustain astronauts aloft and then climb into a Gemini capsule for an imaginary trip beyond Earth's atmosphere. Back on Earth, inspect some of the hardware used to put astronauts and satellites into Earth orbit. Such hands-on experience is emphasized at the Goddard Space Flight Center Visitors Center, reached from the Capital Beltway via Greenbelt and Soil Conservation roads.

In addition, a mockup of command computer banks spotlights the various NASA centers around the country and their missions: aeronautics, space sciences, planetary exploration, earth studies, and astronaut-guided space flight. Other equipment includes five types of satellites and a camera used in space to photograph a supernova. One untouchable display is a 4-billion-year-old moon rock, picked up by astronauts Alan Shephard, Jr., and Edgar Mitchell from Fra Mauro Crater in 1971. Contrasting photographs of space shuttle flights and the primitive rocket experiments of Dr. Robert H. Goddard, considered the founder of American rocketry, show how far science and technology have progressed in a few generations.

A three-person Apollo capsule that has carried astronauts to the moon and back is located on the grounds of the museum. Nearby are a number of sounding rockets, including the tall Delta launch vehicle, which, starting in 1960, put more than 170 payloads into orbit; Iris, used in 1960–1962; and several versions of the Nike (both an active antiaircraft rocket and a test vehicle), including the Javelin, first launched in 1959.

Interpretive programs are held at 1 P.M. every Sunday. Young rocketeers assemble on the first and third Sunday to launch their vehicles under expert supervision. Films are shown on the second Sunday and NASA scientists, engineers, and officials lecture on current topics, such as the space station or the Hubble space telescope, on the fourth Sunday.

The Goddard Center is young as NASA centers go. It was established in 1959 as the first major scientific laboratory devoted entirely to the exploration of space. The Visitors Center is open Wednesday–Sunday from 10 A.M. to 4 P.M.

Agricultural Research Center

A wide-open space of a different sort is the National Agricultural Research Center, where more than 4,000 large farm animals and poultry share 7,000 acres of farmland with 2,500 U.S. Department of Agriculture scientists, engineers, and staff. Farm facilities include research laboratories, barns, greenhouses, poultry houses, mechanical shops, and offices.

The primary function is research into animal and plant reproduction, growth, diseases, and parasites. Guided van tours of the facilities are conducted by public affairs personnel. The van tour usually starts with a visit to the beef cattle and other animals and passes the barns, then turns to the fields and greenhouses where plants and crops are growing. The commentary also discusses phases of the work that cannot easily be seen, including experiments with plant tissue cultures, dwarf fruit trees, vegetables, and animal resistance to different types of insects. The Visitors Center houses exhibits on subjects ranging from entomology to human nutrition.

Tours are conducted by appointment from 8 A.M. to 4:30 P.M. Monday through Friday, year round. The farm lies just outside the Beltway and straddles U.S. Route 1 and the Baltimore-Washington

Parkway (Beltsville exit to Powder Mill Road) about 15 miles from Washington.

Paul E. Garber Facility

The Paul E. Garber Facility of the Smithsonian Institution displays 140 air and space vehicles and conducts tours that include observation of preservation and restoration activities. Tours are held at 10 A.M. Fridays and at 10 A.M. and 2 P.M. Saturdays and Sundays, but arrangement must be made two weeks in advance. A Wings & Things Open House is held in late April. Follow state Route 414 to Silver Hill Road.

Back to the Bay

The Oxon Hill Farm, on Oxon Hill Road off Route 210, presents an opportunity for nearby urban children to observe ordinary domesticated animals in a farm setting. It is open daily from 8 A.M. to 5 P.M. The home of Mary Surratt, who was accused of participating in the conspiracy to assassinate President Lincoln, is located on state Route 381 at Clinton. It is open Thursday through Sunday, except during January and February.

Although Upper Marlboro is currently beyond the Washington suburban band, it is frequently included in the region. Public tobacco auctions occur in April and May. Wild World, at Mitchelville, opens its water slides, wild wave, pools, and other facilities from Memorial Day to Labor Day.

The transitional zone south of the national capital region is, in a way, an appropriate place to end a tour of the Chesapeake Bay area. Gradually, the traffic lessens and the intense urbanization dissolves into a countryside increasingly devoted to forests, farmlands, and the traditional uses of the waterfront. The southern tip of Prince Georges County is a close approximation of what the Chesapeake Bay area used to look like a generation or two ago. There is an awareness, too, that the line of demarcation is still moving.

Appendices

A. Recommended Reading

Books

Barbour, Philip L. *The Three Worlds of Captain John Smith*. New York: Houghton Mifflin, 1964.

Barrick, Susan O., and others. *Chesapeake Bay Bibliography*. Gloucester Point, Va.: Virginia Institute of Marine Science, 1972–1981.

Beverly, Robert. *The History and Present State of Virginia*. Williamsburg: Institute of Early American History, 1947.

Blair, Carvel Hall. *A Guide to Fishing Boats and their Gear*. Cambridge, Md.: Cornell Maritime Press, 1968.

Bodine, A. Aubrey. *Chesapeake Bay and Tidewater*. Baltimore: Bodine and Associates, 1967.

Boorstin, Daniel J. *The Americans: The Colonial Experience*. New York: Random House, 1985.

Brewington, M. V. *Chesapeake Bay: A Pictorial Maritime History*. New York: Bonanza Books, 1953.

Brewington, M. V. *Chesapeake Bay Log Canoes and Bugeyes*. Cambridge: Cornell Maritime Press, 1963.

Brockman, C. Frank. *Trees of North America*. New York: Golden Press, revised 1986.

Brown, Alexander. *Steam Packets on the Chesapeake*. Cambridge: Cornell Maritime Press, 1961.

Burgess, Robert H. *Chesapeake Circle*. Cambridge: Cornell Maritime Press, 1965.

Burgess, Robert H. *This Was Chesapeake Bay*. Cambridge: Cornell Maritime Press, 1965.

Byron, Gilbert. *The War of 1812 on the Chesapeake Bay*. Baltimore: Maryland Historical Society, 1964.

Chapelle, Howard I. *The Baltimore Clipper: Its Origins and Development*. Salem: Dover, 1930.

Cherry, Eloise Heller. *The Complete Chesapeake Bay Retriever.* New York: Hopewell Book House, 1981.

Chesapeake Bay Magazine. *Guide to Cruising on Chesapeake Bay.* Annapolis: Chesapeake Bay Magazine, 1989.

Coggins, Jack. *Ships and Seamen of the American Revolution.* Harrisburg: Stackpole, 1969.

Dashiell, Segar Cofer. *Smithfield: A Pictorial History.* Norfolk: Donning, 1977.

De Gast, Robert. *The Lighthouses of the Chesapeake.* Baltimore: Johns Hopkins University Press, 1973.

Edmunds, Pocahontas Wight. *Tales of the Virginia Coast.* Richmond: The Dietz Press, 1959.

Eller, Ernest McNeill. *Chesapeake Bay in the American Revolution.* Centreville: Tidewater Publishers, 1981.

Ellis, Carolyn. *Fisher Folk.* Lexington: University Press of Kentucky, 1986.

Everett, Rogers. *Wading and Shore Birds.* West Chester: Schiffer Publications, 1988.

Footner, Hulbert. *Rivers of the Eastern Shore.* New York: Farrar & Rinehart, 1944.

Getler, Edward. *Maryland and Delaware Canoe Trails.* Silver Spring: The Seneca Press, 1983.

Godfrey, Robert K., and Jean W. Wooten. *Aquatic and Wetlands Plants of the Southeastern United States.* Athens: University of Georgia Press, 1979.

Goldenberg, Joseph A. *Shipbuilding in Colonial America.* Charlottesville: University of Virginia Press, 1976.

The Gunner's Guide to Maryland's Eastern Shore. Chestertown: The Gunner's Guide, 1988.

Hall, Clayton C., editor. *Narratives of Early Maryland 1633–1684.* New York: Heritage Books, 1988

Handley, Charles O., Jr., and Clyde P. Patton. *Wild Mammals of Virginia.* Richmond: Commission of Game and Inland Fisheries, 1947.

Hill, Norman Allen, editor. *Chesapeake Cruise.* Baltimore: George W. King Printing Co., 1944.

Horton, Tom. *Bay Country.* Baltimore: Johns Hopkins University Press, 1987.

Kenealy, James P. *Boating from Bow to Stern.* New York: Dodd, Mead and Co., 1966.

Kochiss, John M. *Oystering from New York to Boston.* Middletown: Wesleyan University Press, 1974.

Laing, Alexander K. *Seafaring America.* New York: American Heritage Publishing Co., 1974.

Lippson, Alice Jane, and Robert L. Lippson. *Life in the Chesapeake Bay.* Baltimore: The Johns Hopkins University Press, 1984.

Maloney, Elbert S. *Dutton's Navigation and Piloting,* 13th edition. Annapolis: U.S. Naval Institute Press, 1978.

Maryland Seafood Cookbooks (Vols. 1, 2, 3). Annapolis: Department of Economic and Community Development, undated.

Maryland Department of Chesapeake Bay Affairs. *Guide for Cruising Maryland Waters.* Baltimore: 1988.

Meanley, Brooke. *Birds and Marshes of the Chesapeake Bay Country.* Centreville: Tidewater Publishers, 1975.

Meanly, Brooke. *Waterfowl of the Chesapeake Bay Country.* Centreville: Tidewater Publishers, 1982.

Middleton, Arthur Pierce. *Tobacco Coast: A Maritime History of Chesapeake Bay in the Colonial Era.* Newport News: The Mariners Museum, 1953.

Miller, Stephen M. *Early American Waterfowling, 1700s–1930.* Piscatataway, New York: New Century Press, 1986.

O'Neal, William B. *Architecture in Virginia.* Richmond: Virginia Museum, 1968.

Peterson, Roger Tory, and Margaret McKenny. *A Field Guide to Wildflowers of Northeastern and Northcentral North America.* Boston: Houghton Mifflin, 1968.

Phillips, John C. *A Natural History of Ducks* (Vols. 1, 2, 3, 4). Don Mills, Ontario: General Publishing Company, 1986.

Rouse, Parke. *Roll, Chesapeake, Roll.* Norfolk: Historical Society of Norfolk, 1972.

Sanderlin, W. S. *The Great National Project: History of the Chesapeake and Ohio Canal.* Baltimore: Johns Hopkins University Press, 1982.

Sherwood, Arthur W. *Understanding the Chesapeake.* Cambridge: Tidewater Publishers, 1973.

Stone, William T., and Fessenden S. Blanchard. *A Cruising Guide to the Chesapeake.* New York: Dodd, Mead and Co., revised edition, 1987.

Tate, Thad W., and David L. Ammerman, editors. *The Chesapeake Bay in the Seventeenth Century.* Chapel Hill: University of North Carolina Press, 1979.

Terres, John K. *Audubon Society's Encyclopedia of American Birds.* New York: Alfred A. Knopf, 1980.

Tilp, Frederick. *Chesapeake Fact, Fiction and Fun.* New York: Heritage Books, 1988.

Tilp, Frederick. *This Was Potomac River* (second edition). Alexandria: Tilp, 1972.

U.S. Coast Guard Navigation Rules: International-Inland. Washington, D.C.: Department of Transportation annual.

Walsh, Roy E. *Gunning the Chesapeake.* Centreville: Tidewater Publishers, 1960.

Warner, William W. *Beautiful Swimmers.* Boston: Little, Brown and Co., 1976.

Wharton, James. *The Bounty of Chesapeake Bay: Fishing in Colonial Virginia.* Williamsburg: Virginia 350th anniversary Celebration Corp., 1957.

Whitehead, John Hunt. *The Watermen of the Chesapeake Bay.* Richmond: Whitehead, 1979.

Periodicals

Chesapeake Bay Magazine
Notice to Mariners, U.S. Coast Guard, Washington
Motor Boating Magazine
The Skipper Magazine
Yachting Magazine

Newspapers

Baltimore Sun, Baltimore, Maryland
Daily Press, The Times-Herald, Newport News, Virginia
Free Lance Star, Fredericksburg, Virginia
The Virginia Gazette, Williamsburg, Virginia
Virginian Pilot and Ledger-Star, Norfolk, Virginia
Washington Post, Washington Times, Washington, D.C.

Maps

Alexandria Drafting Company, 6440 General Green Way, Alexandria, Virginia (for Northern, Central, and Southern Bay fishing maps).

B. Weather

Chesapeake Bay temperatures are moderate, with mild winters and hot, muggy summers. The southern end of the Bay normally has slightly milder temperatures than the northern section. Averages are about 30 degrees Fahrenheit in January and in the 20s during February, normally the coldest months. Certain days may be colder or warmer, of course. The winter of 1988–89 was unusually mild, with temperatures in the 60s and 70s into January and February. The southern end of the Bay experienced a record high temperature and a foot of snowfall in the same week, but that is most unusual. Temperatures are normally pleasant in October, with colder weather arriving in November. But this shoulder season can be erratic; in 1988, October was colder than November. June temperatures average in the mid-80s, while July and August averages are in the 90s.

Snow falls infrequently, but a few inches can accumulate at times. Normally, the upper bay area experiences more snow than other sections. Rainfall averages from 2½ inches in January to 3.4 inches in June in Washington; Baltimore precipitation usually is slightly higher.

Monthly averages in degrees Fahrenheit at Washington (near the center of the area) are as follows:

	Jan	Feb	Mar	Apr	May	Jun	Jul	Aug	Sep	Oct	Nov	Dec
High	43	44	55	70	70	85	91	92	86	69	57	48
Low	31	29	37	51	60	65	74	74	68	54	41	32

C. Terrain, Habitats, and Flora

The Chesapeake Bay area is a complex system, combining all of the following aspects: deep water where the salinity varies from place to place and from time to time, shoals and mud flats, salt, brackish, and freshwater marshes, fresh and brackish bays, rivers with extensive floodplains, tidal and freshwater rivers, ocean, and upland.

The Bay is part of the coastal plain, where the land is dominated by sandy soil. But there are places where marl exists in large quantities. Borrow pits attest to the existence of rocks. Although the land generally is flat, cliffs overlook the rivers and Bay in a few areas. Shallow beaches crop up in many places. In the south, the plain slopes gently for long distances to the water's edge. In the north, the Bay-front lies only a few miles from the foothills of the mountains. On the ocean side of the Eastern Shore, shifting and stabilized dunes hold back the Atlantic.

Fossils are the primary geological attraction. Indeed, the abundant finds in the area, ranging from 25 to 45 million years in age, are regarded as "magnificent" by some geologists. Among the specimens discovered in quantity in bluffs along most rivers and some sections of the Bay are shark teeth, whale bones, coral, clams, snails, barnacles, moss animals (Bryozoa), seals, and crocodile bones. More unusual finds include mastodon bones, fossilized rabbits, and walrus skulls. Primary sites include the York, James, Rappahannock, and Potomac rivers in Virginia and Calvert Cliffs in Maryland.

Minerals are far less common. Dogtooth calcite crystals are discovered in pits north of Interstate 64 and east of Route 17 in Virginia, where beds of the Yorktown Formation are exposed. These range in size up to half an inch. Gypsum crystals are found in older marine deposits in Westmoreland area. Most rocks are delivered from the mountains and are considered pedestrian. Pieces of orange, green, and gray uniakite and petrified wood are discovered in the gravel of the ancient rivers and occasionally locally along the main rivers.

Gneisses of various grades occur in the Baltimore area. Rock from quarries sometimes contain large calcite crystals up to a foot or more in length, which are unusual. Quartz crystals are less common. The quarry at Port Deposit, Maryland, which produced stone for numerous buildings, delivered a coarse-grained granitic gneiss colored by black mica, starting about 1816. The first buildings in Baltimore may have used similar rock from Jones and Gwynn Falls. The porphyritic gneiss from Ellicott City was used even earlier in the Basilica of the Assumption in Baltimore. Cockeysville marble is a handsome white, crystalline metalimestone; it was used to face the lower section of the Washington Monument in the nation's capital.

The piedmont region west of the Bay area is a prime rockhounding zone. Amelia and Loudoun counties in Virginia are also productive. Dinosaur footprints occur around Culpeper, west of Fredericksburg, and in the nearby hill country. The Gettysburg Basin, north of Washington, D.C., into Pennsylvania, also has produced a fair number of footprints. Only slightly removed from the Bay area are slate, Seneca red sandstone, Potomac marble, serpentinite, Sykesville gneiss, and Setters quartzite deposits.

Ecological features exist independently at times, overlap at others. In the area are large oak-hickory forests, often adjacent to large areas of farmland. A variety of pine trees mix with hardwoods in other areas. The Bay area stands on the cusp between northern and southern varieties, and thus has areas where the two overlap. Bald cypress reaches its northern limit in the area, which also hosts gum forests, swamp forests, bushes, vines, and an extensive variety of wildflowers. Grassland and upland forests at times invade swamps and barrier islands.

As a result of this mingling of habitats, flora and fauna may be distinctive in certain areas, mingle in others. No one area has all the species that inhabit the Bay, though many of them are generally distributed. Migratory species add to the confusion.

The following is a representative list of the flora in and around the Bay:

Pine Family
common juniper
eastern white pine
loblolly pine
pitch pine
pond pine
Virginia pine

Cedar or Cypress Family
American white cedar
bald cypress
eastern red cedar

Poplar and Aspen Family
eastern cottonwood
quaking aspen
swamp cottonwood

Willow Family
bigtooth aspen
black willow
pussy willow
sandbar willow
swamp cottonwood

Wax Myrtle Family
southern bayberry

Walnut Family
bitternut hickory
black walnut
mockernut hickory
pignut hickory
shagbark hickory

Birch Family
American hornbeam
eastern hophornbeam
river birch

Beech Family
Alleghany chinkapin
American beech
American chestnut
bear oak
black oak
blackjack oak
chestnut oak
live oak

overcup oak
pin oak
post oak
red oak
scarlet oak
swamp chestnut oak
water oak
white oak
willow oak

Elm Family

American elm
hackberry
slippery elm

Mulberry Family

fig
Osage-orange
red mulberry

Magnolia Family

magnolia
sweetbay
tulip poplar

Custard-Apple Family

paw-paw

Laurel Family

red bay
sassafras
spicebush

Rose Family

blackberry
black cherry
choke cherry
downy hawthorne
frosted hawthorne
hawthorne
raspberry
shadbush
sweet crabapple
white serviceberry

Witch-Hazel Family

sweet gum
witch-hazel

Sycamore Family

American sycamore

Legume Family

black locust
eastern redbud

Cashew Family

poison ivy
poison oak
poison sumac
shining sumac
staghorn sumac

Holly Family

American holly
gooseberry
inkberry
winterberry
yaupon holly

Maple Family

red maple
sugar maple

Dogwood Family

alternate leaf dogwood
black gum
black tupelo
flowering dogwood

Heath Family

highbush blueberry
huckleberry
mountain laurel
trailing arbutus
wild azalea

Sweetleaf Family

common sweetleaf

Olive Family

devilwood
fringetree
green ash
pumpkin ash
white ash
yellow jasmine

Figwort Family

paulownia

Bumelia Family

persimmon

Honeysuckle Family

American elder
boxelder
possumhaw
nannyberry
honeysuckle
elderberry

Hazel Family

alder

Madder Family

common buttonbush

Vine Family

Virginia creeper

Ginseng Family

angelica tree

White Alder Family

sweet pepperbush

Rue Family

toothache tree

Bignonia Family

trumpet creeper

Mistletoe Family

mistletoe

Grape Family

wild grapes

Mulberry Family

red mulberry

Tea Family

loblolly bay

Fern Family

bay-scented fern
Christmas fern
cinnamon fern
climbing fern
log fern
marsh fern
New York fern
rattlesnake fern
resurrection fern
royal fern
southern lady fern

Cattail Family

narrowleaf cattail
common cattail

Grasses

reed grass
saltmarsh cordgrass
saltmeadow cordgrass
big cordgrass
saltgrass
wild rice
wild celery
eelgrass
red fescue
short dune grass
spike grass
sea oats
fox-tail
wigeon grass

Sedge Family

American threesquare
Olney threesquare

Pondweed Family

Sago pondweed
redhead grass
horned pondweed

Water-Nymph Family

bushy pondweed

Rush Family

black needlerush

Bloodwort Family

redroot

Bladderwort Family

swollen bladderwort

Seaweeds

banded
brown fuzz
coarse red weed
graceful red weed
green-tufted
hollow tube
sea lettuce

Arrowhead Family

broad-leaf arrowhead

Arum Family

arrow arum
Jack-in-the-pulpit

Pickerel Weed Family

pickerel weed
water hyacinth

Lily Family

bell lily
featherbells
greenbriar
morning glory
onion
swamp pink

trillium
yellow pond lily

Composite Family

asters
black-eyed Susan
camphorweed
climbing hempweed
common groundsel
cornflower
dusty miller
goldenrods
groundsel-tree
ironweed
marsh fleabane
ox-eye daisy
salt-marsh fleabane
sunflowers
yarrow

Iris Family

crested dwarf iris
dwarf iris

Barberry Family

mayapple

Buttercup Family

common buttercup
marsh marigold
swamp buttercup
wild columbine

Poppy Family

sea poppy

Bedstraw Family

bluet

Pea Family

clover
fragrant false indigo
lespedezas
partridge pea
wild beans

Mallow Family
marsh hibiscus
marsh mallow
seashore mallow

St. John's-Wort Family
St. John's-wort

Evening Primrose Family
evening primrose
primrose willow

Orchid Family
lady's slipper
showy orchis
small woodland orchis

Bluebell Family
bellflower
cardinal flower
Virginia bluebell

Purslane Family
spring beauty

Milkweed Family
butterfly weed
swamp milkweed

Geranium Family
wild geranium

Buckwheat Family
wild buckwheat

Parsley Family
Queen Anne's lace

Gentian Family
pine barren gentian
rose pink

Mustard Family
bittercress
cut-leaved toothwort

Spiderwort Family
Virginia dayflower

Pink Family
starry campion

Primrose Family
scarlet pimpernel
sea milkwort

Sea Lavender Family
sea lavender

Pitcher-Plant Family
trumpets

Touch-Me-Not Family
jewelweed

Phlox Family
blue phlox
Jacob's ladder

Dogbane Family
periwinkle

Tomato Family
jimsonweed

Violet Family
coast violet
common blue violet
marsh blue violet

Nettle Family
false nettle

Water-Lily Family
yellow pond lily

Goosefoot Family
dwarf glassworts
woody glasswort

D. Wildlife

Wildlife-viewing possibilities are excellent, ranging from butterflies and bumble bees to deer, but vary from place to place and according to changes in habitat. Because of this situation, a single definitive list of the wildlife in the Bay area is impractical. Specific specialties of certain areas are mentioned in the text. The following general list includes other species typical of the area.

Representative Bird Sightings

Loons and Grebes
common loon
red-throated loon
horned grebe
pied-billed grebe
red-necked grebe

Shearwaters and Storm Petrel
Cory's shearwater
greater shearwater
sooty shearwater
Wilson's storm-petrel

Gannet, Pelicans, and Cormorants
northern gannet
American white pelican
brown pelican
great cormorant
double-crested cormorant

Bitterns, Herons, and Ibis
American bittern
least bittern
great blue heron
great egret
snowy egret
little blue heron
tricolored heron
Louisiana heron
green-backed heron
cattle egret
glossy ibis
white ibis
black-crowned night heron
yellow-crowned night heron

Swans, Geese, and Ducks
fulvous whistling duck
tundra swan
greater white-fronted goose
snow goose
brant
Canada goose
wood duck
blue-winged teal
green-winged teal
American black duck
mallard
northern pintail
northern shoveler
gadwall
Eurasian wigeon
American wigeon
canvasback
Redhead
ring-necked Duck
greater scaup
lesser scaup
oldsquaw
black scoter
surf scoter
white-winged scoter

common goldeneye
bufflehead
hooded merganser
common merganser
red-breasted merganser
ruddy duck

Vultures, Hawks, and Falcons

black vulture
turkey vulture
osprey
bald eagle
American swallow-tailed kite
northern harrier
sharp-skinned hawk
Cooper's hawk
northern goshawk
red-shouldered hawk
broad-winged hawk
red-tailed hawk
rough-legged hawk
American kestrel
golden eagle
merlin
peregrine falcon
kestrel

Grouse, Quail, and Turkey

wild turkey
northern bobwhite

Rails and Coots

black rail
clapper rail
king rail
Virginia rail
yellow rail
sora
purple gallinule
common moorhen
American coot

Plovers and Sandpipers

black-bellied plover
lesser golden plover
Wilson's plover
piping plover
semipalmated plover
kildeer
American oystercatcher
long-billed curlew
American avocet
American woodcock
black-necked stilt
greater yellowlegs
lesser yellowlegs
solitary sandpiper
spotted sandpiper
upland sandpiper
willet
whimbrel
Hudsonian godwit
marble godwit
ruddy turnstone
red knot
sanderling
semipalmated sandpiper
western sandpiper
least sandpiper
white-rumped sandpiper
pectoral sandpiper
dunlin
curlew sandpiper
stilt sandpiper
buff-breasted sandpiper
ruff
short-billed dowitcher
long-billed dowitcher
common snipe
American woodcock
Wilson's phalarope
red-necked phalarope
black-necked stilt

Jaegers, Gulls, and Terns

pomarine jaeger

parasitic jaeger
laughing gull
Bonaparte's gull
ring-billed gull
herring gull
Iceland gull
lesser black-billed gull
glaucous gull
great black-backed gull
gull-billed tern
Caspian tern
royal tern
roseate tern
common tern
Forster's tern
least tern
black tern
black skimmer
common Murre

Doves, Cuckoos, Owls, Swifts, and Hummingbirds

rock dove
mourning dove
black-billed cuckoo
yellow-billed cuckoo
common barn owl
eastern screech owl
great horned owl
barred owl
long-eared owl
short-eared owl
northern saw-whet owl
common nighthawk
chuck-will's-widow
whippoorwill
chimney swift
belted kingfisher
ruby-throated hummingbird

Woodpeckers and Flycatchers

red-headed woodpecker
red-bellied woodpecker

yellow-bellied sapsucker
downy woodpecker
hairy woodpecker
northern flicker
pileated woodpecker
eastern wood-peewee
yellow-bellied flycatcher
alder flycatcher
Acadian flycatcher
least flycatcher
willow flycatcher
eastern phoebe
great crested flycatcher
western kingbird
eastern kingbird

Larks and Swallows, Jays and Crows

horned lark
purple martin
northern rough-winged
  swallow
tree swallow
bank swallow
cliff swallow
barn swallow
blue jay
American crow
fish crow

Titmice, Nuthatches, and Wrens

black-capped chickadee
Carolina chickadee
tufted titmouse
red-breasted nuthatch
white-breasted nuthatch
brown-headed nuthatch
brown creeper
Carolina wren
house wren
winter wren
sedge wren
marsh wren

APPENDICES

Kinglets, Thrushes, and Thrashers

golden-crowned kinglet
ruby-crowned kinglet
blue-gray gnatsnatcher
eastern bluebird
veery
gray-chested thrush
Swainson's thrush
hermit thrush
wood thrush
American robin
gray catbird
northern mockingbird
brown thrasher

Waxwings, Shrike, and Starling

water pipit
cedar waxwing
loggerheaded shrike
European starling

Vireos and Wood Warblers

white-eyed vireo
solitary vireo
yellow-throated vireo
red-eyed vireo
blue-winged warbler
golden-winged warbler
Tennessee warbler
orange-crowned warbler
Nashville warbler
northern parula
yellow warbler
chestnut-sided warbler
magnolia warbler
Cape May warbler
black-throated blue warbler
yellow-rumped warbler
black-throated green
  warbler
blackburnian warbler

yellow-throated warbler
pine warbler
prairie warbler
palm warbler
bay-breasted warbler
blackpoll warbler
black-and-white warbler
American redstart
prothonotary warbler
worm-eating warbler
ovenbird
northern waterthrush
Louisiana waterthrush
Kentucky warbler
mourning warbler
common yellowthroat
hooded warbler
Wilson's warbler
Canada warbler
yellow-breasted chat

Tanagers and Sparrows

summer tanager
scarlet tanager
northern cardinal
rose-breasted grosbeak
blue grosbeak
indigo bunting
dickcissel
rufous-sided towhee
American tree sparrow
chipping sparrow
field sparrow
vesper sparrow
lark sparrow
Savannah sparrow
grasshopper sparrow
Henslow's sparrow
sharp-tailed sparrow
seaside sparrow
fox sparrow
song sparrow
swamp sparrow
white-throated sparrow

white-crowned sparrow
dark-eyed junco
Lapland longspur
snow bunting

Blackbirds and Finches

bobolink
red-winged blackbird
eastern meadowlark
yellow-headed blackbird
rusty blackbird
boat-tailed grackle
common grackle
brown-headed cowbird
orchard oriole
northern oriole
purple finch
house finch
red crossbill
white-winged crossbill
common redpoll
pine siskin
American goldfinch
evening grosbeak
house sparrow

Accidental Species

eared grebe
least grebe
western grebe
Audubon's shearwater

Leach's storm-petrel
American white pelican
wood stork
common eider
king eider
sandhill crane
Ross's goose
mute swan
hooded merganser
marsh hawk
barnacle goose
gyrfalcon
Baird's sandpiper
purple sandpiper
snowy owl
northern shrike
little gull
common black-headed gull
sabines gull
dovekie
razorbill
Atlantic puffin
common ground dove
scissor-tailed flycatcher
warbling vireo
Philadelphia vireo
cerulean warbler
Connecticut warbler
clay-colored sparrow
Lincoln's sparrow
Brewer's blackbird
ring-necked pheasant

Mammals

In any forest along the shores of the Chesapeake Bay, the rustle of underbrush is likely to announce the movement of a wild animal. Mammals thrive on land and in the water. White-tailed deer are so abundant they constitute a problem in some areas. The smaller sika deer, introduced only a few decades ago, has prospered. So has the nutria. The Bay area has the largest population of muskrats on the East Coast; more muskrat are taken for commercial purposes than in any other region. A few feral animals still roam the barrier islands in the Atlantic Ocean despite efforts to remove them.

In all, more than a hundred mammals live in the combination of upland and lowland terrain. Thirty-three species of marine mammals inhabit coastal waters. In addition, other species may wander beyond the regular limits of their habitat and into the area. However, it is difficult to compile a single list for the region because the incidence changes according to terrain. The Dismal Swamp, at the southern end of the area, harbors some little-known species, including the meadow vole and southern bog lemming. Blackwater National Wildlife Refuge is one of the places where the endangered Delmarva fox squirrel thrives.

The following is a representative list of animals that may be seen somewhere within the area.

Deer
white-tailed
sika

Opossum
Virginia opossum

Carnivores
beaver
gray fox
red fox
long-tailed weasel
mink
muskrat
raccoon
river otter
striped skunk
southern bog lemming

Rabbits
black-tailed jackrabbit
eastern cottontail rabbit
marsh rabbit

Squirrels
Delmarva fox squirrel
eastern chipmunk
gray squirrel
red squirrel
southern flying squirrel
woodchuck

Shrews and Moles
least shrew
masked shrew
nothern shorttail shrew
southeastern shrew
southern shorttail shrew
eastern mole
star-nosed mole

Nutria and Voles
nutria
meadow vole
pine vole
woodland vole

Mice and Rats
cotton mouse
deer mouse
eastern harvest mouse
golden mouse
house mouse
meadow jumping mouse
white-footed mouse
black rat
hispid cotton rat
Norway rat
rice rat

Bats
big brown bat
eastern pipistrel

evening bat
hoary bat
Keen's bat
little brown bat
red bat
silver-haired bat

Feral Animals

feral cattle
feral hog
feral horse
feral sheep

Aquatic

harbor seal

harp seal
harbor porpoise
rough toothed dolphin
grampus dolphin
bottle-nosed dolphin
saddleback dolphin
goose-beaked whale
common pilot whale
short-finned pilot whale
fin whale

Present but Seldom Seen

black bear
bobcat
false killer whale

Fish

Basses

black sea bass
striped bass
white perch

Sunfishes

bluegill
pumpkinseed
largemouth bass
smallmouth bass
black crappie
white crappie

Perches

yellow perch
tesselated darter

Bluefish

bluefish

Cobia

cobia

Jacks

Florida pompano
blue runner

Drums

black drum
red drum
croaker
silver perch
southern kingfish
northern kingfish
spot
spotted sea trout
weakfish

Wrasses

tautog

Mullets

stiped mullet
white mullet

Porgies

sheepshead
scup

Gar

longnose gar

Sturgeons
Atlantic sturgeon
shortnose sturgeon

Herrings
American shad
blueback herring
gizzard shad
hickory shad
menhaden
threadfin shad

Anchovies
bay anchovies

Pikes
chain pickerel
redfin pickerel

Eels
American eel

Catfishes
white catfish
channel catfish
brown bullhead

Carps and Minnows
carp
goldfish
silvery minnow
shiners

Suckers
white sucker
creek chubbsucker

Killifishes
killifish
mummichog
Sheepshead minnow

Needlefish
Atlantic needlefish

Codfishes
red hake
spotted hake

Silversides
inland silverside
rough silverside

Mackerels
bonito
little tunny

Butterfishes
butterfish
harvestfish

Flounders
summer flounder
winter flounder

Soles
hogchoker

Sharks
bull shark
smooth dogfish
spiny dogfish

Skates, Stingrays
clearnose skate
southern stingray
bluntnose stingray

Jellyfishes
moon jellyfish
sea nettle
southern stingray

Invertebrates

Amphipods

salt marsh flea
beach flea
scuds

Crabs

blue crab
ghost crab
hermit crab
horseshoe crab
Jonah crab
lady crab
marsh crab
marsh fiddler crab
mole crab
mud crab
oyster crab
red-jointed fiddler crab
rock crab
sand fiddler crab
spider crab
wharf crab

Crayfishes

burrowing crayfish
river crayfish

Bivalves

American oyster
angel wing
arks
Asian clam
Atlantic ribbed mussel
Baltic macoma clam
blue mussel
brackish water clam
fallen angel wing
false angel wing
file yoldia
fingernail clams

freshwater mussels
gem clam
hard clam
hooked mussel
jackknife clams
jingle shell
little surf clam
northern dwarf tellin
pill clams
platform mussel
razor clam
softshell clam
surf clam

Shrimps

brown shrimp
flat-browed mud shrimp
grass shrimps
pink shrimp
white shrimp

Snails

baby bubble
barrel bubble
channeled whelk
marsh periwinkle
hornshell snail
impressed odostone
knobbed whelk
lunar dove shell
oyster drill
pouch snail
saltmarsh snail
scallops
seaweed snail
slipper shells
solitary bubble
spindle-shaped turret snail
two-sutured odostone

Other Crustaceans
barnacles

Sea Stars, Sea Cucumbers, and Brittle Stars
burrowing brittle star

common sea star
common sea cucumber
pale sea cucumber
fossil sand dollar

Butterflies

Two of the seven life zones for butterflies cross the Chesapeake Bay area. The Upper Austral zone extends across both shores of the Bay. The northern tip of the Lower Austral zone reaches the lower Bay area. In addition, the variety of habitats in the Chesapeake Bay area—freshwater and saltwater marshes, acidic swamps, mixed forests, bottomland, farmlands being reclaimed by natural foliage and numerous refuges among them—provides the plant life to support a varied population of butterflies.

Like most insects, butterflies are a warm-weather phenomenon. Their growing season is between the last frost in spring and the first in autumn. About 140 species benefit from the mildness of the Bay climate. According to Dr. Paul Opler of the U.S. Fish and Wildlife Service, the Bay acts as a barrier to the movement of northern and southern species. A number of butterflies restricted to hardwood swamps reach their northern limits around Virginia Beach and Great Dismal Swamp. Some northern species stop at the upper end of the Bay.

Opler includes the Great Dismal Swamp and Accomack County in Virginia, certain areas below the Potomac River fall line north of Washington, D.C., and the Pocomoke River swamp in Maryland among the best area for viewing butterflies. Many of the species seen in the area are common throughout the eastern United States. Rare species include King's hairstreak in Suffolk and Accomack County; Hessel's hairstreak, common in the Dismal Swamp; and the duke's slipper, which reaches its northern limit in Chesapeake. A rare species of tiger beetle lives near the Calvert Cliffs in Maryland. It is not unusual to see mating butterflies on the banks of isolated streams such as Dragon Run in Virginia.

One of the largest and most beautiful of Eastern butterflies, the Diana, was once common in southeastern Virginia but has not been seen since 1951.

Among other kinds of butterflies that may be seen in the Bay area are the following:

Hesperiidae Family

silver-spotted skipper
gold-banded skipper
hoary edge
confused cloudy wing
northern cloudy wing
southern cloudy wing
common sooty wing
southern sooty wing
Horace's dusky wing
Juvenal's dusky wing
mottled dusky wing
sleepy dusky wing
wild indigo dusky wing
checkered skipper
clouded skipper
European skipper
least skipper
swarthy skipper
cobweb skipper
cross line skipper
fiery skipper
Leonard's skipper
Peck's skipper
tawny edged skipper
Aaron's skipper
Delaware skipper
mulberry wing
southern golden skipper
yehl skipper
northern broken dash
broken dash
little glassy wing
satchem
broad-winged skipper
sawgrass skipper
dion skipper
duke's skipper
black dash
two-spotted skipper
dun skipper
dusted skipper
Carolina roadside skipper
reversed roadside skipper
roadside skipper
salt marsh skipper
giant yucca skipper

Lycaenidae Family

coral hairstreak
northern hairstreak
gray hairstreak
white m hairstreak
spring azure
eastern tailed blue
little metalmark
American copper
bronze copper
harvester
great purple hairstreak
banded hairstreak
red-banded hairstreak
Edward's hairstreak
king's hairstreak
olive hairstreak
striped hairstreak
Hessel's hairstreak
brown elfin
frosted elfin
Henry's elfin
pine elfin

Libytheidae Family

eastern snout

Papilionidae Family

pipe vine swallowtail
zebra swallowtail
black swallowtail
giant swallowtail
spicebush swallowtail
tiger swallowtail
palamedes swallowtail

Pieridae Family

checkered white

European cabbage
falcate orange tip
clouded sulphur
orange sulphur
dog face
cloudless sulphur
little sulphur
sleepy orange

Nymphalidae Family

great spangled fritillary
meadow fritillary
regal fritillary
silver-bordered fritillary
variegated fritillary
pearl crescent
Baltimore checkerspot

comma merchant
red admiral
question mark
mourning cloak
American painted lady
viceroy
tawny emperor
hackberry
pearly eye
Creole pearly eye
gemmed satyr
Appalachian eyed brown
Carolina satyr
Georgia satyr
little wood satyr
common wood nymph
monarch

Reptiles and Amphibians

SNAKES

The Chesapeake Bay area has many species of snakes. They help preserve the balance in nature by eating insects, small rodents, snails, slugs, amphibians, and reptiles. In turn, they are attacked by weasels, hawks, and owls.

The poisonous copperhead (*Agkistrodon controtrix mokasen*) is abundant in some areas and should be avoided. The snake is primarily nocturnal, eats mostly mice, and seldom is dangerous unless annoyed or stepped on. Stay away from heavy brush, rock piles, and stacks of old boards. Leave if you see one. The dark coloring on its back has an hour-glass shape, the black section of its eyes is a vertical slit similar to that of a cat, and heat-sensory pits separate the nostrils and eyes.

Many people are bitten in wilderness areas every year, and quick, proper treatment is required.

Among nonpoisonous types in the Chesapeake Bay area are the following: eastern worm snake, scarlet snake, black racer, northern ring-necked snake, corn snake, black rat snake, smooth earth, rough earth snake, eastern hognose snake, coastal plain milk snake, milk snake, eastern king snake, northern water snake, rough green snake, eastern brown snake, red-bellied water snake, common garter snake, eastern ribbon snake, and queen snake.

Turtles

Atlantic green
Atlantic loggerhead
eastern box
eastern mud
eastern painted
northern diamondback
  terrapin
red-bellied
snapping
spotted
stinkpot

Lizards and Skinks

broadheaded skink
five-lined skink
ground skink
northern fence lizard

Salamanders

eastern mud salamander

eastern tiger salamander
marbled salamander
red-backed salamander
red-spotted newt
spotted salamander

Toads and Frogs

American toad
bullfrog
chorus frog
eastern narrow-mouthed
  toad
eastern spadefoot toad
fowler's toad
gray treefrog
green frog
northern cricket frog
northern spring peeper
pickerel frog
southern leopard frog

E. Conservation Organizations

1. American Wilderness Alliance, 7600 East Arapahoe Road Suite 114, Englewood, CO 80112 (303/771-0380).
2. American Horticulture Society, 7931 East Boulevard Drive, Alexandria, VA 22308 (703/528-4952).
3. Chesapeake Bay Foundation, 162 Prince George Street, Annapolis, MD 21401 (301/269-0481); 3815 Heritage Building, 1001 East Main Street, Richmond, Virginia 23219 (804/780-1392).
4. Chesapeake Biological Laboratory, P.O. Box 38, Solomons, MD 20688 (301/326-4281).
5. Citizens Program for the Chesapeake Bay, 6600 York Road Suite 109-A, Baltimore, MD 21212 (301/377-6270).
6. National Wildlife Federation, 1412-16th Street NW, Washington, DC 20036 (202/797-6800).
7. National Wildflower Research Center, 2600 FM 973 North, Austin, TX 78725.
8. National Audubon Society, 801 Pennsylvania Avenue, Washington, DC 20004 (202/547-9009).

9. The Nature Conservancy, 1800 North Kent Street, Arlington, VA 22200 (703/841-5300); Brownsville, Nassawaddox, VA 23413 (804/442-3049); 619 High Street, Charlottesville, VA 22901 (804/295-6101).
10. The Wildfowl Trust of North America, P.O. Box 519, Grasonville, MD 21638 (301/827-6694).
11. Sierra Club, 730 Polk Street, San Francisco, CA 94109 (415/776-2211).
12. U.S. Fish and Wildlife Service, Washington, DC 20242 (202/343-5634).
13. Virginia Institute of Marine Science, Gloucester Point, VA 23062 (804/642-7000).
14. Wildlife Management Institute, 1101-14th Street Suite 725, Washington, DC 20005.

F. Additional Information

Maryland

ART MUSEUMS

1. *Baltimore:* Peale Museum, 225 Holiday Street 21202 (301/396-1149); Maryland Institute College of Art, 1300 Mount Royal Avenue 21217 (301/669-9200); Museum of Art, Art Museum Drive 21218 (301/396-7101); Walters Art Gallery, 600 North Charles Street 21201 (301/547-9000).
2. *Salisbury:* North American Wildfowl Art Museum, Salisbury State University, Salisbury 21801 (800/742-4988 or 301/742-4988).
3. *Towson:* Roberts Gallery, Fine Arts Center, Towson State University 21204 (301/321-2807).

BEACHES

1. *Annapolis region:* Bay Ridge Beach Inc., Herndon Avenue, Annapolis 21403 (301/267-6363); Fort Smallwood Park, Fort Smallwood Road, Pasadena 21122 (301/255-5520); Kurtz Pleasure Beach, Paradise Beach, Pasadena 21122 (301/255-1280). Sandy Point State Park, 800 Revell Highway, Annapolis 21401 (301/757-1841); Truxton Park, Primrose Road, Annapolis 21403 (301/263-3506).
2. *Baltimore region:* Mickey's Altoona Beach, 7696 Altoona Beach Road, Glen Burnie 21061 (301/255-5328); Porters New Park, Rocky Point Road, Essex 21221 (301/686-8769); Rocky Point Park, 439 Rocky Point Road, Essex 21221 (301/686-8295).

3. *Eastern Shore:* Betterton Beach, Kent County Parks & Recreation, Chestertown 21620 (301/778-1948); Crystal Beach, mouth of Elk River on Chesapeake Bay, west of Cecilton; Great Marsh, Somerset Avenue, Cambridge 21613; Oxford Town Beach, Oxford 21654 (301/226-5122); Red Point, on Red Point Road west of Route 272, North East; Riverside Beach, Carpenter's Point.

4. *Southern Maryland:* Breezy Point Beach Club & Marina, 5230 Breezy Point Road, Chesapeake Beach 20732 (301/855-1844)); Cedar Hill Park, Leonard's Mill and Shumaker Pond, Wicomico County Recreation & Parks, Youth & Civic Center, Salisbury 21801 (301/548-4900); Elms Beach, St. Mary's County Parks and Recreation, Leonardtown 20650 (301/475-5621 or on-site 301/862-3964); Fishing Creek Joint Venture, intersection of Routes 260 and 261, Chesapeake Beach 20732; Flag Ponds Nature Park, c/o Calvert County Courthouse, Prince Frederick 20678 (301/586-1477); Municipal Beach, between 5th and 7th streets, North Beach 20831 (301/257-6398).

5. *Ocean City:* Assateague Island National Seashore, Rt. 2, Box 293, Berlin 21811 (301/641-2120); Visitors & Convention Bureau, Ocean City 21842 (301/289-8181).

6. Upper Bay: Charleston Manor Beach, off Route 272, Cecil County.

BIKING

Organizations

1. Bicycle Affairs Coordinator, Room 218, Maryland State Highway Administration, P.O. Box 717, Baltimore 21203 (301/333-1663).

2. Trails Coordinator, Department of Parks and Recreation, P.O. Box 1831, Annapolis 21404 (301/987-9600).

3. Bicycle Map Information, Regional Planning Council, 2225 North Charles Street, Baltimore 21218 (301/383-5862).

4. Maryland Forest, Park and Wildlife Services, Department of Natural Resources, Tawes State Office Building, Annapolis 21401 (301/974-3195).

5. Baltimore Office of Promotion & Tourism, 34 Market Place Suite 310, Baltimore 21202 (301/837-4636).

6. Baltimore Bicycling Club, P.O. Box 5906, Baltimore 21208 (301/243-7521).

7. Maryland National Park & Planning Commission, c/o Trails Coordinator/Planning Division, 14741 Governor Oden Bowie Drive, Upper Marlboro 20772 (301/952-3522).

8. Montgomery County Office of Planning & Project Development, c/o Bikeways and Trails Coordinator, 10 Monroe Street 10th Floor, Rockville 20850 (301/251-2177).

9. Salisbury Bicycling Club of Maryland, P.O. Box 66, Allen 21810 (301/742-7957).
10. League of American Wheelmen, 6707 Whitestone Road Suite 209, Baltimore 21207 (301/944-3399).

Routes

1. *Anne Arundel County:* Maryland Business 3, 1.3 miles, 5th Avenue to Hospital Drive in Glen Burnie.
2. *Baltimore County:* MD 45, Timonium Road to Church Lane; MD 139, Baltimore City Line to Kenilworth Avenue; MD 146, Charmuth Road to Pot Spring Road.
3. *Dorchester County:* MD 16, 13 miles, U.S. 50 to Taylor's Island; MD 307, 6 miles, MD 331 at Hurlock to MD 318 at Caroline County line; MD 343, 6.1 miles, Rigby Avenue to Morris Neck Road; MD 392, 4.4 miles, MD 16 at East New Market to Hurlock.
4. *Kent County:* SR 289-20, Chestertown to Rock Hall, SR 445 to Eastern Neck Wildlife Refuge, SR 445-21 to Tolchester Beach, SR 445 to Fairlee Store, SR 298-292-297 to Betterton, SR 292 past Still Pond, SR 566-298 to Harmony Corner, SR 213 to Galena, SR 290-299-313 to Millington Store, SR 291 to Chestertown; same route to Rock Hall and Eastern Neck Refuge, SR 445 to Fairlee Store, SR 20 to Chestertown; MD 213 to Galena, MD 313 across Chester River and past Unicorn Lake, MD 544-213 to Chestertown; SR 289 to Cliff City (diversion on SR 661 to Quaker Neck Landing), return same way; MD 213-448 to Turner's Creek Wharf, return via SR 448-298-Browntown Road-Cherry Lane-291-213; SR 213-298 to Hainesville Store, return via SR 514-20-291-213; MD 213-291-20-Lankford-Pomona Road to Pomona, return via MD 289-213.
5. *Montgomery County:* Old Columbia Pike, 6.1 miles, MD 198 to White Oak Shopping Center; MD 188, 1.7 miles, Elmore Lane to Old Georgetown Road; MD 189, 1.9 miles, MacArthur Boulevard to River Road (MD 190); Md 190, 3.3 miles, Clearwell Drive to Norton Road; MD 410, 1.5 miles, Meadowbrook Lane to Grubb Road to 16th Street; MD 650, 4.5 miles, Randolph Road to Ednor Road.
6. *Prince George's County:* MD 450, MD 197 to Free State Mall; MD 197, Bowie Park-and-Ride to Thunder Hill Road; MD 193, 1.5 miles, Legion Road to 58th Street in Berwyn Heights.
7. *Somerset County:* MD 362, 6 miles, Crisfield Lane to end of state maintenance; MD 413, 13.3 miles, Westover to Crisfield.
8. *Talbot:* MD 33, 10 miles, Easton to St. Michaels; MD 333, 10.5 miles, Easton to Oxford.

9. *Wicomico County:* MD 313, 6 miles, Mardela to Sharptown; MD 349, 7 miles, U.S. 50 in Salisbury to MD 349 near Quantico; MD 350, eight-tenths of a mile, Salisbury city limits to Beaglin Park Drive; MD 675, 2 miles, U.S. 13 to Elizabeth Street in Delmar.
10. *Worcester County:* MD 365, 5.6 miles, Snow Hill to Public Landing; MD 528, 7.7 miles, Ocean City to Delaware state line.

BOATING

Regulations

1. Department of Natural Resources, Licensing and Consumer Services, P.O. Box 1869, Annapolis 21404 (301/976-3211).

Canoeing

1. Greater Baltimore Canoe Club, P.O. Box 591, Ellicott City 21043.
2. C&O Canal National Historical Park: Fletcher's Boathouse (202/244-0461) and Thompson's Boat Center (202/333-9543) at Georgetown and Swain's Lock (301/299-9006), north of Great Falls Visitors Center.
3. Patuxent River Park, RR Box 3380, Upper Marlboro 20772 (301/627-6074).
4. Pocomoke River Canoe Company, Snow Hill 21863 (301/632-3971).

Cruises

1. *Annapolis region:* Chesapeake Marine Tours, P.O. Box 3350, Annapolis 21403 (301/268-7600); Chesapeake Cruising International, 396 Riverside Drive, Pasadena 21122 (301/437-2123).
2. *Baltimore:* American Cruise Lines (800/243-6755); *Baltimore Patriots I & II* (301/685-4288); *Gatsby* (301/467-7778); *Bay Lady* and *Lady Baltimore* (301/727-3113); *Minnie V.* skipjack (301/522-4214); Port Welcome (301/727-3113); *Princess Myrtle Kate* (301/659-6797); Schooner *Clipper City* (301/579-7930); *Schooner Eagle* (301/962-1171); Schooner *Nighthawk* (301/327-7245).
3. *Crisfield: to Tangier Island* — Tangier Island Cruises, 10th and Main Street, Crisfield 21817 (301/968-2338); Tyler's Island Cruises, Smith Island 21858 (301/425-2771). *To Smith Island* — Capt. Larry Laird, Ewell 21824 (301/425-4471); Capt. Alan Tyler, Rhodes Point 21858 (301/425-2771).
4. *Havre de Grace:* Capt. A. L. Price's *Friendship,* Box 723 21078 (301/939-9386).
5. *Ocean City:* Capt. Bill Bunting's *Angler,* Angler Dock 21842 (301/289-7424); *Bay Queen,* Talbot Street Pier 21842 (301/289-

9125); *Capt. Bunting,* Dorchester Street 21842 (301/289-6720); *Miss Ocean City,* North First Street and Bay 21842 (391/289-8234); Talbot Street Pier Inc. 21842 (301/289-9125); *Taylor Maid,* Bahia Marina, 22nd Street 21842 (301/289-8547); *Tortuga,* Bahia Marina, 22nd Street 21842 (301/289-7438).

6. Poolesville ferry (301/394-5200).
7. *Salisbury: Maryland Lady,* P.O. Box 4062, Salisbury 21801 (301/543-2466 or 800/654-5440).

Safety

1. Boating Safety Division, Maryland Department of Natural Resources, Tawes State Office Building, Annapolis 21401 (301/974-3211).
2. District Educational Officer, U.S. Power Squadron District 5, 105 South Winchester Road, Annapolis 21404 (301/974-0618).
3. District Director, U.S. Coast Guard Auxiliary, 5th Coast Guard District, 431 Crawford Street, Portsmouth, VA 23705.

Annapolis Region Marinas

1. Anchor Yacht Basin, Turkey Point Road, Edgewater 21037 (301/281-6440).
2. Annapolis City Marina Inc., 410 Severn Avenue, Annapolis 21403 (301/268-0660).
3. Annapolis Harbor Boat Yard, 326 First Street, Annapolis 21403 (301/267-9050).
4. Annapolis Landing, 922 Klakring Road, Annapolis 21403 (301/269-1903).
5. Annapolis Yacht Basin, Compromise Street, Annapolis 21401 (301/263-3544).
6. Back Creek, Box 48, Annapolis 21404 (301/280-6417).
7. Bert Jabin's Yacht Yard, 7310 Edgewood Road 21403 (301/268-9667).
8. Blue Water, 1024 Carr's Wharf Road, Edgewater 21037 (301/798-6733).
9. Carbacks, 1856 Cedar Road, Pasadena 21122 (301/437-6600).
10. Chesapeake Harbor, 2020 Chesapeake Harbor Drive East, Annapolis 21403 (301/268-1969).
11. Cypress, 350 White Cedar Lane, Severna Park 21146 (301/647-7940).
12. Fairwinds, 1000 Fairwinds Drive, Annapolis 21401 (301/974-0758).
13. Geisler's Point, 7831 S.W. Road, Pasadena 21122 (301/255-9549).
14. Gibson Island Yacht Basin, 487 New York Avenue, Pasadena 21122 (301/255-4114).

15. Hammock Island, 8083 Ventnor Road, Pasadena 21122 (301/437-1870).
16. Horn Point Harbor, 121 Eastern Avenue, Annapolis 21403 (301/263-0550).
17. Magothy, 360 Magothy Road, Severna Park 21146 (301/647-2356).
18. Mears, 519 Chester Avenue, Annapolis 21403 (301/268-8282).
19. Oak Harbor, 7700 Water Oak Road, Pasadena 21122 (301/255-4070).
20. Pier 4, 301-4th Street, Annapolis 21403 (301/269-0933).
21. Port Annapolis, 7074 Bembe Beach Road, Annapolis 21403 (301/269-1990).
22. Rhode River, 3932 Germantown Road, Edgewater 21037 (301/269-0699).
23. Selby Bay Yacht Basin, P.O. Box 635, Edgewater 21037 (301/798-0232).
24. Severn River Yacht Club, 519 Chester Avenue, Annapolis 21403 (301/268-8282).
25. Shipwright Harbor, Deale 20751 (301/867-7686).
26. Turkey Point, 1107 Turkey Point Road, Edgewater 21037 (301/798-1369).
27. White Rocks Yachting Center, 319 Sixth Street, Annapolis 21403 (301/268-5300).

Baltimore Region Marinas
1. Anchorage, 2501 Boston Street 21231 (301/522-4007).
2. Atlantis Marina, 7201 Bucher Road, Dundalk 21219 (301/477-8868).
3. Baltimore Inner Harbor Marina, Baltimore 21201 (301/396-3174).
4. Baltimore Marine Center, 2701 Boston Street 21231 (301/522-1881).
5. Baltimore Yacht Basin, 2600 Insulator Drive 21230 (301/539-8895).
6. Bayview, 2210 Boston Street 21224 (301/276-3424).
7. Boatel Baltimore, 2501 Boton Street 21224 (301/522-0609).
8. Bowley's Quarters, 1700 Bowley's Quarters Road, Middle River 21220 (301/335-3553).
9. Belts Wharf West, 932 Fells Street 21231 (301/342-1110).
10. Chester Cove, 2039 Aliceanna Street 21231 (301/342-1111).
11. Cutter Marine Inc., 1900 Old Eastern Avenue, Essex 21221 (301/391-7245).
12. Galloway Creek Marina Inc., 1414 Burke Road, Middle River 21220 (301/335-3575).

13. Golden Ring Yacht Basin Inc., 400 Wagner Lane, Middle River 21220 (301/687-6149).
14. Gunpowder Falls State Park, Graces Quarters Road, Chase 21220 (301/335-9390).
15. Henderson's Wharf, 1000 Fell Street 21231 (301/269-1755).
16. Inner Harbor Marina, 400 Key Highway 21230 (301/837-5339).
17. Liberty Yacht Club, 64 Old South River Road, Edgewater 21037 (301/266-5633).
18. North Point Marina, 2103 Creek Road, Dundalk 21219 (301/477-2446).
19. Rhode River Marina Inc., 3932 Germantown Road, Edgewater 21037 (301/269-0699).
20. Thames Point, South Wolfe, and Thames streets 21231 (301/327-3105).
21. Tower, 3101 Waterview Avenue 21230 (301/539-2628).
22. Weaver's Marine Service, 730 Riverside Drive, Essex 21230 (301/686-4944).
23. White Rocks Yachting Center, 1402-6th Street, Pasadena 21122 (301/255-3800).

Eastern Shore Marinas

1. Bohemia Bay Yacht Harbor, 1026 Town Point Road, Chesapeake City 21915 (301/885-3601).
2. Georgetown Yacht Basin, Georgetown 21930 (301/648-5112).
3. Goose Creek, P.O. Box 169, Upper Fairmount 21867 (301/651-1193).
4. Gratitude Marina, Route 20, Rock Hall 21661 (301/639-7011).
5. Great Oak Landing, P.O. Box 527, Chestertown 21620 (301/778-5007).
6. Haven Harbor Boatyard and Marina, Gratitude Road, Rock Hall 21661 (301/639-7251).
7. Knapp's Narrows Marina, P.O. Box 277, Tilghman 21671 (301/886-2720).
8. Lankford Bay Marina Inc., Rock Hall 21661 (301/778-1414).
9. Mears Point Marina at Kent Narrows, Grasonville 21638 (301/827-8888).
10. Mears Yacht Haven, Oxford 21654 (301/226-5450).
11. Pelorus Marina, Bayside Avenue, Rock Hall 21661 (301/639-2151).
12. Piney Narrows Yacht Haven, Route 1, Box 72C, Chester 21619 (301/643-6600).
13. Pirates Cove on West River, Galesville 20765 (301/867-2300).
14. Port of Salisbury Marina, 596 West Main Street, Salisbury 21801 (301/548-3176).

15. Queen Anne Marina, 410 Congressional Drive, Stevensville 21666 (301/643-5065).
16. St. Michaels Town Dock Marina, 305 Mulberry Street, St. Michaels 21663 (301/745-2400).
17. Severn Marine Services Inc., P.O. Box 88, Tilghman 21671 (301/886-2159).
18. Spring Cove Marina, Back Creek and Lore Street, Solomons 20688 (301/326-2161).
19. Tolchester Marina, Route 2, Box 503, Chestertown 21620 (301/778-1400).
20. White Rocks Yachting Center, Trappe Landing, Trappe 21673 (301/822-8556).
21. Windmill Point Marina, Walnut Street, Rock Hall 21661 (301/639-2120).
22. Worton Creek Marina, Route 4, Buck Neck Road, Chestertown 21620 (301/778-3282).

National Capital Region Marinas

1. Anacostia, 1900 M Street SE 20003 (202/544-5191).
2. Buzzard Point Boatyard Corp., 2200 1st Street NW 20001 (202/488-8400).
3. Gangplank, 600 Water Street SW 20024 (202/554-5000).
4. Tantallo Marina at Fort Washington, 301-4th Street, Annapolis 21403 (301/858-5515).
5. Washington, 1300 Maine Street SW 20024 (202/554-0222).

Southern Maryland Marinas

1. Aqua-Land Marina, Newburg 20664 (301/259-2123).
2. Benedict Marina, Benedict 20612 (301/274-4429).
3. Blackstone Marina, Hollywood 20636 (301/373-2015).
4. Bohemia Bay Yacht Harbour, 1026 Town Point Road, Chesapeake City 21915 (301/885-2601).
5. Cape St. Mary's Marina, Rt. 1, Box 46, Mechanicsville 20659 (301/373-9834).
6. Cather Marine Inc., Colton's Point 20626 (301/769-3335).
7. Cedar Cove Yacht Basin, Route 249 Valley Lee 20692 (301/994-0500).
8. Clarke's Landing, Hollywood 20636 (301/373-9819).
9. Cobb Island Marina, Cobb Island 20625 (301/259-2032).
10. Combs Creek Marina, Route 2, Box 59, Leonardtown 20650 (301/475-2017).
11. Curley's Point Marina, Clark Road, Piney Point 20690 (301/994-1212).
12. Dennis Point Marina, Drayden 20630 (301/994-2288).

13. Goose Bay Marina, Welcome 20693 (301/934-3812).
14. Harbor Island Marina, Solomons 20688 (301/326-3441).
15. Kopel's Marina, Colton Point 20653 (301/769-3121).
16. Lover's Point Marina, Abells Wharf Road, Leonardtown 20650 (301/475-2063).
17. Point Lookout Marina, Ridge 20680 (301/872-5145).
18. Port Tobacco Marina, Port Tobacco 20677 (301/932-1407).
19. Scheible's Fishing Center, Ridge 20680 (301/872-5185).
20. Solomons Beacon Marina, Lore Road, Solomons 20688 (301/326-3807).
21. Tall Timbers Vacation Club and Marina, Tall Timbers 20690 (301/994-1508).
22. Town Creek Marina, California 20619 (301/862-3553).
23. Town Center Marina, A Street, Solomons 20688 (301/326-2401).
24. Zahniser's, C Street and Back Creek, Solomons Island, MD 20688 (301/326-2166).

Upper Bay Marinas

1. Avalon Yacht Basin, Water and Louisa streets, Charlestown 21914 (301/287-6722).
2. Bohemia River, Town Point Road, Chesapeake City 21915 (301/885-5429).
3. Charlestown, Charlestown 21914 (301/287-8125).
4. Chestnut Point, Chestnut Point Road, Carpenter's Point 21903 (301/642-6634).
5. Craft Haven, Carpenters Point Road, Carpenter's Point 21903 (624-2515).
6. Dockside Yacht Club, Second Street, Chesapeake City 21915 (301/885-5016).
7. Duffy Creek, Duffy Creek Road, Fredericktown 21701 (301/275-2141).
8. Elk Haven, Oldfield Point Road, Elkton 21921 (301/398-3123).
9. Granary, George Street, Fredericktown 21701 (301/648-5112).
10. Harbor North, Court House Point Road, Chesapeake City 21915 (301/885-5656).
11. Lee's, Water Street, Charlestown 21914 (301/287-5100).
12. A. H. Owens & Son, River Road, Perryville 21903 (301/642-6331).
13. Sailing Associates, George Street, Fredericktown 21701 (301/287-2387).
14. Sassafras Boat Company, George Street, Fredericktown 21701 (301/275-8111).
15. Skipjack Cove, Route 213 and Skipjack Road, Fredericktown 21701 (301/275-2122).

16. Tidewater, Bourbon Street, Havre de Grace 21078 (301/939-0950).
17. Triton, Plum Point Road, Elkton 21921 (301/398-7515).
18. Two Rivers Yacht Basin, Town Point Road, Chesapeake City 21915 (301/885-2257).

Ramps

1. *Annapolis region:* Sandy Point State, 800 Revell Highway 21401 (301/757-1841).
2. *Baltimore area:* Broening Park, Middle Branch, Hanover Street, Baltimore 21230 (301/396-3838); Fort Armistead Park, Patapsco River, Department of Planning, 222 East Saratoga Street Room 800, Baltimore 21202 (301/396-4343); Gunpowder Falls State Park, 10815 Harford Road, Glen Arm 21057 (301/592-2897); Loch Raven Reservoir, Providence Road, Towson 21204 (301/252-8755).
3. *Eastern Shore:* Assateague State Park, Rt. 2, Box 293, Berlin 21811 (301/641-2120); Centerville Wharf Landing and Reed's Creek at Centreville; Southeast Creek at Church Hill; Deep Landing and Town Landing at Crumpton; Kent Narrows Marina and Jackson Creek at Grasonville; Wells Creek, Thompson Creek, Shipping Creek, Goodhand Creek, Matapeake State Park, Little Creek and Piney Narrows on Kent Island; Queenstown Landing at Queenstown; Janes Island State Park, Route 2, 40 Alfred Lawson Drive, Crisfield 21817 (301/868-1565); Martinak State Park, Deep Shore Drive, Denton 21629 (301/479-1619); Tuckahoe State Park, Route 21, Box 23, Queen Anne 21657 (301/634-2810); Pocomoke River State Park, Route 3, Box 237, Snow Hill 21863 (301/632-2566).
4. *National capital area:* Bladensburg, Anacostia River on Route 202; C&O National Historical Park, P.O. Box 4, Sharpsburg 21782 (301/739-4200).
5. *Southern Maryland:* Back Creek, off Route 2-4 at Calvert Marine Museum; Chaptico Wharf and Buschwood Wharf, on Wicomico River off Route 238; Colton Point, end of Route 242; Friendship Landing, off Route 424 on Najemoy Creek; Hallows Point, Route 231 at Patuxent River Bridge; Leonardtown, Breton Bay on Route 245; Magruder's Ferry, on Patuxent River north of Milltown Landing; Patuxent River Park, south of Upper Marlboro off Route 382 and near Mt. Calvert on Route 382; Piney Point, St. George's Creek on Route 249; St. Mary's River State Park, Star Route, Box 48, Scotland 20687 (301/872-5688) Solomons, Route 2-4 at Thomas Johnson Bridge; Southern Park on Neale Sound; Sweden Point, on Mattawoman Creek at Small-

wood State Park; Tall Timbers, on Tall Timbers Cove off Route 249.

6. *Upper Bay:* Elk Neck State Park; A. H. Owens & Son, River Road, Perryville; Logan's Wharf, Port Deposit; Port Deposit Marina Park, South Main Street; Richmond's Marina, Greenspring Road, Hacks Point; Riverside Ponderosa Pines, Carpenter's Point Road, Carpenters Point; Shelter Cove Marina, Riverside Drive, Hance Point; Susquehanna State Park, 801 Stafford Road, Havre de Grace 21078 (301/939-0643).

Sailing Schools

1. *Annapolis:* Annapolis Sailing School, 601-6th Street, Annapolis 21403 (301/267-7205 or 800/638-9192); Maiden Voyage Sailing School, 726 Second Street, Annapolis 21403 (301/942-6932); Chesapeake Sailing School, 7074 Bembe Beach Road, Annapolis 21403 (301/269-1593); Severn Sailing Association, P.O. Box 1463, Annapolis 21403 (301/269-6744).
2. *Baltimore area:* Getaway Sailing School, 2701 Boston Street 21231 (301/342-3110); Sailing School of Baltimore, 1800 Bowley's Quarter Road, Middle River 21220 (301/335-7555).
3. *Eastern Shore:* Pelorus, Bayside Avenue, Rock Hall 21661 (301/639-2151).
4. *Southern Maryland:* Solomons Sailing School, Spring Cove Marina, Solomons 20688 (301/586-2612).
5. *Upper Bay area:* Capt. Phineas McHenry Ltd., 24 South Main Street, North East 21901 (301/287-2028).

Yacht Rentals

1. *Annapolis:* Annapolis Luxury Yacht Charters Inc., 98 Green Spring Drive 21403 (301/268-3604); Chesapeake Bay Yacht Charter Association, P.O. Box 4022 21403 (301/269-1594); Cruising Yacht Charters and Charter Club, 410 Westbury Drive 21403 (301/965-5530); Lady Anna Charters, P.O. Box 448, Edgewater 21037 (301/261-1210); Omega Yacht Charters, 410 Severn Ave. #306 21403 (301/268-9305); Pier 7, Route 2, Edgewater 21037 (301/956-2288).
2. *Baltimore:* Harbor Charters by Nautico, Baltimore (301/962-1171).
3. Eastern Shore Yacht Charters, Box 589, Oxford 21654 (301/226-5000).

CAMPING

1. *Annapolis area*
   Edgewater—Camp Letts, P.O. Box 208 21037 (301/798-0440).

Lothian—Duncan's Family KOA Campground, 5381 Sands Road 20711 (301/627-3909).

2. *Baltimore area*

Ellicott City—Patapsco Valley State Park, 8020 Baltimore National Pike 21043 (301/461-5005).

Freeland—Morris Meadows Recreation Farms Inc., 1523 Freeland Road 21053 (301/329-6626).

Glen Arm—Gunpowder Falls State Park, 10815 Harford Road 21057 (301/592-2897).

Havre de Grace—Rocks State Park, 3318 Rocks Chrome Hill Road, Jarrettsville 21084 (301/557-7994); Susquehanna State Park, 801 Stafford Road 21078 (301/939-0643)

3. *Eastern Shore*

Berlin—Eagles Nest, Route 2, Box 465 21811 (301/289-9097).

Chestertown—Duck's Neck Campground, Route 1, Box 262 21620 (301/778-3070).

Delmar—Woodlawn Campground, Route 1, Box 69A 21875 (301/896-2979)

Rock Hall—Ellendale Campsites 21661 (301/639-7485).

Goldsboro—Lake Bonnie Inc., P.O. Box 142 21636 (301/482-8479).

Greensboro—Holiday Park, P.O. Box 277 21639 (301/482-6797).

Madison—Madison Bay Marina and Campground, P.O. Box 41 21648 (301/228-4111).

Nanticoke—Roaring Point Waterfront Campground, P.O. Box B 21840 (301/873-2553).

Princess Anne—Princess Anne Campground, Box 427 21853 (301/651-1520).

Quantico—Sandy Hill Family Camp Inc., Route 1, Box 93 21856 (301/873-2471).

Taylor's Island—Taylor's Island Family Campground, P.O. Box 156 21669 (301/397-3275); Tideland Park Campground 21669 (301/397-3473).

Westover—Lake Somerset Campground, Route 1, Box 11A 21871 (301/957-9897).

4. *National capital region*

College Park—Cherry Hill Campcity, 9530 Rosebill Avenue, College Park 20740 (301/474-5069).

Millarsville—Capitol KOA Campground, P.O. Box 149, 768 Cecil Avenue 21108 (301/923-2771).

5. *Ocean City*—Assateague State Park, Route 2, Box 293, Berlin 21811 (301/641-2120); Bali-Hi Travel Trailer Park, P.O. Box

618 21842 (301/352-5477); Frontier Town, P.O. Box 691, Route 611 21842 (301/641-0880); Ocean City Travel Park, 105-70th Street 21842 (301/524-7601).

6. *Southern Maryland*

Brandywine — Cedarville State Forest, Route 4, Box 106A 20613 (301/888-1622).

Calloway — Take It Easy Ranch 20620 (301/994-0494).

Chesapeake Beach — Breezy Point, 5230 Breezy Point Road 20732 (301/257-2561).

Crisfield — Janes Island State Park, Route 2, Alfred Lawson Drive 21817 (301/968-1565).

Denton — Martinak State Park, Deep Shore Drive 21629 (301/479-1619).

Drayden — Dennis Point Marina and Campground 20630 (301/994-2288).

Leonardtown — Le Grande Estate Camping Resort, Route 1, Box 118A 20650 (301/475-8550).

Prince Frederick — Patuxent Camp Sites, Box 832 20678 (301/586-9880).

Newburg — Aqua-Land Campground, P.O. Box 355 20664 (301/259-2575).

Port Tobacco — Port Tobacco Campground 20677 (301/934-9707).

Queen Anne — Tuckahoe State Park, Route 1, Box 23 21657 (301/634-2810).

Scotland — Point Lookout State Park, Box 48 20687 (301/872-5638).

Snow Hill — Pocomoke River State Park, Route 3, Box 237 21863 (301/623-2566).

Welcome — Goose Bay Marina and Campground, Route 1, Box 1276E 20693 (301/934-3812).

7. *Upper Bay area*

Abingdon — Bar Harbor Campground, 4228 Birch Avenue 21009 (301/679-0880).

Conowingo — Susquehanna Campground, 82 Susquehanna Campground Road 21918 (301/378-2589).

Elkton — Woodlands Camping Resort, P.O. Box 189, Old Oak Neck Road 21921 (301/398-4414).

North East — Elk Neck State Park, Turkey Point Road 21901 (301/287-5333).

Perryville — Chesapeake View Campsites, P.O. Box H 21903 (301/642-6626); Riverside Ponderosa Pines, 1435 Carpenter's Point Road 21903 (301/642-3431).

Ridge — Seaside View 20680 (301/872-4141).

FISHING

Charter and Head Boats

Maryland Charter Boat Association list: Department of Natural Resources, Tidewater Administration, Fisheries Division, 69 Prince George Street, Annapolis 21401 (301/974-3765).

1. *Annapolis area*
   Chesapeake Bay Trawlers, 600 Fairview Avenue 21403 (301/263-2838).

2. *Baltimore area*
   Baltimore Launch & Marine Services, 2202 S. Clinton Street 21224 (301/563-3411); Port of Baltimore Marine Ltd., 2501 Boston Street 21224 (301/327-1800).

3. *Eastern Shore*
   Ocean City — Angler, Angler Dock, Talbot Street 21842 (301/289-7424); *Capt. Bunting,* Dorchester Street 21842 (301/289-6720); *Mariner,* Talbot Street Pier 21842 (301/289-9125); *Miss Ocean City,* North 1st Street 21842 (301/289-8234); *Taylor Maid,* Bahia Marina, 22nd Street 21834 (301/289-7438); *Tortuga,* Bahia Marina, 22nd Street 21842 (301/289-7438). *West Ocean City — Taurus,* South Harbor Road 21842 (301/289-2525). *Tilghman —* All Aboard Charter 21671 (301/482-6558). *Wenona —* Arby's General Store, Main Street 21870 (301/784-2749).

4. *Southern Maryland*
   Avenue — Capt. Frankie Goddard (301/769-2269). *Cobb Island —* Capt. Jim Drummond on Gridiron Street. *Chesapeake Beach —* Rod 'n Reel (301/855-8351). *Drayden —* Dennis Point Marina (301/994-2288). *Point Lookout —* Capt. Brady Bounds (301/872-4342). *Piney Point —* Swann's Hotel (301/994-0774) and Captains Douglas Cornelius (301/994-0347) and Bob Holden (301/994-0269). *Ridge —* Courtney's Marina (301/872-4403), Scheible's (301/872-5185), Trossbach Marina (301/872-5955), Captains Norman Bishop (301/872-5815), Eddie Davis (301/872-5871), Donald Drury (301/872-5217), Tom Drury (301/872-5990), Ray Fenhagen (301/862-5361), Paul Kellam (301/872-5626), and Taft Tippett (301/872-4330). *Scotland —* Hewlett Fishing Center (301/872-5838), Captains Hike Liechlider (301/872-4167), Charles Ridgell (301/872-5133), and Dick Weston (301/872-4464). *St. Inigoes —* Captains Steve Spedden (301/872-5880) and Philip A. Woolford (301/872-5376). *Solomons —* Capt. Bob Clark (301/326-3582); H. M. Woodburn Co. (301/326-3241). *Tall Timbers —* Captains "Mopey" Barber (301/994-1362) and Bob South (301/994-1491). *Valley Lee —* Capt. Joe Scrivener (301/994-1525).

APPENDICES

HISTORIC SITES AND ORGANIZATIONS

Organizations

1. Baltimore County Historical Society, 9811 Van Buren Lane, Cockeysville 21030 (301/666-1876).
2. Charles County Historical Trust, P.O. Box 217, Ironsides 20643 (301/743-7558).
3. Dr. Samuel A. Mudd Society Inc., 69 Matingly Avenue, Indian Head 20640 (301/934-8464).
4. Friends of St. Mary's City, P.O. Box 24, St. Mary's City 20686 (301/826-0990).
5. Historical Society of Charles County, Route 2, Box 65, Indian Head 20640 (301/375-8550).
6. Historical Society of Harford County, 33 Courtland West, Bel Air 21014.
7. Maryland House and Garden Pilgrimage, 1105A Providence Road, Towson 21204.
8. Maryland Indian Heritage Society, P.O. Box 128, Brandywine 20613 (301/888-1566).
9. Society for the Preservation of Federal Hill and Fell's Point, Baltimore, 812 South Ann St., Baltimore 21231 (301/675-6750).
10. State Championship Jousting and Horse Fair, 328 Bush Chapel Road, Aberdeen 21001 (301/272-3086).
11. Talbot County Historical Society, Easton 21601 (301/822-0773).

Individual Sites

1. *Annapolis region:* Banneker-Douglass Museum of Afro-American Life, 84 Franklin Street 21401 (301/974-2894); Governor William Paca House, 186 Prince George Street 21401 (301/263-5553); Hammond-Harwood House, 19 Maryland Avenue 21401 (301/269-1714); London Town Publik House and Garden, Londontown Road, Edgewater 21037 (301/956-4900); State House, State Circle 21401 (301/947-3400); U.S. Naval Academy 21402 (301/267-3363); Victualing House/Maritime Museum, 77 Main Street 21401 (301/263-5553).
2. *Baltimore:* Babe Ruth Birthplace Museum/Maryland Baseball Hall of Fame, 216 Emory Street 21230 (301/727-1539); Basilica of the Assumption, Cathedral and Mallory streets 21201 (301/727-3564); B&O Railroad Museum, 900 West Pratt Street 21223 (301/237-2387); Carroll Mansion, 800 East Leonard Street 21204 (301/396-3523); 1840 House, Lombard and Front streets 21202 (301/396-3279); Evergreen House, 4545 North Charles Street 21210 (301/338-7641); Flag House, 844 East Pratt Street 21202 (301/837-1793); Fort McHenry National Monument,

2400 East Fort Avenue 21230 (301/962-4299); Frigate *Constellation,* Constellation Dock, Inner Harbor 21202 (301/539-1797); H. L. Mencken House, 1524 Hollins Street 21202 (301/396-7997); Homewood House, Charles and 34th streets 21210 (301/235-6882); Jewish Heritage Center, 5700 Park Heights Avenue 21215 (301/732-6400); Maryland Historical Society Museum, 201 West Monument Street 21201 (301/685-3750); Mother Seton House, 600 North Paca Street 21201 (301/728-6464); Mount Clare Mansion, Carroll Park 21230 (301/837-3262); Old Otterbein Church, Conway and Sharp streets 21201 (301/685-4703); Poe House, 203 North Amity Street 21223 (301/396-7932); Robert Long House, 812 South Ann Street 21231 (301/675-6750); St. Paul's Church (301/685-3404); Shot Tower (301/837-5424); Westminster Church (301/328-7228); Zion Lutheran Church (301/727-3939).

3. *Baltimore County:* Hampton National Historic Site, 535 Hampton Lane, Towson 21204 (301/962-0688).

4. *Eastern Shore:* Cambridge Historic District, Chamber of Commerce, Route 50 21613 (301/228-3575); Chestertown Historical District, Kent County Chamber of Commerce, 118 North Cross Street, Chestertown 21620 (301/778-0416); Newtown District, Wicomico County Convention & Visitors Bureau, Civic Center, Glen Avenue, Salisbury 21801 (301/54-3466).

5. *National Capital region:* Clara Barton National Historic Site, National Park Service, 5801 Oxford Road, Glen Echo 20812 (301/492-6243); Montpelier Mansion, Laurel 20708 (301/779-2011); Riverdale 20737 (301/779-2011); Fort Washington 20744 (301/763-4600); Glen Echo Park, Glen Echo 20812 (301/492-6282); Historic Savage Mill (301/498-5751); John Poole House (301/496-8635); Mary Surratt House (301/868-1121); National Colonial Park, Accokeek, MD 20607 (301/283-2115).

6. *Southern Maryland:* Chesapeake Beach Railway Museum, P.O. Box 783, Chesapeake Beach 20732 (301/257-3892); Christ Episcopal Church, Chaptico 20621 (301/884-3451); Historic St. Mary's City, P.O. Box 24, St. Mary's City 20686 (301/862-0990); Jefferson Patterson Park and Museum, Route 2, Box 50A, St. Leonard 20685 (301/586-0050); Old Durham Chapel, Port Tobacco 20677 (301/743-7468); Old Jail, Leonardtown 20650 (301/475-2467); Port Tobacco Courthouse, Port Tobacco 20677 (301/934-4313); Potomac River Museum, Colton's Point 20626 (301/769-2222); Sotterly, The Administrator, Sotterly, Hollywood, MD 20636 (301/373-2280).

7. *Upper Bay region:* Chesapeake City Historical District, South Chesapeake City 21915 (301/885-5233); C&D Canal Museum,

Second Street and Bethel Road, Chesapeake City 21915 (301/ 885-5621); East Nottingham Friends Meeting House, Route 272 and Calvert Road, Calvert 21225 (301/658-6850); Historical Society Museum, 135 East Main Street, Elkton 21921 (301/ 398-0914); Mount Harmon, P.O. Box 65, Earleville 21919 (301/275-2721); Old Bohemia Mission (St. Francis Xavier Roman Catholic Church), Bohemia Church Road, Warwick 21912 (609/299-0582); Partridge Hall, West Main Street, Elkton 21921 (301/398-3816); Rodgers Tavern, Broad Street, Perryville 21903 (301/939-0150); Tory House, Market and Cecil streets, Charlestown 21914 (301/287-8793); Upper Bay Museum, P.O. Box 275, North East 21901 (301/287-5718); West Nottingham Presbyterian Church, 1195 Firetower Road, Colora 21917 (301/658-4596).

Historic Inns and B&Bs

1. *Annapolis region*
   Governor Calvert House, Robert Johnson House and State House Inn, State Circle, Annapolis 21401 (301/263-2641); Maryland Inn and Reynolds Tavern, Church Circle 21401 (301/263-2641).
2. *Baltimore region*
   Shirley-Madison Inn, 205 West Madison Street, Baltimore 21201 (301/728-6550).
3. *Eastern Shore*
   Betterton—Ye Lantern Inn, P.O. Box 310, Ericsson Avenue, 21610 (301/348-5809). *Cambridge*—Sarke Plantation, Route 3, Box 139 21813 (301/228-7020). *Chestertown*—Flyway Lodge, Route 213 South 21620 (301/778-5557); Great Oak Manor, Route 2, Box 766 21620 (301/778-5796); White Swan Tavern, 231 High Street 21620 (301/778-1300); Radcliffe Cross, Quaker Neck Road 21620 (301/778-5540); Widow's Walk Inn, 402 High Street 21620 (301/778-6455).
   Easton—Tidewater Inn, Dover and Harrison streets 21601 (301/822-1300). *East New Market*—Edmondson House, Main Street 21631 (301/943-4471); Friendship Hall, Route 1, Box A 21631 (301/943-4843). *Georgetown*—Kitty Knight House, Route 213 21930 (301/648-5305). *Oxford*—1876 House, 110 N. Norris Street 21654 (301/226-5496); Robert Morris Inn, P.O. Box 70, The Strand 21654 (301/226-5111). *Princess Anne*—Elmwood 21853 (301/651-1066); Washington Hotel & Inn 21853 (301/ 651-2525). *St. Michaels*—Colonel Joseph Kemp House 21663 (301/745-2243). *Snow Hill*—Snow Hill Inn, 104 East Market Street 21863 (301/632-2102).

Tilghman Island — Harrison's Chesapeake House 21671 (301/886-2123). *Vienna* — Governor's Ordinary, Water Street at Church Street 21869 (301/376-3530); Nanticoke Manor House, Church and Water streets 21869 (301/376-3530); The Tavern House, 111 Water Street 21869 (301/376-3347).

4. *National Capital region:* Old Angler's Inn, 10801 MacArthur Boulevard, Potomac 20854 (301/365-2425).
5. *Smith Island*
   Bernice Guy, Ewell 21824 (301/425-2751); Francis Kitchings, Ewell 21824 (301/425-3321); Mrs. Maude Whitelock, Ewell 21824 (301/425-2201).
6. *Upper Bay*
   Bayard House, 11 Bohemia Avenue, Chesapeake City 21915 (301/885-5040).

HUNTING

License and Other Information

1. Licensing and Consumer Services, Department of Natural Resources, Tawes Office Building, Annapolis 21401 (301/269-3195).
2. Maryland Forest, Park, and Wildlife Service, Tawes State Office Building, Annapolis 21401 (301/269-3195).
3. Office of Tourist Development, 217 East Redwood Street, Baltimore 21202 (301/333-6611).

Public Areas

1. Calvert Cliffs State Park (301/888-1622).
2. Chesapeake & Delaware Canal Lands (301/928-3650).
3. Cedarville State Forest (301/888-1622).
4. Chapel Point State Park (301/743-7613).
5. Earleville Wildlife Management Area (301/938-3650).
6. Elk Neck State Park (301/287-5333).
7. Janes Island State Park (301/968-1565).
8. Patuxent River State Park (301/924-2127).
9. Pocomoke State Forest (301/749-2461).
10. Purse State Park (301/743-7613).
11. Rocks State Park (301/557-7994).
12. Seneca Creek State Park (301/924-2127).
13. St. Mary's River State Park (301/872-5688).
14. Tuckahoe State Park (301/634-2810).
15. Wye Island Natural Resources Management Area (301/827-7577).

INFORMATION SOURCES

1. Tourism Council of Annapolis and Anne Arundel County, 152 Main Street, Annapolis 21401 (301/268-8687).
2. Baltimore Office of Promotion & Tourism, 110 West Baltimore Street, Baltimore 21201 (301/752-8632).
3. Baltimore County Chamber of Commerce, 100 West Pennsylvania Avenue, Towson 21204 (301/825-6200).
4. Baltimore County Office of Promotion & Tourism, Courthouse Mezzanine, Towson 21204 (301/832-8040).
5. Calvert County Department of Economic Development, Calvert County Courthouse, Prince Frederick 20678 (301/535-1600).
6. Calvert County Tourism Council, Box 190 Owings 20622 (301/535-1013).
7. Cecil County Office of Planning and Economic Development, County Office Building Room 300, Elkton 21921 (301/398-0200).
8. Charles County Tourism, P.O. Box B, La Plata 20646 (301/645-0559).
9. Discover Harford County, P.O. Box 635, Bel Air 21014 (301/836-8986).
10. Dorchester County Tourism, P.O. Box 307, Cambridge 21613 (301/228-3234).
11. Kent County Chamber of Commerce Inc., P.O. Box 146, Chestertown 21620 (301/778-0416).
12. Ocean City Visitors & Convention Bureau, Inc., P.O. Box 116, Ocean City 21842 (301/289-8181).
13. Prince George's Travel Promotion Council, Inc., 6600 Kenilworth Avenue, Riverdale 20737 (301/927-0700).
14. St. Mary's County Department of Economic and Community Development, P.O. Box 653, Leonardtown 20650 (301/475-5621).
15. Somerset County Tourism Commission, P.O. Box 243, Princess Anne 21853 (301/651-2968).
16. St. Mary's County Chamber of Commerce, Route 5, Box 41A, Mechanicsville 20659 (301/884-2148).
17. Snow Hill Chamber of Commerce, P.O. Box 176, Snow Hill 21863.
18. Talbot County Chamber of Commerce, P.O. Box 1366, Easton 21601 (301/822-4606).
19. Tourism Council of the Upper Chesapeake, P.O. Box 66, Centreville 21617 (301/758-2300).
20. Tri-County Council of Southern Maryland, P.O. Box 1634, Charlotte Hall 20622 (301/884-2144).

21. Wicomico Convention & Visitors Bureau, Glen Avenue Ext., Salisbury 21801 (301/546-3466).

MUSEUMS

1. *Baltimore:* Center for Urban Archeology, 802 East Lombard Street 21202 (301/396-3156); Cloisters Children's, 10440 Falls Road, Brooklandville 21022 (301/823-2250); Courtyard Exhibition Center, 800 East Lombard Street 21202 (301/396-9910); Industry, 1415 Key Highway 21230 (301/727-4808); Lilly Carroll Jackson, 1320 Eutaw Place 21217 (301/523-1208); Lovely Lane, 2200 Paul Street 21218 (301/889-1512); Maritime, Pier 4, Pratt Street 21202 (301/396-5528); National Aquarium, Pier 4, Pratt Street 21202 (301/576-3800); Public Works, 701 Eastern Avenue 21202 (301/396-5565); Science, 601 Light Street 21230 (301/685-2370); Street Car, 1901 Falls Road 21211 (301/547-0264); Zoo, Druid Hill Park 21211 (301/366-5466).
2. *Southern Maryland:* Patuxent Naval Air Station Museum, Lexington Park 20653 (301/863-7418).
3. *National Capital area:* National Capital Trolley Museum, Wheaton (301/384-9797).

NATIONAL PARKS

1. Assateague Island National Seashore, Route 2, Box 294, Berlin 21782 (301/432-5124).
2. Chesapeake and Ohio Canal National Historical Park, Great Falls Tavern, 11710 MacArthur Boulevard, Potomac 20854 (301/299-2026) or P.O. Box 4, Sharpsburg 21782 (301/739-4200); canal boat rides (301/229-2026).
3. Clara Barton National Historic Site, 5801 Oxford Road, Glen Echo 20812 (301/492-6245).
4. Fort McHenry National Monument and Historic Shrine, East Fort Avenue, Baltimore 21230 (301/962-4290).
5. Fort Washington Park, National Capital Parks East, 1900 Anacostia Drive SE, Washington, DC 20020 (301/292-2112).
6. Glen Echo Park, MacArthur Boulevard, Glen Echo 20812 (301/492-6282).
7. Greenbelt Park, 6565 Greenbelt Avenue, Greenbelt 20770 (301/344-3948).
8. Oxon Hill Farm, 6411 Oxon Hill Road, Oxon Hill 20745 (301/839-1177).

STATE PARKS AND FORESTS

1. Assateague, Route 2, Box 293, Berlin 21811 (301/641-2120).

2. Calvert Cliffs, Route 4, Box 106A, Brandywine 20613 (301/888-1622).
3. Cedarville, Route 4, Box 106A, Brandywine 20613 (301/888-1622).
4. Chapel Point State Park, Route 1, Box 64, Marbury 20658 (301/743-7613).
5. Doncaster, P.O. Box 70, Laurel (301/792-7863) or Route 1, Box 425, Indian Head 20640 (301/934-2282).
6. Elk Neck Forest, 130 McKinneytown Road, North East 21901 (301/287-5777).
7. Elk Neck Park, 4395 Turkey Point Road, North East 21901 (301/287-5333).
8. Flag Ponds Nature Park, c/o Courthouse, Prince Frederick 20678 (301/586-1477 or 301/535-5327).
9. Gunpowder Falls, 10815 Harford Road, Glen Arm 21507 (301/592-2897).
10. Janes Island, Route 2, 40 Alfred Lawson Drive, Crisfield 21817 (301/968-1563).
11. Martinak, Deep Shore Road, Denton 21629 (301/479-1619).
12. Merkle Wildlife Sanctuary, 11704 Fenno Road, Upper Marlboro 20772 (301/888-1410).
13. Patapsco Valley, 8020 Baltimore National Pike, Ellicott City 21043 (301/461-5005).
14. Patuxent River, RR, Box 3380, Upper Marlboro 20772 (301/627-6074).
15. Pocomoke, Route 3, Box 237, Snow Hill 21863 (301/632-2566).
16. Point Lookout, Star Route, Box 48, Scotland 20687 (301/872-4342).
17. Rocks, 3318 Rocks Chrome Hill Road, Jarrettsville 21084 (301/557-7994).
18. Sandy Point, 800 Revell Highway, Annapolis 21401 (301/971-1249).
19. Seneca Creek, 11950 Clopper Road, Gaithersburg 20878 (301/924-2127).
20. Severn Run Natural Environmental Area, 800 Revell Highway, Annapolis 21401 (301/757-1841).
21. Smallwood, Route 1, Box 64, Marbury 20658 (301/743-7613).
22. Soldier's Delight Natural Environmental Area, 8020 Baltimore National Pike, Ellicott City 21043 (301/461-5005).
23. St. Clement's Island, Star Route, Box 48, Scotland 20687 (301/872-5688).
24. St. Mary's River, Star Route, Box 48, Scotland 20687 (301/872-5688).

25. Susquehanna, 801 Stafford Road, Havre de Grace 21078 (301/939-0643).
26. Seth, Deep Shore Road, Denton 21629 (301/479-1619).
27. Tuckahoe, Route 1, Box 23, Queen Anne 21657 (301/634-2810).
28. Wicomico, Powellville Work Center, Route 1, Box 136, Parsonburg 21801 (301/835-8686).
29. Wye Oak, Deep Shore Road, Denton 21629 (301/479-1619).

OTHER NATURE AREAS

1. Battle Creek Cypress Swamp Sanctuary, c/o Courthouse, Prince Frederick, MD 20678 (301/535-5327).
2. Jefferson Patterson Park and Museum, SR 2, Box 50A, St. Leonard 20685 (301/586-0050).
3. National Colonial Park, Accokeek 20607 (301/283-2115).
4. Smithsonian Institute for Environmental Studies, Contees Wharf Road, Edgewater 21037 (301/798-4424).

TOURS

1. *Annapolis:* Historic Annapolis Inc., Old Treasury Building, State Circle 21401 (301/267-8149); Maryland State House Tours, Hostess Desk, State House 21401 (301/269-3400); Naval Academy Guide Service, Ricketts Hall 21402 (301/267-3363); The Town Crier, 3 Church Circle Suite 100 21401 (301/268-0239); Three Centuries Tours, 48 Maryland Avenue 21401 (301/263-5401).
2. *Baltimore:* About Town Tours Inc. (301/592-7770); Alexander Tours (301/664-5577); Baltimore Good Times Tours (301/539-3330); Baltimore Rent-A-Tour, 3414 Phillips Drive 21208 (301/653-2998); Masterpieces in Baltimore (301/433-5617); Shoe Leather Safaris (301/764-8067); Women's Civic League (301/837-5424).
3. *National Capital region:* Heritage Tours, 768 Cecil Avenue, Millersville 21109 (301/923-2771).

Virginia

ART MUSEUMS

1. Belmont, the Gari Melchers Memorial Gallery, 224 Washington Street, Falmouth 22405 (703/373-3634).
2. Chrysler Museum, Olney Road & Mowbray Arch, Norfolk 23510 (804/622-1211).
3. Dewitt Wallace Decorative Arts Gallery, 325 Francis Street Williamsburg 23185 (804/220-7554).
4. Fairfax County Council of the Arts (703/642-5173).

5. Afro-American Art Museum, Hampton University, Hampton 23668 (804/727-5308).
6. Hermitage Foundation Museum, 7637 North Shore Road, Norfolk 23505 (804/423-2052).
7. Peninsula Fine Arts Center, Museum Drive, Newport News 23606 (804/596-8175).

BEACHES

1. Assateague Island (804/336-6577).
2. Buckroe Beach (804/727-1101).
3. Cape Charles (804/787-2460).
4. Colonial Beach (804/224-7532).
5. Gloucester Point (804/693-2425).
6. Mathews County Beach (804/725-9817).
7. Naylor's Beach, Northern Neck (804/333-3951).
8. Pohick Bay (703/339-6104).
9. Seashore State Park (804/481-4836).
10. Virginia Beach (804/428-8000).
11. Westmoreland State Park (804/493-8821).
12. White Stone Beach (804/435-1989).
13. Yorktown (804/898-0204).

BIKING

1. State Bicycle Coordinator, Virginia Department of Transportation, 1401 East Broad Street, Richmond, VA 23219 (804/786-2964).
2. Department of Parks & Recreation, City Hall, 2400 Washington Avenue, Newport News, VA 23607 (804/247-8451).
3. George Washington Parkway, McLean 22101 (703/759-2915).
4. Northern Virginia Regional Park Authority, 5400 Ox Road, Fairfax Station 22039 (703/352-5900).
5. Open Road Bicycle Tours Ltd., 1601 Summit Drive, Haymarket 22069 (703/754-4152).

BOATING

Canoeing

1. Canoe Cruisers Association, P.O. Box 572, Arlington 22216 (703/656-2586).

Cruises

1. *Eastern Shore:* Tangier Island Cruises, 2 Market Street, Onancock 23417 (804/787-8220).
2. *Hampton Roads: Hampton—Miss Hampton,* 710 Settlers Landing Road 23667 (803/727-6108). *Newport News*—Harbor Cruises,

Jefferson Avenue and 12th Street 23607 (804/245-1533). *Norfolk — Carrie B.,* Bay Street, Portsmouth 23704 (804/393-4735); *New Spirit,* 501 Front Street 23501 (804/627-7771;) *American Rover,* Suite 15B, Harbor Tower, 1 Harbor Court, Portsmouth 23704 (804/627-7245). *Virginia Beach — Miss Virginia Beach,* Virginia Beach Fishing Center, 5th Street and Pacific Avenue 23451 (804/425-9253).

3. *Middle Peninsula:* Rowe Marine Inc., P.O. Box 219, Achilles 23001 (804/642-4762); Rappahannock River Cruise, Warsaw 22572 (804/333-4656).

4. *Northern Neck: to Tangier —* Hopkins & Brothers Store, 2 Market Street, Onancock 23417 (804/787-8220), Tangier and Chesapeake Cruises Inc., Warsaw 22572 (804/333-4656); *to Smith Island —* Island and Bay Cruises Inc., Route 1, Box 289-R, Reedville, VA 22539 (804/453-3430).

5. *Northern Virginia:* Potomac Party Cruises Inc., Zero Prince Street, Alexandria 22314 (703/683-6076); Potomac Riverboat Co., 205 The Strand, Alexandria 22314 (703/684-0580).

Whitewater Outfitters

1. *Northern Virginia:* Blue Ridge Outfitters of Harper's Ferry, WV 25425 (304/725-3444); Outdoor School of Great Falls 22066 (703/759-7413); Inner Quest of Leesburg 22075 (703/478-1078).

Snorkeling/Scuba Diving

1. Lynnhaven Dive Charter, 1413 North Great Neck Road, Virginia Beach 23454 (804/481-7949).

2. Scuba Ventures, 2247B Great Neck Road, Virginia Beach 23455 (804/481-2132).

CAMPING

1. *Eastern Shore*

   Cape Charles — Cherrystone KOA Holiday Trav-L-Park, P.O. Box 545, Cheriton 23316 (804/331-3063). *Chincoteague —* Camper's Ranch, Ridge and Bunting roads 23336 (804/336-6371); Inlet View, P.O. Box 263 23336 (804/336-5126); Maddox, P.O. Box 82 23336 (804/336-6648); Tom's Cove 23336 (804/336-6498). *Jamesville —* Peaceful Beach 23398 (804/442-3224); Silver Beach 23398 (804/442-6107); *Onancock —* Sandpiper Cove, RFD Box 315 23417 (804/787-7781).

2. *Hampton Roads*

   Hampton — Gordon's Trailer Court, 321 South 1st Street 23664 (804/851-9205); Gosnold's Hope Park, Little Back River Road 23666 (804/727-6161); Grandview Pier Family Camp

Grounds, 54 South Bonita Drive 23664 (804/851-2811). *Newport News*—Newport News Park Campground, 13564 Jefferson Avenue 23603 (804/887-5381). *Virginia Beach*—Holiday Trav-L-Park, 1075 General Booth Boulevard 23451 (804/425-0249); KOA, 1240 General Booth Boulevard 23451 (804/428-1444); North Bay Shore, 3257 Colchester Road 23456 (804/426-7911); Seashore State Park, 2500 Shore Drive 23451 (804/490-3939); Seneca, 144 South Princess Anne Road 23457 (804/426-6241); Surfside at Sandbridge, 3665 South Sandpiper Road 23456 (804/426-2911). *Williamsburg*—Colonial Campgrounds, Route 646 23185 (804/565-2734); Holiday Trav-L-Park, Route 9, Box 249A, Williamsburg 23185 (804/595-2101); Jamestown Beach Campsites 23185 (804/229-7609); KOA, Route 4, Box 340B 23185 (804/565-2907).

3. *Middle Peninsula*

    Gloucester County—Gloucester Point, Route 4, Box 199, Hayes 23072 (301/877-0152). *Mathews County*—New Point, New Point 23125 (804/725-5120). *Middlesex*—Grey's Point Family Campground, P.O. Box 8, Topping 23169 (804/758-2485).

4. *Northern Neck:* Fredericksburg KOA, Route 3, Box 1275 22401 (703/898-7252); Lee Hall, Hague 22469 (804/472-2742); Leedstown, Oak Grove 22443 (804/224-7445); Monroe Bay, Colonial Beach 22443 (804/224-7481); Westmoreland State Park, Route 1, Box 600, Montross 22520 (804/493-8821).

5. *Northern Virginia*

    Bull Run Regional Park, Centreville 22020 (703/631-0550); Burke Lake Park, 7315 Ox Road, Fairfax Station 22039 (703/323-6600); Fredericksburg/Washington KOA, RFD 3, Box 1275, Fredericksburg 22401 (703/898-7252); Lake Fairfax Park, 1400 Lake Fairfax Drive, Reston 22090 (703/471-5415); Pohick Bay Regional Park, 10651 Gunston Road, Lorton 22079 (703/339-6104); Woodland's, 181 Eustace Road, Stafford 22554 (703/659-5452); Yogi Bear's Jellystone Park, 3071 Jefferson Davis Highway, Stafford 22554 (703/659-3447).

FISHING

Charter and Head Boats

Hampton Roads

1. *Hampton:* Captains Dee Johnson (*Reel Time*), Dandy Haven Marina 804/877-2721, Lewis Wiley (*Miss Charlie*), Jones Marina 804/723-0998, Johnny Crabtree (*After Five*), Marina Cove Boat Basin 804/851-0511.

2. *Poquoson:* Capt. Al Hartz (*Sandra*), Al Hartz Marina 804/868-6821.
3. *Norfolk-Virginia Beach: Cobb's Marina* — Captains P. T. Hodges (*Elmon*), Chuck Moltz (*Gusto*), Harry Morgan (*HustlerJr.*), Charles Lovell (*The Screaming Eagle*) 804/588-5401, and Charlie Ward (*Ballyhoo*) 804/464-5830. *D&M Marina* — Captains Kevin Farley (*Big D*), Kevin Seldon (*Nancy Ann*), and H. B. Parker (*Kristen B.*) 804/481-7211. *Fisherman's Wharf Marina* — Captains Marshall Smith (*Marsha Ann*) 804/422-3499, Rick Reid (*Iemanja*) 804/460-3711, Joe Monds (*Alibi*) 804/490-3581, Bob Cozzens (*Great Expectations*), and Milton Sykes 804/460-9443, Charles Alexander (*Wake Breaker*) 804/464-2742; Pee Wee Morris (*Teaser*), Charlie Brown (*Ocean Atlantic*), and Steve Richardson (*Smith Ltd.*) 804/428-2111; Chris Cloverdale (*Abraxas*) 804/428-1000; Jim Rickman (*Cherokee*) 804/473-1633. *Virginia Beach Fishing Center* — Captains Fred Feller (*Sea Sport*) 804/425-9253; Fred Tyler (*Four T's*) 804/425-6088; Tommy English (*Anxious*), Linwood Martens (*Rainbow*), David Wright (*High Hopes*), Joe West (*Mar-Kim*), Jeff Parks (*Miss Virginia Beach*), Albert Bonney (*Bros. Pride*), John Fleet (*Poor Girl*), Wayne Smith (*Follow-The-Sun*), Dennis Johnson (*Chelsea*), Jimmy Seeds (*Our Dream*), Mike Mayo (*Rhonda*), Bill Powell (*Wil Kat*), Bill Moore and Mike Peel (*Pinafore*), Richard Howell (*Obsession*), Mike Romeo (*Ocean Master* and *O Four*), Sam Smith (*Cindy Loo*), Dave Eason (*Virginian*), B. G. Smith (*Hustler*), Billy Carroll (*Top Hook*), and Don Griffith (*Kingfisher*), all 804/425-9253.

Middle Peninsula

1. *Deltaville: Broad Creek* — Captains J. W. Blue (*Susan Carole*) 804/776-6283, B. W. Miller (*Dawn II*) 804/776-9885; Herbert Pinchefsky (*Pretty Lady*) 804/358-8691, Buddy Allen (*Buddy Lee*) 804/776-6694, Buck Hobeck (*Sweet Pea*) 804/776-7804, Bruce Walthall (*Snafu*) 804/776-9841. *Jackson Creek* — Captains Edmond Harriow (*Miss Ruth*) 804/776-9661, Walter Harrow (*Miss Nan*) 804/776-9556, Willie O. Robinson (*Captina O.*) 804/776-9864, Howard McNamara (*Myrtle M.*) 804/776-9786, Edmond Ruark (*Patty Lee II*) 804/776-9394.
2. *Gloucester Point: Sarah's Creek* — Capt. Jimmy Payne (*Florence Marie*) 804/642-2786.
3. *Grey's Point:* Capt. Arthur H. Kidd Sr. (*Pat*) 804/758-2666. *Locklies Marina* — Captains William T. Miller (*Wild Bill*), A. F. Henderson (*Modema*). John D. Miller (*John Boy*), Oscar Fitchett (*Sherwood*), John Homes (*Miss Florence*), Joseph Thornton (*Davea*),

Edward Kidd (*Kathy*), Ben Wormley (*Frances G.*), Robert Miller (*Lee*), John Muse (*Ginger II*), Dale Cook (*Michael C.*), James Thornton (*Miss Ruth*), William Glenn (*Bonita*), and Jim Thompson (*Locklie's Lady*), all 804/758-2871. Wilton Creek (*Piankatank*): Capt. John Willis (*Muriel Eileen*) 804/776-6790.
4. *Tappahannock:* Capt. Bob Handly (*Bunapa II*) 804/443-2339.

Eastern Shore

1. *Cape Charles:* Captains Johnny Netherland (*Mako II*) 804/331-1585, Charles Cook (*SST*) 804/331-1612, Vernon Lewis (*El Pescadore*) 804/331-2058, Don Stiles (*Elizabeth*) 804/336-5433, Monty Webb (*Safari*) 804/331-3235, Walter Lewis (*Nancy May*) 804/331-2369, Ray Cardone (*Miss Jenifer*) 804/464-1669, Adrian Parks (*Klondike I*) 804/331-1228, and Otis Asal (*Buccaneer*) 804/331-2722.
2. *Chincoteague:* Captains Floyd Birch (*Regina S.*) 804/336-6490; Norman Jester (*Roie Lee*) 804/336-6265; Lloyd Reed (*Pinecove*) 804/336-6669; Walter Reed (*Eva K.*) 804/336-5458; Billy Birch (*The Virginian*) 804/336-5430; John Abbaticchio (*Raider*) 804/336-5722; Donald Chernix (*Betty J.*) 804/336-6865; George Taylor (*Osprey*) 804/336-6374; and Steve Finchbaugh (*Canyon Connection*) 804/336-5456.
3. *Oyster:* Captains Buster Hall (*Wanda-Fay*) 804/331-2044, David Bell (*Mary Page*) 804/678-5498, and Jack Brady (*Little Bit*) 804/331-2111.
4. *Quinby:* Captains Nick Nekunas (*Kelly Marie*) 804/665-5011, Archie Doughty, Jr. (*J-Mar*) 804/442-6258, and Charles Roberts (*Timmy Kay*) 804/442-7214.
5. *Sanford*—Capt. J. P. Cutler (*EC II*) 804/824-5068.
6. *Wachapreague*—Captains Bobby Cherrix (*Sea Fox*), Billy Colonna (*Cap'n Bill*), Gordon Eastlake (*Margo A.*), Zed Lewis (*Rebel*), Lawrence Jester, Jr. (*Nomad*), Nat Atkinson (*Foxy Lady*), Buddy Thornton (*Lu-Lu*), Ray Parker (*Sea Bird*), Jimmy Wallace (*Canyon Lady*), Mark Wallace (*Melissa D.*), Sam Parker (*Scorpio*), Bobby Turner (*Bonnie Sue*), Earl Parker (*Virnanjo*), Frank McNeal (*Aqua-Gem*); George McCullough (*Janie-Mac*), Jeff Pitts, and Ken Davenhall, all 804/787-2105.

Northern Neck

1. *Callao area:* Captains John Klar (*Pur Sang*) 804/529-6801; R. L. Dixon (*Gracie D.*) 804/529-6931; Robert Stoner (*Sweet Thing II*) and John K. Stoner (*Sweet Thing*) 804/529-7370; Jim Loop (*20th Century*) 804/529-6622.

2. *Hartfield:* Capt. John C. Willis *(Muriel Ellen)* 804/776-6790.
3. *Lewisetta:* Captains Chuck Obler *(Miss Pam II)* 804/529-6450; David Rowe *(Ken-Ma-Ray)* 804/529-6725; Willie Thomas *(Willie B.)* 804/529-7345; Richard Woodward *(Playtime)* 804/472-3717; Herb Barnes *(Mamie)* 804/472-2486; and Warren Lowery *(Kathy L.)* 804/529-6276.
4. *Lottsburg:* Captains Frank Castle *(Meg C.)* 804/262-2857; Maxwell Davis *(Cin-Cat)* 804/333-3891; and Kelly Fisher *(Blurok)* 804/529-6645.
5. *Reedville: Jett's Hardware* — Captains Danny Wadsworth *(Virginia Breeze)* 804/435-4612, Don Kuykendall *(Don-El)* and Kenny Kuykendall *(Lynch's Point)* 804/580-7452, Fred Biddlecomb *(Dudley)* 804/453-3568, Wayson Christopher *(Betty Jane)* 804/580-5904; John Hudnall *(Earnie Cheryl)* 804/580-7452, Ed Meisenheimer *(Fair Wind)* 804/453-3509; and Francis Swift *(Little Gull)* 804/453-3413. *Smith Point Charter Boat Association* — Captains Fletcher Potts *(Mar-Chelle II)* and Cecil Howdershell *(Mar-Chelle)* 804/453-4554, Richard Wood *(Sunchaser)* 804/222-8819, *Wayne Hennage (Challenger II)* 804/493-8557, Wallace Lewis *(Hiawatha)* 804/453-5852, Danny Crabbe *(Kit)* 804/453-3251, Rick DeVivi *(New Life)* 804/453-7644, Bill Jenkins *(Miss Kathy II)* 804/453-3513, Roy Amburn *(Corsair)* 804/798-5183, Fred Maxwell *(Wahoo)* 804/453-3491, and Tabb Justis *(Captain Tabb)* 804/776-9850. *Smith Point Marina* — Captains Otis Shook, Jr. *(Sherry Jerry)* 804/633-6045, Rap Shepherd *(Southern Belle)* 804/462-7149, Henry Smith *(Iona)* 804/453-4474, Bob Warren *(Sunrise)* 804/453-4639, Don Markwith *(Midnight Sun)* 804/224-7082, Walter Parkinson *(Big Dipper)* 804/224-0896, Russ Burroughs *(Misty Blue)* 804/453-3525, and Jim Hardy *(Misty)* 804/453-4077, Sid Hilton or Robert Taylor *(Crying Shame)* 804/443-2298 or 804/443-3565.
6. *Warsaw:* Capt. William Garland *(Hobo II)* 804/333-4329.

Freshwater Guides

1. Charlie Taylor (Potomac, Rappahannock, etc.) 703/430-4137.
2. Mike Boucher (lower James River) 804/744-2732.

Marinas

1. *Eastern Shore: Cape Charles* — King's Creek 23310 (804/331-3789); Cape Charles Harbor of Refuge 23310 (804/331-2058). *Chincoteague* — R&R 23336 (804/336-6176). *Quinby* — Harbor 23423 (804/442-3651). *Wachapreague* — Wachapreague Seaside 23480 (804/787-4110).
2. *Hampton Roads: Grafton* — Chisman Creek, 821 Railroad Road

23692 (804/898-3000). *Hampton*—Sunset Yachting Center, 4330 Kecoughtan Road 23669 (804/722-3325); Marina Cove, 600 Harris Creek Road 23669 (804/851-0511). *Newport News*—Harborview, 450 Menchville Road 23602 (804/877-9555); James River, 665 Deep Creek Road 23602 (804/930-1909). *Norfolk*—Cobbs, 4524 Dunning Street 23518 (804/588-5401); Harrison's Boat House, 414 West Ocean View Avenue 23503 (804/588-9968); Willoughby Bay, 1651 Bayville Street 23503 (804/588-2663). *Poquoson*—Al Hartz, 127 River Road 23662 (804/868-6821). *Seaford*—Mills, 1742 Back Creek Road 23696 (804/898-4411). *Virginia Beach:* Bubba's, 3323 Shore Drive 23451 (804/481-3513); Lynnhaven Waterway, 2101 North Great Neck Road 23455 (804/481-7517). *Yorktown*—Wormley Creek Marina, 1221 Waterview Road 23692 (804/898-5060).

3. *Middle Peninsula: Gloucester*—Gloucester Point 23072 (804/642-6156); Cook's Landing, Route 2, Hayes 23072; Freeport, Route 673, Gloucester 23072 (804/693-4217). *Middlesex County*—Locklies, Topping 23169 (804/758-2871); Holiday, Achilles 23001 (804/642-2528); Mobjack Bay, Mathews 23118 (804/725-7559); Peninsula Marine, Urbanna 23175 (804/758-5985); Glass Marine, Route 656, Glass 23072 (804/642-2800).

4. *Northern Neck:* Branson's Cove, Coles Point 22442 (804/472-3866); Kinsale Harbour Marina, P.O. Box 189, Kinsale 22488 (804/472-2514); Yeocomico Marina, Kinsale 22488 (804/472-2977).

5. *Northern Virginia:* Marine International, 2121 Military Road, Arlington 22207 (703/243-0496); Prince William, 207 Mill, Occoquan 22125 (703/550-9808); Tyme n' Tyde, 14603 Featherstone Road, Woodbridge 22191 (703/550-7313).

Fishing Piers

1. *Norfolk:* Harrison's, 414 West Ocean View Avenue, Norfolk 23503 (804/587-9630); Ocean View, 300 East Ocean View Avenue, Norfolk 23503 (804/587-5276); Willoughby Bay, 1525 Bayville Street, Norfolk 23503 (804/588-2663).

2. *Peninsula:* Buckroe Beach, Resort Boulevard, Hampton 23664 (804/851-9146); Grandview, South Bonita Drive, Hampton 23664 (804/851-2811); James River, James River Bridge, Newport News 23607 (804/247-0364).

3. *Virginia Beach:* Lynnhaven Inlet, 2350 Starfish Road 23455 (804/481-7071); Sea Gull, Chesapeake Bay Bridge-Tunnel, Cape Charles 23310 (804/464-4641); Virginia Beach, 15th and Ocean Front, Virginia Beach 23451 (804/428-2333).

Ramps (State Maintained)

1. *Eastern Shore*
   Accomack—Chesconnessex, SR (State Route) 655 three miles north of Onancock; Folly Creek, SR 651 three miles from Accomac; Onancock, end of SR 178; Quinby, end of SR 727; Saxis, end of SR 695; Wishart Point, SR 695 two miles from Atlantic. *Northampton*—Cape Charles, SR T-1100; Morley's Wharf, SR 606 four miles west of Exmore; Oyster, SR 1802; Red Bank, SR 617 east of Nassawaddox; Willis Wharf, SR 603 east of Exmore.

2. *Hampton Roads*
   Charles City—Morris Creek, SR 621 five miles southeast of Holdcroft. *Chesapeake*—Great Bridge, SR 168; Dismal Swamp, SR 17. *Hampton*—Fox Hill, end of Dandy Point Road. *Isle of Wight*—Joyners Bridge, SR 611 four miles north of Franklin; Tyler's Beach, SR 686 nine miles northwest of Smithfield. *Newport News*—Denbigh, SR 173. *Norfolk*—Willoughby, View Street at Ocean View. *Suffolk*—Lake Curtis, SR 626. *Surry*—Lawnes Creek, SR 650 five miles north of Bacon Castle. *Virginia Beach*—Back Bay, Mill Landing Road; Owl Creek Municipal, General Booth Boulevard; Pocahontas-Trojan, Bay Landing Road. *York*—Messick, SR 171 in Poquoson; Tide Mill, SR 600 two miles northeast of Tabb.

3. *Middle Peninsula*
   Essex—Hoskin's Creek, Dock Street, Tappahannock. *Gloucester*—Deep Point, SR 606 eight miles southeast of Glenns; Gloucester Point, Route 1208; Tanyard, SR 617; Warehouse, SR 621. *King & Queen*—Melrose, SR 602 four miles from King and Queen Court House; Waterfence, SR 611 nine miles north of West Point. *King William*—Aylett, SR 600; Lester Manor, SR 672 eight miles south of King William Courthouse; West Point, SR 23. *Mathews*—Gwynn's Island, SR 223; Town Point, SR 615. *Middlesex*—Mill Creek, SR 799 three miles north of Hartfield; Mill Stone, SR 608 six miles north of Church View; Saluda, SR 618.

4. *Northern Neck*
   Northumberland—Coopers, SR 707 five miles west of Burgess; Shell, SR 657 two miles southeast of Reedville. *Richmond*—Carter's Wharf, SR 622 six miles southeast of Montross; Simonson, SR 606 six miles south of Farnham; Totusky, SR 3 three miles southeast of Warsaw. *Westmoreland*—Bonum's Creek, SR 763 five miles north of Kinsale; Colonial Beach, SR T-1156.

5. *Northern Virginia: Fairfax*—Lake Burke, SR 123, seven miles south of City of Fairfax.

HIKING

1. Virginia Trails Association, 13 West Maple, Alexandria 22301 (703/548-7490).
2. Northern Virginia Regional Park Authority, 5400 Ox Road, Fairfax Station 22039 (703/352-5900).

HISTORIC SITES AND ORGANIZATIONS

Organizations

1. Historic Fredericksburg Foundation Inc., P.O. Box 162, Fredericksburg 22401 (703/371-4504).
2. Historic Garden Week in Virginia, 12 East Franklin Street, Richmond 23219 (804/643-7141).
3. The Center for Historic Preservation, Mary Washington College, Fredericksburg 22401 (703/899-4037).

Leading Attractions

1. *Eastern Shore*

   Accomac — Historic District, Eastern Shore of Virginia Tourism Commission, P.O. Box 147, Accomac 23301 (804/787-2460).

   Cape Charles — Historic District, Cape Charles/Northampton County Chamber of Commerce, 207 Mason Avenue 23310 (804/331-2304).

   Eastville — Historic District (same address and telephone as *Accomac*).

   Onancock — Kerr Place, 69 Market Street 23417 (804/787-8012); Hopkins & Brother Store, 2 Market Street, 23417 (804/787-8220).
2. *Hampton Roads*

   Hampton — Casemate Museum, Ft. Monroe 23651 (804/727-3935); Langley NASA Museum, Langley Laboratory, National Aeronautics and Space Administration 23665 (804/865-2855).

   Newport News — Army Transportation Museum, Fort Eustis 23604 (804/878-1109); The Mariners Museum, Museum Drive 23606 (804/595-0368).

   Norfolk: Hampton Roads Naval Museum, Norfolk Naval Station 23511 (804/444-3827); Hunter House Victorian Museum, 240 West Freemason Street 23510 (804/623-9814); MacArthur Memorial, MacArthur Square 23510 (804/441-2965); Moses Myers and Willoughby-Baylor houses, East Freemason Street 23510 (804/622-1211); St. Paul's Church, 201 St. Paul Boulevard 23510 (804/627-4353). *Portsmouth* — Naval Shipyard Museum, P.O. Box 850 23795 (804/393-8591).

   Virginia Beach — Adam Thoroughgood House, 1636 Parish

Road 23455 (804/622-1211); Lynnhaven House, 4405 Wishart Road 23455 (804/460-1688).

Yorktown — National Historical Park, P.O. Box 210, Yorktown 23690 (804/898-3400); Victory Center, P.O. Box 1976, Yorktown, VA 23690 (804/887-1776).

3. *Middle Peninsula*

Middlesex — County Courthouse, P.O. Box 158, Saluda, VA 23149 (804/758-5540).

4. *Northern Neck*

Fredericksburg — James Monroe Law Office, 908 Charles Street 23401 (703/373-8426); Kenmore, 1201 Washington Ave. 22401 (703/373-3381); Mary Washington House, 1200 Charles Street 23401 (703/373-1569); Museum & Cultural Center, P.O. Box 922 22404 (703/371-5668); Rising Sun Tavern, 1304 Caroline Street 23401 (703/371-1494).

Irvington — Christ Church 22480 (804/438-6855).

King George County — St. Paul's Episcopal Church, King George 22458 (703/663-3085).

Lancaster — Mary Ball Memorial Museum and Library, P.O. Box 97 22503 (804/462-7280).

Stratford — Stratford Hall Plantation 22558 (804/493-8038).

5. *Northern Virginia*

Alexandria — Carlyle House, 121 North Fairfax Street 22314 (703/549-2997); Christ Church, 118 North Washington Street 22314 (703/549-1450); Collingwood Library and Museum on Americanism, 801 East Boulevard Drive 22308 (703/765-1652); Fort Ward Museum and Park, Department of Parks and Cultural Activities, 1108 Jefferson Street 22314 (703/838-4848); Gadsby's Tavern, 132 North Royal Street 22314 (703/838-4242); George Washington Masonic National Shrine, 101 Calahan Drive 22301 (703/683-2007); Old Presbyterian Meeting House, 321 South Fairfax Street 22314 (703/549-6670).

Fairfax — Sully Plantation, 3701 Pender Drive, Fairfax 22030 (703/737-1794).

Great Falls — Colvin Mill Historic Site, 10017 Colvin Run 22066 (703/759-2771).

Herndon — Dranesville Tavern, 1119 Leesburg Pike 22070 (703/759-5241).

Lorton — Gunston Hall 22079 (703/550-9220).

McLean — Claude Moore Colonial Farm, 6310 Georgetown Pike 22101 (703/442-7557).

Mount Vernon — Mount Vernon 22121 (703/780-2000); Woodlawn, P.O. Box 37 22121 (703/557-7880).

Historic Inns and B&Bs

1. *Eastern Shore*

    Cape Charles—Sea Gate, 9 Tazewell Street 23310 (804/331-2206); Pickett's Harbor, P.O. Box 97AA, Cape Charles 23310 (804/331-2212). *Eastville*—Eastville Inn 23347 (804/678-5551). *Wachapreague*—Burton House, 11 Brooklyn Street 23480. *Willis Wharf*—E. L. Willis & Co. 23486 (804/442-4225).

2. *Hampton Roads*

    Hampton—Chamberlin Hotel, Old Point Comfort 23651 (804/723-6511).

    Smithfield—Smithfield Inn and Tavern, 112 East Main Street 23430 (804/357-0244).

3. *Middle Peninsula*

    Gloucester—Seawell's Ordinary, Ordinary 23131 (804/642-3635).

4. *Northern Neck*

    Montross—Inn at Montross, Courthouse Square 22520 (804/493-9097). *Lancaster*—The Inn at Levelfields, P.O. Box 216 22503 (804/435-6887). *Morattico*—Holly Point 22523 (804/462-7759). *Warsaw*—Greenwood, Route 2, Box 50 22572 (804/333-4353).

5. *Northern Virginia: Alexandria*—Historic homes, 819 Prince Street 22314 (703/683-2159); Old Gadsby's Tavern, 138 North Royal Street 22314 (703/548-1288); *Clifton*—Hermitage, 7134 Main Street 22024 (703/266-1623). *Occoquan*—Rockledge, 410 Mill Street 22125 (703/690-3377). *Mount Vernon*—Cedar Knoll Inn, P.O. Box 34 22121 (703/360-7880).

6. *Tangier*—Hilda Crockett's Chesapeake House 23440 (804/891-2331).

HUNTING

License and Other Information

1. Department of Game and Inland Fisheries, P.O. Box 11104, Richmond 23230 (804/257-1000).

Public Places

1. Back Bay Hunting Area, 737 acres, blinds allocated by lottery. Area Manager, Department of Game and Inland Fisheries, P.O. Box 7100, Virginia Beach 23457.

2. Chickahominy Wildlife Management Area, 5,111 acres in Charles City County, deer, turkey, waterfowl, quail and small animals, floating wildlife blinds only. WMA Supervisor, Route 1, Box 115, Charles City 23030.

3. Chincoteague National Wildlife Refuge. Refuge Manager, P.O. Box 62, Chincoteague 23336.
4. False Cape State Park, 3,412 acres in Virginia Beach, limited waterfowl. Area Manager, Commission of Game and Inland Fisheries, P.O. Box 7100, Virginia Beach 23457.
5. Great Dismal Swamp Refuge Manager, Box 349, Suffolk 23434.
6. Hog Island Waterfowl Management Area, 3908 acres in Surry County, waterfowl and bow hunting for deer. Area Manager, Department of Game and Inland Fisheries, Surry 23883.
7. Mockhorn Island Wildlife Management Area, 9,452 acres in Northampton County, rail and waterfowl. WMA Supervisor, P.O. Box 212, Hallwood 23359.
8. Pettigrew Wildlife Management Area, 934 acres in Caroline County, deer, quail, and small animals. WMA Supervisor, Route 4, Box 126F, Amelia 23002.
9. Rugged Island Wildlife Management Area, 1,537 acres in Isle of Wight County, waterfowl and deer. WMA Supervisor, Surry 23883.
10. Saxis Wildlife Management Area, 5,775 acres in Accomack County, rail, waterfowl and deer. WMA Supervisor, P.O. Box 212, Hallwood 23339.
11. *Military areas that admit some civilians:* Marine Corps Development and Education Command, Quantico (703/640-5523 or 640-5218) and Fort A. P. Hill Military Reservation in Caroline County (804/633-8300 or 633-8219).
12. *Private lands that permit some hunting: Hampton Roads and Middle Peninsula areas,* Hunting Permits, Chesapeake Corporation, Box 311, West Point 23181; Continental Forest Investments, Inc., P.O. Box 1041, Hopewell 23860; and Flippo Lumber Corporation, Box 38, Doswell 23047. *In the Northern Neck,* Hunting Permits, Chesapeake Corporation, Box 942, Warsaw 22572; Glatfelter Pulp Wood Company, District Manager, Box 868, Fredericksburg 22404; and Flippo. *On the Eastern Shore,* Hunting Permits, Chesapeake Corporation, P.O. Box 300, Pokomoke City, MD 21851.

Guides

Ducks, Geese, Fish
1. Pedro Cartright, 3993 Melby Creek Road, Virginia Beach 23456 (Back Bay) (804/426-6418).
2. Lake Chesdin Guide Service (Chesdin, Gaston, Anna) (804/520-1367).
3. Dean Davis (Back Bay waterfowl), 1317 Ship's Cabin Road, Virginia Beach, VA (804/426-2061).

4. Sonny Gregory (Back Bay waterfowl), 4052 Muddy Creek Road, Virginia Beach 23457 (804/426-6659).
5. Andy Linton, Chincoteague 23336 (804/336-6717).
6. Dardin Lovett (Back Bay bass/waterfowl), Muddy Creek Road, Virginia Beach 23457 (804/426-6415).
7. Earl Parker, Wachapreague 23480 (804/787-3341).
8. Ray D. Shepherd (Rappahannock River fish/waterfowl), P.O. Box 47, Monticello 22523 (804/462-7149).
9. Tom Smith (Eastern Shore geese), Eastville 23347 (804/678-5416).
10. Jimmy Wallace, Wachapreague 23480 (804/787-3272).
11. Tom Webb, Route 183, Jamesville 23398 (804/442-7684).

INFORMATION SOURCES

Chambers of Commerce

1. Alexandria, P.O. Box 359, Alexandria 22311 (703/549-1000).
2. Annandale, 7263 Maple Place, Annandale 22003 (703/256-7232).
3. Arlington, 4600 N. Fairfax Drive Suite 120, Arlington 22203 (703/625-2400).
4. Chesapeake Council-Hampton Roads Chamber of Commerce, P.O. Box 1776, Chesapeake 23320 (804/547-2118).
5. Chincoteague, P.O. Box 258, Chincoteague 23336 (804/336-6161).
6. Colonial Beach, 2 Boundary Street, Colonial Beach 22443 (804/224-7531).
7. Eastern Shore of Virginia, P.O. Box 147, Accomac 23301 (804/787-2460).
8. Fairfax City, 10856 Main Street, Fairfax 22030 (703/591-5550).
9. Fairfax County, 8100 Oak Street Suite 32, Dunn Loring 22027 (703/573-9458).
10. Greater Falls Church, P.O. Box 491, Falls Church 22046 (703/532-1050).
11. Fredericksburg-Stafford-Spotsylvania, P.O. Box 7476, Fredericksburg 22401 (703/373-9400).
12. Gloucester, P.O. Box 296, Gloucester 23061 (804/693-2425).
13. Hampton Roads, P.O. Box 327, Norfolk 23501 (804/622-2312).
14. Herndon, P.O. Box 327, Herndon 22070 (703/437-5556).
15. Isle of Wight/Smithfield, P.O. Box 38, Smithfield 23430 (804/357-3502).
16. Kilmarnock, Box 1357, Kilmarnock 22482 (804/435-1111).
17. Mathews, Box 1126, Mathews 23109 (804/725-4026).
18. Norfolk Council-Hampton Roads, P.O. Box 327, Norfolk 23501 (804/622-2312).

19. Virginia Peninsula, P.O. Box 7267, Hampton 23666 (804/838-4182).
20. Portsmouth Council-Hampton Roads, P.O. Box 70, Portsmouth 23704 (804/397-3453).
21. Prince William, P.O. Box 495, Manassas 22110 (703/368-4813).
22. Springfield, P.O. Box 823, Springfield 22150 (703/971-1977).
23. Suffolk Council-Hampton Roads, 1001 West Washington Street, Suffolk 23434 (804/539-2111).
24. Tappahannock, P.O. Box 156, Tappahannock 22560 (804/443-2717).
25. Urbanna, Drawer C, Urbanna 23175 (804/758-5540).
26. Virginia Beach Council-Hampton Roads, 4512 Virginia Beach Boulevard, Virginia Beach 23462 (804/490-1221).
27. Warsaw-Richmond County, Route 2, Box 115, Warsaw 22572 (804/333-4436).
28. West Point Area Improvement Association, P.O. Box 1035, West Point 23181.
29. White Stone, White Stone 22578 (804/435-1989).
30. Williamsburg Area, P.O. Drawer HQ, Williamsburg 23185 (804/662-4118).

Visitor Bureaus

1. Alexandria Tourist Council, 221 King Street, Alexandria 22314 (703/549-0205).
2. Arlington Visitors Service, 100 North 14th Street, Arlington 22201 (703/558-2536) or Arlington County information, 735-18th Street, Arlington 22204 (703/521-0772).
3. Cape Charles Director of Planning and Development, P.O. Box 391, Cape Charles 23310 (804/331-4820).
4. City of Fairfax Public Information Office, Room 311, City Hall, 10455 Armstrong St. 22030 (703/385-7855).
5. Fairfax County Tourism & Convention Bureau, 8300 Boone Boulevard Suite 450, Vienna 22180 (703/790-0600).
6. Fredericksburg Tourism, 706 Caroline Street, Fredericksburg 22401 (703/373-1776).
7. Hampton Department of Conventions and Tourism, 710 Settlers Landing Road, Hampton 23669 (804/727-6108).
8. Norfolk Convention & Visitors Bureau, 208 East Plume Street, Norfolk 23510 (804/441-5266).
9. Northampton Planning and Zoning, Courthouse, Eastville, VA 23347 (804/678-5872).
10. Virginia Peninsula Tourism & Conference Bureau, Patrick Henry International Airport, Newport News 23602 (804/881-9777).

11. Portsmouth Tourism, 801 Crawford Street, Portsmouth 23704 (804/393-8804).
12. Prince William County Office of Economic Development, 1 County Complex Court, Prince William 22192 (703/335-6680).
13. Virginia Beach Convention Bureau, P.O. Box 136, Virginia Beach 23458 (804/428-8000).
14. Williamsburg Area Tourism & Conference Bureau, P.O. Drawer GB, Williamsburg 23187 (804/253-0192).

MUSEUMS

1. *Eastern Shore:* Oyster Museum, Beach Road, Chincoteague 23336 (804/336-6117); Refuge Waterfowl Museum, Maddox Boulevard, Chincoteague 23336 (804/336-5800).
2. *Hampton Roads: Hampton*—Syms-Eaton Museum & Kecoughtan Indian Village, 418 West Mercury Boulevard 23669 (804/727-6348). *Newport News*—Mariners, Museum Drive 23606 (804/595-9398); War Memorial Museum of Virginia, 9385 Warwick Boulevard 23607 (804/247-8523); Virginia Living, 524 J. Clyde Morris Boulevard 23601 (804/595-1500). *Portsmouth*—The Portsmouth Museums, P.O. Box 850 23705. *Virginia Beach*—Maritime Historical, 24th and Oceanfront 23451 (804/422-1587); Virginia Marine Science, 717 General Booth Boulevard 23451 (804/425-3474).
3. *Northern Neck:* Montross Museum, Courthouse Square, Montross 22520 (804/493-8770).
4. *Northern Virginia:* U.S. Army Corps of Engineers Museum, 16th and Belvoir Road, Fort Belvoir 22060 (703/664-3171); Marine Corps Air-Ground Museum, Quantico 22134 (703/640-2606).

PARKS AND NATURAL AREAS

National

1. Assateague Island National Seashore, Virginia District Ranger, P.O. Box 38, Chincoteague 23336 (804/336-6577).
2. Back Bay National Wildlife Refuge, P.O. Box 6286, Virginia Beach 23456 (804/721-2412).
3. Chincoteague National Wildlife Refuge, Box 62, Chincoteague 23336 (804/336-6122).
4. Colonial National Historic Park, P.O. Box 210, Yorktown 23690 (804/898-3400).
5. Eastern Shore of Virginia National Wildlife Refuge, Route 1, Box 122B, Cape Charles 23310 (804/331-2760).
6. Fredericksburg and Spotsylvania National Military Park, Lafayette Boulevard and Sunken Road 22401 (703/373-4461).

7. George Washington Birthplace National Monument, RR 1, Box 717, Washington's Birthplace 22443 (804/224-1732).
8. George Washington Memorial Parkway, c/o Turkey Run Park, McLean 22101 (703/759-2169).
9. Great Falls Park, P.O. Box 66, Great Falls 22066 (703/285-2966).
10. Great Dismal Swamp, P.O. Box 349, Suffolk 23434 (804/986-3705).
11. Mackay Island National Wildlife Refuge, Knotts Island, NC 27950.
12. Manassas (Bull Run) National Battlefield Park, P.O. Box 1830 Manassas 22111 (703/754-7107).
13. Mason Neck National Wildlife Refuge, 14416 Jefferson Davis Highway Suite 20A, Woodbridge 22191 (703/690-1297).
14. Prince William National Forest Park, P.O. Box 209, Triangle 22171 (703/221-7181).

State

1. Virginia Division of Parks & Recreation, 1201 Washington Building, Richmond 23219 (804/786-1712).
2. Caledon Natural Area, Route 2, Box 1124, King George, VA 22485 (703/663-3861).
3. Chippokes Plantation State Park and Charles C. Steirly Heron Rookery, 23883 (804/294-3625).
4. False Cape State Park, Washwoods 23456 (804/426-7128).
5. George Washington Grist Mill State Historical Park, 5514 Mount Vernon Memorial Highway, Alexandria 22309 (703/780-3383).
6. Leesylvania State Park, Woodbridge, VA 22192 (703/670-0372).
7. Mason Neck State Park, 7301 High Point Road, Lorton 22079 (703/339-7256).
8. Parkers Marsh Natural Area, c/o Seashore State Park, 2500 Shore Drive, Virginia Beach 23459 (804/481-2131).
9. Seashore State Park Natural Area, 2500 Shore Drive, Virginia Beach 23451 (804/481-4836 or 804/481-2131).
10. Westmoreland State Park, Route 1, Box 600, Montross 22520 (804/493-8821).
11. Wreck Island Natural Area, 2500 Shore Drive, Virginia Beach 23451 (804/481-2131).
12. York River State Park, 5526 Riverview Road, Williamsburg 23185 (804/564-9057).

Other

1. *Hampton:* Bluebird Gap Farm, Parks Department 23369 (804/

727–6739); Grandview Refuge, Parks Department, City Hall 23669 (804/727-6347).

2. *Newport News:* Newport News Park, 13564 Jefferson Avenue 23602 (804/977-5211); Virginia Living Museum, 524 J. Clyde Morris Boulevard 23601 (804/595-1900).
3. *Norfolk:* Botanical Gardens, Airport Road 23518 (804/855-0194); Zoo, 3500 Granby Street 23504 (804/441-2706).
4. *Northern Virginia:* Fairfax County Park Authority, 4030 Hummer Road, Annandale 208033 (703/941-5000); Fraser Preserve, 2126 North Rolfe Street, Arlington 22209 (703/528-4952); Northern Virginia Regional Parks, 5400 Ox Road, Fairfax Station 22039 (703/352-5900); Pohick Bay Park, 10651 Gunston Road, Lorton 22079 (703/339-6100 or 703/528-5406 for canoe tours).
5. *Suffolk:* Bennett's Creek Park, Shoulders Hill Road 23435 (804/484-3984).
6. *Williamsburg:* Busch Gardens–The Old Country 23187 (804/220-2896).

RESORTS

1. *Northern Neck:* Tides Inn, Irvington 22480 (804/438-5000); Windmill Point Marine Resort, Windmill Point 22578 (804/435-1166).

TOURS

1. *Norfolk:* Naval Base (804/444-7955); free trolley shuttle bus (804/632-3222).
2. *Northern Neck:* Litchfield Ordinary and Tours, Wicomico Church 22579 (804/580-2236)
3. *Virginia Beach:* Wilderness E.A.S.T. (canoe, kayak, and bike trips), 847 Seahawk Circle Suite 104, Virginia Beach 23452 (804/427-3278).

District of Columbia

ART MUSEUMS

1. Arthur M. Sackler Gallery (Smithsonian), 1050 Independence Avenue SW 20560 (202/357-2104).
2. Corcoran Gallery of Art, 17th Street and New York Avenue NW 20006 (202/638-3211).
3. Freer Gallery of Art (Smithsonian), 12th Street and Jefferson Drive SW 20560 (202/357-2104).
4. Hirshhorn Museum & Sculpture Garden (Smithsonian), 7th Street and Independence Avenue SW 20560 (202/357-3235).

5. Howard University Gallery of Fine Arts, 2455-6th Street NW 20059 (202/636-7070).
6. Hillwood, 4155 Linnean Avenue NW 20008 (202/686-5807).
7. Museum of Modern Art of Latin America, 201-18th Street 20006 (202/789-0019).
8. National Gallery of Art, 6th Street and Constitution Avenue 20565 (202/737-4215).
9. National Museum of Women in the Arts, 13th Street and New York Avenue 20005 (202/783-5000).
10. National Museum of African Art (Smithsonian), 950 Independence Avenue SW 20560 (202/357-4600).
11. National Museum of American Art (Smithsonian), 8th and G streets NW 20560 (202/357-3111).
12. National Portrait Gallery (Smithsonian), 8th and F streets 20560 (202/357-2747).
13. Phillips Collection, 1600-21st Street NW 20009 (202/387-2151).
14. Renwick Gallery (Smithsonian), 17th Street at Pennsylvania Avenue 20560 (202/357-3111).

BIKING

1. Washington Area Bicyclist Association, 530 Seventh Street SE, Washington, DC 20003 (202/544-5349).
2. Bicycle Coordinator, Washington Department of Public Works, 2000-14th Street NW 7th Floor, Washington, DC 20009 (202/939-8016).
3. Commercial and Shenandoah Bicycle Touring, P.O. Box 65292, Washington, DC 20035.
4. Potomac Peddlers Touring Club, P.O. Box 23601, L'Enfant Plaza, Washington, DC 20026 (202/363-8687).
5. Bicycle Federation, 1818 R Street NW, Washington, DC 20009 (202/332-6986).

BOATING

Canoeing

1. Canoe Cruisers Association, P.O. Box 572, Arlington, VA 22216 (703/656-2586).

Cruises

1. *The Spirit of Washington,* 6th and Water streets SW 20024 (302/554-8000).

Marinas (see also *Northern Virginia, Suburban Maryland*)

1. Anacostia, 1900 M Street SE 20003 (202/544-5191).
2. Buzzard Point, 2200-1st Street NW 20001 (202/488-8400).

3. Gangplank, 600 Water Street SW 20024 (202/554-5000).
4. Washington, 1300 Maine Street 20024 (202/554-0222).

CAMPING (see also *Northern Virginia, Suburban Maryland*)

1. Chesapeake & Ohio Canal National Historic Park, P.O. Box 4, Sharpsburg, MD 21782 (302/739-4200).
2. Duncan's KOA, 5381 Sands Road, Lothian, MD 20711 (301/627-3909).
3. Greenbelt Park, 6501 Greenbelt Road, Greenbelt, MD 20770 (301/344-3948).
4. Lake Fairfax Park, 1400 Lake Fairfax Drive, Fairfax, VA 22090 (703/471-5415).
5. Prince William Forest Park, P.O. Box 209, Triangle, VA 20770 (301/344-3948).

HISTORIC SITES AND ORGANIZATIONS

1. Anderson House, 218 Massachusetts Avenue NW 20008 (202/785-0540).
2. B'nai Brith Klutznick Museum, 1640 Rhode Island Avenue NW 20036 (202/857-6583).
3. *Churches:* Franciscan Monastery, 14th and Quincy streets NE 20017 (202/526-6800); Islamic Center, 2551 Massachusetts Avenue NW 20008 (202/332-8343); National City Christian Church, Thomas Circle NW 20005 (202/232-03239); National Shrine of the Immaculate Conception, 4th Street and Michigan Avenue 20017 (202/526-8300); New York Avenue Presbyterian Church, 1313 New York Avenue NW 20005 (202/393-3700); St. John's Episcopal Church, Lafayette Square 20006 (202/347-8766); Washington National Cathedral, Massachusetts and Wisconsin avenues NW 20016 (202/537-6200).
4. Columbia Historical Society, 1307 New Hampshire Avenue NW 20036 (202/785-2068).
5. D.A.R. Constitution Hall and Museum, 1776 D Street NW 20006 (202/628-1776).
6. Decatur House, 748 Jackson Place NW 20006 (202/842-0920)
7. Folger Shakespeare Library, 201 East Capitol Street 20003 (202/544-7077).
8. Ford's Theater and Lincoln Museum, 511-10th Street NW 20004 (202/426-6924).
9. London Brass Rubbing Center, Washington Cathedral, Wisconsin, and Massachusetts avenues NW 20016 (202/364-9303).
10. Martin Luther King Library, 981 G Street NW 20001 (202/727-0321).
11. National Archives, 8th Street and Constitution Avenue NW 20508 (202/532-3183).

12. Octagon House, 18th Street and New York Avenue NW 20006 (202/638-3105).
13. Old Stone House, Georgetown (202/426-6851).
14. White House, 1600 Pennsylvania Avenue NE 20002—regular tours (202/456-2200 or 202/456-7041); garden tours (202/456-2200); Easter Egg hunt (202/456-2200).
15. Woodrow Wilson House Museum, 2340 S Street NW 20008 (202/387-4062).

Historic Inns and B&Bs

1. The Bed and Breakfast League Ltd., 3939 Van Ness Street NW 20008 (202/363-7767).
2. Kalorama Guest House at Woodley Park, 2700 Cathedral Avenue NW 20008 (202/667-6369).
3. Morrison-Clark, Massachusetts Avenue and 11th Street 20001 (202/898-1200).
4. Victorian Accommodations, 1309 Rhode Island Avenue NW 20005 (202/234-6292).

INFORMATION SOURCES

1. National Capital Parks-East, 1900 Anacostia Drive SE 20020.
2. Smithsonian Institution, 1000 Jefferson Drive SW 20560 (202/357-2700).
3. Washington Convention & Visitors Bureau, 1212 New York Avenue NW, Washington, DC 20005 (202/789-7000).

MONUMENTS

1. Jefferson Memorial (202/485-9666).
2. Lincoln Memorial (202/426-6841).
3. U.S. Navy Memorial (703/524-0830).
4. Vietnam Veterans Memorial (202/426-6841).
5. Washington Monument (202/426-6841).

MUSEUMS

1. Anacostia Neighborhood Museum (Smithsonian), 1901 Fort Place SE 20020 (202/287-3369).
2. Armed Forces Medical Museum, Walter Reed Army Medical Center, Washington 20036 (202/576-2348).
3. Arts and Industries Building (Smithsonian), 900 Jefferson Drive SW 20560 (202/357-2700).
4. Barney Studio House, 2306 Massachusetts Avenue NW 20560 (202/357-3111).
5. Bethune Museum-Archives, 1318 Vermont Avenue NW 20005 (202/332-9201).

6. Bureau of Engraving and Printing, 14th and C streets SW 20228 (202/447-9709).
7. Capital Children's Museum, 800-3rd Street NE 20002 (202/543-8600).
8. Department of Interior Museum, C Street 20240 (202/343-2743).
9. Federal Bureau of Investigation, E Street 20535 (202/324-3447).
10. National Air & Space Museum (Smithsonian), 6th Street and Independence Avenue SW 20560 (202/357-1400).
11. National Building Museum, F Street 20001 (202/272-2448).
12. National Geographic Society, 17th and M streets NW 20036 (202/857-7588).
13. National Museum of American History (Smithsonian), 14th Street and Constitution Avenue NW 20560.
14. National Museum of Natural History (Smithsonian), 10th Street and Constitution Avenue NW 20560 (202/357-2747).
15. National Museum of Women in the Arts, 13th Street and New York Avenue NW 20005 (202/783-5000).
16. Textile Museum, 2320 S Street NW 20008 (202/667-0441).
17. Washington Dolls House and Toy Museum, 5236-44th Street NW 20015 (202/244-0024).
18. Wonderlight Collection of Holography/Art, Science and Technology Institute, 2018 R Street NW 20009 (202/667-6322).

NATURE CENTERS

1. Ansel Adams Collection, 1400 Eye Street NW 20005 (202/785-0540).
2. Dumbarton Oaks, 1703-32nd Street NW 20007 (202/338-8278).
3. Kenilworth Aquatic Gardens, Kenilworth Avenue and Douglas Street NE 20019 (202/426-6905).
4. National Aquarium, Commerce Building 20235 (202/377-2825).
5. National Arboretum, 3501 New York Avenue NE 20002 (202/475-4815).
6. National Zoological Park, 3000-block Connecticut Avenue NW 20008 (202/673-4953).
7. Rock Creek Park: Nature Center, 5200 Glover Road NW 20015 (202/426-6829); horse rentals (202/362-0117); Pierce Mill (202/426-6908); Art Barn (202/426-6719).
8. Roosevelt Memorial, Turkey Run Park, George Washington Memorial Parkway, McLean, VA 22101 (202/285-2601)
9. U.S. National Arboretum, 3501 New York Avenue NE 20002 (202/475-4815).
10. U.S. Botanic Gardens, Maryland Avenue and First Street SW 20024 (202/225-8333).

TOURS

1. All About Town, 519-16th Street NW 20001 (202/393-1616).
2. Benefit Tours of Foreign Embassies (202/636-4225).
3. Capital Tours Ltd., 1517-27th Street NW 20001 (202/393-3696).
4. Gray Line, 4th and E streets SW 20004 (202/479-5900).
5. Gold Line Inc., 333 E Street SW 20024 (202/479-5900).
6. Old Town Trolley Tours, 3150 V Street NE 20018 (202/269-3020).
7. Tourmobile Sightseeing, 1000 Ohio Drive SW 20024 (202/554-5100).

Index

433

Prince Georges County, Maryland, 64, 76, 93, 364
Prince William County, Virginia, 308; forest park, 310–12
Pruitt, Mrs. Eva, 164
Pungoteague, Virginia, 176, 184, 185
Purcellville, Virginia, 316

Quantico, Maryland, 145
Queen Anne, 216
Queen Anne's County, Maryland, 29, 115, 123–27, 129; historical society, 124
Queenstown, Maryland, 124
Quinby, Virginia, 173, 176, 185, 190

Ramsey, Lt. Col. Nathaniel, 109
Redbank, Virginia, 190
Reed, Dr. Walter, 267
Reedville, Virginia, 27, 165, 167, 184, 284, 301
Reliance, Maryland, 142
Remington Farms Wildlife Management Demonstration Area, 120, 121
Reptiles and amphibians, 70, 140, 188, 313
Reston, Virginia, 309
Revolutionary War, 13, 14, 39, 48, 59, 60, 83, 96, 97, 99, 102, 108, 109, 110, 119, 120, 123, 129, 134, 138, 143, 153, 205, 224, 229, 230, 241, 256, 260, 266, 270, 271, 272, 277, 322, 330, 343
Rhodes Point, Maryland, 155, 167
Richie, Thomas, 274
Richmond, Virginia, 14, 33, 184
Richmond County, Virginia, 284, 293–95
Ridge, Maryland, 83
Rittenhouse, William, 126
Rivers: Anacostia, 24, 347; Back, 55, 239; Blackwater, 25, 139, 224; Bohemia, 112; Chester, 16, 21, 31, 116, 117, 118, 120, 121, 123; Chickahominy, 25, 201; Chickamacomico, 141; Choptank, 18, 24, 26, 31, 126, 131, 138, 142; Coan, 285, 302; Corrotoman, 295, 296;

Delaware, 110; Dragon Run, 25, 264, 269–70; Eastern Bay, 129; Elizabeth, 18, 205, 208, 209, 210, 224, 242; Elk, 18, 110, 112; Great Wicomico, 301; Gunpowder, 24, 55–56; Hampton, 237, 238; Honga, 137; James, 4, 11, 12, 14, 18, 24, 25, 26, 32, 198, 201, 232, 233, 235, 236, 238, 240, 243, 248; Little Choptank, 18; Little Wicomico, 301; Lynnhaven, 216; Machipongo, 185; Magothy, 26; Manokin, 18, 152; Miles, 18, 21, 132; Nansemond, 224, 225; Nanticoke, 25, 137, 141, 143; North Landing, 224; Northwest, 223; Occoquan, 315, 316; Ohio, 316; Pagan, 228; Pamunkey, 249; Patapsco, 18, 24, 43, 44; Patuxent, 15, 25, 65, 73, 74, 76, 80, 82; Piankatank, 19, 270; Pocomoke, 12, 18, 25, 26, 137, 148, 149, 150, 151; Porpotank, 267; Port Tobacco, 94; Potomac, 16, 19, 22, 24, 26, 64, 80, 83, 85, 87, 90, 93, 95, 96, 100, 210, 275, 281, 282, 286, 289, 290, 293, 302, 309, 315, 316, 324, 341, 342, 349, 357, 360, 361; Rappahannock, 19, 34, 235, 274, 275, 276, 281, 285, 294, 297, 298; Rhode, 63; St. Mary's, 88; Sassafras, 12, 102, 112, 113, 116; Severn, 19, 25, 26, 58, 62, 267; South, 26, 62; Susquehanna, 3, 4, 10, 26, 31, 101, 106, 107, 108, 109; Transquaking, 25; Tred Avon, 18, 21, 130, 135; Tuckahoe, 26; West, 133; Wicomico, 18, 26, 87, 93, 143, 145, 151, 152; Wye, 18; York, 19, 235, 247, 248, 260, 262, 265, 266, 267
Rochambeau, Comte de, 257, 260
Rochester, Minnesota, 144
Rockefeller, John D., Jr., 256, 257
Rock Hall, Maryland, 116, 117–18, 120
Rockville, Maryland, 357–58
Rogers, Col. John, 108; Randolph, 343
Rolfe, John, 234, 252

Please note that area codes for Maryland phone numbers in the Chesapeake Bay area have changed from 301 to 410.